IELTS 必須英単語 4400

英単語3300
英熟語1100

Perfect Your Vocabulary for IELTS with These 4400
Most Commonly Appearing Words And Idioms in the Test

林 功 著・監修　小玉英央 著

Isao Hayashi & Hideo Kodama
LINGO L.L.C. / Johnan Academy Group

べレ出版

はじめに

　筆者が代表を務める LINGO L.L.C.（1998 年設立）で，従来の TOEFL 講座に加えて，IELTS 対策講座を初開講したのが 2004 年の春，当時はまだ IELTS の試験会場は都内でも飯田橋の東京理科大の一ヵ所だけだったと記憶しています。従って，レベル別の対策講座を開講していた学校も，ブリティッシュカウンシルと LINGO L.L.C. の 2 校だけだったようです。その後，IELTS は，英検（日本英語検定協会）を中心とする各関係者の尽力により，留学希望者間での認知度も上がり，ここ数年の受験者数の増加には驚異的なものがあります。

　従って本書の目指すところは，このように増え続ける IELTS 受験者のための実践的な英語運用力養成です。特に本書では，LINGO L.L.C. の 10 年以上に及ぶレベル別 IELTS 対策講座を通して蓄積された知識・技術・経験を基に，≪聞く・読む・書く・話す≫の英語 4 技能習得に奏功する単語・熟語を 4400 余網羅しました。

　本書を作るにあたり，実践的な単語・熟語集として，より深く，正確に現行の IELTS に対応するために，今おそらく日本国内で最も IELTS の内容と出題傾向，そして教授法を研究している LINGO の IELTS 主任講師小玉英央に，本書に深くかかわってもらうことを要請しました。具体的には，収録単語熟語の選別や例文作成，IELTS 本試験絡みの重要コメントなどを主に彼に担当してもらいました。最近は LINGO の受講生が，一開催で 30 名程度 IELTS 本試験を受験しますが，その教え子たちに混じって，小玉先生も定期的に本試験を受験し，出題傾向と難易度をくまなく確認して教案や教材に活かしています。その経験とこだわりの深さが本書の至るところに活かされています。例えば，各単語・熟語の語義や用法の記憶定着を確実なものとするために，同じ単語でも意味・用法が違えば敢えて別々に掲載し，記憶の混同を避けていますし，付記としての「コメント」で注意を促しています。

　また英語のアウトプット（Writing / Speaking）能力とインプット（Listening / Reading）能力の両方の養成を意識し，紙面と録音では英語フレーズと和訳の順序を入れ替えるなどして，学習者の「使い勝手」と「成果」の連動を強く意識しました。ぜひ，「本書の効果的な使い方」や「演習を通しての語彙の増強」にしっかり目を通してから，本書を使い切ってください。その先には必ず「実り多き留学」が見えてくると確信しております。

2016 年 5 月　黄金週間の或る夜半に

林　功

IELTS 必須英単語 4400 ［目次］

IELTS 概要　005

1. 本書について　006

2. 本書の効果的な使い方　008

3. 演習を通しての語彙の増強　010

4. IELTS について　010

- IELTS とは ……010
- Academic Module と General Module ……010
- IELTS for UKVI について ……010
- テストのスコア ……011
- 日本でのテスト日程と申し込み ……011
- テスト当日の流れ ……011

5. 各セクションの問題形式　012

- **Academic Module**
  Listening……013　Reading……013　Writing……013　Speaking……014
- **General Module**
  Reading……014　Writing……014

IELTS 必須英単語　015

Group A……015　Group B……051　Group C……167　Group D……269

IELTS 必須英熟語　297

索引　391

●音声のダウンロード方法　421

IELTS概要

1. 本書について

・本書の特徴
本書には過去問を中心に抽出した IELTS 頻出の単語・熟語が収録されています。単語は難易度ごとに 4 グループに分けてあります。

・単語の分類
Group A：IELTS の受験者全員が覚えるべき基礎単語です。スペリングや使い方まで覚えましょう。
Group B：Overall 5.5 〜 6.0 を目指す人もここまでは必須です。
Group C：Overall 6.5 〜 7.5 を目指す人はここまで覚えてください。
Group D：さらに上を目指す人のための単語です。

・単語レイアウト

見出し語／[発音記号]

単語・発音	語義／フレーズ	同意表現
potential [pəténʃəl]	形 潜在的な，起こり得る potential customers 潜在的な客 ＊名詞「可能性，将来性」＝ possibility も覚える。	latent ← 同義語
primary [práɪmèri]	形 主要な；第 1 位の a primary concern 一番懸念している点 ＊ⓢ 理由を聞かれたら The primary reason is that SV が使える。	major
content [kántent]	名 含有量，容量；中身 alcoholic content アルコール含有量 ← 英語フレーズ／フレーズの和訳 ＊ the content of the lecture なら「講義の要旨」と訳す。	proportion
satisfy [sǽtəsfàɪ]	動（必要，条件）を満たす satisfy his curiosity 彼の好奇心を満足させる ＊ satisfy needs / demand「需要を満たす」で覚えよう。 ← コメント	meet
race [réɪs]	名 人種；民族 regardless of race, religion, or sex 人種，宗教，性別にかかわりなく	people(s)

セミコロンは第1義、第2義を区別する
カンマの場合はほぼ同義

・熟語レイアウト

見出し語		
熟語	語義／例文	同意表現／コメント
get the better of ~	~に打ち勝つ　←　意味 I want to get the better of him in the sociology exam. 私は社会学の試験で彼に打ち勝ちたい。	= beat ~
get through with ~	~を片付ける，~をやり遂げる I got through with my term paper at 11pm. 私は11時に期末レポートをやり遂げた。	= have done with ~　英語フレーズ／フレーズの和訳
get to ~	~に到着する She got to the small country in Africa after a long trip. 彼女は長旅の末にアフリカの小国に到着した。	= arrive at [in] ~ / reach ~
get [bring] ~ under control	~を抑えつける，~をコントロールする The government got the riot under control. 政府は暴動を抑えつけた。	
get used [accustomed] to ~ [~ ing]	~に[~することに]慣れる He got used to living in China. 彼は中国で生活するのに慣れました。	= getは「~になる」というニュアンス。be動詞だと状態を表す。

同義語／反義語／コメント

凡例

名：名詞　　動：動詞　　形：形容詞　　副：副詞　　助：助動詞　　前：前置詞

関副：関係副詞　　連結：連結詞

＊IELTSでの出題例やその単語にまつわる注意事項やコメントがあります。
　各セクションに関連するコメントは次の記号で表します。
　L：Listening　　R：Reading　　W1：Writing Task1　　W2：Writing Task2
　S：Speaking　　[英]：イギリス英語　　[米]：アメリカ英語　　⇔：反義語

＊赤シートを使うと見出し語から語義や同義語を，英語フレーズからフレーズの和訳をテストできます。

・収録音声について

本書の単語・熟語はすべて，「見出し語」→「フレーズの和訳」→「英語フレーズ」という順に収録されています。単に語義を覚えるだけではなく，アウトプット(WritingとSpeaking)にも使える語彙を増やすことを目的としています。

2. 本書の効果的な使い方

次の方法でインプット（ListeningとReading）だけでなく，アウトプット（WritingとSpeaking）でも使える力をつけることを目指してください。効率よく，しかも確実に全4セクションに対応する技能を身につけるためには，ただ本を眺めているだけではダメです。目はもちろん，耳や口や手を使う練習を組み合わせて覚えていきましょう。

＜まずはインプット用に＞

1. ペースの決定

覚えるべきページ数と期限から逆算して，1週間に何ページ覚えるかを決めます。例えば，3カ月（約13週間）でGroup AからGroup B（150ページ）を覚える場合，1週間に12ページ（144個）を覚えることになります。

2. 語義を知っている単語を消す

1週間の始めに，その週に覚えるべきすべての単語・熟語の見出し語を見て，語義が分かるかどうかをテストします。赤シートで隠しながら進めると簡単です。意味を知っていたものは鉛筆で見出し語の左側にチェックマークを入れていきます。

3. 平日は朝晩，全範囲に触れる

平日5日間は毎日，朝晩の2回は1週間に覚えるべき全範囲の単語・熟語に触れるようにしましょう。次の練習をバランスよく組み合わせてください。電車の中など隙間時間にやることができます。初日に消したものはあまり見る必要はなく，印が付いていないものを中心に取り組んでください。

- **本を見て…**　「見出し語」から「語義」が分かるかの確認
- **本を見て…**　「英語フレーズ」から「フレーズの和訳」が分かるかの確認
- **本を見て…**　「語義」から「同義語」が分かるかの確認
　　　　　　　※赤シートで隠すと同義語の頭文字だけが見えるのでヒントとなります。

- **音声を聞いて…**　「語義」や「英語フレーズ」のリピート　※電車内であれば，心の中で
- **音声を聞いて…**　「フレーズの和訳」から「英語フレーズ」を言う練習

4．週末は平日にはできない練習を

平日は無理でも週末には机に向かって勉強できる時間が取れるという方も多いはずです。週末は上記練習の他、次の練習をしてください。

- **音声を聞いて…**　「語義」や「英語フレーズ」を声を出してリピート
- **音声を聞いて…**　「語義」を聞いて、スペリングの書き取り練習

5．再度テストして正解したものを消す

1週間の最後に全範囲のテストを行います。見出し語を見て、語義と同義語が出てくるかのテストです。語義が分かったら見出し語の左側に、同義語が分かったら同義語の右にチェックマークを書き込むとよいでしょう。ここで見出し語の語義はすべてチェックが入ることを目指します。入らなかったものは翌週の範囲にプラスします。

6．その後も1週間に1度は全てチェック

次週には次の範囲に移りますが、前の範囲に全く触れないのでは時間とともに忘れてしまいます。1週間に1度は、今までに覚えてきたすべての単語・熟語で見出し語を見て語義が分かるかどうかを確認してください。

＜アウトプット用に＞

WritingやSpeakingで使うには語義からその単語・熟語が出てくるだけでは不十分です。使い方まで覚えなければなりません。そのためには、本書のフレーズを丸ごと覚えて使うようにしましょう。アウトプット用に使える単語・熟語を増やすには、次の練習をしてください。特に熟語はSpeakingで使えると高評価です。

- **本を見て…**　「フレーズの和訳」から「英語フレーズ」を言う練習
- **音声を聞いて…**　「英語フレーズ」を書き取る、声に出してリピートする練習
- **音声を聞いて…**　「フレーズの和訳」から「英語フレーズ」を言う練習

覚えた単語・熟語はWritingやSpeakingの練習で積極的に使いましょう。

3. 演習を通しての語彙の増強

本書での学習が単語・熟語の勉強のすべてではありません。Listening, Reading, Writing, Speaking の演習問題を通して語彙の増強に努めてください。問題の中で分からない単語や熟語に出会ったときがチャンスです。演習後に必ず自作のノートに書き留めておいてください。

次のようなノートを作ることをお勧めします。

見出し語 同義語の頭文字	語義 同義語
retain = k	維持する = keep

こうしておけば，語義や同義語を同時に覚えられます。

また，Writing や Speaking で使いたい単語・熟語が見つかったら，フレーズごと抜き出してアウトプット用のノートにまとめておきましょう。

4. IELTS について

・IELTS とは

International English Language Testing System の略で，イギリス，オーストラリア，ニュージーランド，カナダ，シンガポールへの留学・就労・移住希望者などを主な対象とした英語能力判定テストです。アメリカの大学でも受け入れが広がっています。

・Academic Module と General Module

一般的に留学を目指す人は Academic Module を，移住を目指す人は General Module を受けます。Listening と Speaking は両 Module 共通問題で，Reading と Writing のみ問題が異なります。

・IELTS for UKVI について

イギリスビザ取得を目的に IELTS を受験する場合，通常の IELTS（日本では日本英語検定協会，または日本スタディ・アブロード・ファンデーションから申し込む）ではなく，ブリティッシュカウンシル経由で申し込む IELTS for UKVI（UK Visas and

Immigration）が必要になることがあります。イギリスの大学や大学院に Foundation Course や Presessional Course から入学する際は UKVI が求められることが多いです。その場合, 通常の IELTS のスコアではビザ取得はできませんので注意が必要です。詳しくは, 出願先の教育機関にご確認ください。イギリス以外の国に留学する場合は通常の IELTS を使います。通常の IELTS も UKVI も問題は全く同じで, 申し込みの手続きが違うだけです。

・テストのスコア

テスト結果は 1.0 〜 9.0 まで, 0.5 刻みのバンドスコアで通知されます。4 つのセクション別のスコアと Overall（OA）のスコアが成績表に記されます。一般的には大学留学は OA5.5 〜 6.5, 大学院留学は OA6.5 〜 7.5 を出願基準としている学校が多いです。また, セクション別の指定スコアがあると難易度が上がりますので注意してください。

Overall は 4 セクションのバンドスコアの平均値から算出されます。平均点の 0.25 は 0.5 に, 0.75 は 1.0 に繰上げとなります。また, 0.125 は 0.0 に 0.615 は 0.5 に繰り下げられます。

スコアの例

Listening	Reading	Writing	Speaking	Overall
6.5	6.5	5.0	5.0	平均 5.75 → 6.0
7.5	8.0	6.5	6.5	平均 7.125 → 7.0

・日本でのテスト日程と申し込み

〈通常の IELTS〉
　IDP
　https://ieltsjp.com/ielts-test-dates/

　日本英語検定協会
　https://www.eiken.or.jp/ielts/

〈IELTS for UKVI〉
　日本英語検定協会（ペーパー版のみ）
　https://www.eiken.or.jp/ielts/ukvi/

　British Council（コンピューター版のみ）
　https://www.britishcouncil.jp/exam/ielts-uk-visa-immigration/register

・テスト当日の流れ（ペーパー版）

Writing, Reading, Listening の3セクションは午前中にいっせいに行われます。Speaking は人により集合時間が異なります。1-day なら3セクション終了後、2-day なら指定された日に設定されます。時間帯は受験票にて通知されます。

※身分証明書となるパスポートだけは絶対に持って行ってください。3セクションの試験でも Speaking のときでも忘れると受験ができません。

〈3 セクション〉

8:30～9:00（実施団体により異なる）	控え室に集合
9:00 頃まで	順次、試験教室に入室
9:15 頃～10:15 頃	Writing
10:25 頃～11:25 頃	Reading
11:35 頃～12:20 頃	Listening

12:30 頃には解散となります。集合から解散まで約4時間です。

各セクションのテストが終わると試験官が問題・解答用紙の配布や回収をする時間があります。ただし、このときにトイレに出ることは許されません。Writing が始まってからは Listening が終わるまでの間でトイレに行けるのは Writing と Reading の試験時間内のみとなります。自分の試験時間を削らなければなりません。

〈Speaking〉

試験開始 20 分前が集合時間。試験は移動なども含めて約 20 分で終わります。集合から解散まで約 40 分です。

・テスト結果（ペーパー版）

Writing, Reading, Listening のテストの 13 日後にオンラインで確認できます。成績証明書 (Test Report Form) はその数日後に指定した住所に届きます。

・CDI（Computer-delivered IELTS）について

CDI は IELTS のコンピューター版テストです。Listening, Reading, Writing の3セクションを試験会場のコンピューター上で解きます。問題形式はペーパー版と全く同じです。Writing はタイピングとなりますので、手書きのペーパー版よりも取り組みやすいかもしれません。Speaking だけはペーパー版と同様の対面式の試験となります。成績証明書は 3～5 日間後に発行されます。

CDI の受験については LINGO L.L.C. ウェブサイトのコラムをご覧ください。

https://www.lingollc.com/column/i6.thml

5. 各セクションの問題形式

〈Academic Module〉

• Listening

時間	約 40 分（音声が約 30 分＋解答用紙に記入する時間が 10 分）
問題数	40 問（10 問× 4 セクション）
問題形式	スペリングを書き取る問題と記号で答える選択問題がある。ペーパー版では音声が流れているときは答えを問題冊子にメモしておき，最後に 10 分間が与えられ，答えを解答用紙に写す。
採点方法	1 問 1 点で 40 点満点をバンドスコアに変換。30 問正解で 7.0，23 問正解で 6.0 が目安。

• Reading

時間	60 分
問題数	40 問（13 〜 14 問× 3 パッセージ）
問題形式	抜き出し，選択，段落の見出しをつけるなど多岐にわたる。リスニングとは違い，解答用紙に答えを写す時間は別途与えられない。時間内に解答用紙に答えを書いていく必要がある。
採点方法	1 問 1 点で 40 点満点をバンドスコアに変換。30 問正解で 7.0，23 問正解で 6.0 が目安。

• Writing

時間	60 分（Task1 と Task2 の時間配分は自由に決められる）
問題数	Task1 と Task2 の 2 題
問題形式	Task1 はグラフ，表，地図，プロセスの中から 1 つが出題され，その内容を文章で説明する。Task2 は課題に対する自分の考えを述べる。ペーパー版では両 Task とも制限時間内で手書きする。
採点方法	4 つの観点（タスク到達度・対応，一貫性，語彙，文法）が 25 ％ずつを占める。Task2 は Task1 より配点が高い。Task1 は 150 単語，Task2 は 250 単語以上書かなければ減点となる。

• Speaking

時間	11〜14分(パートごとに制限時間が決まっている)
問題数	3パート
問題形式	ネイティブの試験官と1対1の面接試験。Part1は身近な話題の質疑応答, Part2は2分間のスピーチ, Part3は一般的な話題についての議論。
採点方法	4つの観点(流暢さと一貫性, 語彙, 文法, 発音)が25％ずつを占める。

〈General Module〉

　ListeningとSpeakingはAcademic Moduleと共通問題です。

• Reading

時間	60分
問題数	40問(5パッセージ) ※最初の4パッセージはやや短く, 各6〜8問が, 最後のパッセージは長く, 約13問が出題される。
問題形式	抜き出し, 選択, 段落の見出しをつけるなど多岐にわたる。
採点方法	1問1点で40点満点をバンドスコアに変換。34問正解で7.0, 30問正解で6.0が目安。

• Writing

時間	60分(Task1とTask2の時間配分は自由に決められる)
問題数	Task1とTask2の2題
問題形式	Task1は指定された状況に合わせて手紙を書く。Task2は課題に対する自分の考えを述べる。
採点方法	4つの観点(タスク到達度・対応, 一貫性, 語彙, 文法)が25％ずつを占める。Task2はTask1より配点が高い。Task1は150単語, Task2は250単語以上書かなければ減点となる。

※IELTSに関する情報は2021年9月現在のものです。

IELTS必須英単語
Group A

Track 001

単語・発音	語義／フレーズ	同意表現
potential [pəténʃəl]	形 潜在的な, 起こり得る potential customers 潜在的な客 ＊名詞「可能性, 将来性」= possibility も覚える。	latent
primary [práɪmèri]	形 主要な；第1位の a primary concern 一番懸念している点 ＊S 理由を聞かれたら The primary reason is that SV が使える。	major
content [kάntent]	名 含有量, 容量；中身 alcoholic content アルコール含有量 ＊ the content of the lecture なら「講義の要旨」と訳す。	proportion
satisfy [sǽtəsfàɪ]	動 (必要, 条件)を満たす satisfy his curiosity 彼の好奇心を満足させる ＊ satisfy needs / demand「需要を満たす」で覚えよう。	meet
race [réɪs]	名 人種；民族 regardless of race, religion, or sex 人種, 宗教, 性別にかかわりなく	people(s)
religion [rɪlídʒən]	名 信仰, 宗教 separation between politics and religion 政教分離	faith
negative [négətɪv]	形 否定的な；消極的な a negative reply 否定的な回答 ＊W2 disadvantages を negative aspects と書き換えよう！	rejecting
traditional [trədíʃənl]	形 伝統的な；従来の a traditional Irish folk song 伝統的なアイルランド民謡 ＊ traditional ideas は「従来の考え」と訳すことが多い。	conventional
pollution [pəlúːʃən]	名 汚染；公害 environmental pollution 環境汚染 ＊ pollutant は「汚染物」。	contamination
democratic [dèməkrǽtɪk]	形 民主主義の build a democratic system 民主主義的体制を確立する	self-governing
predominate [prɪdάːmənèɪt]	動 (力・数・影響力で)優位を占める a district where Labour predominates 労働党が優位を占める地区	prevail
advance [ədvǽns]	動 前進する；前払いする The army advanced towards the town. 軍隊は町へ向かって前進した。 ＊ in advance は「事前に」。	move

Track 002

単語・発音	語義／フレーズ	同意表現	難易度
evidence [évədəns]	名 証拠；根拠 circumstantial evidence 状況証拠　＊「証拠」は不可算なので、「2つの証拠」は two pieces of evidence（不可算）。	proof	A
prove [prú:v]	動 証明する；判明する prove a yeti's existence scientifically 雪男の存在を科学的に証明する	demonstrate	
consist [kənsíst]	動 〜から成り立つ；〜に本質がある The audience consisted entirely of teenagers. 観客はすべて10代の若者で成り立っていた。 ＊言い換えると受身で be composed of 〜。	comprise	
ready-made [rédi-méɪd]	形 既製の ready-made clothes 既製服 ＊ ready-made meal はスーパーで売っている調理済みの食事。	ready-to-wear	B
manufacture [mæ̀njəfǽktʃər]	動 製造する，生産する manufacture laser printers レーザープリンタを製造する ＊「製造者」manufacturer の綴りに注意。rを付けるだけ！	produce	
catch [kǽtʃ]	動 見つける，目撃する；間に合う catch someone stealing my watch 私の時計を盗んでいるところを見つける	discover	
creativity [krì:eɪtívəti]	名 創造性 be rich in creativity and artistry 創造性と技術が豊かである	originality	C
construction [kənstrʌ́kʃən]	名 建設，建築；構造 be under construction 建設中である ＊動詞は construct。	building	
brief [brí:f]	形 簡潔な；短い give a brief explanation of the theory その理論について簡潔な説明をする	short	
experiment [ɪkspérəmənt]	名 実験 conduct an experiment 実験を行う	test	D
ironically [aɪrá:nɪkəli]	副 皮肉を込めて ironically enough 何とも皮肉なことには ＊形容詞は ironic。	sarcastically	
attract [ətrǽkt]	動 引き付ける attract a lot of attention 大いに注目を集める ＊名詞は attraction。形容詞 attractive「魅力的な」も覚える。	capture	

17

単語・発音	語義／フレーズ	同意表現
enemy [énəmi]	名 敵, かたき, 敵対者 natural enemies 天敵	foe
differ [dífər]	動 異なる；意見が合わない Our views differ greatly in important ways. 我々の考えは重要な点で大いに違う。	vary
ultimately [ʌ́ltəmətli]	副 最終的には, 結局；根本的には lead a business ultimately to success 事業を最終的に成功へと導く	finally
visible [vízəbl]	形 目に見える visible to the naked eye 肉眼で見える	perceptible
exceed [iksí:d]	動 上回る, しのぐ exceed one's expectations 期待を上回る ＊W1 The rate exceeded the target.「レートは目標値を上回った」。	surpass
plastic [plǽstɪk]	形 プラスチック製の；柔軟な a plastic bag ビニール袋	vinyl
desire [dɪzáɪər]	名 強い願望, 欲望；要望 satisfy a desire 欲求を満たす ＊ meet a desire も「欲求を満たす」。	wish
recruitment [rɪkrú:tmənt]	名 新入社員募集；新兵募集 the recruitment of a new employee 新入社員の募集 ＊ recruit するのは企業。学生がするのは job hunting。	enlisting
retirement [rɪtáɪərmənt]	名 退職, 引退 a retirement allowance 退職金 ＊W2 S enjoy life after retirement「引退後の人生を楽しむ」。	resignation
lifetime [láɪftàɪm]	名 一生, 生涯；形 一生の, 終身の the chance of a lifetime 一生で最高のチャンス ＊ the lifetime employment system で「終身雇用制度」。	lifespan
invention [ɪnvénʃən]	名 発明, 考案；発明品 take out a patent for invention 発明の特許を取得する ＊ invent はものを発明する以外に「考案する」の意もある。	innovation
editor [édətər]	名 編集者, 校訂者 an editor in chief 編集長	compiler

Track 004

単語・発音	語義／フレーズ	同意表現	難易度
acceptance [əkséptəns]	名 支持，容認；受け入れ gain widespread acceptance 幅広い支持を得る	support	A
punish [pʌ́nɪʃ]	動 罰する，刑をもって処する punish those convicted by a fine それらの既決囚に罰金を科す	penalize	
control [kəntróʊl]	動 制御する，操作する，支配する This knob controls the volume. このつまみで音量を制御します。	operate	
emotion [ɪmóʊʃən]	名 感情，情緒；感動 how to express honest emotion on stage 舞台で偽りのない感情を表す方法	feeling	B
average [ǽvərɪdʒ]	形 平均的な，平均の the average score in the class クラスの平均点	mean	
assumed [əs(j)úːmd]	形 仮定した；見せかけの assumed innocence 推定無罪　＊assume「引き受ける； ふりをする」も覚えよう！assume responsibility「責任を引き受ける」。	presumed	
duty [d(j)úːti]	名 義務；職務 the notions of right and duty 権利と義務という概念 ＊職務という意味では task が同義語。	obligation	C
practise [prǽktɪs]	動 練習する；実践する practise the piano ピアノの練習をする ＊[米]では practice。名詞は[英][米]ともに practice。	work out	
progressive [prəgrésɪv]	形 進歩的な；漸進的な the progressive wing of the Labour Party 労働党の進歩派	liberal	
independence [ìndɪpéndəns]	名 独立；自活 gain independence from Britain イギリスから独立する	self-government	D
factor [fǽktər]	名 要因 factors contributing to global warming 地球温暖化の要因 ＊[S]There are many factors involved.「多くの要素がある」。	cause	
atmosphere [ǽtməsfɪər]	名 大気；雰囲気 the ozone layer in the atmosphere 大気のオゾン層 ＊[S] in a casual atmosphere「気楽な雰囲気で」。	air	

19

単語・発音	語義/フレーズ	同意表現
sufficiently [səfíʃəntli]	副 十分に recover sufficiently to go out 外出できるほど十分に回復する ＊adequately も同義語。	enough
tiny [táɪni]	形 とても小さな a tiny amount of money わずかな額の金	diminutive
consider [kənsídər]	動 よく考える consider all the facts あらゆる事実を考慮する ＊W2 consider A as B「A を B とみなす」。	think
beyond [bɪjánd]	前 ～を越えて；～以外に matters beyond his understanding 彼の理解を超える事柄	over
manmade [mǽn-méɪd]	形 人工の manmade diamond 人造ダイヤモンド	synthetic
survival [sərváɪvl]	名 生き延びること a survival rate 生存率	endurance
motivation [mòʊtəvéɪʃən]	名 動機 an increase in motivation やる気の増大	motive
profit [prá:fət]	名 利益 profit and loss 会計損益 ＊W2 企業の利益。benefit（利点）と混同しないように！	gain
ancestor [ǽnsestər]	名 祖先，先祖 The two species have evolved from a common ancestor. その2種は共通の祖先から進化した。 ＊⇔ descendant「子孫，末裔」。	predecessor
settlement [sétlmənt]	名 入植，定住；植民地 the settlement of the American West アメリカ西部への入植 ＊多義なので settler「開拓移民」も併せて覚えよう！	immigration
characteristic [kèrəktərístɪk]	名 特徴，特質 interesting characteristics of the man その男の興味深い特徴 ＊ property, trait も同義語。	feature
permanent [pə́:rmənənt]	形 永続的な permanent residency 永住権 ＊ on a permanent basis「永久的に」。	lasting

Track 006

単語・発音	語義／フレーズ	同意表現	難易度
shallow [ʃǽlou]	形 浅い a shallow sea 浅い海	shoal	A
hang [hǽŋ]	動 吊るす hang ~ from a tree branch ～を木の枝に吊るす ＊ⓈI have ~ hang over one's head「～が頭を悩ませる」。	suspend	
branch [brǽntʃ]	名 枝；支流 Monkeys swing from branch to branch. 猿が枝から枝へ跳び移る。 ＊企業の「支店」という意味もある。	bough	
autumn [ɔ́ːtəm]	名 秋 beautiful autumn leaves 美しい秋の紅葉 ＊［英］では fall より autumn の方が一般的。	fall	B
recover [rɪkʌ́vər]	動 回復する recover from a cold 風邪が治る ＊ recover from ~「～が治る」で from を忘れないように！	recuperate	
courage [kə́ːrɪdʒ]	名 勇気 courage to face the reality 現実に向き合う勇気	bravery	
insurance [ɪnʃʊ́ərəns]	名 保険 fire insurance 火災保険 ＊Ⓛ 発音と綴りのギャップに注意！	hedge	C
escape [ɪskéɪp]	動 逃れる escape from prison 脱獄する ＊W2 avoid「避ける」と混同しないように！	flee	
permit [pərmít]	動 許可する permit the use of weapons 武器の使用を認める	allow	
fear [fíər]	名 恐怖 overcome fear 恐怖に打ち勝つ ＊Ⓢ for fear that SV「SV を恐れて」。	dread	D
origin [ɔ́ːrədʒɪn]	名 起源, 由来, 素性 the origin of all mankind 全人類の起源 ＊ of ~ origin「～系の, ～にもとを発する」	source	
record [rékərd]	名 記録 accounting records 会計記録	document	

Track 007

単語・発音	語義／フレーズ	同意表現
memorise [méməràɪz]	動 暗記する memorise vocabulary 単語を暗記する	learn ~ by heart
amateur [ǽmətʃʊ̀ər]	形 素人の an amateur astronomer アマチュア天文家 ＊スペリングに注意！	non-professional
maintenance [méɪntənəns]	名 維持；メンテナンス maintenance and repair costs 維持修繕費	upkeep
huge [hjúːdʒ]	形 巨大な；大量の a huge amount of work 大変な労力 ＊S big よりは huge を使いたい。	immense
highland [háɪlænd]	名 高地 highland climate 高地気候	upland
overpopulation [òʊvərpɑ̀ːpjəléɪʃən]	名 人口過剰 suffer from overpopulation 人口過剰に悩む	surplus population
border [bɔ́ːrdər]	名 境界（線） a national border 国境 ＊意外とスペリングを間違えやすい単語。	boundary
scenario [sənériòʊ]	名 筋書き；脚本 a scenario for economic recovery 経済復興への筋書き	synopsis
destruction [dɪstrʌ́kʃən]	名 破壊；撲滅 environmental destruction by human activities 人間の活動による環境破壊	demolition
core [kɔ́ːr]	名 中心部，核 the core of the problem 問題の核心	centre
pronounce [prənáʊns]	動 発音する；公表する pronounce each word distinctly 一語一語はっきりと発音する	articulate
double [dʌ́bl]	動 2倍にする double the size サイズを2倍にする ＊動詞以外に形容詞，副詞，名詞としても使える。	duplicate

Track 008

単語・発音	語義／フレーズ	同意表現	難易度
per [pər]	前 ～につき per day 1日につき ＊W1 per の後に冠詞を付けないように。	a	A
preventive [prɪvéntɪv]	形 予防の, 防止する；妨げる as a preventive measure 予防対策として	preventative	
standard [stǽndərd]	名 基準, 標準；正直, 誠実 set the standard for water quality 水質基準を設定する ＊ criterion も同義語として覚えたい。	norm	
correlation [kɔ̀:rəléɪʃən]	名 相互関係 correlation between A and B　AとBの相関関係	mutuality	B
interest [íntərəst]	名 利息；興味 interest rates 利子率	finance	
blind [bláɪnd]	形 盲目の a blind person 盲目の人	sightless	
debt [dét]	名 借金 debts to pay off 払うべき借金 ＊ get into debt「借金する」。	borrowing	C
foundation [faʊndéɪʃən]	名 基盤；財団 economic foundation 経済的基盤	base	
draw [drɔ́:]	動 描く；線を引く draw a graph グラフを描く ＊R draw a conclusion のように「引き出す」も頻出。	sketch	
sliding [sláɪdɪŋ]	形 事情に応じて変わる, スライドする sliding scale fees スライド制料金	adjustable	D
extent [ɪkstént]	名 程度, 範囲 to some extent ある程度 ＊W2 To what extent do you agree? でおなじみ。	degree	
tuition [t(j)u(:)íʃən]	名 教授；授業料 private tuition in English 英語の個人教授	school fee	

Track 009

単語・発音	語義／フレーズ	同意表現
delight [dɪláɪt]	名 大喜び, 楽しみ be speechless with delight 喜びで何も言えない	pleasure
alter [ɔ́:ltər]	動 変える；変わる alter one's diet for one's health 健康のために食事を変える	change
partly [pá:rtli]	副 部分的に partly right but mostly wrong 部分的に正しいが, ほとんど間違っている　＊W2 I partly agree という立場が有効なことも。	partially
undoubtedly [ʌndáʊtɪdli]	副 疑いなく undoubtedly guilty 疑いなく有罪の	no doubt
advantage [ədvǽntɪdʒ]	名 利点, メリット the advantage of good education よい教育の利点 ＊W2 benefits, positive aspects で書き換える。	benefit
significance [sɪgnífɪkəns]	名 重要性；意義 historical significance of the Industrial Revolution 産業革命の歴史的重要性	importance
industrialisation [ɪndʌ̀striəlaɪzéɪʃən]	名 工業化, 産業化 rapid industrialisation and urbanisation 急速な工業化と都市化	having industries
prevention [prɪvénʃən]	名 防止；予防 the prevention of cruelty to animals 動物への虐待防止 ＊「防止策」は preventive measures.	deterrence
precondition [prì:kəndíʃən]	名 前提条件 require as a precondition 前提条件として求める	prerequisite
compare [kəmpéər]	動 比較する；例える compare between the advantages and disadvantages メリットとデメリットを比較する	contrast
chief [tʃí:f]	形 最高位の；主要な Chief Executive Officer 最高経営責任者（CEO） ＊S The chief factor is that SV「主な要素は SV だ」。	principal
urban [ɔ́:rbən]	形 都会の a larger urban population より多い都市部の人口 ＊⇔ rural	city

24

Track 010

単語・発音	語義／フレーズ	同意表現	難易度
coal [kóʊl]	名 石炭 a coal mine 炭鉱	anthracite	A
ingredient [ɪŋgríːdiənt]	名 材料；構成要素 mix the ingredients for a pancake パンケーキの材料を混ぜる	constituent	
burst [bə́ːrst]	名 爆発，破裂 a burst in population of China 中国の人口爆発	explosion	
rural [rúərəl]	形 田舎の a quiet rural life 静かな田舎の生活 ＊⇔ urban	country	B
class [klǽs]	名 階級；水準 a class discrimination 階級差別	rank	
medical [médɪkl]	形 医学の，医術の medical staff in the hospital その病院の医療スタッフ		
last [lǽst]	動 もつ，続く This battery lasts a long time. この電池は長もちする。	continue	C
introduce [ìntrəd(j)úːs]	動 導入する；紹介する introduce a new system 新しい制度を導入する	bring in	
device [dɪváɪs]	名 装置；工夫 a built-in safety device 内蔵安全装置 ＊「工夫，手段」では method, strategy も同義語。	mechanism	
astonishing [əstɑ́nɪʃɪŋ]	形 驚くほどの，目覚ましい an astonishing number of books in the national library 国立図書館の驚くべき数の本	surprising	D
wheel [wíːl]	名 輪；車輪 a four-wheel drive car 四輪駆動車	disc	
aid [éɪd]	名 援助，救援 financial aid for international students 留学生への財政的援助　＊ aid organisations「援助団体」。	assistance	

単語・発音	語義／フレーズ	同意表現
recreational [rìːkriéɪʃənl]	形 娯楽の recreational activities during the vacation 休暇中の娯楽活動	relaxative
budget [bʌ́dʒət]	名 予算 cut the annual budget 年間予算を減らす ＊W2 allocate the budget「予算を割り当てる」を使えるように。	financial plan
luxury [lʌ́gʒəri]	名 ぜいたく the luxuries of the rich お金持ちのぜいたく	profusion
income [ínkʌm]	名 収入 a gap between income and expenses 収入と支出の差	earnings
imply [ɪmpláɪ]	動 暗示する, ほのめかす His silence implied agreement. 彼の沈黙は同意を暗示した。	implicate
inequality [ìnɪkwάːləti]	名 不平等 the inequality between the rich and the poor 貧富間の不平等	imbalance
selective [səléktɪv]	形 選択的な；選択能力のある a new type created through selective breeding 選択育種で生み出された新種	elective
greet [gríːt]	動 迎え入れる；挨拶する greet the prize winner with applause 受賞者を拍手で迎え入れる	welcome
praise [préɪz]	動 称賛する praise an achievement 功績を称賛する	admire
breath [bréθ]	名 息, 呼吸 breath alcohol test 呼気アルコール検査 ＊動詞は e を加えて breathe。発音注意！	breathing
system [sístəm]	名 制度, 体制 a social security system 社会保障制度	establishment
physician [fɪzíʃən]	名 医者, 内科医 consult a physician 医者にかかる	doctor

Track 012

単語・発音	語義／フレーズ	同意表現	難易度
treatment [tríːtmənt]	名 取り扱い；治療 equal treatment for men and women 男女平等な取り扱い	handling	A
accidental [æksədéntl]	形 不慮の, 偶然の an accidental death 不慮の死 ＊⇔ intentional「故意の」。	incidental	
pill [píl]	名 錠剤 a sleeping pill 睡眠薬 ＊薬では painkiller「鎮痛剤」が頻出。	tablet	
poet [póuət]	名 詩人 quote a poet 詩人の言葉を引用する	writer of verse	B
existence [ɪgzístəns]	名 存在 believe in the existence after death 死後の存在を信じている	being	
distant [dístənt]	形 遠い；離れた distant future 遠い将来	remote	
volcano [vɑːlkéɪnoʊ]	名 火山 eruption of a volcano 火山の爆発 ＊L volcanic ash「火山灰」は書けるように！		C
court [kɔ́ːrt]	名 裁判所 the Supreme Court 最高裁判所	judicatory	
latter [lǽtər]	形 後の latter half of the century 世紀の後半 ＊⇔ former	posterior	
desert [dézərt]	名 砂漠；不毛の土地 turn to desert 砂漠化する　＊ deserted island「無人島」。L 砂漠は何もないからsが1つ。dessert（デザート）は多いと嬉しいからsが2つ。	sands	D
patronage [pǽtrənɪdʒ]	名 後援 under the patronage of ～ ～の後援のもとに	sponsorship	
nuclear [n(j)úːkliər]	形 原子力の nuclear weapons 核兵器 ＊ nuclear family「核家族」も覚えよう！	atomic	

27

単語・発音	語義／フレーズ	同意表現
resident [rézəərdənt]	名 居住者, 在住者 conflicts between local residents and the police 地元住民と警察の対立 ＊ dweller も同義語として一緒に覚える。	inhabitant
concentration [kὰ:nsəntréɪʃən]	名 集中 concentration of attention 注意集中	convergence
volatile [vá:lətl]	形 揮発性の volatile oil 揮発性油	explosive
territory [térətɔ̀:ri]	名 領土, 領域 internationalised territory 国際管理化地域	realm
uncomfortable [ʌnkʌ́mftəbl]	形 心地よくない；気詰まりな uncomfortable silence 気まずい沈黙	unpleasant
thermometer [θərmá:mətər]	名 温度計, 寒暖計 The thermometer registers minus nine. 温度計はマイナス９度を示している。	heat indicator
interior [ɪntíəriər]	形 内部の interior air temperature 室内気温	internal
bounce [báʊns]	動 跳ね返す；跳ね返る A ball hit the ground and bounced. 球は地面に当たって跳ね返った。	rebound
spring [spríŋ]	名 泉；湧水 hot springs 温泉	fountain
seed [síːd]	名 種（たね） sow seeds in a field 畑に種をまく	pip
grain [gréɪn]	名 穀物；粒子 grain harvest 穀物収穫高	cereal
equator [ɪkwéɪtər]	名 赤道 a tropical island near the equator 赤道に近い熱帯の島	equatorial line

Track 014

単語・発音	語義／フレーズ	同意表現	難易度
alarmingly [əláːrmɪŋli]	副 驚くほどに finish in an alarmingly short time 驚くほど短時間で終える	surprisingly	A
radically [rǽdɪkli]	副 根本的に；過激に be radically different from his idea 彼の意見と根本から異なる	fundamentally	
exceptionally [ɪksépʃənəli]	副 並外れて；例外的に an exceptionally talented artist 並外れた才能のある芸術家	extraordinarily	
positive [pɑ́ːzətɪv]	形 肯定的な，前向きの；楽観的な feel positive about the new policy 新方針を前向きに受けとめる	affirmative	B
bandage [bǽndɪdʒ]	名 包帯 apply a bandage to a wound 傷に包帯をする	dressing	
valuable [vǽljuəbl]	形 貴重な；高価な offer valuable lessons 貴重な教訓を与える ＊invaluable も「貴重な」の意味。	precious	
tale [téɪl]	名 物語 fairy tales おとぎ話	story	C
up-to-date [ʌ́ptədéɪt]	形 最新の provide up-to-date information 最新情報を提供する ＊cutting-edge も同義語。state-of-the-art は「技術が最先端の」。	latest	
frustration [frʌstréɪʃən]	名 欲求不満；挫折 get rid of the frustration 欲求不満を解消する	discontent	
lead [líːd]	動 導く；仕向ける lead a person to success 人を成功に導く ＊「鉛」という意味では発音が変わる。	conduce	D
mentally [méntli]	副 精神的に be mentally and physically exhausted 心身ともに疲れ果てている	spiritually	
lease [líːs]	動 賃借する；賃貸する lease the land from a farmer 農民から土地を借りる	let	

29

単語・発音	語義／フレーズ	同意表現
guilty [gílti]	形 有罪の；罪悪感のある be found guilty of murder 殺人で有罪となる ＊名詞は guilt。	non-innocent
rear [ríər]	名 後部；背後 rear of the head 後頭部 ＊「(子供を)育てる；(動物を)飼育する」という意味もある。	back
sail [séɪl]	動 航行する sail around the world 世界一周の航海をする	navigate
dense [déns]	形 (濃度が)濃い；(密度が)高い be encompassed with a dense fog 深い霧に包まれる	thick
seek [síːk]	動 探し求める seek a better life より良い生活を求める	quest
burn off [bə́ːrn ɔ́(ː)f]	動 消費する；焼き払う burn off extra calories 余分なカロリーを消費する	burn away
lung [lʌ́ŋ]	名 肺，肺臓 develop lung cancer 肺がんを発症する	pulmonis
discount [dìskáʊnt]	動 無視する；割り引く discount rumours 噂を無視する	disregard
variation [vèəriéɪʃən]	名 変化，変動 variation in DNA sequence DNA 配列の変化 ＊形容詞 varying「変化する」も覚える。	fluctuation
signal [sígnl]	動 信号を送る；前兆となる；合図する signal for a rescue 救援を求める合図を送る	sign
globalisation [glòʊbəlaɪzéɪʃən]	名 グローバル化；世界化 globalisation of capital market 資本市場のグローバル化	internationalisation
boom [búːm]	名 一時的流行；にわか景気 real estate investment boom 不動産投資ブーム ＊ boom years は「好況の時期」。	fad

Track 016

単語・発音	語義／フレーズ	同意表現	難易度
productive [prədʌ́ktɪv]	形 生産的な have a productive conversation 実りのある会話をする ＊名詞は productivity。	fruitful	A
prehistoric [prì:hɪstɔ́:rɪk]	形 有史以前の，大昔の prehistoric mammoths 太古のマンモス ＊ pre- は「前」を表す。pre-war「戦前」。	ancient	
chain [tʃéɪn]	名 連鎖；鎖 a food chain 食物連鎖	series	
liver [lívər]	名 肝臓 liver cancer 肝臓がん		B
kidney [kídni]	名 腎臓 transplantation of a kidney 腎臓移植		
loss [lɔ́(:)s]	名 失うこと；損失；敗北 loss of memory 記憶喪失	deprivation	
switch [swítʃ]	動 切り替える；打ち据える switch direction in life 人生の方向を変える	shift	C
majority [mədʒɔ́:rəti]	名 大多数，大部分 the majority of people 大多数の人々 ＊⇔ minority「少数」。	large number	
accountant [əkáʊntnt]	名 会計士 a certified public accountant 公認会計士	book-keeper	
dominant [dɑ́:mənənt]	形 支配的な；主要な the dominant party 第1党	most influential	D
deliver [dɪlívər]	動 （演説などを）行う，（意見を）述べる；届ける deliver an address 演説を行う	pronounce	
range [réɪndʒ]	動 変動する；並べる The prices range from 5 pounds to 10 pounds. 価格は5〜10ポンドまで様々だ。	vary	

31

Track 017

単語・発音	語義／フレーズ	同意表現
revolution [rèvəlúːʃən]	名 大変革, 革命；（天体の）公転 the information revolution 情報革命	dramatic change
expect [ɪkspékt]	動 期待する；予期する expect a miracle 奇跡を期待する ＊W1 be expected to で未来の予想値を表す。	anticipate
upward [ʌ́pwərd]	副 上に向かって, 上向きに Oil prices rise upward. 原油価格が上昇する。 ＊W1 形容詞なら have an upward trend「上昇傾向にある」。	up
adequate [ǽdɪkwət]	形 十分な；適した adequate food supply 十分な食糧供給 ＊ enough ということだが, suitable の意もある。	sufficient
costly [kɔ́(ː)stli]	形 高価な, 費用のかさむ；犠牲の大きい a costly jewel 高価な宝石	expensive
gigantic [dʒaɪgǽntɪk]	形 巨大な a gigantic enterprise 巨大企業	huge
critic [krítɪk]	名 批評家 a literary critic 文芸批評家	reviewer
worthy [wə́ːrði]	形 価値のある be worthy of praise 称賛に値する	deserving
inner [ínər]	形 内面的な inner resources 内に秘めた力量	internal
logical [lɑ́ːdʒɪkl]	形 論理的な, 理にかなった logical thinking 論理的思考 ＊⇔ illogical「非論理的な」。	reasoned
justify [dʒʌ́stəfàɪ]	動 正当化する justify one's claim 自身の主張を正当化する	give grounds for
overconfidence [óʊvərkɑ́ːnfədəns]	名 過信, うぬぼれ the risk of overconfidence 過信の危険性	excessive trust

単語・発音	語義／フレーズ	同意表現	難易度
competition [kɑ̀:mpətíʃən]	名 競争；競争相手 intense competition 激しい競争	rivalry	A
initial [ɪníʃəl]	形 当初の；初めの the initial step 第1段階 ＊ initially appealing とくれば、「最初は魅力的だったが」。	beginning	
comfort [kʌ́mfərt]	名 快適さ；満足 live in comfort 快適に暮らす	ease	
adjust [ədʒʌ́st]	動 適応する；調節する adjust to the new way of life 新しい生活様式に適応する	adapt	B
wealthy [wélθi]	形 裕福な a wealthy young widow 裕福な若き未亡人	rich	
civilisation [sìvələzéɪʃən]	名 文明；文明化 origins of civilisation 文明の起源 ＊精神的な面を強調するなら culture。	culture	
demonstrate [démənstrèɪt]	動 明らかに示す；証明する As this clearly demonstrates, このことが明らかに示すように,	show	C
escalate [éskəlèɪt]	動 段階的に拡大［激化］する stop the war from escalating 戦争の拡大を止める	enlarge	
abundant [əbʌ́ndənt]	形 豊富な；大量の abundant natural resources 豊富な天然資源	plentiful	
entrepreneur [ɑ̀:ntrəprənə́:r]	名 起業家, 事業家；興行主 success stories of young entrepreneurs 若き企業家たちの成功談	businessman	D
ring [ríŋ]	動 電話する ring for a taxi 電話してタクシーを呼ぶ ＊［英］会話表現（［米］では call）。	call	
centre [séntə]	名 中心地；中心 city centre 町の中心部 ＊［英］（［米］では downtown）。	heart	

単語・発音	語義／フレーズ	同意表現
bother [bάːðər]	動 わざわざ〜する；悩ます Don't bother to write. わざわざお手紙はいりません。	trouble
brilliant [bríljənt]	形 素晴らしい；優秀な a brilliant performance 素晴らしい演技 ＊[英]は excellent の意でよく使う。	impressive
extend [ɪksténd]	動 延長する；広げる Clarification extends the shelf life of milk. 浄化が牛乳の保存期間を延ばす。	lengthen
pregnant [prégnənt]	形 妊娠して；妊娠中の six months pregnant 妊娠6カ月	expectant
pulse [pʌ́ls]	名 脈拍, 心拍；躍動 take one's pulse 脈を取る	heartbeat
principal [prínsəpl]	形 主な, 最も重要な one of Britain's principal industries 英国の最重要産業の1つ ＊「校長先生」の意味もある。	chief
welfare [wélfèər]	名 福祉, 福利, 幸福；生活保護 the child's welfare 児童福祉	well-being
applicant [ǽplɪkənt]	名 志願者, 応募者 200 applicants for the job その職に対する200人の応募者	candidate
servant [sə́ːrvnt]	名 奉仕者；使われる人；使用人 civil servants 公務員	employee
pudding [pʊ́dɪŋ]	名 プディング；デザート traditional plum pudding 伝統的なプラムプディング	sweet
cheque [tʃék]	名 小切手 cash a cheque 小切手を現金に換える	check
domesticate [dəméstɪkət]	動 飼い慣らす, 家畜化する Dogs were domesticated much earlier. 犬ははるかに早く家畜化された。	tame

Track 020

単語・発音	語義／フレーズ	同意表現	難易度
capital [kǽpətl]	名 資本（金），資産，元金；首都 plenty of capital to start a new business 多額の新事業開設資金 ＊もちろん「首都」という意味もある。	funds	A
chick [tʃík]	名 （ニワトリの）ひよこ；ひな a newly hatched chick 孵化したばかりのひよこ	nestling	
nourish [nə́:rɪʃ]	動 育てる，養う；促進する nourish a baby 赤ちゃんを育てる	foster	
vacuum [vǽkju:m]	名 真空，真空状態 an experiment in a vacuum 真空状態での実験 ＊R emptiness との書き換えに注意！	void	B
unpleasant [ʌnpléznt]	形 不愉快な，嫌な unpleasant noises from the street 通りの不愉快な騒音 ＊⇔ pleasant	disagreeable	
proofreading [prú:frí:dɪŋ]	名 校正 editing and proofreading 編集と校正 ＊論文提出の話題では「見直し」のこと。	emendation	
pity [píti]	名 哀れみ；残念なこと feel pity for starving children 飢えた子供たちを哀れむ	compassion	C
service [sə́:rvəs]	名 礼拝，宗教儀式 a church service on Sunday 日曜の礼拝	ceremony	
rob [rá:b]	動 強奪する，奪う rob a bank 銀行強盗をする ＊名 robbery「強盗（行為）」も併せて覚える。	burgle	
flat [flǽt]	名 アパート，マンション rent a furnished flat 家具付きアパートを借りる ＊［英］a ground-floor flat「1階の部屋」。	apartment	D
semester [səméstər]	名 学期 the autumn (spring) semester 秋(春)学期 ＊［英］では term の方がおなじみ。	term	
fee [fí:]	名 料金，手数料 an admission fee 入場料，入学金 ＊ fare「乗車料金」，toll「通行料」も覚えよう！	charge	

35

Track 021

単語・発音	語義／フレーズ	同意表現
remote [rimóut]	形 遠い，人里離れた vacation on a remote tropical island 遠く離れた熱帯の島での休暇	distant
snowfall [snóufɔ:l]	名 降雪；降雪量 a heavy snowfall 大雪	snowing
polar [póulər]	形 極地の；正反対の a polar bear 北極熊 ＊Antarctica（南極）や Arctic（北極）の話題で頻出。	arctic
constant [kánstənt]	形 絶えず続く；不変の constant noise of a big city 大都会の絶え間ない騒音	continual
donate [dóuneit]	動 寄付する，提供する donate money to a charity 慈善団体にお金を寄付する ＊donate food のようにお金以外にも使う。	contribute
height [háit]	名 高さ，高度；高所 measure the height of a mountain 山の高さを測る ＊発音もスペリングも注意。「高い所」の場合，heights とすることが多い。	elevation
width [wídθ]	名 幅，広さ 1.5 feet in width 幅 1.5 フィート	wideness
passionate [pǽʃənət]	形 情熱的な；激しい a passionate love of opera オペラへの情熱的な愛	ardent
portrait [pɔ́:rtreit]	名 肖像画，ポートレート paint portraits of celebrities 有名人の肖像画を描く	representation
watercolour [wɔ́:tərkÀlə]	名 水彩絵の具；水彩画 paint with watercolours 水彩絵の具で描く	water paint
landscape [lǽndskèip]	名 景色，風景；地形 beautiful landscapes in the countryside 田舎の美しい風景 ＊「地形」の意味が盲点。	scenery
biography [baiáːgrəfi]	名 伝記；経歴 read a biography of Thomas Edison エジソンの伝記を読む	life story

Track 022

単語・発音	語義／フレーズ	同意表現	難易度
collection [kəlékʃən]	名 選集；収集物 a collection of poems 詩集 ＊garbage collection は「ごみの収集」。	anthology	A
passage [pǽsɪdʒ]	名 文章の一節；通路 write a short passage 短い文章を書く ＊W1 be connected by a passage「通路でつながれている」。	extract	
ecology [ɪkάːlədʒi]	名 生態学；生態環境 ecology class 生態学の授業		
professional [prəféʃənl]	名 専門家 a licensed professional 免許を持った専門家	expert	B
landlord [lǽndlɔ̀ːrd]	名 家主 the landlord of the house その家の家主	property owner	
ground floor [gráʊnd flɔ́ːr]	名 1階 a ground floor of the department store 百貨店の1階 ＊[英] lower ground floor は「地下1階」。	first floor	
staircase [stéərkèɪs]	名 階段 a dark and narrow staircase 暗くて狭い階段	stairs	C
replace [rɪpléɪs]	動 〜を取り換える，〜に取って代わる replace old equipment 古い設備を取り換える ＊W1 地図の課題は be replaced by 〜が便利。	take the place of	
postcode [póʊstkòʊd]	名 郵便番号 fill in the postcode 郵便番号を記入する ＊[L] イギリスでは「CB2 1TN」のように数字と英文字が混在する。	zip code	
pupil [pjúːpl]	名 生徒，児童 the number of pupils 生徒数 ＊発音注意！[i]の音なし。	student	D
promote [prəmóʊt]	動 促進する，増進する；昇進させる promote gender equality 男女平等を促進する	encourage	
regulation [règjəléɪʃən]	名 規則，規制；調節 comply with the regulations 規則を遵守する	rule	

Track 023

単語・発音	語義／フレーズ	同意表現
grateful [gréɪtfl]	形 感謝する，ありがたく思う grateful to you あなたに感謝する	appreciative
guardian [gáːrdiən]	名 保護者，監視者 a signature of the guardian 保護者の署名	protector
cottage [kátɪdʒ]	名 小屋 a holiday cottage 休暇用の小屋	cabin
basic [béɪsɪk]	形 必要最低限の，基本の basic human rights 基本的人権	fundamental
gather [gǽðər]	動 推測する，推断する；集める from what I can gather, 私の察するところ， ＊I gather that SV では suppose や understand に近い意味。	infer
youngster [jʌ́ŋstər]	名 若者 popular among youngsters 若者に人気がある ＊「子供」に近い意味。	juvenile
retail [ríːteɪl]	名 小売り retail industry 小売業界	
fabric [fǽbrɪk]	名 繊維 waterproof fabrics 防水繊維	material
harmless [háːrmləs]	形 無害の；悪意のない harmless insects 害のない虫	nontoxic
prepare [prɪpéər]	動 用意する；調理する prepare dinner 夕食の用意をする ＊形容詞 prepared は ready とほぼ同じ意味。	arrange
judge [dʒʌ́dʒ]	動 推測する，判断する；裁判する judging from his clothes 彼の服装から判断すると	guess
beforehand [bɪfɔ́ːrhǽnd]	副 事前に，あらかじめ get ready beforehand あらかじめ準備をしておく	in advance

Track 024

単語・発音	語義／フレーズ	同意表現	難易度
print [prínt]	動 活字体で書く, 印刷する print one's name 活字体で自分の名前を書く	write in block letters	A
bleach [blíːtʃ]	動 漂白する, 脱色する blinds bleached by the sun 太陽によって色褪せたブラインド	whiten	
seasick [síːsìk]	形 船酔いした He got seasick. 彼は船酔いした。	shipsick	
committee [kəmíti]	名 委員会 hold a committee meeting 委員会を開く	board	B
cinema [sínəmə]	名 映画館 visit the local cinema 地元の映画館に行く ＊[英]（[米]では movie theater）。	movie theatre	
subtitled [sʌ́btàɪtld]	形 字幕付きの a movie subtitled in Japanese 日本語で字幕の付けられた映画	captioned	
clay [kléɪ]	名 粘土 mould a rabbit with clay 粘土でウサギを作る ＊ mould 「型に入れて〜を作る」。	paste	C
requirement [rɪkwáɪərmənt]	名 必須要件 meet the requirements 要件を満たす	demand	
fortune [fɔ́ːrtʃən]	名 財産, 富 make a fortune 財産を築く	wealth	
online [áːnlàɪn]	副 オンライン上で make an application online オンライン上で申し込む ＊W2 buy something online のように副詞として使うと便利。	on the Internet	D
renew [rɪn(j)úː]	動 更新する renew a driver's license 運転免許を更新する	update	
original [ərídʒənl]	形 元の, 原形の；独創的な original documents 原本	initial	

39

単語・発音	語義／フレーズ	同意表現
encyclopaedia [ɪnsàɪkləpíːdiə]	名 百科事典 Encyclopaedia of Australian Wildlife オーストラリア野生生物の百科事典	cyclopaedia
migration [maɪgréɪʃən]	名 移動, 移住 seasonal migration 季節ごとの移動	travel
supernatural [sùːpərnǽtʃərəl]	形 超自然の, 人間離れした supernatural phenomena 超常現象	paranormal
refundable [rɪfʌ́ndəbl]	形 払い戻し可能な a refundable deposit 払い戻し可能な保証金 ＊refund は動詞と名詞の両方がある。	reimbursable
immigrant [ímɪgrənt]	名 移民, 移住者, 入植者 illegal immigrants into US 米国への不法移住者 ＊外国への移民は emigrant。	settler
rent [rént]	名（家／土地の）賃貸料 pay rent for the room 家賃を支払う	rental fee
magical [mǽdʒɪkəl]	形 魅惑的な a magical voice 魅惑的な声	charming
cave [kéɪv]	名 洞窟, 洞穴 cave art of ancient cultures 古代文化の洞窟画	hole
appointment [əpɔ́ɪntmənt]	名 約束, 予約；任命, 選任 cancel an appointment 約束を取り消す	engagement
register [rédʒɪstər]	動 登録する, 登記する register a birth 出生を登録する	enrol
temporary [témpərèri]	形 一時的な, 臨時の temporary workers 臨時職員	transient
scholarship [skáːlərʃɪp]	名 奨学金 a scholarship for international students 留学生のための奨学金	grant

Track 026

単語・発音	語義／フレーズ	同意表現	難易度
award [əwɔ́ːrd]	動 授与する award prises 賞を与える	grant	A
nursing [nə́ːrsɪŋ]	名 看護；保育 the School of Nursing 看護学部	care	
introductory [ìntrədʌ́ktəri]	形 入門的な an introductory course of English 英語入門講座	elementary	
warning [wɔ́ːrnɪŋ]	名 警告, 注意 a tornado warning 竜巻警報	caution	B
demand [dɪmǽnd]	名 需要；要求 a huge demand for educational reforms 教育改革に対する大きな要求	need	
employment [ɪmplɔ́ɪmənt]	名 雇用 full-time employment 常勤雇用 ＊R employee「従業員」, employer「雇用主」も併せて覚える。	hiring	
advertisement [ǽdvɚ́ːtɪsmənt]	名 広告, 宣伝 a TV advertisement for a new product 新製品のテレビ宣伝　＊[英]と[米]で発音が異なる。	advert	C
companion [kəmpǽnjən]	名 仲間, 友人；伴侶 a travel companion 旅の道連れ	friend	
wheelchair [wíːəltʃèər]	名 車椅子 get around in a wheelchair 車椅子で動き回る	Bath chair	
box office [bɑ́ksɑ̀fɪs]	名 切符売り場 buy a ticket at the box office 窓口でチケットを買う	ticket window	D
ache [éɪk]	名 痛み, 疼き complain of aches and pains あちこちの痛みを訴える	pain	
period [píəriəd]	名 時代 the colonial period 植民地時代 ＊W1 during the period「その期間に」をよく使う。	era	

41

単語・発音	語義／フレーズ	同意表現
referee [rèfərí:]	名 審判 a fair referee 公正な審判	umpire
chaos [kéɪɑːs]	名 無秩序；大混乱 chaos after the war 戦後の大混乱 ＊英語では「カオス」とは読まない。	disorder
quotation [kwoʊtéɪʃən]	名 引用 quotations from the Bible 聖書からの引用	citation
domain [doʊméɪn]	名 領域, 範囲；領土 the domain of science 科学の領域	field
herd [hə́ːrd]	名 群れ a herd of elephants 象の群れ	huddle
legacy [légəsi]	名 遺産 a historical legacy 歴史的遺産	heritage
bribe [bráɪb]	動 賄賂を贈る bribe a government official 政府の役人に賄賂を贈る	boodle
survey [sərvéɪ]	名 調査；概観 conduct a survey 調査を実施する	examination
unsatisfactory [ʌ̀nsætəsfǽktəri]	形 満足できない unsatisfactory results 不満足な結果	deficient
tan [tǽn]	動 (肌を)日焼けさせる；(獣皮を)なめす tan one's skin 日焼けする	sunburn
sleeveless [slíːvləs]	形 袖なしの a sleeveless shirt 袖なしのシャツ	short-sleeve
stock [stάk]	名 株式；在庫 a stock market 株式市場 ＊R share も「株式」の意味で使われる。	equity

Track 028

単語・発音	語義／フレーズ	同意表現	難易度
folk [fóuk]	形 民族の；民間の folk tales 民話	ethnic	A
well-balanced [wél-bǽlənst]	形 バランスのよい a well-balanced meal バランスの取れた食事	proportionate	
meaningful [míːnɪŋfl]	形 意味を持つ a meaningful dialogue 有意義な対話 ＊「意味のない」は meaningless。	significant	
attempt [ətémpt]	動 企てる；努力する attempt to climb Mt. Everest エベレスト登頂を試みる ＊名詞でも使われる。	try	B
broadly [brɔ́ːdli]	副 大ざっぱに；広範囲に broadly speaking 大まかに言って	largely	
preview [príːvjùː]	名 試写（会）；下見 a sneak preview 覆面試写会	trailer	
mention [ménʃən]	動 言及する, 触れる；のことを書く Now that you mention it, I haven't seen him. そう言えば, 彼に会わないね。	refer to	C
delay [dɪléɪ]	動 遅らせる delay a flight in a storm 嵐でフライトを遅らせる	detain	
divorce [dɪvɔ́ːrs]	名 離婚 get a divorce 離婚する	separation	
objective [əbdʒéktɪv]	形 客観的な objective data 客観的データ ＊⇔ subjective「主観的な」。	detached	D
so-called [sóukɔ́ːld]	形 いわゆる so-called high society いわゆる上流社交界	what is called	
vote [vóut]	名 票, 投票 the casting vote 決定投票	ballot	

43

Track 029

単語・発音	語義／フレーズ	同意表現
lighthouse [láɪthàʊs]	名 灯台 a lighthouse keeper 灯台守	beacon
reef [ríːf]	名 礁，岩礁 coral reef サンゴ礁	chain of rocks or coral
fade [féɪd]	動 弱まる；薄くなる；消えていく The glory gradually faded. その栄光は徐々に消えていった。	wither
precious [préʃəs]	形 貴重な a precious moment 貴重な時間	valued
masterpiece [mǽstəpìːs]	名 傑作 a classic masterpiece 最高級の名作	masterwork
carpentry [káːrpəntri]	名 大工仕事；木工細工 home carpentry 日曜大工	woodwork
ambulance [ǽmbjələns]	名 救急車 Please call an ambulance. 救急車を呼んでください。	emergency car
tomb [túːm]	名 墓，墓穴；墓石 He was buried in the family tomb. 彼は一家の墓に埋葬された。	grave
accurately [ǽkjərətli]	副 正確に accurately predict the future 未来を正確に予測する ＊「時間通りに」は punctually を使う。	exactly
attitude [ǽtət(j)ùːd]	名 態度；姿勢 take a negative attitude 消極的な態度をとる ＊「考え方」の意味もある。	manner
ceiling [síːlɪŋ]	名 天井 a chandelier hanging from the ceiling 天井から吊るされているシャンデリア　＊L 発音に注意！	roof
celebrate [séləbrèɪt]	動 祝う；褒めたたえる celebrate a victory 勝利を祝う	commemorate

Track 030

単語・発音	語義／フレーズ	同意表現	難易度
continuity [kɑ̀:ntən(j)ú:əti]	名（時間的・空間的）連続, 継続 historical continuity 歴史的連続性	sequence	A
diet [dáɪət]	名食事；ダイエット a healthy and balanced diet 健康でバランスの取れた食事 ＊R「減量」で出ることは稀で、ほとんどが「食生活」の意味。	meal	
emergency [ɪmə́:rdʒənsi]	名緊急事態, 非常事態 an emergency call 緊急招集	exigency	
encourage [ɪnkə́:rɪdʒ]	動促進する, 奨励する；励ます encourage communication コミュニケーションを促す ＊W2 encourage O to V「OがVするよう勧める」は便利。	promote	B
flow [flóʊ]	動流れる flow back 逆流する	stream	
indicator [índəkèɪtər]	名表示機器；表すもの a wind indicator 風向計 ＊[英]では「車の方向指示器」も意味する。[米]だと blinker。	index	
memorable [mémərəbl]	形忘れられない a memorable event 忘れられない出来事	unforgettable	C
monologue [má:nəlɔ̀(:)g]	名独白 conduct a monologue 独り言を言う ＊L Section2 と 4 は monologue。1 と 3 は conversation。	soliloquy	
overwork [óʊvərwə́:rk]	名働き過ぎ overwork death 過労死	working too hard	
souvenir [sù:vəníər]	名土産 a souvenir shop 土産物店	home-coming gift	D
subject [sʌ́bdʒekt]	名主題 a familiar subject なじみ深いテーマ	theme	
supportive [səpɔ́:rtɪv]	形支えとなる supportive evidence 裏付けとなる証拠	supporting	

45

Track 031

単語・発音	語義／フレーズ	同意表現
surround [səráʊnd]	動 取り囲む be surrounded by a wall of 〜 〜の壁に囲まれている	encompass
theme [θíːm]	名 テーマ a theme park テーマパーク ＊Ⓛ 発音注意。聞き取りにくい。	subject
unstable [ʌnstéɪbl]	形 不安定な an unstable political situation 不安定な政情 ＊⇔ stable	precarious
unwise [ʌnwáɪz]	形 あさはかな an unwise statement 軽率な発言	ill-advised
display [dɪspléɪ]	動 展示する；表す be displayed in a museum 美術館に展示される	exhibit
dramatically [drəmǽtɪkəli]	副 劇的に A car navigation system has dramatically improved. カーナビは劇的に向上した。	drastically
gradually [grǽdʒuəli]	副 徐々に gradually come to like it 徐々にそれが好きになる	step by step
overweight [óʊvərwèɪt]	形 太り過ぎの She is 3 pounds overweight. 彼女は3ポンド太り過ぎです。	exceed
rapidly [rǽpɪdli]	副 急速に a rapidly changing society 急速に変貌を遂げる社会 ＊W1 increase rapidly = soar を覚えたい。	quickly
sharply [ʃáːrpli]	副 急に sharply drop 急落する ＊W1「急落する」は plunge を使えると高評価。	acutely
sink [síŋk]	動 沈む sink into the sea 海に沈む	submerge
slump [slʌ́mp]	名 落ち込み；不況 slump in sales 販売不振	decline

46

Track 032

単語・発音	語義／フレーズ	同意表現	難易度
trend [trénd]	名 傾向，流行 a fashion trend ファッション傾向	vogue	A
unemployment [ʌ̀nɪmplɔ́ɪmənt]	名 失業 unemployment insurance 失業保険	joblessness	
export-import [ɪkspɔ́ːrt-ɪmpɔ́ːrt]	形 輸出入の export-import policies 輸出入政策		
rank [ræŋk]	名 階級；身分 rise through the ranks 出世する	grade	B
tax [tæks]	名 税金 income tax 所得税 ＊W2 impose a tax を使えるように。	duty	
thus [ðʌs]	副 したがって；このように He is the eldest son and thus heir to the title. 彼は長男，それゆえ跡取りです。	therefore	
underground [ʌ́ndərgràʊnd]	名 地下鉄 take the underground 地下鉄に乗る ＊[英]。	tube	C
woodland [wʊ́dlənd]	名 森林地帯 woodland ecosystem 森林生態系	timberland	
merchant [mə́ːrtʃənt]	名 商人 a retail merchant 小売商人	merchandiser	
canal [kənǽl]	名 運河，水路 rivers interconnected by canals 運河によって相互に結ばれている河川	waterway	D
map [mæp]	動 地図を描く；綿密に計画する map out a new project 新事業の計画を練る	chart	
binoculars [bɪnɑ́kjələr]	名 双眼鏡 binoculars for bird watching バードウォッチングのための双眼鏡	field glasses	

47

単語・発音	語義／フレーズ	同意表現
subway [sʌ́bwèɪ]	名 地下道；[米]地下鉄 a pedestrian subway 歩行者用地下道 ＊[英]。	underpass
wheat [hwíːt]	名 小麦 a wheat field 小麦畑 ＊ oat「カラスムギ」, barley「大麦」も併せて覚える。	
coastline [kóʊstlàɪn]	名 海岸線 along the coastline 海岸線沿いに	shoreline
sculpture [skʌ́lptʃər]	名 彫刻 ice sculpture 氷の彫刻 ＊ statue で言い換えられることもある。	carving
innocence [ínəsəns]	名 無罪 plead innocence 無罪を主張する	guiltlessness
reunion [riːjúːnjən]	名 再会；同窓会 reunion of separated families 離散家族の再会 ＊ family reunion「（クリスマスなどの）家族との再会」。	meeting again
restriction [rɪstríkʃən]	名 制限, 限定；制約 restriction of diet 食事制限	limitation
tribe [tráɪb]	名 部族, 種族 raid an enemy tribe 敵の部族を襲撃する	race
prairie [préəri]	名 大草原 a flat desolate prairie 何もない荒涼たる原野 ＊ A Little House on the Prairie「大草原の小さな家」。	great plain
sustain [səstéɪn]	動 持続させる；支える；屈しない sustain a close relationship 緊密な関係を維持する ＊ sustainable「持続できる」も併せて覚える。	maintain
constitution [kɑ̀ːnstət(j)úːʃən]	名 憲法 the Constitution of the United States 合衆国憲法 ＊ the Constitution of ～で「～憲法」。	principle
cement [səmént]	動 固める；セメントで接着する cement our friendship 我々の友情を固める	join

Track 034

単語・発音	語義／フレーズ	同意表現	難易度
organic [ɔːrgǽnɪk]	形 有機的な；基本的な an organic vegetable grower 有機野菜栽培農家 ＊「器官の」や「基本的な」が盲点かもしれない。	relating to living organisms	A
fertiliser [fə́ːrtəlàɪzər]	名 肥料, 化学肥料；受精媒介者 chemical fertilisers 化学肥料 ＊fertilise「肥沃にさせる」からきているので簡単。	manure	
balance [bǽləns]	名 残高 have a balance of £20,000 in the bank account その銀行口座に2万ポンドの残高がある ＊キャンパスでの預金に関する会話で頻出。	remainder	
once [wʌ́ns]	接 いったん～すると Once you cross the line いったん一線を越えると ＊副詞なら「かつて；1度」の意味。	as soon as	B
slot [slɑ́ːt]	名 時間帯；位置 the prime-time slot ゴールデンタイム枠 ＊time slot「時間帯」が覚えやすい。	space	
appreciate [əpríːʃièɪt]	動 評価する；感謝する His artistry was appreciated after his death. 彼の芸術性は死後に評価された。	appraise	
transit [trǽnsət]	名 通過, 乗り換え；輸送, 運輸 a transit check-in counter（空港の）乗り継ぎカウンター ＊a transit lounge は，「（空港の）通過旅客用待合室」。	traffic	C
contact [kɑ́ːntækt]	名 付き合い；接触 various professional contacts いろいろな職業人との付合い ＊動詞「連絡をとる」の場合は, with 不要の他動詞。	communication	
flourish [flə́ːrɪʃ]	動 繁茂する；繁栄する Ferns flourish even in the rock crevices. シダは岩の割れ目でも繁茂する。	thrive	
intensity [ɪnténsəti]	名（光・熱の）強さ；（気候などの）激しさ measure the intensity of radiation 放射線強度を測る	strength	D
doom [dúːm]	動 運命づける；確実に破滅させる I'm doomed. 私は破滅だ。	destine	
interactive [ìntərǽktɪv]	形 双方向性の；対話方式の digital interactive broadcasting デジタル双方向放送 ＊英語のままでよく耳にしているので意外と盲点になる単語。	reciprocal	

49

| 単語・発音 | 語義／フレーズ | 同意表現 |

access
[ǽkses]

名接近；手立て

approach

give citizens independent access to the candidates
国民に，候補者への独自の接触方法を与える
＊この意味での access には，動詞の用法がない。have access to 名詞, get access to 名詞「利用する；利用できる」。

IELTS必須英単語
Group B

Track 036

単語／発音	語義／フレーズ	同意表現
inevitable [ɪnévətəbl]	形 避けられない，不可避の；必然の inevitable consequences 避けられない結果 ＊ unavoidable も同義語。	inescapable
shrink [ʃríŋk]	動 縮む Most glaciers have been shrinking. ほとんどの氷河が縮小中だ。　＊R decrease, diminish との書き換えに注意。	contract
adopt [ədɑ́:pt]	動 採用する adopt a variety of approaches 様々な方法を採用する ＊ adapt「適応する」と間違えないように。	accept
accumulation [əkjù:mjəléɪʃən]	名 蓄積 accumulation of fat under the skin 皮下脂肪の蓄積 ＊ snow accumulation は「積雪」。	build-up
satellite [sǽtəlàɪt]	名 衛星 observation of Jupiter's satellites 木星の衛星観測	moon
omit [oʊmít]	動 除外する omit a name from the list リストから名前を除外する ＊ emit「放出する」と混同しないように！	exclude
broad [brɔ́:d]	形 大まかな；広々とした a broad prediction 大まかな予測	rough
complex [kà:mpléks]	形 複雑な a complex structure 複雑な構造 ＊ perplexing も同義語。	complicated
genetic [dʒənétɪk]	形 遺伝子の；起源の，発生の genetic engineering 遺伝子工学 ＊ genetics「遺伝学；遺伝的特徴」も頻出。	hereditary
basis [béɪsɪs]	名 基礎，根拠，基準 form the basis of a theory 理論の基礎を作る	foundation
examine [ɪgzǽmən]	動 調査する，検査する examine the sample サンプルを調べる ＊「調査する」は investigate, explore, scrutinise も覚えたい。	inspect
raw [rɔ́:]	形 生の；加工していない raw materials 原材料	crude

Track 037

単語／発音	語義／フレーズ	同意表現	難易度
process [prá:ses]	動 加工（処理）する process food 食品を加工する	deal with	A
absorb [əbzɔ́:rb]	動 吸収する absorb moisture 水分を吸収する ＊absorb a language で「言語を身につける」。	assimilate	
advancement [ədvǽnsmənt]	名 進歩；昇進 advancement in technology 技術の進歩	progress	
resource [rí:sɔ:rs]	名 財源，資源 pool resources 資金を出し合う ＊「財源」という意味が盲点。	fund	B
contribute [kəntríbju:t]	動 貢献する；一因となる contribute to the sales 売り上げに貢献する　＊マイナスのことにも使う。W2 contribute to の後は名詞。動詞ではない。	play a part in	
rate [réɪt]	名 率；速度 the unemployment rate 失業率 ＊W2 ratio は「(2者の)比率」の意。むやみに書き換えないように！	proportion	
degree [dɪgrí:]	名 学位；程度 earn an associate degree in economics 経済学準学士号を取る　＊「程度」の意味もある。	title	C
recognise [rékəgnàɪz]	動 認識する recognise him by his voice 声で彼だと分かる	perceive	
merely [míərli]	副 単に It is merely because I like him. それはただ私が彼を好きだからだ。 ＊W1 a mere 10%「たった10%」。	simply	
reproduce [rì:prəd(j)ú:s]	動 繁殖する reproduce by laying eggs 産卵によって繁殖する ＊multiply, propagate の類義語も覚えたい。	breed	D
obtain [əbtéɪn]	動 得る，手に入れる obtain a promotion 昇進を手に入れる	gain	
chew [tʃú:]	動 噛む，咀嚼する Digestion begins with chewing. よく噛むことで消化が始まる。 ＊chewing gum で覚えよう！	masticate	

53

単語／発音	語義／フレーズ	同意表現

estimate
[éstəmèɪt]

動 見積もる，推定する
roughly estimate the amount 額を大雑把に見積もる
＊W1 be estimated to V で未来の予測を表す。

evaluate

substance
[sʌ́bstəns]

名 物質
a chemical substance 化学物質
＊ chemicals「化学薬品」の書き換えで出題されることも。

material

moss
[mɔ́(:)s]

名 コケ
A rolling stone gathers no moss. 転がる石には苔が生えない。
＊L 書き取り問題に出そうな単語。

liverwort

application
[æplɪkéɪʃən]

名 応用，適用，利用；申し込み
the application of scientific principles 科学的原理の応用
＊L application form「申込書」の記入は Section1 で頻出。

use

determine
[dɪtə́ːrmən]

動 決定する
Your score on IELTS determines your class.
IELTS の点でクラスが決まります。

fix

nevertheless
[nèvərðəlés]

副 それにもかかわらず
I'm feeling ill; nevertheless I'll come.
気分が悪い，それでも伺います。

nonetheless

precise
[prɪsáɪs]

形 正確な
precise figures 正確な数字

exact

shore
[ʃɔ́ːr]

名 岸，海岸
on shore 上陸して

coast

radiation
[rèɪdiéɪʃən]

名 放射線，放射能；(光の)放射
high doses of radiation that damage cells
細胞を損なう多量の放射線

radioactive rays

tough
[tʌ́f]

形 硬い，破れにくい
the tough skin of a reptile 爬虫類の硬い皮膚
＊L「(肉などが)噛み切れない」という意味でも出る。

hard

contain
[kəntéɪn]

動 含む
contain some alcohol アルコールがいくらか入っている

include

moist
[mɔ́ɪst]

形 湿った
moist air 湿った空気
＊ damp（発音注意）も同意語で覚えよう！

wet

Track 038

54

Track 039

単語／発音	語義／フレーズ	同意表現	難易度
scarce [skéərs]	形 乏しい, 不十分な, 不足している Plums are scarce because of the bad weather. 悪天候でプラムは品薄です。＊名詞 scarcity も頻出。	short	A
proportion [prəpɔ́:rʃən]	名 割合, 比率；釣り合い the proportion of men to women in population 人口の男女比	ratio	
priority [praiɔ́:rəti]	名 優先, 優先権 give human life the highest priority 人命を最優先する	precedence	
capacity [kəpǽsəti]	名 能力, 才能；収容能力 a great capacity for remembering facts 事実を記憶する偉大な能力	ability	B
proper [prá:pər]	形 適切な, 正しい；固有の a proper diet 正しい食事 ＊polite「礼儀正しい」の意味もある。	appropriate	
order [ɔ́:rdər]	名 秩序, 整頓；順序 be in good order 秩序立っている	system	
fundamental [fʌ̀ndəméntl]	形 基本的な, 根本的な defend a fundamental human right 基本的人権を守る ＊同義語 rudimentary も覚えたい。	basic	C
right [ráit]	名 権利 fight for equal rights 平等の権利のために戦う	title	
obligation [à:bligéiʃən]	名 義務, 責務；恩義 fulfil a legal obligation 法律上の義務を果たす	duty	
state [stéit]	名 国家；州 the three requisites of a state 国家の3要素 ＊「状態」の意も重要。state of mind「精神状態」。	nation	D
ensure [inʃúər]	動 確実にする；確保する ensure the safety 安全を確保する	make sure	
liberal [líbərəl]	形 自由主義の；寛大な a liberal and unconventional family 自由主義で型破りな家族	unbiased	

55

Track 040

単語／発音	語義／フレーズ	同意表現
whole [hóʊl]	形 全体の, すべての the whole nation 国民全体	all
realisation [rìːəlaɪzéɪʃən]	名 認識, 悟ること；実現 a realisation of the imminent danger 迫り来る危険の認識	awareness
evident [évədənt]	形 明白な, はっきり分かる especially evident in this case この場合, 特に明白である	obvious
establishment [ɪstæblɪʃmənt]	名 機関, 組織, 会社；設立, 確立 a research establishment 研究機関	organisation
remark [rɪmάːrk]	動 言う, 述べる as has just been remarked ただいま言われたように	say
mammal [mǽml]	名 哺乳類 Mammals are fed with their mothers' milk. 哺乳類は母乳で育つ。	suckler
indicate [índəkèɪt]	動 ほのめかす；指し示す A sneeze indicates a cold. くしゃみは風邪の兆候である。	show
resemble [rɪzémbl]	動 似ている not resemble either of one's parents 両親のどちらにも似ていない　＊他動詞なので前置詞は不要。	look like
particular [pərtíkjələr]	形 特定の；特有の choose one particular subject 特定の1科目を選ぶ	specific
peak [píːk]	動 頂点に達する Stock prices peaked then. 株価はそのときピークに達した。 ＊W1 名詞・動詞の両方で使えるように。	culminate
decline [dɪkláɪn]	動 低下する；丁寧に断る Our profit declined temporarily. 我々の利益は一時低下した。 ＊W1 自動詞 decrease の書き換えに使う。	dwindle
inspection [ɪnspékʃən]	名 調査, 点検 a closer inspection より詳しい調査	examination

Track 041

単語／発音	語義／フレーズ	同意表現	難易度
significantly [sɪgnífɪkəntli]	副 著しく，はっきりと；意味深く significantly reduce one's body fat 体脂肪を著しく減らす ＊W1 considerably, remarkably と書き換えられる。	remarkably	A
sensitive [sénsətɪv]	形 敏感な，神経過敏の sensitive to light 光に対して敏感な	susceptible	
activate [ǽktəvèɪt]	動 活性化させる activate the brain 脳を活性化させる	revitalise	
nerve [nə́ːrv]	名 神経 the optic nerve 視神経 ＊ get on one's nerves「(人の)神経に障る」。	neuron	B
cell [sél]	名 細胞；基本組織 the nucleus of a cell 細胞核		
component [kəmpóʊnənt]	名 構成要素；部品 a vital component 重要な要素	ingredient	
specific [spəsífɪk]	形 特定の，明確な a specific candidate 特定の候補者	particular	C
tease [tíːz]	動 からかう tease a person about his height 身長のことで人をからかう	make fun of	
seal [síːl]	名 オットセイ，アザラシ juvenile fur seals 幼いキタオットセイ ＊R 動詞の seal「密封する」も知っておきたい。		
glance [glǽns]	名 ちらりと見ること at first glance ひと目見てすぐに	glimpse	D
unquestionably [ʌnkwéstʃənəbli]	副 疑いなく，間違いなく， It is unquestionably true. 間違いなく真実である。	indubitably	
curiosity [kjùəriɑ́ːsəti]	名 好奇心；せんさく好き out of curiosity 好奇心から（が原因で）	inquisitiveness	

Track 042

単語／発音	語義／フレーズ	同意表現
expand [ɪkspǽnd]	動 拡大する；発展させる Vocabulary expands through reading. 語彙は読書で増える。	extend
overcome [òʊvərkʌ́m]	動 克服する，打ち勝つ overcome injury 怪我を克服する	surmount
status [stǽtəs]	名 地位；身分 an improvement in the status of women 女性の地位向上 ＊L 発音注意。「スタタス」と読むこともある。	standing
detect [dɪtékt]	動 見抜く；探知する detect diseases early 病気を初期に発見する ＊ lie detector「うそ発見器」。	notice
initiative [ɪníʃətɪv]	名 率先，主導権；独創力 on one's own initiative 率先して	enterprise
outline [áʊtlàɪn]	動 要点を述べる；輪郭を描く outline the programme プログラムの概要を述べる ＊W2 outline（骨子）を決めてから書き始めるのが重要。	summarise
marked [máːrkt]	形 際立った，著しい a marked difference 際立った相違	noticeable
vital [váɪtl]	形 とても重要な；絶対に必要な vital for health 健康にとって非常に大切な ＊ essential, integral など同義語多数。	crucial
regardless [rɪgáːrdləs]	形 気にかけない，無頓着な regardless of sex 性別に関係なく ＊W2 使うときには of を忘れないように。	unconcerned
dull [dʌ́l]	形 どんよりした，陰気な a dull sky どんよりした空	murky
drastic [drǽstɪk]	形 徹底的な；過激な drastic changes 激烈な変化	extreme
ultraviolet [ʌ̀ltrəváɪələt]	形 紫外線の，紫外の ultraviolet rays 紫外線	of sunrays

Track 043

単語／発音	語義／フレーズ	同意表現	難易度
ordinary [ɔ́:rdənèri]	形 普通の，ありふれた ordinary citizens 一般の市民	standard	A
expose [ɪkspóʊz]	動 触れさせる；さらす expose students to radical ideas 学生を過激な思想に触れさせる	subject	
mood [mú:d]	名 気分；雰囲気 not in the mood for joking 冗談を言う気分ではない	temper	
arithmetic [ərɪ́θmətìk]	名 算数；計算（能力） reading, writing, and arithmetic 読み書きと計算	calculation	B
optimistic [à:ptɪmɪ́stɪk]	形 楽観的な an optimistic projection 楽観的な予想 ＊⇔ pessimistic	positive	
suicide [sú:əsàɪd]	名 自殺 commit suicide 自殺する	killing oneself	
irritable [ɪ́rɪtəbl]	形 怒りっぽい，短気な an irritable disposition 怒りっぽい性格 ＊ irritate は「イライラさせる」。	bad-tempered	C
reactive [riǽktɪv]	形 敏感な，すぐ反応する make people more reactive 人を敏感にする	sensitive	
possibly [pá:səbli]	副 おそらく possibly the most difficult おそらく最も難しい	perhaps	
aggressive [əgrésɪv]	形 積極的果敢な；攻撃的な aggressive pricing 攻めの価格設定 ＊いい意味「積極的な」でも悪い意味でも使われる。	competitive	D
essential [ɪsénʃəl]	形 不可欠な；本質的な an essential cause of human aggression 人間の攻撃性に不可欠な要因　＊ critical, integral も同義語。	necessary	
tension [ténʃən]	名 緊張，緊迫状態；伸張 ease racial tensions 民族間の緊張を和らげる	strain	

59

Track 044

単語／発音	語義／フレーズ	同意表現
rebound [rɪbáʊnd]	動 立ち直る；跳ね返る rebound from the loss 損失から立ち直る	recover
minority [maɪnɔ́:rəti]	名 少数派；少数民族 the rights of racial minorities 人種的少数派の権利	a small group
refuse [rɪfjú:z]	動 拒絶する；辞退する flatly refuse to have surgery 手術を受けることをきっぱり断る	turn down
shift [ʃíft]	動 転嫁する；移す shift the blame 責任を転嫁する ＊R change との書き換えに気づくように！	impute
identity [aɪdéntəti]	名 身元；本人であること the murderer's identity 殺人犯の素性	antecedents
cite [sáɪt]	動 引用する；例証する cite an adage 格言を引用する	quote
athlete [ǽθli:t]	名 運動選手；元気で活発な人 athletes competing in the Olympics オリンピックで競い合う運動選手	sportsman
impressive [ɪmprésɪv]	形 感銘を与えるほどの；印象的な the pianist's impressive performance ピアニストの感動的な演奏	touching
instantly [ínstəntli]	副 直ちに，すぐに He went to bed and instantly fell asleep. 彼は床について直ちに寝入った。	immediately
analysis [ənǽləsɪs]	名 分析，分解，検討 make a close analysis of the fossils 化石を綿密に分析する	dissection
comprehend [kà:mprɪhénd]	動 理解する；含む comprehend the intention 意図を理解する	understand
equipment [ɪkwípmənt]	名 装備，機器；知識 the equipment necessary for mountaineering 登山に必要な装備	apparatus

Track 045

単語／発音	語義／フレーズ	同意表現	難易度
foreseeable [fɔːrsíːəbl]	形 予見可能な foreseeable risks 予見可能な危険 ＊R foreseeable future「（予測できる）近い未来」。	predictable	A
inadequate [ɪnǽdəkwət]	形 不適切な an inadequate diet 不適切な食事	inappropriate	
pioneer [pàɪəníər]	動 先駆けとなる；開拓する Who pioneered the use of vaccine? ワクチンを最初に使ったのは誰か。	initiate	
joint [dʒɔ́ɪnt]	名 関節；継ぎ目 the top two joints of her ring finger 彼女の薬指の上部2関節	articulation	B
equation [ɪkwéɪʒən]	名 方程式 a second degree equation 二次方程式		
remain [rɪméɪn]	動 〜のままである remain the same 同じ状態のままである ＊W1 The rate remained stable.「レートは変わらないままだった」。	stay	
generation [dʒènəréɪʃən]	名 世代 future generations 後の世代の人々	age	C
endangered [ɪndéɪndʒərd]	形 絶滅寸前の endangered species 絶滅危惧種	vanishing	
critical [krítɪkl]	形 危篤の；危機の，重大な in a critical condition 危篤状態で ＊「重大な」は integral, significant など同義語が多数ある。	serious	
confidence [kάːnfədəns]	名 信頼；自信 crisis of confidence 信頼の危機	trust	D
alongside [əlɔ́ːŋsáɪd]	副 前 そばに；並んで A car drew up alongside. 1台の車が横付けに止まった。	next to	
voluntary [vάːləntèri]	形 自発的な voluntary retirement 希望退職	spontaneous	

61

単語／発音	語義／フレーズ	同意表現
effectively [ɪféktɪvli]	副 効果的に, 有効に use time effectively 時間を有効に活用する ＊R「事実上」という意味で出ることも。	efficiently
preserve [prɪzə́ːrv]	動 保存する；保護する preserve a heritage 文化遺産を守る	conserve
harmful [hɑ́ːrmfl]	形 有害な, 害を及ぼす be harmful to health 健康に対して有害だ	detrimental
excessive [ɪksésɪv]	形 過度の, 過大な excessive consumption of alcohol アルコールの過剰摂取 ＊⇔ moderate	undue
hazard [hǽzərd]	名 危険 be exposed to a hazard 危険にさらされている ＊ danger も同義語。	risk
accessible [æksésəbl]	形 接近できる；利用できる be accessible by the Internet インターネットでアクセス可能である	approachable
adaptation [æ̀dæptéɪʃən]	名 適応；適応能力 adaptation to the environment 環境に対する適応	adjustment
assign [əsáɪn]	動 割り当てる；任命する assign a duty 任務を割り当てる ＊ assignment は「任務」。もちろん「課題」の意味も。	allot
blame [bléɪm]	動 責任を負わせる；非難する blame youth crime on unemployment 若者の犯罪を失業のせいにする	reproach
surpass [sərpǽs]	動 上回る, しのぐ surpass expectations 予想を上回る ＊W1 surpass the rate of 〜 「〜のレートを上回る」。	exceed
reduce [rɪd(j)úːs]	動 減らす；まとめる reduce a budget 予算を削る	decrease
efficiency [ɪfíʃənsi]	名 効率；能率 fuel efficiency 燃費（燃料の効率）	effectiveness

Track 047

単語／発音	語義／フレーズ	同意表現	難易度
emphasis [émfəsɪs]	名 強調 emphasis on the economy 経済重視 ＊put/lay/place emphasis on ～「～を強調する」。	accentuation	A
bless [blés]	動 (通例 be ～ ed)恩恵を受ける，祝福される be blessed with good weather 天候に恵まれている	endow	
imaginative [ɪmǽdʒənətɪv]	形 想像力に富んだ；想像の an imaginative writer 想像力豊かな作家	inventive	
character [kǽrəktər]	名 登場人物；性格 fascinating characters in his novel 彼の小説の魅力的な登場人物	persona	B
interpretation [ɪntə̀ːrprətéɪʃən]	名 解釈 interpretation of the Constitution 憲法解釈	construction	
cheat [tʃíːt]	動 カンニングする；だます be caught cheating on an exam カンニングしているのを見つけられる	copy	C
myth [míθ]	名 神話；根拠のない説 a creation myth 天地創造の神話 ＊「根拠のない説」の意味に関する出題も多い。	legend	
generalisation [dʒènərəlaɪzéɪʃən]	名 一般化；一般論 make sweeping generalisation おおまかに一般化する	universalisation	
observation [àːbzərvéɪʃən]	名 観察，観測；観察記録 make a close observation of planets 惑星の緻密な観察を行う	observance	
otherwise [ʌ́ðərwàɪz]	副 違ったふうに；さもなければ He seems to think otherwise. 彼は違ったふうに考えているようだ。	in a different way	D
inquiry [ɪnkwáɪəri]	名 質問；調査 a letter of inquiry 問い合わせの手紙	question	
methodology [mèθədáːlədʒi]	名 方法論 methodology of science 科学的方法論	procedure	

63

単語／発音	語義／フレーズ	同意表現
naive [nɑːíːv]	形 単純な, 世間知らずの；純真な have a naive faith in a rumour うわさを単純に信じ込む ＊「考えが甘い」という意もある。	innocent
modify [mɑ́ːdəfàɪ]	動 修正する, 変更する；緩和する modify a document 文書に修正を加える ＊類義語が多く, このグループは最頻出。	alter
hence [héns]	副 それゆえに；今から先 The earth is round. Hence, there is night and day. 地球は丸い。ゆえに昼夜が存在する。	therefore
apparent [əpérənt]	形 明白な；見たところ apparent contradiction 明らかな矛盾	evident
fascinating [fǽsənèɪtɪŋ]	形 魅力的な；うっとりさせる a fascinating book 興味の尽きない本 ＊ interesting, intriguing と同義語でプラスの意味。	enchanting
remarkable [rɪmɑ́ːrkəbl]	形 注目に値する；際立った another remarkable characteristic もう1つの注目すべき特性	noteworthy
crow [króʊ]	名 カラス as black as a crow カラスのように真っ黒で	raven
species [spíːʃiːz]	名 （生物学的な）種；人類 a rare species of spider 希少種のクモ ＊《単複同形》。	specific kind
habitual [həbítʃuəl]	形 常習の；習慣的な, いつもの a habitual gambler ギャンブル常習者	chronic
cunning [kʌ́nɪŋ]	形 ずるい, 悪賢い as cunning as a fox 狐のように悪賢い ＊人だと「ずるい」, ものだと「巧妙な」。	crafty
insect [ínsekt]	名 昆虫 an insect repellent 防虫剤 ＊「殺虫剤」は insecticide。	bug
row [róʊ]	名 （横並びの）列；座席の列 three days in a row 3日間連続で ＊ in a row ＝ consecutively「連続で」。	sequence

Track 048

64

Track 049

単語／発音	語義／フレーズ	同意表現	難易度
tear [téər]	動 引き裂く tear a cardboard box to pieces 段ボール箱をずたずたに引き裂く　＊「涙」とは発音が異なる。	rip	A
progression [prəgréʃən]	名 進行, 前進；進歩 progression of cancer がんの進行	procession	
instruction [instrʌ́kʃən]	名 指示, 指図；教えること provide verbal instructions 口頭で指示を与える ＊ rigid instruction は「厳しい教育」。	direction	
clip [klíp]	動 (はさみなどで)切る；刈る clip an article (新聞などから)記事を切り抜く	cut	B
ample [ǽmpl]	形 豊富な, 十分な；広大な offer ample evidence 十分な証拠を提示する	plentiful	
proof [prú:f]	名 証明；証拠 have proof of identity 身元を証明するものを持っている	evidence	
workmanship [wə́:rkmənʃip]	名 出来栄え；(職人の)すぐれた技量 be of excellent workmanship 素晴らしい出来栄えである	craftsmanship	C
in-between [ìn-bɪtwí:n]	形 中間の, 中間的な at that in-between age, neither a child nor an adult 子供でも大人でもない中間の年齢で	intermediate	
reveal [rɪví:l]	動 漏らす, 明らかにする reveal industrial secrets 企業秘密を漏らす ＊W1 the graph shows ＝ the chart reveals と書き換える。	disclose	
sophisticated [səfístɪkeɪtɪd]	形 洗練された；精巧な a sophisticated manner beyond one's years 年齢をしのぐ洗練された物腰　＊「高度な」という意味では advanced と同義語。	refined	D
resourceful [rí:sɔ̀:rsfl]	形 機略にすぐれた, やりくり上手の resourceful ways of thinking 臨機応変な思考法	witty	
well [wél]	名 井戸 an oil well 油田, 油井(せい)	font	

65

Track 050

単語／発音	語義／フレーズ	同意表現
functional [fʌ́ŋkʃənl]	形 機能的な；機能上の，職務上の play a functional role 機能的な役割を果たす ＊function は名詞でも動詞としても使える。	functionable
property [prɑ́:pərti]	名 資産；特性 inherit real property 不動産を相続する ＊「資産」「特性」どちらの意味でも頻出。	assets
foresight [fɔ́:rsàit]	名 先見の明，洞察力 a person of foresight 先見性のある人	vision
wedge [wédʒ]	名 くさび；くさび形のもの drive a wedge into the crack 割れ目にくさびを打ち込む	chock
crack [krǽk]	名 割れ目，裂け目，ひび This wine glass has a crack in it. このワイングラスにはひびがある。	cleavage
retain [rɪtéɪn]	動 保持する manage to retain a solid majority 何とか安定過半数を保持する	hold
encounter [ɪnkáʊntər]	名 出会い，遭遇 a chance encounter 偶然の出会い	meeting
evolution [èvəlú:ʃən]	名 進化，進化論；発展 the evolution of multicellular species 多細胞生物の進化 ＊動詞は evolve。	development
lateral [lǽtərəl]	形 横からの，側面の；外側の lateral collision 側面からの衝突	side
specialisation [spèʃəlaɪzéɪʃən]	名 専門化；専門科目，専門分野 job specialisation 職務の専門化	becoming specialised
extraordinary [ɪkstrɔ́:rdənèri]	形 非凡な，並外れた；異常な an extraordinary talent 並外れた才能	unusual
fixed [fíkst]	形 固定した；一定の fixed asset tax 固定資産税 ＊fix は「修理する；固定する；決定する」の多義語。	steady

Track 051

単語／発音	語義／フレーズ	同意表現	難易度
plenty [plénti]	名 多量, 多数；豊富さ give plenty of thought to the future 将来についてじっくり考える	abundance	A
twig [twíg]	名 小枝 snap a twig into two 小枝をポキッと2つに折る	branchlet	
rib [ríb]	名 あばら骨 a cracked rib ひびの入ったあばら骨 ＊R 植物の「茎」という意味もある。	costa	
retrieve [rɪtríːv]	動 回収する retrieve cargoes from the wreck of a sunken ship 沈没船の残骸から積荷を回収する	recover	B
declare [dɪkléər]	動 宣言する；断言する declare war on an enemy 敵に宣戦布告する	proclaim	
humble [hʌ́mbl]	形 謙虚な show a humble attitude 謙虚な態度を示す ＊「粗末な, 質素な」という意味もある。	modest	
evil [íːvl]	形 邪悪な；有害な be possessed by an evil spirit 悪霊にとりつかれている ＊発音注意！	malicious	C
emotive [ɪmóʊtɪv]	形 感情的な；感情の avoid emotive language 感情的な言葉を避ける	emotional	
rubbish [rʌ́bɪʃ]	名 ごみ；廃棄物 a rubbish dump ごみ捨て場 ＊[英]「ごみ箱」は rubbish bin。	trash	
vast [vǽst]	形 広大な vast areas of farmland 広大な農地	immense	D
landfill [lǽndfìl]	名 (埋め立て式)ごみ処理(場)；埋め立て(地) a rubbish landfill 埋め立て式ごみ処理場	dump	
victim [víktɪm]	名 犠牲者, 被害者；えじき unsuspecting victims of fraud 疑うことを知らない詐欺の被害者	sufferer	

67

単語／発音	語義／フレーズ	同意表現
charge [tʃáːrdʒ]	動 請求する；(責任を)負わせる charge a commission 手数料を取る	demand
criticise [krítɪsàɪz]	動 非難する；批評する，批判する criticise the government's policy or actions 政府の政策や行動を批判する	reproach
prompt [práːmpt]	動 促す；誘発する prompt fears of infestation of lice シラミの蔓延という不安をあおる	encourage
choke [tʃóʊk]	動 窒息する；窒息させる choke to death on food 食べ物で詰まらせて窒息死する	suffocate
slash [slǽʃ]	動 削減する slash a budget 予算を削減する	cut
reuse [rìːjúːs]	名 再利用 promote reuse of paper 紙の再利用を進める	recycle
usage [júːsɪdʒ]	名 使用，利用 the effective usage of resources 資源の有効利用	use
on-the-spot [áːn-ðiː-spàːt]	形 現場での on-the-spot investigation 現場検証	on-site
qualification [kwàːləfɪkéɪʃən]	名 資格，適性 professional qualifications 職業適性 ＊ qualified は「資格がある」。	requisite
prospect [práːspekt]	名 見込み，可能性；客になりそうな人 This plan offers no prospects. この計画は成功の見込みゼロだ。　＊ possibility との言い換えに注意。	expectation
dialogue [dáɪəlɔ̀(ː)g]	名 対話；会談 a constructive dialogue between leaders 指導者間の建設的な対話	conversation
occasional [əkéɪʒənl]	形 時折の；予備の an occasional smoker 時々喫煙をする人	casual

Track 053

単語／発音	語義／フレーズ	同意表現	難易度
revision [rɪvíʒən]	名 改正, 改訂 revision of the constitution 憲法改正	amendment	A
conference [kάːnfərəns]	名 会議, 相談 the conference on disarmament 軍縮会議	convention	
determination [dɪtɔ̀ːrmənéɪʃən]	名 決意 express a strong determination 強い決意を表明する	resolution	
acquire [əkwáɪər]	動 獲得する；習得する acquire a good reputation 良い評価を得る	attain	B
suitable [súːtəbl]	形 適切な, ふさわしい take suitable measures 適切な方策を取る	appropriate	
mode [móʊd]	名 様式, 方法；流行 a preferred mode of behaviour 好ましい行動様式 ＊mode of transport は「交通手段」。	fashion	C
vary [véəri]	動 様々である, 異なる；変化する vary according to age and sex 年齢や性別によって様々である	differ	
resign [rɪzáɪn]	動 辞める, 辞職する resign from office 役職を辞める ＊resign oneself「身を任せる, 甘んじて従う」も併せて。	abdicate	
flooded [flʌ́dɪd]	形 浸水した a flooded house 浸水家屋	inundated	
expectation [èkspektéɪʃən]	名 予想；期待される状態 beyond expectation 予想以上に	forecast	D
cultivate [kʌ́ltəvèɪt]	動 育む；耕す cultivate a long-term relationship 長期的な関係を築く	nurture	
wage [wéɪdʒ]	名 賃金 a minimum wage 最低賃金	pay	

Track 054

単語／発音	語義／フレーズ	同意表現
allowance [əláuəns]	名 (一定額の)手当て an allowance for housing 住宅手当	benefit
firm [fə́ːrm]	名 会社 a family-run firm 家族経営会社 ＊形容詞は「安定した」。firm stock prices「安定した株価」。	company
colleague [káːliːg]	名 同僚, 仲間 get along with a colleague 同僚とうまくやっていく ＊Ⓢ go drinking with my colleagues「同僚と飲みに行く」。	co-worker
eagerly [íːgərli]	副 熱心に, ひたむきに；しきりに eagerly await the reply ひたむきに返事を待つ	earnestly
gain [géin]	動 得る gain insight from experience 経験から洞察力を得る	acquire
net [nét]	形 正味の；最終的な net income after tax 税引後純利益	after deductions
sum [sʌ́m]	名 合計 the sum of cash flows 入出金合計	total
succeed [səksíːd]	動 引き継ぐ succeed to the throne 王位を継承する ＊同意語を overtake「追い抜く」と間違えないように。	take over
fasten [fǽsn]	動 締める；留める Fasten your seat belt when seated. 着席中はシートベルトを着用してください。	tighten
wonder [wʌ́ndər]	動 〜だろうかと思う；不思議に思う I wonder if [whether] I could use this dictionary. この辞書を借りてもいいですか。	ponder
reliable [riláiəbl]	形 信頼できる；頼りになる reliable information about current affairs 時事問題に関する信頼できる情報	dependable
jam [dʒǽm]	名 渋滞；込み合い be stuck in a heavy traffic jam ひどい交通渋滞にはまっている	crowding

Track 055

単語／発音	語義／フレーズ	同意表現	難易度
firmly [fɚ́ːrmli]	副 しっかりと，堅く；断固として keep ～ firmly in mind ～をしっかりと心に留める	tightly	A
weigh [wéɪ]	動 比較考察する；重みで圧する weigh up the pros and cons 賛否両論を比較検討する	consider	
meanwhile [míːnwàɪl]	副 その間に；話は変わって一方 Meanwhile, start boiling the water. その間にお湯を沸かしてください。　＊W1 つなぎ言葉として使える。	meantime	
durable [d(j)ʊ́ərəbl]	形 耐久性のある，長持ちする durable and inexpensive products 丈夫で安価な製品 ＊名詞 durability も覚える。	lasting	B
patent [peitnt]	名 特許(権)，専売特許 file an application for a patent 特許出願書を提出する	exclusive right	
neat [níːt]	形 こぎれいな，整頓された keep a room neat and tidy 部屋をこぎれいにきちんとしておく ＊ nice and neat で覚えよう。	orderly	
distinguish [dɪstíŋgwɪʃ]	動 区別する；見分ける distinguish between right and wrong 善悪の区別をする	differentiate	C
rationalise [rǽʃənəlàɪz]	動 合理化する rationalise the legal procedure 法的手続を合理化する	streamline	
stroke [stróʊk]	名 一撃，ひと打ち；ひとかき give a finishing stroke とどめの一撃を加える	blow	
dictation [dɪktéɪʃən]	名 口述筆記，書き取り；命令 take dictation at eighty words a minute 1 分で 80 語の口述筆記をする	transcription	D
spring [spríŋ]	動 跳ねる，跳ぶ；急に起こる spring out of bed ベッドから跳ね起きる	leap	
strike [stráɪk]	動 打つ；攻撃する He struck her a blow in the face with his elbow. 彼は彼女の顔に肘打ちを加えた。	hit	

Track 056

単語／発音	語義／フレーズ	同意表現
instinct [ínstiŋkt]	名 本能；天性, 直感 instinct for self-preservation 自己防衛本能 ＊ intuition も同意語。	inherent aptitude
prevailing [prɪvéɪlɪŋ]	形 広まっている；優勢な challenge the prevailing view 一般的な考え方に疑問を呈する　＊R 動詞 prevail「流行する；圧倒する」も覚える。	predominant
widespread [wáɪdspréd]	形 広まった gain widespread support from public 人々から幅広い支持を得る	wide-ranging
renowned [rɪnáʊnd]	形 名高い be renowned for its geysers 間欠泉で名高い	famous
ignore [ɪgnɔ́:r]	動 無視する, 知らないふりをする totally ignore warnings 警告を完全に無視する ＊ neglect も類義だが,「意図的」ではない。	disregard
manner [mǽnər]	名 態度；方法 behave in a more responsible manner より責任ある態度で振る舞う　＊「礼儀；習慣」という意味では manners とする。	attitude
infant [ínfənt]	名 乳児；幼児 Sudden Infant Death Syndrome (SIDS) = cot death 乳児突然死症候群	baby
odd [á:d]	形 奇妙な, 異常な；はんぱな an odd way to behave 奇妙な振る舞い ＊ bizarre, unusual など同義語は多い。	peculiar
incorrect [ìnkərékt]	形 正しくない an incorrect use of monitoring equipment 監視装置の間違った使い方	wrong
relieve [rɪlí:v]	動 取り除く, 軽減する；救済する help to relieve stress ストレスを解消するのに役立つ ＊S relieve stress は何かと使える。	alleviate
combat [ká:mbæt]	動 戦う, 立ち向かう；やめさせる combat global warming 地球温暖化問題に立ち向かう	battle
strengthen [stréŋkθn]	動 強くする, 強化する；増強する strengthen one's stomach muscles 腹筋を強化する	reinforce

Track 057

単語／発音	語義／フレーズ	同意表現	難易度
immune [ɪmjúːn]	形 影響を受けない；免疫のある be immune from taxation 税金を免れている ＊immune system で「免疫システム」。	exempt	A
respectable [rɪspéktəbl]	形 立派な，社会的地位のある；上品な hold a respectable position れっきとした地位を有する	estimable	
decade [dékeɪd]	名 10 年間 continue for decades 何十年にもわたって続く	decennium	
conduct [kάːndʌkt]	動 実施する；導く conduct experiments on animals 動物実験を行う ＊W2 conduct research on ～「～の調査を行う」。	carry out	B
cure [kjúər]	動 治す，治療する；(悪癖を)取り除く cure a serious disease 重病を治す	heal	
star [stάːr]	動 主役を演じる a film starring Anthony Hopkins アンソニー・ホプキンス主演の映画　＊現在分詞・過去・過去分詞では r を重ねる。	play the lead	
belly [béli]	名 腹，腹部；内部の空洞 crawl along on one's belly 腹ばいになって進む	stomach	C
inspiration [ìnspəréɪʃən]	名 インスピレーション，ひらめき；刺激 draw inspiration from the countryside 田園地帯からひらめきを得る	afflatus	
premise [prémɪs]	名 前提，仮定；家屋敷 on the major premise that all A's are B's すべての A は B だという大前提に基づき　＊premises「土地, 建物, 施設」も頻出。	assumption	
physiology [fìziάːlədʒi]	名 生理；生理学 look at the underlying physiology of the thyroid gland 甲状腺の隠れた生理に目を向ける　＊psychology と勘違い注意。	bionomy	D
anxiety [æŋzáɪəti]	名 心配，不安；願望 growing public anxiety over air pollution 大気汚染への人々の増大する不安	concern	
weaken [wíːkən]	動 弱める；弱くなる Stress weakens an immune system. ストレスが免疫システムを弱める。　＊「強める」は strengthen。	enfeeble	

単語／発音	語義／フレーズ	同意表現
appetite [ǽpətàɪt]	名 食欲；欲求, 意欲 suffer from loss of appetite 食欲不振に苦しんでいる	desire for food
digestion [daɪdʒéstʃən]	名 消化, 消化力；理解 poor digestion and heartburn 消化不良と胸焼け ＊ingestion「摂取」してから digestion「消化」すると覚えよう！	assimilation
surgery [sə́:rdʒəri]	名 手術 perform emergency surgery 緊急手術を行う ＊[英]なら「医院；診療時間」という意味にもなる。	operation
propose [prəpóʊz]	動 提案する；企てる propose a novel idea 斬新なアイデアを提案する	put forward
elderly [éldərli]	形 年配の, 初老の bedridden elderly people 寝たきり老人 ＊W2 the elderly で「高齢者」。	old
nearly [níərli]	副 ほとんど, もう少しで nearly die from poisoning 中毒によりもう少しで死にかける ＊W1 about, approximately と同じく「約」を表す。	virtually
gender [dʒéndər]	名 （社会的・文化的な）性 gender bias against women 女性に対する性差別	sex
consumer [kəns(j)ú:mər]	名 消費者 health-conscious consumers 健康を気にする消費者	purchaser
current [kə́:rənt]	形 現在の the current rate of exchange 現在の為替相場 ＊L 書き取り問題では名詞「流れ」で出題される。	present
segment [ségmənt]	名 部分；断片 a large segment of the population 人口の大部分	section
pleasant [plézənt]	形 心地よい；楽しい a pleasant aromatic odour 心地よい芳香 ＊発音注意！	pleasing
actual [ǽktʃuəl]	形 実際の, 現実に存在する a true story based on actual events 実際の出来事に基づいた実話	real

Track 059

単語／発音	語義／フレーズ	同意表現	難易度
hire [háɪər]	動 雇う hire a live-in maid 住み込みのメードを雇う	employ	A
preference [préfərəns]	名 好み，他よりも好きであること；優先 identify customer preference 客の嗜好を見きわめる	predilection	
tendency [téndənsi]	名 傾向 have a tendency to jam 故障する傾向がある ＊W1 show an increasing tendency「上昇傾向を示す」。	inclination	
associate [əsóuʃièɪt]	動 結び付ける；連想する associate words with meanings 単語と意味を結び付ける	connect	B
nap [nǽp]	名 うたた寝；昼寝 take a nap after lunch 昼食後に昼寝する	slumber	
laziness [léɪzinəs]	名 怠惰 give in to laziness 怠け心に負ける	indolence	
energetic [ènərdʒétɪk]	形 精力的な；強力な a capable and energetic officer 有能で精力的な将校	tireless	C
subtract [səbtrǽkt]	動 差し引く subtract 3 from 9 9から3を差し引く	take away	
primarily [praɪmérəli]	副 第一に；主として work primarily with guest workers 主に外国人労働者と一緒に働く	mainly	
suburban [səbə́:rbən]	形 郊外の a large suburban shopping mall 郊外型大規模ショッピングセンター　＊suburb は名詞。	out-of-town	D
disturb [dɪstə́:rb]	動 かき乱す，混乱させる；不安にする disturb the neighbourhood 近所を騒がせる	upset	
improvement [ɪmprú:vmənt]	名 改善；改良点 There's still room for improvement. まだ改善の余地がある。	reformation	

75

Track 060

単語／発音	語義／フレーズ	同意表現
permission [pərmíʃən]	名 許可 get permission to use the passage その文章の使用許可を得る	authorization
suspect [səspékt]	動 ではないかと思う，嫌疑をかける suspect that weapons are hidden there 武器がそこに隠されているのではと思う	distrust
flexibility [flèksəbíləti]	名 柔軟性；曲げやすいこと have flexibility in deciding the policy 方針の決定において柔軟性を持つ	pliability
intense [inténs]	形 激しい，猛烈な；感情的な cause intense pain 激痛を引き起こす	strong
circle [sə́ːrkl]	名 サークル，仲間，団体，〜界 the unhealthy atmosphere in academic circles 学界の不健全な雰囲気	social group
commit [kəmít]	動 （罪などを）犯す；委託する commit a crime 罪を犯す	carry out
violation [vàɪəléɪʃən]	名 違反；侵害 in violation of international law 国際法に違反して	breach
inclined [ɪnkláɪnd]	形 乗り気である；かかりやすい I'm inclined to agree with him this time. 今回は彼に同意したい。	disposed
statistics [stətístɪks]	名 統計，統計資料；統計学 Statistics show that the population is decreasing. 統計によると，人口は減っている。	figures
inexperienced [ìnɪkspíəriənst]	形 経験の浅い too inexperienced to recognise danger 経験不足で危険を認識できない	inexpert
bend [bénd]	動 曲げる；曲がる The river narrows and bends sharply. 川は狭くなり急に曲がっている。	flex
mature [mət(j)ʊ́ər]	形 成熟した；熟した be mature for one's age 若いのにしっかりしている	grown-up

Track 061

単語／発音	語義／フレーズ	同意表現	難易度
nod [nάd]	動 居眠りする；うなずく Even Homer sometimes nods. ホメロスでさえ時には居眠りをする。　＊名人もたまにはまずいことをする, という諺。	nap	A
convert [kənvə́ːrt]	動 転換する, 変換する convert a solid into a gas 固体を気体に変換する	change	
popularity [pὰːpjulǽrəti]	名 人気 popularity poll 人気投票	vogue	
droplet [drάːplət]	名 滴 water droplets 水滴	drop	B
crystal [krístl]	名 結晶；水晶 snow crystals 雪の結晶		
particle [pάːrtɪkl]	名 微粒子 elementary particle 素粒子	molecule	
accomplish [əkάːmplɪʃ]	動 成し遂げる, 成就する accomplish a mission 任務を成し遂げる	achieve	C
combine [kəmbáɪn]	動 混合する combine two ideas into one 2つのアイデアを1つに組み合わせる	mix	
attach [ətǽtʃ]	動 添える；くっつける attach a file to an e-mail ファイルをEメールに添付する	append	
reservoir [rézərvwὰːr]	名 貯水池 an irrigation reservoir 灌漑用貯水池	catchment	D
stream [stríːm]	名 流れ swim against the stream 川の流れに逆らって泳ぐ ＊[英]では「能力別クラス」の意味もある。	current	
split [splít]	動 割る, 分ける split a nation 国家を分断する	divide	

77

Track 062

単語／発音	語義／フレーズ	同意表現
glide [gláɪd]	動 滑らかに動く glide through the air 滑空する	slide
trail [tréɪl]	名 小道；跡 a mountain trail 山道	path
crop [krá:p]	名 作物, 収穫物；全収穫高 harvest crops 作物を収穫する ＊harvest にも名詞と動詞の両方がある。	harvest
undergo [ʌ̀ndərgóʊ]	動 （変化・困難を）経験する undergo hardship 苦難を経験する	experience
concern [kənsə́:rn]	名 懸念, 心配；関心 considerable public concern 一般の人々の重大な懸念	worry
calculate [kǽlkjəlèɪt]	動 計算する；評価する；判断する calculate an average 平均値を算出する	compute
extremely [ɪkstrí:mli]	副 極端に extremely delicate subject 極めて取り扱いにくい問題	exceedingly
fortunately [fɔ́:rtʃənətli]	副 幸いにも fortunately for all of us 私たち全員にとって幸運なことに	luckily
compressor [kəmprésər]	名 圧縮機 an air compressor 空気圧縮機	compactor
level [lévl]	形 平らな level surface 水平面	flat
throughout [θruáʊt]	前 ～の間中ずっと；～の至る所で throughout one's life 生涯を通じて ＊W1 during とは違い「期間中ずっと」を表すので注意！	all through
return [rɪtə́:rn]	名 報酬, お返し；返答 The average rates of return are 10 %. 平均利益率は 10％です。　＊W2 in return「お返しに」。	profit

Track 063

単語／発音	語義／フレーズ	同意表現	難易度
logging [lɔ́(ː)gɪŋ]	名 木材の切り出し illegal logging in national forests 国有林の違法伐採	cutting of trees	A
generate [dʒénərèɪt]	動 生み出す generate electricity 発電する	produce	
trunk [trʌ́ŋk]	名 (木の)幹 decayed tree trunks 朽ちた木の幹	stem	
awaken [əwéɪkən]	動 目覚める；覚醒する awaken from a dream 夢から目覚める	wake up	B
conductor [kəndʌ́ktər]	名 指揮者 a conductor of an orchestra オーケストラの指揮者	director	
imitate [ímətèɪt]	動 真似する imitate human speech 人間の言葉を真似る	simulate	
force [fɔ́ːrs]	動 強要する force a confession 無理やり白状させる ＊W2 force O to V「OがVするよう強制する」。	compel	C
improvise [ímprəvàɪz]	動 即興で演奏する；即席に作る improvise on the melody メロディを即興で演奏する	extemporise	
engage [ɪngéɪdʒ]	動 関与する；従事する Don't engage in politics. 政治に関わるな。 ＊ be engaged in 〜「〜に携わっている」の形でよく出る。	get involved	
operation [ɑ̀ːpəréɪʃən]	名 操業, 操作；実施, 施行 machine operation 機械操作	handling	D
bold [bóʊld]	形 大胆な；ずうずうしい a bold and detailed plan 大胆にして綿密な計画	daring	
tame [téɪm]	動 飼い慣らす tame a wild animal 野生動物を飼い慣らす	domesticate	

単語／発音	語義／フレーズ	同意表現
mutually [mjúːtʃuəli]	副 相互に mutually beneficial for both countries 両国にとって互いに有益な	reciprocally
beneficial [bènəfíʃəl]	形 有益な, ためになる beneficial to health 健康に有益な ＊W2 be beneficial to 名詞。不定詞は不可。	advantageous
descend [dɪsénd]	動 下る, 降りる；〜の子孫である descend the stairs slowly 階段をゆっくり下る ＊「上がる」は ascend。	fall
track [trǽk]	動 跡をたどる track the footprints 足跡を追う	follow
archaeology [àːrkiάːlədʒi]	名 考古学 learn archaeology and history 考古学と歴史を学ぶ	study of material remains
keen [kíːn]	形 (感覚が)鋭い；熱心な keen interest 強い関心 ＊L be keen on 〜「〜に乗り気である」。	intense
relative [rélətɪv]	形 相対的な relative merits of both approaches 両方法の相対的価値 ＊W1 The figures were relatively high.「その数字は比較的高かった」。	comparative
facility [fəsíləti]	名 設備, 施設 recreational facilities 娯楽施設	installation
physical [fízɪkl]	形 肉体の physical and mental state 心身の状態	bodily
fossil [fάːsl]	名 化石 fossil energy 化石エネルギー	petrifaction
bush [búʃ]	名 低木；(低木の)茂み hide behind a bush 茂みの陰に隠れる	thicket
pasture [pǽstʃər]	名 牧草地 common pasture 共同放牧場	grazing

Track 065

単語／発音	語義／フレーズ	同意表現	難易度
approximately [əprá:ksəmətli]	副 およそ approximately one million years ago およそ100万年前 ＊W1 「約」は approximately が最もフォーマル。	roughly	A
handful [hǽndfùl]	名 ひと握り only a handful of people ほんの少数の人々	fistful	
beneath [bɪní:θ]	前 〜の真下に beneath the surface of the sea 海面下に	under	
dig [dɪ́g]	動 （穴などを）掘る dig a hole in a garden 庭に穴を掘る	excavate	B
self-sustaining [sélfsəstéɪnɪŋ]	形 自立する self-sustaining economy 自立経済	self-sufficient	
multiply [mʌ́ltəplàɪ]	動 増殖する；掛け算する multiply at an explosive rate 爆発的速度で増殖する ＊ multiple は形容詞。	reproduce	
overlap [òʊvərlǽp]	動 重なる overlap one another 互いに重なり合う	lap	C
former [fɔ́:rmər]	形 前の the former prime minister 前首相	previous	
integral [íntɪgrəl]	形 不可欠な an integral component 不可欠な構成要素 ＊ essential, necessary など同義語多数。	indispensable	
enrich [ɪnrítʃ]	動 （質・価値を）高める enrich quality of life 生活の質を高める	enhance	D
seldom [séldəm]	副 めったに〜しない seldom eat at home 家ではめったに食事をしない	rarely	
inescapable [ìnəskéɪpəbl]	形 逃れられない an inescapable problem 避けて通れない問題	unavoidable	

Track 066

単語／発音	語義／フレーズ	同意表現
threaten [θrétn]	動 脅かす threaten peace and stability 平和と安定を脅かす	menace
meadow [médoʊ]	名 草地 alpine meadows 高山草原	grass field
quantity [kwɑ́:ntəti]	名 量；分量, 数量 a vast quantity of information 膨大な量の情報 ＊quantitive/quantitative research「定量調査」。	amount
commodity [kəmɑ́:dəti]	名 商品；日用品 commodity prices 物価	goods
removal [rɪmúːvl]	名 除去 stain removal 染み抜き ＊「転居」の意味もある。[英] removal van「引っ越しトラック」。	disposal
overstocking [óʊvəstɑ̀:kɪŋ]	名 過剰在庫 prevent overstocking 供給過剰を防止する	excess inventory
moderate [mɑ́:dərət]	形 穏健な moderate alcohol drinking 適度な飲酒 ＊W1 「穏やかに上がった」increased moderately。	temperate
legally [líːɡəli]	副 法律的に be legally permitted 法律上許されている	juridically
likelihood [láɪklihʊ̀d]	名 可能性 estimate the likelihood 可能性を予測する	possibility
insecure [ìnsɪkjʊ́ər]	形 安全でない feel insecure 不安を感じる	unsafe
outwards [áʊtwərdz]	副 外側に look outwards 外に目を向ける	outside
subordinate [səbɔ́:rdənət]	名 部下 a direct subordinate 直属の部下	junior staff

Track 067

単語／発音	語義／フレーズ	同意表現	難易度
ritual [rítʃuəl]	名（宗教的）儀式 a symbolic ritual 象徴儀礼	rite	A
virtue [vớːrtʃuː]	名美徳，徳，善；長所 virtue and vice 美徳と悪徳	goodness	
clarity [klérəti]	名明晰さ；明快さ remember with surprising clarity 意外なほど明晰に覚えている	lucidity	
reward [rɪwɔ́ːrd]	名報酬 reward and punishment 賞罰 ＊動詞でも使う。	repayment	B
asset [ǽset]	名資産，財産；利点 cultural assets of a nation 国の文化財 ＊be asset to ～「～に役立つ」。	property	
instance [ínstəns]	名事例 for instance 例えば	example	
repetitive [rɪpétətɪv]	形繰り返しの repetitive movement 反復運動 ＊W2 repetitive だと減点対象。	repeating	C
stick [stík]	動突き刺す；貼り付ける stick a knife ナイフを突き刺す ＊stick to ～「～にこだわる」。	stab	
inventive [ɪnvéntɪv]	形発明の（才のある），創意に富む an inventive design 創意に富んだデザイン	original	
store [stɔ́ːr]	動蓄える store a large amount of data 大量のデータを蓄える	stock	D
frontal [frʌ́ntəl]	形正面の a frontal collision 正面衝突	head-on	
conscious [kɑ́ːnʃəs]	形意識のある；意図的な conscious behaviour 意図的な行為	deliberate	

83

単語／発音	語義／フレーズ	同意表現
fatigue [fətí:g]	名 疲労 metal fatigue 金属疲労 ＊fatigued = very tired = exhausted は有効な書き換え。	tiredness
depressed [dɪprést]	形 意気消沈した be depressed about life 人生を悲観している	dispirited
phenomenon [fɪná:mənà:n]	名 現象 a paranormal phenomenon 超常現象 ＊複数形は phenomena。	event
severely [sɪvíərli]	副 ひどく be severely injured 重傷を負う	badly
sticky [stíki]	形 粘着性のある sticky tape 粘着テープ ＊「頭に残りやすい」という意味でも使う。	gluey
involve [ɪnvá:lv]	動 ～と関わる be deeply involved with the fraud 詐欺と深く関わっている	engage
unit [jú:nɪt]	名 構成単位 unit cost 単位当たり原価	constituent
predictable [prɪdíktəbl]	形 予測可能な predictable consequences 予想できる結果	foreseeable
conform [kənfɔ́:rm]	動 従う；一致する conform to the standard 規範に従う ＊「（規則やパターンに）従う」という意味。	comply
tap [tǽp]	名 蛇口, 栓 turn the tap on 蛇口を開ける ＊Ⓡ 動詞だと「開発する, 利用する」の意味。	faucet
unite [ju(:)náɪt]	動 合体する unite against terrorism テロに対して団結する	consolidate
standardise [stǽndərdàɪz]	動 標準化する, 規格化する standardise the fat content of dairy products 乳製品の脂肪分を標準化する	systematise

Track 069

単語／発音	語義／フレーズ	同意表現	難易度
heartily [hάːrtəli]	副 心から heartily congratulate a person on 〜 〜に関して人を心から祝福する	cordially	A
buzz [bʌ́z]	名 ざわめき；騒音 the buzz of the bees 蜂のざわつき ＊L buzzy は「酔っぱらった」。	bombination	
miraculous [mərǽkjələs]	形 奇跡的な a miraculous victory 奇跡的な勝利	phenomenal	
authority [əθɔ́ːrəti]	名 権力, 権威；権威者 people in authority 権力のある人々 ＊複数形の場合, British authorities「英国当局」のように使う。	power	B
physics [fíziks]	名 物理学 laws of physics 物理法則	physical science	
solid [sάːlɪd]	形 固体の solid baby food 固形離乳食	solid-state	
acid [ǽsɪd]	形 酸性の；酸味のある acid rain 酸性雨	acidic	C
pharmacy [fάːrməsi]	名 薬局 a pharmacy practitioner 薬剤師	chemist	
restraint [rɪstréɪnt]	名 抑制 restraint of free speech 言論の自由の制限	constraint	
multiple [mʌ́ltəpl]	形 複合的な multiple acts of terror 同時多発テロ ＊動詞は multiply。	compositive	D
sequence [síːkwəns]	名 順序, 次第；連続 the sequence of events leading up to murder 殺人に至る事の次第	succession	
sac [sǽk]	名 嚢(のう) air sac 気嚢[鳥類の肺に付属する空気袋]	bladder	

Track 070

単語／発音	語義／フレーズ	同意表現
thermal [θə́ːrml]	形 熱の，温度の；保温用の a thermal spring 温泉	thermic
shrub [ʃrʌ́b]	名 低木 garden shrubs 庭の潅木（かんぼく）	bush
distinct [dɪstíŋkt]	形 他と異なる；独特な two distinct categories 2つの全く異なる種類 ＊単純な different との書き換えにも注意。	discrete
obscure [əbskjúər]	形 ぼんやりした an obscure answer あいまいな返事	vague
rust [rʌ́st]	名 さび a rust preventive さび止め	corrosion
free [fríː]	形 〜を免れた a duty-free shop 免税店	exempt
nutrient [n(j)úːtriənt]	名 栄養物，栄養素，栄養剤 absorb nutrients from the soil 土壌から栄養物を吸収する	nourishment
deficiency [dɪfíʃənsi]	名 欠乏；欠陥 calorie deficiency カロリー不足 ＊R lack との書き換えに注意。	insufficiency
similarly [símələrli]	副 同様に similarly priced products 同じような価格の商品 ＊W1 同じ傾向を示すものを導入する際に文頭で使う。	likewise
shady [ʃéɪdi]	形 陰の多い the shady side of the street 道の陰になっている側	shadowy
unpromising [ʌnprɑ́ːməsɪŋ]	形 （成功などの）見込みがない unpromising prospect 見込みのない展望	hopeless
hedge [héd͡ʒ]	名 生け垣 a windbreak hedge 防風垣	planting fence

86

単語／発音	語義／フレーズ	同意表現	難易度
spectacular [spektǽkjələr]	形 壮観な, 目覚ましい spectacular achievements 目覚ましい業績	striking	A
upright [ʌ́praɪt]	形 直立の an upright posture 真っすぐな姿勢	erect	
coarse [kɔ́ːrs]	形 粗い；粗野な a coarse particle 粗い粒子	rough	
leathery [léðəri]	形 革状の leathery skin ガサガサの肌	coriaceous	B
optimum [ɑ́ptəməm]	形 最適な an optimum amount 最適量	optimal	
disaster [dɪzǽstər]	名 大災害；大惨事 prevent natural disasters 自然災害を防ぐ	calamity	
destroy [dɪstrɔ́ɪ]	動 破壊する；台無しにする Their offices were destroyed by bombing. 彼らの事務所は爆撃で破壊された。	demolish	C
pessimistic [pèsəmístɪk]	形 悲観的な a pessimistic view of life 悲観的な人生観 ＊⇔ optimistic	gloomy	
humankind [hjúːmənkàɪnd]	名 人類, 人間 progress of humankind 人類の進歩 ＊ mankind は差別的と考える人もいるので, この単語が使われる。	human beings	
alternate [ɔ́ːltərnèɪt]	動 交互に行う alternate writing with reading 執筆と読書を交互にする	take turns	D
fragile [frǽdʒaɪl]	形 壊れやすい fragile economy 脆弱な経済 ＊ brittle も同義語。	frail	
fertile [fə́ːtaɪl]	形 肥沃な；多産の fertile agricultural land 肥沃な農耕地 ＊⇔ sterile / barren	rich	

単語／発音	語義／フレーズ	同意表現
swollen [swóulən]	形 膨らんだ swollen legs 　むくんだ脚 ＊ swell「腫れる；増加させる」の過去分詞。「増水した」という意味にもなる。	puffy
wreck [rék]	動 破壊する, 難破させる；駄目にする The building was wrecked by the explosion. 建物は爆発によって破壊された。	demolish
low-lying [lóu-làiŋ]	形 低地の low-lying costal areas 　低地にある沿岸地域	lower
conflict [káːnflɪkt]	名 対立, 争い；不一致 conflict between religion and science 　宗教と科学の対立	struggle
shortage [ʃɔ́ːrtɪdʒ]	名 不足 shortage in labour 　人手不足	lack
globe [ɡlóub]	名 地球；球体 across the globe 　全世界で	earth
consumption [kənsʌ́mpʃən]	名 消費；消費量 domestic consumption 　国内消費	use
despair [dɪspéər]	名 絶望；失望 be in the depths of despair 　失意のどん底にある	hopelessness
revolve [rɪváːlv]	動 （周りを）回転する；循環する The earth revolves on its axis. 地球は軸を中心に回転している。	rotate
commentary [káːməntèri]	名 解説；注釈 a news commentary 　時事解説	comment
profound [prəfáund]	形 深い profound knowledge 　深い知識 ＊ profound change は「抜本的な変更」。	deep
denial [dɪnáɪəl]	名 否定；拒否, 拒絶 make a formal denial 　公式に否定する	negation

Track 073

単語／発音	語義／フレーズ	同意表現	難易度
humanity [hjuːmǽnəti]	名 人間らしさ；人類 crimes against humanity 人道に反する犯罪	humanness	A
consequence [kɑ́ːnsəkwèns]	名 結果 consequences of global warming 地球温暖化の結果 ＊consequence, outcome, result はセットで覚える。	result	
conjunction [kəndʒʌ́ŋkʃən]	名 共同；結合 in conjunction with a famous researcher 有名な研究者と共同で	combination	
explode [ɪksplóʊd]	動 爆発する explode violently 激しく爆発する	blow up	B
refugee [rèfjudʒíː]	名 難民 a refugee camp 難民収容所 ＊アクセント注意！	displaced person	
disintegration [dɪsìntəgréɪʃən]	名 崩壊, 分裂 disintegration of a society 社会の崩壊	dissolution	
sweep [swíːp]	動 一掃する；（ほうきなどで）掃く sweep away the corrupt elite 墜落したエリート集団を一掃する	clear	C
aftermath [ǽftərmæ̀θ]	名 （災害などの）余波, 影響 the aftermath of a war 戦争の余波 ＊悪いことが起きた後の状態を表す。	backwash	
controversy [kɑ́ːntrəvə̀ːrsi]	名 論争 political controversy 政治論争 ＊R controversial「論争を巻き起こす」。	disagreement	
counter [káʊntər]	形 反対の, 反撃の a counter flow 逆流	anti	D
fold [fóʊld]	動 折り畳む fold a paper into four parts 紙を4つに折り畳む ＊W1 increase twofold は「2倍に増える」。	upfold	
immense [ɪméns]	形 莫大な, 広大な an immense amount of time and effort 莫大な時間と労力	huge	

89

Track 074

単語／発音	語義／フレーズ	同意表現

longevity
[lɑːndʒévəti]
名 寿命
decrease the longevity 寿命を縮める
life duration

gross
[gróʊs]
形 総計の, 全体の；ひどい
Gross Domestic Product 国内総生産（GDP）
total

tariff
[tǽrɪf]
名 関税
tariff liberalisation 関税自由化
duty

gulf
[gʌ́lf]
名 大きな隔たり；湾
gulf between rich and poor 貧富の大きな差
chasm

acknowledge
[əknάːlɪdʒ]
動 認める
acknowledge the achievement 功績を認める
＊acknowledgement(著者からの協力者に対する)謝辞の意でも用いる。
recognise

reverse
[rɪvə́ːrs]
動 反対にする, ひっくり返す
reverse directions 方向を(180度)転換する
invert

notion
[nóʊʃən]
名 概念
a notion that the Earth is round 地球は丸いという考え
idea

faith
[féɪθ]
名 信頼；信念
faith in government 政府への信頼
＊faithful は形容詞「信頼できる」と名詞「信者」の意味。
belief

withdraw
[wɪðdrɔ́ː]
動 撤回する；(預金を)引き出す
The newspaper withdrew the allegations.
その新聞は主張を撤回した。
retract

indefinitely
[ɪndéfənətli]
副 無期限に
be postponed indefinitely 無期限に延期される
unlimitedly

deception
[dɪsépʃən]
名 詐欺；だますこと
money gained by deception 詐欺で得られたお金
＊動詞 deceive も頻出。
deceit

credibility
[krèdəbíləti]
名 信頼性
credibility as an expert 専門家としての信頼性
believability

単語／発音	語義／フレーズ	同意表現	難易度
adolescent [ædəlésnt]	形 青春期(10代)の adolescent boys and girls 青春期(10代)の男女 ＊名詞で出ることも。	teenage	A
potentially [pəténʃəli]	副 潜在的に potentially harmful substances 潜在的に有害な物質	possibly	
antibiotic [æ̀ntibaɪɑ́:tɪk]	名 抗生物質 antibiotics like penicillin ペニシリンのような抗生物質	antibacterial agent	
instrumental [ìnstrəméntl]	形 助けとなる, 役に立つ be instrumental in establishing 〜 〜創設において助けとなる	helpful	B
identify [aɪdéntəfàɪ]	動 特定する, 識別する identify the cause of the death 死因を特定する	confirm	
sibling [síblɪŋ]	名 兄弟姉妹 parents and siblings 親兄弟(姉妹)	brothers and/or sisters	
dairy [déəri]	名 乳製品; 搾乳場 low-fat dairy products 低脂肪の乳製品 ＊W2 daily「毎日の」と綴りを混同しないように！	milk product	C
antipode [æntɪpòʊd]	名 正反対のもの The antipode of love is hate. 愛と正反対のものは憎しみ。	opposite	
predominantly [prɪ:dɑ́mənəntli]	副 大部分は, 主に predominantly Muslim communities 大部分がイスラム教徒の地域	mainly	
preconception [prì:kənsépʃən]	名 先入観, 偏見 the gap between preconceptions and reality 先入観と現実のギャップ	prejudice	D
array [əréɪ]	名 ずらりと並んだもの, 大群; 配列 a vast array of goods in the megastore 巨大ストアにずらっと並んだ商品　＊an array of 〜「たくさんの〜」の形でよく出る。	alignment	
extensive [ɪksténsɪv]	形 広範囲にわたる; 大規模な the professor's extensive academic knowledge その教授の広い学術知識	broad	

Track 075

Track 076

単語／発音	語義／フレーズ	同意表現
hemisphere [héməsfìər]	名 半球 areas in the northern hemisphere 北半球の地域	half-sphere
downturn [dáuntə̀ːrn]	名 下降；沈滞 an economic downturn 経済の下降	decline
demographic [dèməgrǽfɪk]	形 人口統計の a demographic shift towards an older population 人口統計の高齢化　＊population に関係する単語だと覚える。	populational
enrolment [ɪnróulmənt]	名 入学, 登録 enrolment in a school 学校への入学 ＊[英]では l（エル）が 1 つだけ！[米]では 2 つ！	registration
compensate [ká:mpənsèɪt]	動 補償する；相殺する compensate the deficit 損失を補償する	make up
wield [wíːld]	動 （影響などを）及ぼす,（権力などを）振るう The government wields enormous power. 政府が大きな力を及ぼす。	exert
anthropology [æ̀nθrəpá:lədʒi]	名 人類学 major in social anthropology 社会人類学を専攻する	study of human beings
drive [dráɪv]	動 追う, 駆逐する drive away the enemy 敵を追い払う ＊W2 drive O to V「O が V せざるを得ないようにする」。	move
epidemic [èpədémɪk]	名 流行, 伝染（病） epidemics of influenza インフルエンザの流行	outbreak
waterborne [wɔ́ːtərbòun]	形 水性の；水上の waterborne paint 水性塗料	water-based
static [stǽtɪk]	形 静止した static electricity 静電気	stationary
halve [hǽv]	動 半分にする halve the price as a special discount　特別割引として半額にする　＊W1 the sales halved「売上が半分になった」。	decrease by half

Track 077

単語／発音	語義／フレーズ	同意表現	難易度
incidence [ínsədəns]	名 発生率；発生 a higher incidence of cancer among smokers 喫煙者の高いがん発生率	occurrence	A
agent [éɪdʒənt]	名 因子, 作用物質 a cancer-causing agent がん因子（発がん性物質）	factor	
prevalence [prévələns]	名 普及, 流行 a high prevalence rate 高い普及率	pervasiveness	
coincidence [koʊínsədəns]	名 偶然の一致；同時発生 by an amazing coincidence 驚くほどの偶然で	accident	B
purify [pjúərəfàɪ]	動 浄化する, 清める Trees purify the air. 木々が空気を浄化する。	clean	
inconsistency [ìnkənsístənsi]	名 不一致, 矛盾 inconsistency between words and deeds 言行の不一致	incompatibility	
heighten [háɪtn]	動 高める；強める heighten awareness of the importance 重要性の認識を高める	enhance	C
measure [méʒər]	名 手段, 方策 a measure to stop global warming 温暖化を止める手段 ＊S take measures against ～「～に対して手を打つ」。	means	
devote [dɪvóʊt]	動 捧げる, 専念する devote one's time to achieving goals 目的達成に時間を捧げる ＊ devote A to B「AをBに捧げる」の形で使う。Bは不定詞ではなく名詞。	dedicate	
shelter [ʃéltər]	名 避難所 a need for food, shelter and clothing 衣食住の必要性	refuge	D
household [háʊshòʊld]	名 世帯, 家庭 a large household of ten persons 10人の大世帯 ＊「家事」は housework や household tasks。	family unit	
finding [fáɪndɪŋ]	名 発見 a remarkable new finding by scientists 科学者による注目すべき新発見	discovery	

93

Track 078

単語／発音	語義／フレーズ	同意表現
expenditure [ɪkspéndɪtʃər]	名 支出, 消費；経費 avoid unnecessary expenditure 不必要な支出を避ける ＊ outlay, expense, spending も同義語として覚える。	spending
tricky [tríki]	形 狡猾な, 巧妙な；扱いにくい victims of the tricky diplomacy 狡猾な外交術の犠牲	artful
fair [féər]	形 公正な, 公平な a fair judgement 公正な判断 ＊ a fair amount of ～「かなりの量の～」も覚えたい。	righteous
molecule [má:ləkjù:l]	名 分子 DNA molecules DNA 分子 ＊「原子」は atom。	particle
ethical [éθɪkl]	形 倫理道徳上の；倫理道徳的な face ethical dilemmas 倫理上のジレンマに直面する	moral
wary [wéəri]	形 用心深い, 慎重な be wary of strangers 見知らぬ人に用心する	cautious
dispute [dɪspjú:t]	名 論争, 口論 resolve the dispute between two groups 2グループの論争を解決する	argument
ongoing [á:ngòuɪŋ]	形 進行中の, 継続している Don't ignore the ongoing crisis. 今ある危機を見過ごすな。 ＊ ongoing research「継続中の調査」などの表現は頻出。	current
hesitancy [hézətənsi]	名 ためらい, 躊躇 hesitancy and doubt about a war 戦争へのためらいと疑い	scruple
deficient [dɪfíʃənt]	形 欠けている, 不足した stop a diet deficient in vitamins ビタミン不足の食事をやめる　＊似ている deficit は, 主に「会計の」不足。	lacking
pest [pést]	名 害虫, 有害生物 an effective means of pest control 効果的な害虫駆除方法　＊ pesticide は「農薬」。	injurious insect
proponent [prəpóunənt]	名 支持者 a proponent of democracy 民主主義の支持者 ＊「反対者」は opponent。	advocate

Track 079

単語／発音	語義／フレーズ	同意表現	難易度
malnutrition [mæln(j)uːtríʃən]	名 栄養失調, 栄養不足 die from malnutrition 栄養失調で亡くなる	undernourishment	A
lessen [lésn]	動 少なくする, 減らす lessen the risk of cancer がんのリスクを減らす	decrease	
found [fáʊnd]	動 設立する a school founded in 1890　1890年に設立された学校 ＊fund「資金；資金を出す」やfindの過去・過去分詞形と混同しないように！	establish	
remedy [rémədi]	名 治療(薬)；特別補習 Chinese herbal remedy 漢方治療(薬) ＊「改善策」という意味でも出る。solutionも同義語。	therapy	B
symptom [símptəm]	名 兆候, 症状 a symptom of ageing 老化の兆候	sign	
represent [rèprɪzént]	動 表す；代表する Wind direction is represented by arrows. 風向は矢で表される。	symbolise	
incredible [ɪnkrédəbl]	形 信じられない；途方もない an incredible number of stars in a galaxy 銀河の中のおびただしい数の星	unbelievable	C
dissolve [dɪzάːlv]	動 溶ける；溶かす dissolve in water 水に溶ける	solve	
stand [stænd]	動 我慢する；持ちこたえる stand hard work 激務に耐える ＊bear, tolerateも一緒に覚える。	endure	
conventional [kənvénʃənl]	形 慣習の；伝統の challenge conventional thinking 従来の考え方に挑戦する ＊新しいこととの対比で使われる場合も多い。	traditional	D
clinical [klínɪkəl]	形 臨床の clinical experiment 臨床実験	bedside	
unconscious [ʌnkάːnʃəs]	形 無意識の an unconscious bias 無意識の偏見	senseless	

Track 080

単語／発音	語義／フレーズ	同意表現
lengthy [léŋkθi]	形 非常に長い lengthy illness 長患い	prolonged
underlying [ˌʌndərláiiŋ]	形 根本的な, 基本的な；裏に隠れた an underlying cause of the rising crime rate 増加する犯罪率の根本的原因	fundamental
stimulate [stímjəlèit]	動 刺激して〜させる；刺激する stimulate discussion among students 学生たちの議論を促す	encourage
medication [mèdikéiʃən]	名 薬物；投薬 medication abuse 薬物乱用	drug
asthma [ǽsmə]	名 ぜんそく preventive care for asthma ぜんそく予防治療	
inexpensive [ìnikspénsiv]	形 安価な a small and inexpensive car 小型の低価格車 ＊economical, budget も同義語。	cheap
revival [riváivl]	名 復活；再生 revival of militarism 軍国主義の復活	resurgence
sacred [séikrəd]	形 神聖な a sacred war 聖戦 ＊発音注意！	holy
addict [ǽdikt]	名 （薬物などの）中毒者, 常用者 a drug addict 麻薬中毒者	junkie
lava [lɑ́ːvə]	名 溶岩 lava flow 溶岩流	molten rock
isolated [áisəlèitid]	形 孤立した isolated from one another お互いに孤立している	lone
icecap [áiskæp]	名 氷冠；万年雪 the polar icecap 極地の万年雪	permanent snow

Track 081

単語／発音	語義／フレーズ	同意表現	難易度
carve [káːrv]	動 彫る；切り開く carve a name in stone 名前を石に刻む	engrave	A
impoverish [ɪmpávərɪʃ]	動 貧しくする an impoverished neighbourhood 貧民区	make ~ poor	
heritage [hérətɪdʒ]	名 遺産 World Heritage 世界遺産	inheritance	
murmur [máːrmər]	動 つぶやく；ざわめく murmur a complaint ブツブツ文句を言う	mutter	B
crust [krʌ́st]	名 地殻 movement of the earth's crust 地殻変動	geosphere	
boast [bóʊst]	動 自慢する boast about one's position 自分の地位を自慢する	brag	
flourishing [fláːrɪʃɪŋ]	形 繁栄している a flourishing new industry 勢いが盛んな新産業	prosperous	C
erupt [ɪrʌ́pt]	動 噴火する；吹き出す The volcano may erupt at any moment. その火山はいつ噴火してもおかしくない。	burst	
subsequent [sʌ́bsɪkwənt]	形 それに続く subsequent generation 次世代 ＊R subsequently「その後」。手順を示すときに使う。	following	
avalanche [ǽvəlæntʃ]	名 雪崩；殺到 an avalanche danger in the snowy mountain 雪山での雪崩の危険	snowslide	D
stubborn [stʌ́bərn]	形 頑固な make a stubborn resistance 頑強に抵抗する ＊「考えを変えられないこと」を表すことも。	headstrong	
superiority [suːpəriɔ́ːrəti]	名 優越，優勢 superiority of Western civilisation 西洋文明の優位性	predominance	

単語/発音	語義/フレーズ	同意表現
intimidate [ɪntímədèɪt]	動 おびえさせる be intimidated by terrorist threats テロの脅威におびえる	frighten
short-sighted [ʃɔ̀ətrt-sàɪtɪd]	形 近視の；近視眼的な a short-sighted and misguided policy 近視眼的で誤った方針	myopic
sabotage [sǽbətàːʒ]	名 妨害工作 a deliberate act of sabotage 意図的な妨害行為	obstruction tactics
grand [grǽnd]	形 壮大な a grand project 壮大な計画	magnificent
spill [spíl]	動 こぼす spill milk on the floor 床にミルクをこぼす ＊ cry over spilt milk「過ぎたことを後悔する」。	slop
cargo [káːrgoʊ]	名 貨物，積荷 an air cargo 航空貨物	freight
chemical [kémɪkl]	形 化学的な，化学の chemical reaction 化学反応 ＊ chemicals は「化学物質」。	chemic
strip [stríp]	動 はぎ取る，取り除く strip the wallpaper off the walls 壁から壁紙をはがす	tear off
implication [ìmpləkéɪʃən]	名 影響，関わり；暗示 This has implications for women. このことは女性に影響がある。 ＊複数形 implications「影響」は頻出。	effect
amid [əmíd]	前 〜の真ん中に；〜の最中に hurry home amid the storm 嵐の真っ只中で家路を急ぐ	in the middle of
ventilation [vèntəléɪʃən]	名 換気（装置） ventilation and air-conditioning system 換気空調システム ＊ vent は「通気口」。	air infiltration
odour [óʊdə]	名 におい body odour 体臭	smell

単語／発音	語義／フレーズ	同意表現	難易度
uncharted [ʌ̀ntʃɑ́ːrtəd]	形 未知の；地図に載っていない uncharted territory 未知の領域	unmapped	A
await [əwéɪt]	動 期待して待つ await the arrival of peace 平和の到着を待ち望む	expect	
immediately [ɪmíːdiətli]	副 すぐに immediately after the accident 事故直後に	right away	
sediment [sédəmənt]	名 堆積物；沈殿物 a thick layer of sediment 厚い堆積層	deposit	B
feature [fíːtʃər]	名 特徴 learn topographic features 地形の特徴を覚える	characteristic	
ratio [réɪʃoʊ]	名 比率, 割合；釣り合い the ratio of teachers to students 生徒に対する先生の比率　＊W1「比」の意味なので使わない方が無難。	proportion	
trace [tréɪs]	動 たどる, 跡を追う；捜し出す trace his family tree to the 17th century 彼の家系図を17世紀までたどる	track down	C
hydrothermal [hàɪdroʊθə́ːrml]	形 熱水の a hydrothermal vent 熱水噴出孔	of hot water	
expedition [èkspədíʃən]	名 遠征；探検隊 an expedition to the North Pole 北極探検 ＊「調査旅行」の意味で使われることが多い。	exploration	
hover [hʌ́vər]	動 空中に舞う；うろつく hover over the building ビルの上空にとどまる	float	D
bedrock [bédrɑ̀ːk]	名 基盤；岩盤 financial bedrock 財政基盤	base	
underneath [ʌ̀ndərníːθ]	前 〜の下に underneath the surface 表面下で	below	

Track 084

単語／発音	語義／フレーズ	同意表現
tremendous [trɪméndəs]	形 (大きさ・量・程度など)ものすごい do tremendous damage to the community その地域に甚大な被害を及ぼす	enormous
seismic [sáɪzmɪk]	形 地震の an active seismic zone 活発な地震帯	seismal
microorganism [màɪkroʊɔ́:gənàɪzm]	名 微生物 a disease-causing microorganism 病気を引き起こす微生物	microbe
pollutant [pəlú:tənt]	名 汚染物質 hazardous air pollutants 有害大気汚染物質	contaminant
organism [ɔ́:rgənìzm]	名 有機体；生物 a pathogenic organism 病原体	living being
scant [skǽnt]	形 乏しい have scant experience 経験に乏しい	scarce
liberate [líbərèɪt]	動 解放する liberate a country from the occupation 占領から国を解放する	free
trap [trǽp]	動 閉じ込める；捕らえる trap lions in a cage ライオンを檻に閉じ込める	snare
compound [ká:mpaʊnd]	名 複合物, 化合物 an organic compound 有機化合物	composition
sphere [sfíər]	名 球体 a celestial sphere 天球 ＊「(社会の中の)身分」という意味もある。	globe
axis [ǽksɪs]	名 軸 the axis of rotation of the earth 地球の自転軸 ＊複数形は axes なので注意。	axle
plot [plá:t]	名 筋書き, 構想 the plot for a movie 映画の筋書き	scenario

Track 085

単語／発音	語義／フレーズ	同意表現	難易度
horizontal [hɔ̀:rəzá:ntl]	形 水平線の；水平の horizontal to vertical ratio 縦横比率	level	A
latitude [lætət(j)ùːd]	名 緯度 a high latitude 高緯度	parallel	
distort [dɪstɔ́ːrt]	動 曲げる；歪める distort the truth 真実を歪める ＊名詞は distortion。	twist	
whereas [weəræz]	接 であるのに；[文頭で]なるがゆえに I'm short, whereas my siblings are all tall. 私は背が低いが，兄弟はみんな高い。　＊W1 対比するときに便利。	while	B
prominence [prá:mənəns]	名 卓越；突出 achieve prominence 有名になる ＊形容詞は prominent。	eminence	
botany [bɑ́:təni]	名 植物学；植生 pharmaceutical botany 薬用植物学 ＊ botanical gardens「植物園」の話も出題例あり。	phytology	
mummy [mʌ́mi]	名 ミイラ a well-preserved mummy 保存状態のよいミイラ	a body embalmed for burial	C
native [néɪtɪv]	形 原産の；原住の，土着の be native to South America 南米原産である ＊名詞の場合は be a native of 〜。	indigenous	
hostile [hɑ́:stl]	形 敵意のある take a hostile action 敵対行為をする ＊L 発音注意！ [hɑ́staɪl] と読むこともある。	inimical	
insulting [ɪnsʌ́ltɪŋ]	形 侮辱的な make an insulting remark 侮辱的な言葉を口にする	scornful	D
accuse [əkjúːz]	動 責める，非難する；告発する accuse him of misconduct 彼を不正行為で非難する	blame	
fraud [frɔ́ːd]	名 詐欺 accounting fraud 粉飾決算（不正会計） ＊発音注意！　聞き逃しやすい。	dupery	

101

単語／発音	語義／フレーズ	同意表現
trace [tréɪs]	名 跡, 痕跡 vanish without a trace 跡形もなく消えてなくなる	vestige
cemetery [sémətèri]	名 墓地 be buried at a cemetery for war dead 戦没者墓地に埋葬される	graveyard
fragment [frǽgmənt]	名 一片；破片 a fragment of a poem 詩の断片	piece
abdomen [ǽbdəmən]	名 腹部；腹腔 acute pains in one's abdomen 腹部の激痛	belly
artefact [ɑ́ːrtəfækt]	名 （自然物に対して）人工物；人工的な遺物 archaeological artefacts in the British Museum 大英博物館蔵の考古学的遺物	relic
arrogance [érəgəns]	名 傲慢, 尊大, 横柄 intolerable arrogance 耐えられない傲慢さ	haughtiness
exclude [ɪksklúːd]	動 排除する；締め出す exclude all other possibilities 他のすべての可能性を除外する	rule out
sublime [səbláɪm]	形 崇高な a sublime idea 崇高な理念	lofty
brochure [bróʊʃùər]	名 パンフレット, 小冊子；チラシ request a free brochure 無料パンフレットを請求する ＊W1 General Module では brochure を請求する手紙を書くことも。	pamphlet
arouse [əráʊz]	動 （感情などを）喚起する；刺激する arouse suspicion and anger 疑念と怒りをかき立てる	evoke
inspire [ɪnspáɪər]	動 （感情などを）引き出す inspire confidence and trust 自信と信頼を呼び起こす	elicit
ascertain [æ̀sərtéɪn]	動 確かめる；突き止める ascertain the exact location 正確な場所を突き止める	confirm

Track 087

単語／発音	語義／フレーズ	同意表現	難易度
comprise [kəmpráɪz]	動 含む；〜からなる comprise 25% of the total population 全人口の25％を占める	make up	A
tightrope [táɪtròʊp]	名 綱渡りのような状況 walk a diplomatic tightrope 綱渡り外交をする	knife-edge situation	
footnote [fʊ́tnòʊt]	名 脚注 add a footnote 脚注を付ける	bottom note	
allusion [əlúːʒən]	名 ほのめかし，（さりげない）言及 make an allusion to Shakespeare それとなくシェークスピアを引用する	hint	B
assonance [ǽsənəns]	名 （音の）類似，類音 make an assonance 母音韻を踏む	vowel rhyme	
default [dɪfɔ́ːlt]	名 不履行；怠慢；初期設定 default on debts 債務の不履行	failure(to pay/act)	
rage [réɪdʒ]	名 激怒，憤慨 explode with rage 怒りが爆発する	fury	C
due [d(j)úː]	形 当然支払うべき；提出期限がきた Payment is due on the 1st of September. 支払いは9月1日が期限です。	owing	
resort [rɪzɔ́ːrt]	動 頼る〔訴える〕；しばしば行く Extremists resorted to violence. 過激派は暴力に訴えた。	rely	
dehumanisation [diːhjùːmənəzéɪʃən]	名 人間性の喪失；非人間化 dehumanisation by war 戦争による人間性の喪失	becoming inhuman	D
evasive [ɪvéɪsɪv]	形 回避的な；言い逃れの take an evasive action 回避のための手段をとる	avoiding	
collision [kəlíʒən]	名 衝突；食い違い a head-on collision 正面衝突	crash	

103

Track 088

単語／発音	語義／フレーズ	同意表現
dreadful [drédfl]	形 恐ろしい a dreadful car accident 恐ろしい自動車事故	horrific
gruesome [grúːsəm]	形 陰惨な；身の毛がよだつ a gruesome crime scene おぞましい犯罪現場	appalling
bestow [bɪstóu]	動 授ける, 贈る bestow an honorary degree on her 彼女に名誉学位を授与する ＊ give と置き換えればよい。	endow
witness [wítnəs]	動 目撃する；証言する witness a major change 大きな変化を目の当たりにする ＊ eyewitness で「目撃者」。	see
startling [stáːrtlɪŋ]	形 仰天させるような, 驚くべき reveal startling facts 衝撃的な事実を明らかにする ＊ surprising, astonishing も併せて覚える。	shocking
deliberately [dɪlíbərətli]	副 わざと, 意図的に deliberately ignore the question 質問を故意に無視する ＊Ⓡ on purpose / consciously との書き換えに気づくように。	intentionally
chilling [tʃílɪŋ]	形 身も凍るような；冷え冷えする a chilling ghost story 身も凍るような怪談	scary
assault [əsɔ́ːlt]	名 猛攻撃 Troops began an assault. 軍隊が攻撃を開始した。	attack
verbally [vɔ́ːrbli]	副 言葉で be abused verbally 言葉で虐待を受ける	by words
dim [dím]	形 薄暗い in the dim light 薄明かりの中で	dusky
precede [prɪsíːd]	動 先行する, 先立つ precede the discovery of uranium ウランの発見に先行する	come before
uphill [ʌphíl]	形 骨の折れる；上り坂の uphill struggle 苦しい戦い（悪戦苦闘）	laborious

Track 089

単語／発音	語義／フレーズ	同意表現	難易度
meek [míːk]	形 おとなしい；柔和な be as meek as a lamb 極めて従順である	mild	A
horrific [hɔːrífɪk]	形 恐ろしい, ぞっとするような horrific terrorist acts 恐ろしいテロ行為	frightening	
midst [mídst]	名 真っ最中；真ん中 in the midst of the night 真夜中に	middle	
turbulence [tə́ːrbjələns]	名 乱気流；(社会的)混乱；動揺 severe turbulence during the flight 飛行中の激しい乱気流 ＊社会の「激動」なら同意語は upheaval。	rough air currents	B
suspend [səspénd]	動 一時停止する suspend a license 免許を一時停止にする	stop temporarily	
tumble [tʌ́mbl]	動 転倒する tumble from a horse 馬から転げ落ちる	fall down	
spiral [spáɪrəl]	形 らせん状の, 渦巻きの spiral galaxies 渦巻き銀河	voluted	C
maze [méɪz]	名 迷路 in a maze 当惑して；途方に暮れて	labyrinth	
vine [váɪn]	名 つる植物；ブドウの木 a thorn-covered vine トゲだらけのつる植物	bine	
fractured [frǽktʃər]	形 砕けた suffer a fractured jaw あごを骨折する	shattered	D
hunger [hʌ́ŋgər]	名 飢え, 飢餓；渇望 have a hunger for knowledge 知識に飢えている	starvation	
hut [hʌ́t]	名 小屋；山小屋 thatched hut 草ぶきの小屋・草庵 ＊L hat と聞き間違えないように。	cabin	

単語／発音	語義／フレーズ	同意表現
discomfort [dɪskʌ́mfərt]	名 不快(感), 不便 relieve stomach discomfort 胃の不快感を軽減する	unpleasantness
erect [ɪrékt]	動 建設する；直立させる, 立てる erect a television antenna on the roof 屋根にテレビのアンテナを立てる	construct
metabolism [mətǽbəlìzm]	名 (新陳)代謝；物質交代 the medicine speeding up alcohol metabolism アルコール代謝を速める薬品	metabolic process
hiccup [híkʌp]	名 しゃっくり get rid of hiccups しゃっくりを止める ＊「ちょっとした問題」の意味も。	singultation
sentence [séntns]	動 判決を下す sentence the old man to death その老人に死刑判決を下す ＊「文」以外の意味も覚える。	decern
persistence [pərsístəns]	名 粘り強さ；固執 require persistence and patience 粘り強さと忍耐を必要とする ＊動詞 persist, 形容詞 persistent。	tenacity
disprove [dɪsprúːv]	動 反証する；誤りを立証する disprove an old theory 古い理論を反証する	rebut
weak-willed [wíːk-wíld]	形 意志の弱い be too weak-willed to stand 意志が弱くて我慢できない	weak-minded
defect [díːfekt]	名 欠点；不足；不具合 a defect in the software そのソフトウェアの欠陥	fault
subtle [sʌ́tl]	形 微妙な notice a subtle change in weather 天候のかすかな変化に気づく ＊発音注意。b は読まない。	slight
corporate [kɔ́ːrpərət]	形 法人の, 企業の abolish the corporate income tax 法人所得税を撤廃する	incorporated
conversely [kənvə́ːrsli]	副 逆に言えば；反対に, 対照的に Conversely, to be unmarried may be easier. 逆に言えば, 独身の方が楽かも。	reversely

Track 091

単語／発音	語義／フレーズ	同意表現	難易度
firsthand [fə́:rsthǽnd]	形 直接の，じかの firsthand experience 直接の体験	direct	A
collaborative [kəlǽbərèɪtɪv]	形 協力による；合作の collaborative research with spirited scientists 気鋭の科学者との共同研究	cooperative	
peer [píər]	名 同輩，同僚；(能力などが)同等の人 my peers in the class クラスの同級生	fellow	
simulated [símjəlèɪtɪd]	形 模造の；真似た a simulated pearl 模造真珠	mock	B
empower [ɪmpáʊər]	動 (権限や能力)を与える be empowered by the law 法律によって権限を与えられる	authorise	
module [má:dʒu:l]	名 (英国)大学の履習単位；測定基準(単位) ten core modules in the course コースの主要10モジュール(単位)	unit	
consensus [kənsénsəs]	名 総意，合意 need a national consensus 国民の総体的合意を必要とする	agreement	C
cohesion [koʊhí:ʒən]	名 結束，団結 build cohesion in a team チームの結束を築く *W2 代名詞をうまく使うと cohesive な文が書ける。	unity	
persuade [pərswéɪd]	動 説得する persuade him to change his mind 考えを変えるよう彼を説得する	prevail on	
resolve [rɪzá:lv]	動 解決する；決定する resolve a conflict 対立(紛争)を解決する	settle	D
commence [kəméns]	動 始まる，始める；(学位など)を受ける The holidays commence on Saturday. 休日は土曜に始まる。	begin	
procedure [prəsí:dʒər]	名 手順；手続き follow the proper procedure ふさわしい手順を踏む *L 書き取り問題のためにスペリングは正確に覚える。	course of action	

単語／発音	語義／フレーズ	同意表現
capable [kéɪpəbl]	形 能力のある computer capable of understanding human speech 言語理解能力のあるコンピュータ	able
convince [kənvíns]	動 納得させる cannot convince everyone 全員を納得させることはできない ＊「私が〜を確信する／している」は I am convinced that SV 〜が定番。	persuade
spot [spá:t]	動 見つける spot an unknown micro-organism 未知の微細生物を見つけ出す　＊find も同義語。	detect
whip [wíp]	名 鞭；鞭のような物 use a whip on a horse 馬に鞭を振るう	lash
propel [prəpél]	動 進ませる, 推進する a ship propelled by steam 蒸気で進む船	move forwards
magnify [mǽgnəfàɪ]	動 拡大する magnify an object 500 times 物体を500倍に拡大する	enlarge
deter [dɪtə́:r]	動 抑止する；思いとどまらせる the way to deter war 戦争を抑止する方法	discourage
swallow [swá:loʊ]	動 のみ込む Snakes swallow their prey whole. ヘビは獲物をまるのみにする。	eat up
discourage [dɪskə́:rɪdʒ]	動 やめさせる；がっかりさせる discourage children from smoking 児童の喫煙をやめさせる　＊W2 discourage O from 〜 ing の形を覚える。	deter
intriguing [ɪntrí:gɪŋ]	形 魅力的な；とても興味深い be pulled into an intriguing story 魅力的な物語に引き込まれる　＊発音注意！	fascinating
tissue [tíʃu:]	名 組織；ちり紙 living tissues of an animal 動物の生きた組織	matter
span [spǽn]	動 及ぶ, 広がる；橋渡しをする span from East to West 東西に及ぶ	extend

単語／発音	語義／フレーズ	同意表現	難易度
estuary [éstʃuèri]	名 河口 the Thames estuary テムズ川の河口	river mouth	A
content [kəntént]	形 満足して be content with the success その成功に満足している	satisfied	
photosynthesise [phòutousínθəsàɪz]	動 光合成する enough light for plants to photosynthesise 植物が光合成をするために十分な日光　＊名詞は photosynthesis。		
devour [dɪváʊər]	動 むさぼり食う devour the prey 獲物をむさぼる	eat	B
feed [fíːd]	動 常食とする；食べ物を与える Cattle feed mainly on grass. 牛は主に草を食べる。 ＊ feed は「食事を与える；食べる」と他動詞・自動詞の両方あるので注意。	live on ～	
flush [flʌ́ʃ]	動 水をどっと流す；(顔が)赤らむ flush the toilet トイレの水を流す	wash	
habitat [hǽbəitæ̀t]	名 生息地 live in a wet habitat 湿った生息地に住む ＊ inhabit「住む」や inhabitant「住民」などを考えると易しい。	natural territory	C
shellfish [ʃélfiʃ]	名 甲殻類動物 shellfish allergy 甲殻類アレルギー	crustacean	
strand [strǽnd]	動 座礁する；座礁させる；途方に暮れさせる a stranded ship 座礁した船 ＊ whale stranding（鯨が浜に打ち上げられること）がよく出る。	run aground	
proceeding [prəsíːdɪŋ]	名 進行；処置；手続き hinder the proceedings 進行を妨げる	procedure	D
streak [stríːk]	名 筋，線 a streak of light in the sky 空に一条の光	line	
aquaculture [ǽkwəakʌ̀ltʃər]	名 養殖(魚介類) oyster aquaculture 牡蠣の養殖	cultivation	

Track 094

単語／発音	語義／フレーズ	同意表現
reluctance [rɪlʌ́ktəns]	名 気が進まないこと, 不本意 show reluctance to eat raw fish 刺身を口にしたがらない	unwillingness
farm [fɑ́ːrm]	名 養殖場；農場 an eel farm 鰻の養殖場	nursery
manual [mǽnjuəl]	形 手を使う, 手動の；手引書の a manual transmission on a car 手動変速装置 ＊® manual workers は「肉体労働者」。	hand-operated
striking [stráɪkɪŋ]	形 際立った, 目立つ；ストライキ中の a woman of striking beauty 際立った美女	noticeable
institution [ìnstət(j)úːʃən]	名 機関, 組織；設立；制度 an academic institution 学術機関	organisation
emerging [ɪmə́ːrdʒɪŋ]	形 新興の emerging markets in Asia アジアの新興市場	rising
govern [gʌ́vərn]	動 支配する, 統治する govern a nation 国を治める	rule
crammer [krǽmər]	名 塾, 予備校 attend a crammer to prepare for entrance exams 入学試験準備で予備校に通う	preparatory school
prestige [prestíːʒ]	名 威信, 面子；名声 enhance national prestige 国威を高める	status
vicious [víʃəs]	形 冷酷な, 非道の；悪徳の a vicious killer in the novel 小説の中の冷酷な殺人者 ＊vicious circle「悪循環」も頻出。	brutal
preferably [préfərəbli]	副 むしろ；もしできれば Want an assistant, preferably a young man. 助手募集, なるべくなら若者希望。	ideally
division [dɪvíʒən]	名 部門；区分；分割 the sales division 販売部門 ＊division of labour は「労働の区分, 分業」。	section

110

Track 095

単語／発音	語義／フレーズ	同意表現	難易度
forecasting [fɔ́:rkæstɪŋ]	名 予報, 予測 weather forecasting 天気予報	prediction	A
resurface [rɪsə́:rfəs]	動 再浮上する；再舗装する The problem resurfaced. その問題が再び表面化した。	happen again	
sense [séns]	動 感じる, 気づく；探知する sense danger and warn 危険を感じて警告する	discern	
conceivable [kənsí:vəbl]	形 考えられる, 想像できる every conceivable reason 考えられるすべての理由	imaginable	B
ashore [əʃɔ́:r]	副 陸上に（で） go ashore from a ship 船から上陸する	on (to) land	
twist [twíst]	名 急変, 急展開；ねじれ surprising twists in a story 物語の驚くべき急展開	turn	
roaring [rɔ́:rɪŋ]	形 目覚ましい, 活気のある；ほえる a roaring success 目覚ましい成功	terrific	C
house [háʊs]	名 会社, 商店 a publishing house 出版社 ＊動詞「収容する」の意味も覚える。動詞は発音も注意！	company	
command [kəmǽnd]	動 命ずる, 指揮する command his men 部下に命じる ＊ have a good command of English「英語の運用能力が高い」。	order	
fuel [fjúːəl]	動 活気づける, あおる fuel the economic boom 好景気をあおる ＊Ⓛ スペリングは書けるように！	stimulate	D
nourishment [nə́:rɪʃmənt]	名 栄養（物）；養育 provide sufficient nourishment 十分な栄養を与える	nutrition	
frighten [fráɪtn]	動 ぎょっとさせる, 怖がらせる be frightened at a big spider 大きなクモにぎょっとする	scare	

111

Track 096

単語／発音	語義／フレーズ	同意表現
demanding [dɪmǽndɪŋ]	形 骨の折れる；要求の厳しい a demanding job 骨の折れる仕事 ＊⒮ My work / boss is demanding. は使えそう。	difficult
fanatical [fənǽtɪkəl]	形 熱狂的な fanatical soccer fans 熱狂的なサッカーファン	enthusiastic
handle [hǽndl]	動 扱う Handle with care. 取り扱い注意。	treat
off-limits [ɔ́(ː)f-límɪts]	形 立ち入り禁止の an off-limits area 立ち入り禁止区域	no-entry
nonetheless [nʌnðəlés]	副 それでもなお，それにもかかわらず Nonetheless, he survived. それでもなお彼は生き延びた。	nevertheless
derive [dɪráɪv]	動 得る；引き出す derive pleasure from reading 読書から楽しみを得る	obtain
bidding [bídɪŋ]	名 せり，入札 The bidding began at £10,000. せりは1万ポンドで始まった。	auction
uncertainty [ʌnsə́ːrtnti]	名 不確かさ uncertainty about the future 未来についての不確かさ	unpredictability
inability [ìnəbíləti]	名 無能，無力 inability to speak 言葉を話すことができないこと ＊Ⓦ2 inability to V「Vする能力がないこと」。	incapability
irrationally [ɪrǽʃənli]	副 理不尽に；不合理に behave irrationally 理不尽に振る舞う ＊ illogically も同義語。	unreasonably
blossom [blɑ́ːsəm]	動 開花する；栄える blossom in spring 春に花が咲く ＊Ⓡ The business blossomed. だと「商売が栄えた」。	bloom
self-fulfilling [sélf-fʊlfílɪŋ]	形 自己達成の；予言通りに成就される a self-fulfilling prophecy 自己達成的予言	—

単語／発音	語義／フレーズ	同意表現	難易度
prophecy [prá:fəsi]	名 予言 a gift of prophecy 予言能力 ＊動詞は prophesy だが発音注意！	prediction	A
poll [póʊl]	名 世論調査；投票（結果） ABC News poll ABC ニュースの世論調査	survey	
respondent [rɪspá:ndənt]	名 回答者 the respondents to this survey この調査の回答者	answerer	
overestimate [òʊvəréstəmèɪt]	動 過大評価する overestimate one's own ability 自分の能力を過信する	overrate	B
decisive [dɪsáɪsɪv]	形 決定的な；果断な decisive proof 決定的証拠	conclusive	
hold [hóʊld]	名 影響力，支配力 have a hold over children 子供への影響力がある	influence	
party [pá:rti]	名 関係者，当事者；団体 all parties concerned すべての関係者	those concerned	C
acquisition [ækwəzíʃən]	名 習得，取得；買収 language acquisition 言語習得	learning	
cherish [tʃérɪʃ]	動 大事にする；かわいがる cherish a memory 思い出をいつくしむ	treasure	
colour [kʌ́lə]	動 影響を及ぼす；特徴付ける be coloured by prejudice 先入観に影響される ＊「色をつける」から連想できる。influence も同義語。	affect	D
accustom [əkʌ́stəm]	動 慣れさせる，なじませる I'm not accustomed to being treated like that. そんな処遇には慣れていません。	familiarise	
possession [pəzéʃən]	名 所有物，財産；所有，占有 lose all one's possessions すべての財産をなくす	belongings	

Track 097

単語/発音	語義/フレーズ	同意表現
billion [bíljən]	名 10億 4.6 billion years ago 46億年前 ＊million「100万」とtrillion「1兆」の間。	milliard
school [skúːl]	名 (学問・芸術の)流派, 学派 the Platonic school of philosophy プラトン派哲学 ＊「魚の群れ(をつくる)」というschoolもまれに出る。	group
admittedly [ədmítɪdli]	副 明らかに；一般が認めるように Admittedly, he is not well. 明らかに, 彼の状態はよくない。	obviously
insuperable [ɪnsúːpərəbl]	形 克服できない, 乗り越えられない insuperable difficulties 克服不能な困難	insurmountable
ought [ɔ́ːt]	助 当然すべきである Yes, you ought to help the elderly. そう, 老人を助けるべきだよ。 ＊助動詞だが, to do が続く。	should
affluent [ǽfluənt]	形 裕福な a very affluent neighbourhood 非常に裕福な地域 ＊rich も同義語。	wealthy
compel [kəmpél]	動 無理やり〜させる compel a person to resign 人を無理やり辞職させる ＊W2 compel O to V の形で使う。	force
downside [dáʊnsàɪd]	名 不利な面；底側 the downside of the hotel そのホテルの欠点 ＊W2 disadvantage の書き換えとして drawback と併せて覚える。	disadvantage
norm [nɔ́ːrm]	名 基準, 標準；標準労働量 conform to the norms of behaviour 行動基準に従う	standard
customary [kʌ́stəmèri]	形 習慣的な；慣習の It is customary to eat turkey for Christmas dinner. クリスマスの晩餐は七面鳥が定番。	habitual
extinct [ɪkstíŋkt]	形 絶滅した；(火などが)消えた danger of becoming extinct 絶滅の危機 ＊go extinct「絶滅する」。go＋形容詞の形を覚える。	exterminated
game [géɪm]	名 (狩猟の)獲物；(攻撃の)目標 game such as wild deer 例えば野生の鹿などの獲物	quarry

Track 099

単語／発音	語義／フレーズ	同意表現	難易度
disperse [dɪspə́:rs]	動 散らばらせる，散らばる；消散する The seeds are dispersed by the wind. 種は風で散らばる。	dissipate	A
obstacle [ɑ́:bstəkl]	名 障害物，邪魔(物) put obstacles in the way of her marriage 彼女の結婚を邪魔する	barrier	
fatality [feɪtǽləti]	名 (事故などによる)死者(数)；必然 the number of traffic fatalities 交通事故による死者の数	casualty	
ground [gráʊnd]	名 根拠，理由；前提 discrimination on grounds of age 年齢に基づく差別 ＊W2 on the grounds that SV「SV という理由で」。	reason	B
enquiry [ɪnkwáɪəri]	名 問い合わせ；調査 make enquiries 問い合わせる	inquiry	
bill [bíl]	名 法案，議案；紙幣 the draft of the new bill 新法案の草稿 ＊ pay the bill で「費用を支払う」。	measure	
practitioner [præktíʃənər]	名 開業者，専門家 general practitioners 一般開業医 ＊「開業医」を表すことが多い。	specialist	C
impatient [ɪmpéɪʃənt]	形 我慢できない；しきりにしたがる be impatient of delay 遅延が我慢できない	restless	
chronic [krɑ́:nɪk]	形 慢性の；長期にわたる a chronic back pain 慢性的な背中の痛み	persistent	
incapacitate [ìnkəpǽsətèɪt]	動 (健康・能力・資格)を奪う He was incapacitated by an accident. 彼は事故で身障者となった。	disable	D
immobile [ɪmóʊbl]	形 動かせない，動けない；静止した His injury made him completely immobile. 彼は怪我で活動不能となった。	unmovable	
spine [spáɪn]	名 背骨；とげ，針 damage one's spine 背骨を傷める	backbone	

115

Track 100

単語／発音	語義／フレーズ	同意表現
posture [pɑ́:stʃər]	名 姿勢, ポーズ；心構え The change in posture made language possible. 姿勢の変化が言語を可能にした。	position
corridor [kɔ́:rədər]	名 廊下, 通路, 回廊；回廊地帯 Go along the corridor and up the stairs. 廊下を進んでから階段を上れ。　＊発音注意！	passageway
insufficient [ìnsəfíʃənt]	形 不十分な, 不足な；不適当な insufficient to pay for the expense 経費を払うには不十分である	deficient
query [kwíəri]	名 質問, 疑問；疑惑 in answer to your query あなたのご質問にお答えして	question
nursery [nɔ́:rsəri]	名 苗木屋；託児所；育児室 buy tomato plants at the nursery 園芸店でトマトの苗木を買う　＊R nursery school「保育園」。	garden centre
questionnaire [kwèstʃənéər]	名 アンケート用紙, 質問票；調査 fill in a questionnaire アンケート用紙に記入する	question sheet
conical [kɑ́:nɪkəl]	形 円錐形の a conical mountain 円錐形の山	cone-shaped
glue [glú:]	名 接着剤, のり a strong glue for plastics プラスチック用の強力接着剤	adhesive
impose [ɪmpóʊz]	動 （義務・罰を）課す；押し付ける impose protective tariffs on foreign imports 輸入品に保護関税を課す	charge
straightforward [strèɪtfɔ́:rwərd]	形 簡単な；（言動などが）率直な a straightforward job 簡単な仕事	uncomplicated
deposit [dɪpɑ́:zət]	名 保証金, 頭金；預金 a deposit to cover possible damage 損害補償用の保証金　＊L 手付金の意味で頻出。	security
entitle [ɪntáɪtl]	動 権利・資格を与える be entitled to receive health insurance 健康保険の権利が与えられる	qualify

Track 101

単語／発音	語義／フレーズ	同意表現	難易度
annual [ǽnjuəl]	形 毎年の, 年1回の the annual rainfall in London ロンドンの年間雨量 * L an annual fee of £10 = £10 per year。	yearly	A
livestock [láɪvstɑ̀:k]	名 家畜 herd the livestock 家畜の群れを集める	cattle	
ostrich [ɑ́:strɪtʃ]	名 ダチョウ；現実逃避者 an ostrich farm ダチョウ飼育場		
breed [brí:d]	動 繁殖させる；飼育する breed dogs and sell them as pets 犬を繁殖飼育しペットとして売る　* breed-bred-bred の変化。	reproduce	B
pale [péɪl]	形 (色が)薄い, 淡い；薄暗い pale yellow 薄い黄色	light	
fatty [fǽti]	形 脂肪質の, 脂っこい；ひどく太った a fatty substance 脂肪分の多い物質	oily	
fashion [fǽʃən]	名 やり方, 流儀；流行 speak in a very strange fashion とても変わった話し方でしゃべる * be in fashion で「流行している」。	manner	C
hide [háɪd]	名 皮；自身の安全 make coats out of animal hides 動物の皮で外套を作る	skin	
margin [mɑ́:rdʒɪn]	名 利幅, 余白 good profit margins 良い利幅	markup	
gadget [gǽdʒɪt]	名 ちょっとした(便利な)機器, 仕掛け the gadgets James Bond used ジェームス・ボンドが使った便利な器具	appliance	D
intent [ɪntént]	名 目的, 意図 prove criminal intent 犯意を証明する	aim	
flash [flǽʃ]	動 点灯する, 点滅させる flash a torch 懐中電灯をつける	light up	

Track 102

単語／発音	語義／フレーズ	同意表現
squeeze [skwíːz]	動 (狭い場所に)無理に入る；絞る squeeze into a crevice 割れ目に入り込む ＊economic squeeze 経済的締め付け(名詞)も併せて覚える。	push into
burglar [bə́ːrglər]	名 強盗，住居侵入者 arrest a burglar 強盗を逮捕する	housebreaker
draft [dræft]	名 下書き，草稿 write a first draft 最初の草稿を書く ＊L Section3 では draft に関する相談の場面が頻出。	outline
dash [dæʃ]	動 急ぐ；突進する，驀進する dash off the article just before the deadline 締切間際に記事を急ぎ仕上げる	hasten
astray [əstréɪ]	副 正道を踏み外して；道に迷って be led astray by one's bad friends 悪友に惑わされて道を誤る	into error
teller [télər]	名 (銀行の)受付係 a bank teller 銀行の窓口係	clerk
transaction [trænsǽkʃən]	名 取引，売買；処理 a profitable transaction 儲かる取引	deal
confused [kənfjúːzd]	形 困惑した，混乱した be confused about his words 彼の言葉に困惑する ＊perplexed も一緒に覚える。	puzzled
sympathetic [sìmpəθétɪk]	形 同情的な offer a person a sympathetic ear 親身になって人の話を聞く	thoughtful
queue [kjúː]	名 (順番待ちの)列 wait in a queue 列を作って待つ	line
drawback [drɔ́ːbæk]	名 欠点，障害 The main drawback is the high cost. 主な欠点は高いコストだ。 ＊W2 disadvantage の書き換えになる。	downside
accordance [əkɔ́ːrdns]	名 一致，調和；授与 in accordance with the rules ルールに従って(と調和して)	agreement

Track 103

単語／発音	語義／フレーズ	同意表現	難易度
illegal [ilíːgl]	形 違法の，非合法の an illegal drug 違法薬品	illicit	A
theft [θéft]	名 盗み，窃盗 be convicted of theft 窃盗罪の判決を受ける ＊「起訴される」は indicted。	stealing	
misfortune [misfɔ́ːrtʃən]	名 不幸，災難 endure many misfortunes 多くの不幸に耐える	hardship	
sensational [senséiʃənl]	形 驚くべき；扇情的な；素晴らしい a movie based on a sensational crime 驚くべき犯罪に基づく映画	amazing	B
venue [vénjuː]	名 開催地；現場 a big concert venue 大きなコンサート会場	place for something	
refer [rifɔ́ːr]	動 〜のことを言う；参照する refer to the matter そのことについて言う ＊Lrefer 人 to 場所「(人)を(場所)へ向かわせる」。	mention	
intensive [inténsiv]	形 集中的な；激しい，強い an intensive language course in summer 夏の集中語学講座	thorough	C
enthusiastic [inθ(j)ùːziǽstik]	形 熱心な，熱狂的な；狂信的な enthusiastic football supporters 熱狂的なサッカーファン ＊Sbe enthusiastic about 〜「〜に熱中している」も使える。	avid	
ultimate [ʌ́ltəmət]	形 最終の，究極の；最大の an ultimate decision by the president 大統領による最終決定	eventual	
submit [səbmít]	動 提出する；服従させる submit an assignment by due date 期限までに課題を提出する	hand in	D
residence [rézədəns]	名 住宅，家；居住 the British Prime Minister's official residence 英国首相の公邸	home	
minimal [mínəml]	形 最小の maximum profit at minimal cost 最小コストでの最大利益	minimum	

119

Track 104

単語／発音	語義／フレーズ	同意表現
personnel [pə́:rsənél]	名 職員；人事課 hire security personnel 警備職員を雇う	staff
iceberg [áɪsbə:rg]	名 氷山 only the tip of the iceberg 氷山のほんの一角	a mountain of ice
sledge [slédʒ]	名 そり go by dog-sledge 犬ぞりで行く ＊[米] sled。	sleigh
build-up [bíldʌp]	名 蓄積；増加；増強 the build-up of CO_2 in the atmosphere 大気中の CO_2 の蓄積	accumulation
shipping [ʃípɪŋ]	名 輸送 a price including the cost of shipping 送料込みの価格	transport
cupboard [kʌ́bərd]	名 戸棚, 食器棚 built-in wardrobes and cupboards 備え付けの箪笥と戸棚 ＊発音注意！ bの音に重なるため, pの音が聞こえない。	cabinet
roundabout [ráʊndəbàʊt]	名 環状交差路 Slow down at the roundabout. 環状交差点ではゆっくり。 ＊[英]（[米]では traffic circle）。	rotary
raise [réɪz]	動 (資金を)集める, 育てる raise money for a research project 研究事業の資金を集める	collect
refreshment [rɪfréʃmənt]	名 軽い飲食物, スナック；元気回復 serve drinks and refreshments 飲物と軽食を出す	snacks
depict [dɪpíkt]	動 描写する, 表現する depict everyday lives in the novel 日常生活を小説に描く	illustrate
abstract [æbstrǽkt]	形 抽象的な, 観念的な an abstract and difficult poem 抽象的で難解な詩	notional
scenery [sí:nəri]	名 風景；舞台背景 the wonderful scenery of the Swiss Alps スイスアルプスの素晴らしい風景	landscape

Track 105

単語／発音	語義／フレーズ	同意表現	難易度
pile [páɪl]	名 大量, 沢山；積み重ね a pile of work 山のような仕事	lot	A
portray [pɔːrtréɪ]	動 表現する；肖像を描く portray the essence 最も重要な点を表現する	represent	
harsh [hɑ́ːrʃ]	形 厳しい the harsh environment of the Arctic 北極の厳しい環境	severe	
utterly [ʌ́tərli]	副 全く utterly useless 全く役に立たない	completely	B
estate [ɪstéɪt]	名 財産；地所, 私有地 a real estate agent 不動産業者 ＊L Section1 に不動産の話題で出ることも。	property	
outnumber [àʊtnʌ́mbər]	動 〜に数で勝る Boys outnumber girls. 男子が女子より多い。 ＊W1 数の大小を比較するときに使いたい。	exceed	C
magnificent [mægnífəsənt]	形 素晴らしい, 壮大な a magnificent building 壮大な建物	wonderful	
orientate [ɔ́ːriəntèɪt]	動 適応させる, 正しい位置に置く orientate oneself to one's new way of life 新しい生活様式に適応する	adapt	
stunning [stʌ́nɪŋ]	形 とても美しい, 魅力的な；驚くべき a stunning view of the lake 湖の素晴らしい眺め	impressive	
scheme [skíːm]	名 計画, 配置 a business scheme 事業計画	plan	D
Human Resources [hjúːmən ríːsɔ̀ːrs]	名 人事部 a human resources manager 人事部長	the personnel	
refine [rɪfáɪn]	動 〜に磨きをかける, 〜を精製する refine one's own mind 自分の心を磨く	improve	

121

Track 106

単語／発音	語義／フレーズ	同意表現
proficiency [prəfíʃənsi]	名 上達, 習熟 a degree of proficiency 習熟度	ability
monolingual [mὰːnoəlíŋgwəl]	名 1カ国語だけ話す人 be brought up as a monolingual 1カ国語だけ話す人として育てられる	
publicity [pʌblísəti]	名 知名度, 評判；宣伝広報 receive much publicity 大きな注目を集める	attention
council [káʊnsl]	名 地方自治体, 評議会 the city council 市議会	local authority
breakdown [bréɪkdὰʊn]	名 内訳；分析；故障 a breakdown of expenses 費用の内訳	detail
grant [grǽnt]	名 助成金, 奨学金 government grants for research 政府の研究助成金	subsidy
cosmopolitan [kὰːzməpáːlətən]	形 国際的な, 洗練された cosmopolitan atmosphere in the big city 大都会の国際的な雰囲気	international
laidback [léɪdbǽk]	形 のんびりした laidback environment in the countryside 田舎ののんびりした環境	relaxed
nasty [nǽsti]	形 不快な, たちの悪い a nasty smell from the garbage 生ごみの嫌な臭い	disgusting
stall [stɔ́ːl]	名 屋台, 露店 stalls selling food 食べ物を売る屋台	stand
narrow [nérou]	動 絞り込む；範囲を狭くする narrow down the cause 原因を絞り込む	limit
hypothesis [haɪpáːθəsɪs]	名 仮説, 前提 prove the hypothesis 仮説を証明する	supposition

Track 107

単語／発音	語義／フレーズ	同意表現	難易度
precipitation [prɪsìpɪtéɪʃən]	名 降水(量)；急落下 precipitation percentage 降水確率	rainfall	A
qualitative [kwá:lətèɪtɪv]	形 質的な qualitative identity 質的同一性	subjective	
numerous [n(j)ú:mərəs]	形 沢山の，数多くの；多数からなる on numerous occasions 多くの場合に	many	
inconclusive [ìnkənklú:sɪv]	形 決定的でない inconclusive debates 結論の出ない議論	indecisive	B
noteworthy [nóʊtwə̀:rði]	形 注目すべき a noteworthy fact 注目すべき事実	remarkable	
trek [trék]	名 トレッキング，山麓歩き，小旅行 go trek in Nepal ネパールでトレッキングをする	hike	C
sustainable [səstéɪnəbl]	形 持続可能な；維持できる sustainable development (環境を害せず)持続可能な開発	maintainable	
assert [əsə́:rt]	動 主張する；断言する She asserted her innocence. 彼女は無実を主張した。	insist	
signpost [sáɪnpòʊst]	名 道標，道しるべ a signpost at the fork 分かれ道の道標	notice	
abrupt [əbrʌ́pt]	形 不意の，突然の an abrupt death from a heart attack 心臓発作による突然の死　＊sudden も同義語。	unexpected	D
criterion [kraɪtíəriən]	名 基準 criteria of safety 安全基準 ＊複数形は criteria。	standard	
settle [sétl]	動 解決する；定住する make every effort to settle the dispute 論争を解決するために，あらゆる努力をする	resolve	

123

単語／発音	語義／フレーズ	同意表現
commitment [kəmítmənt]	名 約束, 責任, 義務；献身, 傾倒 make a big emotional commitment 重大な心情的約束を結ぶ	promise
boundary [báundəri]	名 境界線, 端 the boundary between two countries 2つの国の境界線	borderline
plain [pléɪn]	名 平野 across the great plains 大平原を横切って	grassland
scope [skóʊp]	名 範囲 expand the scope of one's business 事業の範囲を拡張する	extent
logistics [lədʒístɪks]	名 事業の計画・実行, 物流 Logistics went well. 計画はうまくいった。 ＊an international logistics business「国際物流事業」。	management, planning
informative [ɪnfɔ́ːrmətɪv]	形 有益な, 情報の an informative article 参考になる記事	educational
abandon [əbǽndən]	動 諦める, 見捨てる abandoned dogs 捨て(られた)犬 ＊throw away「(ごみ箱に)捨てる」との違いに注意。	give up
tow [tóʊ]	動 レッカー移動させる；引っ張る My car was towed away. 私の車はレッカー移動された。 ＊違法駐車に対する掲示でも頻出の単語。	pull
make [méɪk]	名 製造者, メーカー the make and model 製造者とモデル	brand
flat tyre [flǽt táɪər]	名 パンク get a flat tyre タイヤがパンクする ＊Ⓛ「タイヤ」はtireでもtyreでもOK。	blowout
windscreen [wìndskríːn]	名 (車の)フロントガラス；風防 a crack in the windscreen フロントガラスの亀裂 ＊[米] windshield。	windshield
shipwreck [ʃíprèk]	動 難破させる The vessel was shipwrecked. その船は難破した。	sink

Track 109

単語／発音	語義／フレーズ	同意表現	難易度
portfolio [pɔːrtfóuliòu]	名 作品集, ポートフォリオ submit a portfolio 作品集を提出する ＊「所有株一覧」を表すこともある。	a collection of works	A
postgraduate [pòustgrǽdʒuèit]	形 大学院の postgraduate courses 大学院課程 ＊大学の学部レベルは undergraduate。	graduate	
overstretch [òuvərstrétʃ]	動 ～を伸ばし過ぎる The facilities were overstretched. 施設は拡張され過ぎた。	overextend	
nature [néitʃər]	名 性質, 本質 the nature of laughter 笑いの本質	character	B
relief [rɪlíːf]	名 安心, 安堵；(苦痛・心配の)軽減 breathe a sigh of relief 安堵のため息をつく	reassurance	
definite [défənət]	形 明確な, 決定的な definite evidence 明確な証拠	obvious	
tone [tóun]	動 (肌・筋肉を)整える, 引き締める a beautifully toned body 美しく引き締まった肉体	tighten	C
ethnic [éθnɪk]	形 民族の；民族特有の many different ethnic groups たくさんの異なる民族グループ	racial	
project [prədʒékt]	動 計画する, 推定する New roads are projected to be constructed. 新しい道路が建設される計画だ。	plan	
excursion [ɪkskə́ːrʒən]	名 小旅行, 遠足 a school excursion 修学旅行	journey	D
tick [tík]	動 チェックマークを付ける tick the box 四角にチェックマークを入れる		
last-minute [lǽst mínət]	形 直前の, 間際の a last-minute change 直前の変更 ＊S I'm a last-minute person.「私は期限ギリギリにやる人です」。		

125

Track 110

単語／発音	語義／フレーズ	同意表現
petrol [pétrəl]	名 石油 a petrol station ガソリンスタンド ＊［英］。	gasoline
placement [pléɪsmənt]	名 職業紹介；配置 job placement services 職業斡旋サービス	positioning
mark [máːrk]	動 採点する；印を付ける；表す mark a student's work 学生の学業を採点する	grade
visual [víʒuəl]	名 映像, 画像 create interesting visuals 面白い映像を制作する	graphic
tight [táɪt]	形 余裕がない, 詰まった；窮屈な on a pretty tight budget かなり逼迫した予算で	insufficient
waterway [wɑ́ːtərwèɪ]	名 水路, 運河 waterway shipping 水路の輸送	canal
artificial [ɑ̀ːrtəfíʃəl]	形 人工的な, 作り物の an artificial satellite 人工衛星 ＊「わざとらしい；模造の」の意味もある。artificial flowers は「造花」。	synthetic
rub [rʌ́b]	動 こすれる, こする, ふく Badly fitting shoes can rub painfully. 合わない靴はこすれて痛いかも。	chafe
sprinkle [spríŋkl]	動 まき散らす sprinkle water 水をまく	scatter
head [héd]	動 先頭に立つ, 率いる；向ける Most single-parent families are headed by women. ほとんどの片親家族は女性が率いる。	lead
soothing [súːðɪŋ]	形 落ち着かせる, 安心させる have a soothing effect on children 子供を落ち着かせる効果がある	restful
migratory [máɪgrətɔ̀ːri]	形 （動物が）移住性の；遊牧する migratory birds 渡り鳥	migrant

単語／発音	語義／フレーズ	同意表現	難易度
load [lóʊd]	動 (荷物を)積む load a cargo 貨物を積む	pack	A
rectangular [rektǽŋgjələr]	形 長方形の a rectangular-shaped room 長方形の部屋	oblong	
customs [kʌ́stəmz]	名 関税, 税関 pay customs on imported cigarettes 輸入タバコに関税を払う	tariff	
upcoming [ʌ́pkʌ̀mɪŋ]	形 もうすぐやってくる upcoming events 近日開催のイベント	approaching	B
concession [kənséʃən]	名 譲歩, 許容 make minimal concessions 最低限譲歩する ＊[英]「割引き」の意味もある。a student concession「学生割引」。	compromise	
pensioner [pénʃənər]	名 年金受給者 become a pensioner at 65 65歳で年金受給者になる	annuitant	
eligible [élədʒəbl]	形 資格のある, ふさわしい be eligible for retirement benefits 退職金の資格がある	suitable	C
major [méɪdʒər]	動 〜を専攻する major in sociology 社会学を専攻する	specialise	
charge [tʃɑ́ːrdʒ]	名 責任 be in charge of sales 営業を担当している	responsibility	
sewage [súːɪdʒ]	名 下水, 汚水 sewage disposal 下水処理	waste	D
marsh [mɑ́ːrʃ]	名 沼地 ponds and marshes 池と沼	bog	
gravel [grǽvl]	名 砂利 a gravel road 砂利道	hoggin	

Track 112

単語／発音	語義／フレーズ	同意表現
outflow [áʊtflòʊ]	名 流出 pollution outflow 汚染の流出	effluence
waterfowl [wɔ́ːtərfàʊl]	名 水鳥 a habitat for waterfowl 水鳥の生息地	water bird
swamp [swɑ́ːmp]	名 沼 muddy like a swamp 沼のようにどろどろ	marsh
bear [béər]	動 耐える；運ぶ bear a burden 負担に耐える *かなりの多義語。bear in mind that ～は「～を心に留める」。	endure
troublesome [trʌ́blsəm]	形 煩わしい，困難な deal with a troublesome situation 面倒な状況に対処する	annoying
despite [dɪspáɪt]	前 ～にもかかわらず despite the material wealth 物質的な豊かさにもかかわらず *W1 使い方に注意! despite ＋名詞。although ＋ SV。	notwithstanding
swipe card [swáɪp kɑ́ːrd]	名 磁気カード a swipe card to enter the building ビルに入るための磁気カード	magnetic card
valid [vǽlɪd]	形 有効な；正当な a valid passport 有効期限内のパスポート *⇔ invalid「無効な」。	good
voucher [váʊtʃər]	名 引換券，割引券 a gift voucher ギフト券	coupon
unbeatable [ʌnbíːtəbl]	形 無敵の；最良の the most unbeatable football team 最強のサッカーチーム	unmatched
directory [dəréktəri]	名 住所録；人名簿 the London phone directory ロンドンの電話帳	index
supervise [súːpərvàɪz]	動 監督する，指揮を執る supervise an examination 試験を監督する	oversee

Track 113

単語／発音	語義／フレーズ	同意表現	難易度
vocational [voʊkéɪʃənl]	形 職業の，職務上の a vocational school 専門学校	occupational	A
compromise [kámprəmàɪz]	動 妥協する，譲歩する compromise to avoid a further argument 更なる論争を避けるために妥協する	meet each other halfway	
well-being [wélbíːɪŋ]	名 満足な状態，幸福 pray for one's well-being 人の幸せを願う	happiness	
disorder [dɪsɔ́ːrdər]	名 (体の)不調，障害 suffer from a panic disorder パニック障害に苦しむ	disease	B
eventuality [ɪvèntʃuǽləti]	名 起こり得る事態；成り行き preparation for all eventualities あらゆる事態に対する準備	contingency	
worn-out [wɔ́ːrn áʊt]	形 使い古した，疲れ切った worn-out shoes 使い古しの靴 ＊wear には動詞「すり減る」，名詞「磨耗」の意味がある。	ragged	
astronaut [ǽstrənɔ̀ːt]	名 宇宙飛行士 astronauts aboard the Apollo 11 アポロ 11 号搭乗の宇宙飛行士　＊astronomer「天文学者」と間違えないように。	spaceman	C
hardy [háːrdi]	形 丈夫な，頑丈な a hardy breed of sheep 丈夫な品種のヒツジ	sturdy	
account [əkáʊnt]	名 記述，説明；預金口座 an account of the incident 事件についての説明 ＊動詞用法 account for ～「～を説明する；～を占める」あり。	description	
buffet [bəféɪ]	名 ビュッフェ，バイキング buffet lunch at a hotel ホテルの昼食バイキング	smorgasbord	D
self-catering [sélf kéɪtərɪŋ]	形 自炊の a self-catering accommodation 自炊式の宿泊施設		
glow [glóʊ]	動 光る，輝く A star glows. 星が輝く。 ＊「栄光」は glory。	shine	

Track 114

単語／発音	語義／フレーズ	同意表現
firefly [fáɪərflàɪ]	名 蛍 firefly flashing 蛍の瞬き	glow-worm
dazzling [dǽzəlɪŋ]	形 (眩しいくらい)見事な；眩しいばかりの dazzling performance 見事なパフォーマンス	impressive
countless [káʊntləs]	形 無数の countless numbers of people 無数の人々	innumerable
damp [dǽmp]	形 湿気のある, ジメジメした a damp climate in June 6月のジメッとした気候 ＊dump(どさっと下ろす)と混同しないように！	humid
raft [rǽft]	名 いかだ, ゴムボート an emergency rubber raft 救命用ゴムボート	floater
punctual [pʌ́ŋktʃuəl]	形 時間を厳守する Be always punctual for an appointment. 常に約束の時間を守りなさい。 ＊「時間通り」に accurate はダメ。	on time
injection [ɪndʒékʃən]	名 注射, 注入 a preventive injection 予防注射	shot
prescription [prɪskrípʃən]	名 処方箋；規定 a prescription for pain medication 痛み止めの処方箋	instruction
relocate [rìːlóʊkeɪt]	動 移転する relocate the firm to NY ニューヨークに会社を移転する ＊W1 地図で be relocated to ～「～に移転する」を使えるように。	move
note [nóʊt]	動 注意する, 注目する Please note that ～. ～にご注意ください。	observe
intake [ínteɪk]	名 摂取(量) the intake of oxygen 酸素の摂取(量)	ingestion
diploma [dɪplóʊmə]	名 卒業(修了)証 a high school diploma 高校の卒業証書	certificate

Track 115

単語／発音	語義／フレーズ	同意表現	難易度
certificate [sərtífɪkət]	名 証明書, 免状 a teaching certificate 教員免許状	licence	A
tutorial [t(j)u:tɔ́:riəl]	名 個別指導 an English tutorial 英語の個別指導 ＊L tutor「個人指導教員」は書けるように！	lesson	
guarantee [gèrəntí:]	動 保証する Diligence guarantees success. 勤勉なら成功間違いない。	ensure	
book [búk]	動 予約する book a suite room スイートルームを予約する	reserve	B
prosper [prá:spər]	動 繁栄する；成功する；利益を得る The Asian personal computer market is prospering. アジアのPC市場は繁栄中だ。	thrive	
vegetation [vèdʒətéɪʃən]	名 植物, 草木 vegetation of tropical rainforests 熱帯雨林の草木	plants	
hospitality [hɑ̀:spətǽləti]	名 おもてなし, 歓待 thanks for hospitality おもてなしへの感謝	warmth	C
standby [stǽndbàɪ]	形 予備の；待機中の a standby battery 予備のバッテリー（電池）	reserve	
unforeseen [ʌ̀nfɔːrsíːn]	形 予期しない, 不測の an unforeseen accident 不慮の事故	unpredicted	
urgent [ə́:rdʒənt]	形 緊急の；差し迫った be in urgent need of medical attention 医学治療を緊急に必要としている	immediate	D
consult [kənsʌ́lt]	動 助言を求める, 相談する consult a doctor 医者に診てもらう	seek advice	
notification [nòʊtəfɪkéɪʃən]	名 通知 an official notification 正式な通知	announcement	

単語／発音	語義／フレーズ	同意表現
reptile [réptl]	名 爬虫類 Sea turtles are marine reptiles. 海亀は海の爬虫類だ。	Reptilia
lizard [lízərd]	名 トカゲ be made of lizard skin トカゲ革で作られている	saurian
comet [ká:mɪt]	名 彗星 Halley's Comet ハレー彗星	
parallel [pérəlèl]	名 類似点；平行線[面] have parallels in 〜 〜に類似点を持つ	equivalent
workforce [wə́ːrkfɔ̀ːrs]	名 総労働力（人口） highly skilled workforce 高いスキルの労働力	personnel
stiff [stíf]	形（競争・風が）激しい；筋肉がこった stiff competition 激しい競争	harsh
self-evident [sèlf-évədənt]	形 明白な a self-evident truth 自明の理	obvious
submerged [sʌbmə́ːrdʒd]	形 水中の, 水面下の；秘密の a submerged floating tunnel 水中トンネル ＊動詞は submerge「〜を沈める」。	underwater
by-product [báɪ-prɑ̀ːdəkt]	名 副産物；副作用 a hazardous by-product 有害な副産物	side effect
overflowing [òʊvərflóʊɪŋ]	形 あふれ出る overflowing with joy 喜びにあふれている	overfull
station [stéɪʃən]	動 配置する guards stationed at the gate 門に配備された警備員	assign
noble [nóʊbl]	形 高貴な；貴族の the noble class 貴族階級	aristocratic

Track 117

単語／発音	語義／フレーズ	同意表現	難易度
obedient [oʊbíːdiənt]	形 従順な obedient to authority 権力に対し従順な	submissive	A
merge [mə́ːrdʒ]	動 合併する；溶け込ませる merge two companies 2社を合併する	amalgamate	
gaping [géɪpɪŋ]	形 大きく開いた a gaping wound 大きな傷口 ＊gapping と間違えないこと！	widely open	
apparatus [æpərǽtəs]	名 器具, 装置；機関, 組織 experimental apparatus in the laboratory 研究室の実験装置	instrument	B
delta [déltə]	名 三角州；三角形のもの a river mouth delta 河口三角州	alluvial deposit at a river mouth	
tram [trǽm]	名 路面電車 a mountain tram 登山電車	streetcar	
municipal [mjuː(ː)nísəpl]	形 地方自治体の the municipal waste dump 市営ごみ捨て場	communal	C
pane [péɪn]	名 窓ガラス；窓枠 a large clear pane 大きく透明な窓ガラス	sheet of glass	
shatter [ʃǽtər]	動 打ち砕く shatter someone's hopes 人の希望を打ち砕く ＊自動詞だと「粉々になる」。	smash	
inclusion [ɪnklúːʒən]	名 算入, 加入, 包含 his inclusion in the team 彼のチームへの加入	counting	D
bulky [bʌ́lki]	形 かさばった a bulky dictionary 分厚い辞書	voluminous	
self-reliance [sélf-rɪláɪəns]	名 自立 economic self-reliance 経済的自立	autonomy	

133

Track 118

単語／発音	語義／フレーズ	同意表現
fare [féər]	名 乗車料金 a round-trip fare 往復運賃 ＊toll「通行料」も覚える。	transportation cost
conviction [kənvíkʃən]	名 確信，信念；有罪判決 religious convictions 宗教的信念	belief
endure [ɪnd(j)ʊ́ər]	動 耐える；(物が)持ちこたえる endure hardship 苦難に耐える ＊名詞 endurance「耐久力」。	bear
wear off [wéər ɔ́(:)f]	動 すり減る；消える Novelty wears off someday. 目新しさはいつかはなくなる。	wear down
equitable [ékwətəbl]	形 公平な；正当な an equitable distribution of profits 公平な配分	fair
prolong [prəlɔ́:ŋ]	動 引き延ばす prolong life expectancy 平均寿命を延ばす	extend
vigour [vígər]	名 活力 full of vigour 元気いっぱいで ＊形容詞 vigourous「活気あふれる」。	vitality
mortal [mɔ́:rtl]	形 死ぬべき運命の a mortal disease 死に至る病	deadly
fan [fǽn]	動 扇形に広がる fan out in all directions 八方に広がる ＊名詞では「扇子」の意味もある。	stretch
courteous [kə́:rtiəs]	形 礼儀正しい；丁寧な a courteous attitude 礼儀正しい態度	polite
crisp [krísp]	形 パリッとした a crisp shirt パリッとした皺のないシャツ	crispy
favourably [féɪvərəbli]	副 好意的に impress someone favourably 人に好感を与える	agreeably

Track 119

単語／発音	語義／フレーズ	同意表現	難易度
marvellous [máːrvələs]	形 素晴らしい；驚くべき a marvellous opportunity 素晴らしい機会	fantastic	A
vacancy [véɪkənsi]	名 欠員；空室 There is still one vacancy on the school board. 教育委員会にまだ1人欠員あり。	opening	
utensil [juː(ː)ténsl]	名 器具 kitchen utensils 台所用具	tool	
arise [əráɪz]	動 起こる, 生じる, 現れる New problems arise daily. 日々新たな問題が生じている。 ＊W2 自動詞で「（主語が）起きる」と使う。	occur	B
arrangement [əréɪndʒmənt]	名 準備, 手配；話し合い；配置 the arrangement for our trip 私たちの旅行の手配	preparation	
identical [aɪdéntɪkl]	形 全く同じの identical twins 一卵性双生児	same	
penalise [píːnəlàɪz]	動 罰する penalise someone for 〜 〜の理由で（人を）罰する	punish	C
transitional [trænzíʃənl]	形 過渡期の, 移り変わる a transitional government 暫定政府	transitive	
controversial [kɑ̀ːntrəvə́ːrʃəl]	形 論争上の, 議論の余地のある a controversial topic 賛否の分かれる話題 ＊トーン的にはマイナスの意味で, 名詞は controversy。	contentious	
fine [fáɪn]	名 罰金 a traffic fine 交通違反の罰金 ＊動詞だと「罰金を科す」。	penalty	D
standstill [stǽndstìl]	名 停止, 行き詰まり The traffic came to a standstill. 交通が渋滞した。	stop	
restore [rɪstɔ́ːr]	動 元の状態に戻す；復帰させる restore a good relationship 良好な関係を回復する ＊名詞 restoration「修復」。	reinstate	

135

Track 120

単語／発音	語義／フレーズ	同意表現
restrict [rɪstríkt]	動 制限する, 限定する；自由を奪う restrict the number of students per class 1クラスの生徒数を制限する	limit
irresponsible [ìrɪspá:nsəbl]	形 無責任な an irresponsible remark 無責任な発言	feckless
drain [dréɪn]	名 流出；排水溝 a brain drain 頭脳流出	outflow
conserve [kənsə́:rv]	動 節約する；保護する, 保存する conserve limited energy 限りあるエネルギーを節約する	preserve
starvation [stɑ:rvéɪʃən]	名 飢餓 death from starvation 餓死	famine
orbit [ɔ́:rbət]	名 軌道 an orbit period 軌道周期	trajectory
ignorance [ígnərəns]	名 無知, 無学 display one's ignorance 無知をさらけ出す	illiteracy
degrade [dɪgréɪd]	動 品位を下げる, 堕落させる Don't degrade yourself by lying. 嘘で自分の品位を下げるな。	demean
namely [néɪmli]	副 すなわち He is extraordinarily talented, namely charisma. 彼には類まれな才能がある, すなわちカリスマ性だ。	that is to say
reckless [rékləs]	形 向こう見ずな reckless driving 向こう見ずな運転	brash
offside [ɔ́(:)fsáɪd]	名 オフサイド, 反則の位置；右側 beat the offside trap オフサイドトラップを打ち破る ＊もっぱらスポーツ用語として使用。	foul
incidentally [ìnsədéntəli]	副 偶然に discover incidentally 偶然発見する ＊文頭で使うと「ところで」の意味。	accidentally

Track 121

単語／発音	語義／フレーズ	同意表現	難易度
colonial [kəlóuniəl]	形 植民地の the colonial period 植民地時代	of settlement	A
nucleus [n(j)ú:kliəs]	名 核；中心部 an atom nucleus 原子核	core	
crush [kráʃ]	動 押しつぶす，圧搾する crush grapes for wine ワイン作りのためにブドウをつぶす	squash	
ornament [ɔ́:rnəmənt]	名 装飾品 an interior ornament 室内装飾	decoration	B
chamber [tʃéimbər]	名 部屋，室；会議場 the king's burial chamber 王の埋葬室	room	
aisle [áil]	名 通路 an aisle seat （乗り物の）通路側の席 ＊飛行機で aisle seat を頼む人も多いはず。発音注意。	lane	C
correspond [kɔ̀:rəspá:nd]	動 一致する；対応する His deeds and words correspond. 彼の言動は一致している。	accord	
bombard [bɑ:mbá:rd]	動 砲撃する；(質問などで)攻め立てる bombard the enemy 敵を砲撃する	bomb	
disabled [diséibld]	形 体に障害のある；身体障害者の aids for disabled people 障害のある方々への援助 ＊W2 the disabled で「体の不自由な方々」。	handicapped	D
highlight [háilàit]	動 強調する highlight a problem 問題を浮かび上がらせる	emphasise	
PIN [pín]	名 暗証番号 enter one's PIN 自分の暗証番号を入力する ＊ PIN は Personal Identification Number の略語。	password	
glamorous [glǽmərəs]	形 魅惑的な glamorous movie stars 魅力的な映画スター	fascinating	

単語／発音	語義／フレーズ	同意表現
china [tʃáɪnə]	名 陶磁器；瀬戸物 a china vase 磁器の花瓶	porcelain
coral [kɔ́ːrəl]	名 サンゴ a coral reef サンゴ礁	
expel [ɪkspél]	動 追放する；除名する expel a student from school 生徒を退学させる	oust
in-depth [índépθ]	形 徹底的な, 掘り下げた in-depth research 徹底的な調査	thorough
notably [nóʊtəbli]	副 顕著に notably different 著しく異なる	remarkably
cater [kéɪtər]	動 (料理を)仕出しする cater for a party パーティーの仕出しをする	provide a supply of (food)
realm [rélm]	名 領域 beyond the realm of possibility 可能な範囲を超えて ＊field, sphere も同義語。	region
enclose [ɪnklóʊz]	動 同封する；囲む enclose a check 小切手を同封する ＊手紙で Enclosed is ～ は「～を同封します」。	include
jar [dʒɑ́ːr]	名 瓶；つぼ half a jar of peanut butter 瓶半分のピーナツバター	pot
temperate [témpərət]	形 温暖な；控えめな a temperate zone 温帯	mild
bait [béɪt]	名 (釣りの)餌；おとり, 誘惑 artificial bait for trout fishing ます釣り用の擬似餌 ＊発音注意！	lure
acoustic [əkúːstɪk]	形 音の；聴覚の acoustic effects in a theatre 劇場の音響効果	auditory

単語／発音	語義／フレーズ	同意表現	難易度
fin [fín]	名 ヒレ shark fin soup フカヒレスープ	flipper	A
handsome [hǽnsəm]	形 立派な；ハンサムな a handsome house 立派な家 ＊人以外にも使う。	good-looking	
imposing [ɪmpóuzɪŋ]	形 壮大な, 印象的な, 堂々とした an imposing ceremony 盛大な式典	grand	
sniff [sníf]	動 匂いを嗅ぐ sniff out the truth 真相を探り出す	snuff	B
spit [spít]	動 唾を吐く spit in someone's face 人の顔に唾を吐きかける	ptyalise	
admire [ədmáɪər]	動 称賛する admire someone's outstanding talent 人の傑出した才能を称賛する	acclaim	C
aim [éɪm]	動 目指す, 目標とする；狙う aim at being a novelist 小説家を目指す ＊R 設問では goal, purpose での書き換えが多い！	purpose	
caring [kéərɪŋ]	形 思いやりのある, 面倒見のよい nurses' caring attitude 看護師たちの思いやりのある態度	tender	
celebrity [səlébrəti]	名 有名人；高名 a celebrity scandal 有名人のスキャンダル	personage	
competitive [kəmpétətɪv]	形 競争力のある；競争の at competitive prices 他より安い値段で ＊動詞は compete。間違えやすいので念のため。	rivalrous	D
excitable [ɪksáɪtəbl]	形 興奮しやすい an excitable person 興奮しやすい人	irritable	
fully [fúli]	副 十分に fully understand 十分に理解する　＊R NG 問題では要注意。本文で「完全に」か判断できなければ Not Given。	amply	

Track 124

単語／発音	語義／フレーズ	同意表現
gap [gǽp]	名 ギャップ；割れ目 a gap between ideal and reality 理想と現実のギャップ	break
headline [hédlàɪn]	名 見出し a front page headline 一面トップの見出し	heading
influential [ìnfluénʃəl]	形 影響力のある an influential newspaper 影響力のある新聞	weighty
landmark [lǽndmàːrk]	名 画期的な出来事 a landmark discovery 画期的な発見 ＊「歴史的建造物」の意味もある。	breakthrough
materialistic [mətìəriəlístɪk]	形 物質主義の materialistic values 物質主義的価値観	worldly-minded
narration [nəréɪʃən]	名 物語ること direct narration 直接話法	discourse
noticeable [nóʊtəsəbl]	形 目立つ a noticeable change 目に見える変化	detectable
one-sided [wʌ́nsáɪdɪd]	形 一方だけの one-sided love 片思い	unilateral
pedestrian [pədéstriən]	名 歩行者 a pedestrian bridge 歩道橋	footer
reasonable [ríːznəbl]	形 道理にかなった a reasonable price 適正価格	rational
rest [rést]	名 残り the rest of one's life 人生の残り ＊ the 〜だと「残り」, a 〜だと「休息」の場合が多い。	remainder
roughly [rʌ́fli]	副 おおよそ roughly speaking 大ざっぱに言えば ＊W1「約，およそ」で使う。	approximately

Track 125

単語／発音	語義／フレーズ	同意表現	難易度
routine [ruːtíːn]	名 決まり切った仕事 a daily routine 日課	mundane task	A
sociable [sóuʃəbl]	形 社交的な a sociable person 社交家 ＊[S] 人を説明するときに便利。	amiable	
spontaneous [spɑːntéɪniəs]	形 自発的な spontaneous behaviour 自発的行動	voluntary	
strategy [strǽtədʒi]	名 戦略 corporate strategy 企業戦略　＊[W2] strategies to deal with the problem 「問題に対処する戦略」。	scheme	B
diagram [dáɪəgræm]	名 図，図表；図式 a 3D diagram 立体図	schema	
dip [díp]	動 (少し)浸す dip a pen in ink ペンをインクにちょっとつける ＊[W1] 「一時的な下落」を表す。	immerse	
enormously [ɪnɔ́ːrməsli]	副 極めて；法外に enormously difficult 極端に難しい	tremendously	C
eventually [ɪvéntʃuəli]	副 最終的に Eventually we reached our goal. 最終的に目標に達した。	finally	
illustrate [íləstrèɪt]	動 説明する illustrate the theory by an example　例を挙げて理論を説明する　＊[W1] the graph illustrates 〜 「グラフは〜を示す」。	exemplify	
leap [líːp]	動 跳ぶ leap a barrier 障害を飛び越える	jump	D
mobility [moʊbíləti]	名 移動性 population mobility 人口移動 ＊[R] 「動きやすさ」のこと。「引っ越しのしやすさ」を表すことも。	migration	
occupancy [ɑ́ːkjəpənsi]	名 占有，居住；収容能力 an occupancy rate （客室・座席などの）稼働率 ＊[W2] occupation 「職業」とは違う。	possession	

Track 126

単語／発音	語義／フレーズ	同意表現
overtake [òʊvərtéɪk]	動 追い越す overtake one's rival ライバルを追い越す ＊W1 overtook the rate of ～「～のレートを上回った」。	pass
pie chart [páɪ tʃɑ̀ːrt]	名 円グラフ create a pie chart 円グラフを作る	circle graph
soar [sɔ́ːr]	動 急上昇する soar by 20% 20％分急上昇する ＊W1 動詞でも名詞でも使える。	skyrocket
steeply [stíːpli]	副 急に fall steeply from 60% to 25% 60％から25％に急落する	precipitously
table [téɪbl]	名 表 a data table データ表	chart
accommodate [əkɑ́ːmədèɪt]	動 収容する；宿泊させる This hotel can accommodate 1,000 guests. このホテルは 1,000 人収容できる。	lodge
disapproval [dìsəprúːvl]	名 不賛成，反対意見；不承認 strong disapproval of the law その法律への強い反対	disapprobation
figure [fígjər]	名 総額；数量 export-import figures 輸出入額 ＊W1 the figure for Japan のように前置詞は for を使う。	sum
internal [ɪntə́ːrnl]	形 国内の；内部の the internal affairs of another country 他国の内政 ＊⇔ external	domestic
liquor [líkər]	名 蒸留酒 a liquor licence 酒類販売許可証	spirit
path [pǽθ]	名 小道；進路 a path to success 成功への道のり	track
region [ríːdʒən]	名 地域，地方；領域，分野 Arctic regions 北極地域	area

単語／発音	語義／フレーズ	同意表現	難易度
respectively [rɪspéktɪvli]	副 それぞれ ～ and … respectively ～と…をそれぞれに ＊W1 数字を並べて書くときに使う。	each	A
savings [séɪvɪŋz]	名 貯蓄 a savings account 定期預金口座［英］ ＊［米］なら普通預金口座。	nest egg	
sneeze [sníːz]	名 くしゃみ fight off a sneeze くしゃみを我慢する	sternutation	
-goer [góʊər]	名 ～によく行く人 a cinema-goer 映画によく行く人	frequenter	B
turnround [tə́ːrəràʊnd]	名 (方向などの)転換；突然の好転 turnround in public opinion 世論の大きな変化	reversal	
vehicle [víːəkl]	名 乗り物 a recreational vehicle RV車	car	
whisper [wíspər]	動 ささやく whisper a charm into someone's ear 耳元でまじないをささやく	murmur	C
contract [kəntrǽkt]	動 縮小する；短縮する contract a muscle 筋肉を収縮させる	shrink	
destination [dèstənéɪʃən]	名 目的地, 行き先 one's final destination 最終目的地	terminus	
scholar [skáːlər]	名 学者 a dedicated scholar 研究熱心な学者	academic	D
astronomer [əstráːnəmər]	名 天文学者 space discoveries made by astronomers 天文学者による宇宙に関する発見	stargazer	
theology [θi(ː)áːlədʒi]	名 神学 a college of theology 神学校	divinity	

Track 128

単語／発音	語義／フレーズ	同意表現
abbey [ǽbi]	名 大修道院 pray in an abbey 修道院で祈る	monastery
vineyard [vínjərd]	名 ブドウ園 a family-run vineyard 家族経営のブドウ園	vinery
cosmic [kά:zmɪk]	形 宇宙の cosmic physics 宇宙物理学	universal
revitalise [rìváɪtəlàɪz]	動 再生させる revitalise local economy 地域経済を再活性化させる	rejuvenate
circuit [sə́:rkət]	名 回路, 回線；円周 an electric circuit 電気回路	circle
wait [wéɪt]	動（お店で）給仕をする, 給仕する He spent the summer waiting tables. 彼は給仕をやりながら夏を過ごした。	serve
shorthand [ʃɔ́:rthænd]	名 速記 a shorthand typist 速記者	stenography
nanny [nǽni]	名 乳母 be raised by a nanny 乳母に育てられる	nurse
assemble [əsémbl]	動 組み立てる；集める assemble many parts into the machine 多くのパーツを組み立てて, その機械を作る	put together
promptly [prά:mptli]	副 即座に promptly respond to 〜 〜に即座に対応する	quickly
challenge [tʃǽlɪndʒ]	動 異議を申し立てる；挑戦する challenge a policy 方針に異議を申し立てる	defy
thoroughly [θə́:rouli]	副 徹底的に discuss 〜 thoroughly 〜を徹底的に議論する ＊「しっかりと」という意味。	completely

単語／発音	語義／フレーズ	同意表現	難易度
deficit [défəsɪt]	名 不足；欠損 a trade deficit 貿易赤字 ＊⇔ surplus(trade surplus 貿易黒字)。	shortage	A
board [bɔ́ːrd]	名 役員；役員会 a board meeting 取締役会議	executive officer	
cliff [klíf]	名 崖，絶壁 drop off a cliff 崖から落ちる	precipice	
peninsula [pənínsələ]	名 半島 at the tip of the peninsula 半島の突端で	chersonese	B
cape [kéɪp]	名 岬 sail around a cape 岬を回って航行する	ness	
still [stíl]	形 静止した a still image 静止画	static	
judge [dʒʌ́dʒ]	名 判事，裁判官；審判員 a High Court judge 高等法院判事	judicator	C
inflame [ɪnfléɪm]	動 火をつける；刺激する inflame public opinion 世論をあおる	ignite	
furnish [fə́ːrnɪʃ]	動 供給する；(家具を)備え付ける furnish the library with new books 図書館に新しい本を供給する　＊アパートなどが「家具付き」の場合も, furnished。	supply	
well-rounded [wélráʊnded]	形 包括的で多方面にわたる；均整の取れた formation of a well-rounded character バランスの取れた豊かな人間性の形成	all-round	D
density [dénsəti]	名 密度；濃度 separate substances with different densities 密度の違う物質を分離する　＊文脈から「濃度」か「密度」かを見極めたい。	solidity	
symmetry [símətri]	名 対称；調和 bilateral symmetry 左右対称 ＊⇔ asymmetry「非対称」。	balance	

Track 130

単語／発音	語義／フレーズ	同意表現
renovate [rénəvèɪt]	動 改築する，復元する renovate a historic building 歴史的建造物を改修する	refurbish
dividend [dívədènd]	名 配当金；配当；配当率 a dividend of 2% 2％の配当	share
saw [sɔ́ː]	動 のこぎりで切る saw a tree down のこぎりで木を切り倒す	cut with a saw
convey [kənvéɪ]	動 伝える convey thoughts and ideas 考えや意見を伝達する	communicate
dissent [dɪsént]	動 （宗教上などで）意見を異にする This is where I dissent from the general opinion. ここが全体的意向と私の異なる点だ。	disagree
diverse [dəvə́ːrs]	形 多様な；相違した people from diverse backgrounds 多様な経歴の人々 ＊ different や various あたりと組み合わせて記憶。	various
conspicuous [kənspíkjuəs]	形 目立つ make oneself conspicuous by wearing gaudy clothes 派手な服を着て自分を目立たせる	noticeable
expire [ɪkspáɪər]	動 （契約・期限が切れて）無効になる My driver's licence expired last month. 私の運転免許は先月失効した。	run out
malfunction [mælfʌ́ŋkʃən]	動 機能不全を起こす cause computers to malfunction コンピュータの故障を引き起こす　＊ mal- は「悪い；不完全な」の接頭辞。	break down
distinction [dɪstíŋkʃən]	名 相違，差別，特徴；気品 without distinction of sex or age 性別や年齢の差別なく	difference
elaborate [ɪlǽbərət]	形 入念な；精巧な an elaborate plan 入念な計画 ＊「細工が細かい」場合と「注意深い」場合あり。	detailed
overwhelm [òʊvərwélm]	動 圧倒する；参らせる be overwhelmed by US military power 米国の軍事力に圧倒される	overpower

Track 131

単語／発音	語義／フレーズ	同意表現	難易度
irrelevant [ɪréləvənt]	形 不適切な，見当違いの a point irrelevant to the argument 的外れな論点 ＊⇔ relevant「適切な；要点をついた」も頻出度が高い。	irrelative	A
undue [ʌnd(j)úː]	形 過度の，必要以上の；不当な give undue weight to ～ ～を重視し過ぎる ＊ undue risks「無用なリスク」は覚えよう！	unnecessary	
shot [ʃɑ́ːt]	名 写真，スナップ a close-up shot クローズアップ写真 ＊「注射」の意味もある。	photo	
undertake [ʌ̀ndərtéɪk]	動 引き受ける，請け負う undertake a challenging task 困難な仕事を引き受ける	assume	B
sport [spɔ́ːrt]	名 楽しみ spoil someone's sport 人の楽しみに水を差す	pastime	
platform [plǽtfɔ̀ːrm]	名 基盤；演壇 create a stable platform 安定した基盤を築く	base	
concrete [kάːnkriːt]	形 具体的な，明確な concrete evidence 具体的な証拠 ＊⇔ abstract	specific	C
sprout [spráʊt]	動 芽を出す；(急に)成長する，出現する The young leaves sprout in spring. 若葉は春に芽吹く。	germinate	
literally [lítərəli]	副 文字通り literally translate to ～ 文字通りに訳せば～となる ＊ exactly でも言い換えられる「強意語」の仲間。	in a literal sense	
camouflage [kǽməflɑ̀ːʒ]	名 偽装，迷彩；ごまかし camouflage and mimicry 偽装と擬態 ＊ camouflage と mimicry はどう違うのか。	disguise	D
equate [ɪkwéɪt]	動 同一視する，同等とみなす equate money with happiness お金を幸福と同一視する	identify	
embrace [ɪmbréɪs]	動 喜んで受け入れる；含む embrace the new religion 新しい宗教を進んで受け入れる	accept	

147

単語／発音	語義／フレーズ	同意表現
excel [ɪksél]	動 勝る, 秀でる excel in foreign languages 外国語において優れている	surpass
edible [édəbl]	形 食べられる, 食用の an edible mushroom 食べられるきのこ	eatable
stumble [stʌ́mbl]	動 偶然出くわす；つまずく stumble on information about ～ 期せずして～の情報を得る	come across
tidal [táɪdl]	形 潮の, 干満［潮流］の；潮任せの tidal currents 潮流 ＊ tidal wave は「津波（seismic sea wave）」でなく「高潮」。	flowing
speculate [spékjəlèɪt]	動 推測する；思惑売買をする speculate about her disappearance 彼女の失踪原因を推測する　＊「熟考する」「思惑売買をする」の意味にも注意！	conjecture
hinder [híndər]	動 邪魔をする；妨げる hinder people from understanding one another 人々が互いに理解するのを妨げる	hamper
innovation [ìnəvéɪʃən]	名 革新, 刷新, 新導入 latest technology innovation 最新の技術革新	renovation
canine [kéɪnaɪn]	形 イヌ科の, 犬の a canine tooth 犬歯 ＊ K-9 と書く人もいる。	dog
bury [béri]	動 埋める Some Chinese kings were buried in jade suits. 中国王の中には翡翠でできた喪服を着て埋葬された者もあった。	plant
tolerate [tɑ́:lərèɪt]	動 我慢する, 耐える；容認する There is a limit to what a man can tolerate. 我慢するのにも限界がある。　＊同意語が多く, 頻出。	endure
genre [ʒɑ́:nrə]	名 （芸術などの）ジャンル, 様式 the science fiction genre 空想科学小説ジャンル	category
mine [máɪn]	動 採掘する, 掘る mine a mountain for gold 金を採るために山を掘る ＊名詞だと coal mine「炭鉱」がおなじみ。	dig

Track 133

単語／発音	語義／フレーズ	同意表現	難易度
hassle [hǽsl]	名 わずらわしい事；混乱；激論 Sending email means less hassle than phoning. メールを送る方が電話するより厄介ではない。	trouble	A
incentive [ɪnséntɪv]	名 刺激策；報奨金 early retirement incentive plan 早期退職優遇制度	inducement	
treason [tríːzn]	名 反逆罪；裏切り be arrested for treason 反逆罪で逮捕される	rebellion	
reflection [rɪflékʃən]	名 映った姿；反射，反響 one's own reflection in a mirror 鏡に映った自分自身の姿 ＊「反射」「反映」「熟考」と多義なので，文脈で決定する。	image	B
edit [édət]	動 （原稿・映画などを）編集する edit the film 映画を編集する	check	
collide [kəláɪd]	動 衝突する The van collided head on with a lorry. ライトバンはトラックと正面衝突した。　＊自動詞なので with を伴う。	crash	
census [sénsəs]	名 （人口の）一斉調査；国勢調査 conduct a traffic census 交通量一斉調査を行う	survey	C
stump [stʌ́mp]	名 演台；切り株 a stump speech （遊説中の政治家の）街頭演説	platform	
periodically [pìəriáːdɪkəli]	副 周期的に，定期的に periodically update the web page 定期的にHPを更新する　＊ at regular intervals でも書き換え可能。	regularly	
numerical [n(j)uːmérɪkl]	形 数の，数的な，計算の in descending numerical order 数が大から小の順（降順）で　＊「小説」ではありません。形容詞。	numeral	D
withdraw [wɪðdrɔ́ː]	動 撤退する；脱退する withdraw from the business 事業から撤退する	retreat	
dedicate [dédəkèɪt]	動 （時間・精力を）捧げる，専念する dedicate one's life to helping the poor 貧困者の救済に一生を捧げる	devote	

149

単語／発音	語義／フレーズ	同意表現
wharf [wɔ́ːrf]	名 埠頭, 波止場；岸壁 come alongside the wharf 埠頭に接岸する	pier
sort [sɔ́ːrt]	動 分類する sort ~ into alphabetical order ～をアルファベット順に分類する	classify
grasp [grǽsp]	動 理解する, つかむ grasp what someone's getting at 人が何を言おうとしているのか理解する	understand
retreat [rɪtríːt]	動 後退する, 退却する retreat inside oneself 自分の殻に引きこもる	retire
compact [kəmpǽkt]	動 固める, 圧縮する compacted and compressed snow 固められ圧縮された雪	compress
presume [prɪzúːm]	動 推定する, 仮定する be presumed innocent until proved guilty 有罪と立証されるまでは無罪と推定される	presuppose
reinforce [rìːɪnfɔ́ːrs]	動 強化する reinforce a cooperative relationship 協力的な関係を強化する	strengthen
neutral [n(j)úːtrəl]	形 中立の；中性の a permanent neutral country 永世中立国	impartial
dogma [dɔ́(ː)gmə]	名 教義, 信条, 独断 Roman Catholic dogma ローマカトリックの教義	belief
defer [dɪfɔ́ːr]	動 延期する, 据え置く defer the decision 決定を延ばす ＊ deferment「延期」。入学延期や支払延期に使う。	postpone
originally [ərídʒənəli]	副 もともとは；元来；独自に；独創的 as originally planned もともとの予定通りに ＊「もともとは」が「独創的に」より要注意。	initially
tune [t(j)úːn]	動 (調子を)合わせる tune a piano ピアノを調律する	adjust

Track 135

単語／発音	語義／フレーズ	同意表現	難易度
jot [dʒá:t]	動 書き留める jot down the address 住所をメモする ＊口語表現。	write down	A
perspective [pərspéktɪv]	名 見方, 観点, 展望 take a different perspective 異なった視点に立つ ＊W2 from my perspective「私の見解では」。	viewpoint	
strive [stráɪv]	動 ～しようと努力する, 励む strive for a goal 目標に向かって努力する ＊W2 S strive for ～「～に向けて努力する」。	endeavour	
loot [lú:t]	動 略奪する loot the company's assets 会社の資産を横領する	plunder	B
injustice [ɪndʒʎstəs]	名 不正 fight social injustice 社会的不正と闘う	iniquity	
pursuit [pərs(j)ú:t]	名 仕事, 職業；趣味；追求, 追跡 be a teacher by pursuit 職業としては教師である ＊複数形で「仕事」を表すことが多い。	occupation	
dissipate [dísəpèɪt]	動 消散させる；霧散する The sun gradually dissipated the mist. 太陽が少しずつ霧を晴らした。	scatter	C
lament [ləmént]	動 嘆き悲しむ；残念に思う lament the death of ～ ～の死を悼む	deplore	
invariably [ɪnvé(ə)riəbli]	副 いつも変わらず invariably make a mistake 常に間違いを犯す	constantly	
carnivore [ká:rnəvɔ̀:r]	名 肉食動物 "Carnivore" and "carnival" have something in common.「肉食動物」と「謝肉祭」には共通点がある。	predator	D
boost [bú:st]	動 向上させる, 増加させる, 高める boost athletes' speed and endurance 選手のスピードと持久力を向上させる　＊W2 boost sales「売上を伸ばす」。	increase	
missionary [míʃənèri]	名 宣教師；伝道師 Francis Xavier, the first Christian missionary to Japan 最初に来日したキリスト教宣教師, フランシスコ・ザビエル	propagandist	

Track 136

単語／発音	語義／フレーズ	同意表現

resin
[rézn]
图 ヤニ, 樹脂
pine resin 松ヤニ
rosin

bankruptcy
[bǽŋkrʌptsi]
图 破産, 失墜
file for bankruptcy 破産を申告する
＊W2 スペルミスに注意！
insolvency

fluctuation
[flʌ̀ktʃuéɪʃən]
图 絶え間ない変化, 不安定；流動
Plants are affected by fluctuations in temperature.
植物は気温の変化に影響される。
change

blur
[blə́ːr]
動 ぼやける, ぼやけさせる
The rain blurred our field of vision. 雨で視界がぼやけた。
＊ ed や ing 形で r が重なるので要注意。
haze

plaster
[plǽstər]
图 漆喰（しっくい）；ばんそうこう
be made of wood and plaster 木造モルタル造りである
whitewash

cue
[kjúː]
图 きっかけ, 合図
a cue for more quarrels 更なる口論のきっかけ
signal

paddle
[pǽdl]
動 オールでこぐ；手足でこいで進む
paddle a boat on a lake 湖でボートをこぐ
＊ puddle「水たまり」と区別しよう！
row

emigrate
[éməgrèɪt]
動（他国へ）移住する
emigrate from Britain to America 英国から米国へ移住する
＊「移民となって出て行く」なので, immigrate と区別可能。
relocate

humidity
[hjuːmídəti]
图 湿気；湿度
unbearable humidity 耐え難い湿気
＊L humility「謙虚」と聞き間違えないように。
dampness

run
[rʌ́n]
動 経営する, 運営する
run a Japanese restaurant abroad
海外で日本料理店を経営する
operate

raid
[réɪd]
图 襲撃
an indiscriminate air raid 無差別空襲
assault

faculty
[fǽkəlti]
图 能力, 教授団, 学部
the faculty of understanding complex issues
複雑な問題を理解する能力
ability

Track 137

単語／発音	語義／フレーズ	同意表現	難易度
peculiarity [pɪkjùːliérəti]	名 特性；特異性 exhibit a remarkable peculiarity 際立った特性を示す	idiosyncrasy	A
tip [típ]	名 有益な情報, 助言；先, 先端 provide some tips on doing business 商売のヒントを提供する　＊ finger tip「指先」。	clue	
bulletin [búlətn]	名 告示, 公報, 短いニュース, 会報 job openings on the bulletin board 掲示板に載っている求人　＊「短いニュース；速報」の語義もあり。	report	
sparse [spáːrs]	形 点在する；まばらな sparse vegetation 点在する草木	thin	B
stray [stréɪ]	形 さまよっている, 道に迷った a stray dog 野良犬 ＊ stray sheep「迷える羊」はご存じのはず。	wandering	
stabilise [stéɪbəlàɪz]	動 安定させる stabilise financial markets 金融市場を安定させる ＊ stable「安定した」から, すぐ想起できるはず。	steady	
legible [lédʒəbl]	形 判読できる write in a legible hand 読みやすくはっきりとした字で書く ＊⇔ illegible	readable	C
optical [áːptɪkl]	形 視覚の；光学の due to an optical illusion 目の錯覚によって	visual	
navigate [nǽvəgèɪt]	動 航行する navigate by the stars 星を頼りに航海する	sail	
abuse [əbjúːs]	名 濫用, 悪用；虐待 financial abuses in the campaign 選挙運動における資金濫用	misuse	D
crevice [krévɪs]	名 狭い割れ目, 裂け目 Mosses thrive even in rock crevices. 苔は岩の狭い割れ目でもすくすく育つ。	fissure	
condensation [kàːndenséɪʃən]	名 凝縮, 凝結 Condensation is the reverse of vaporisation. 凝縮は蒸発の逆です。　＊「集中」か「凝縮」か「濃縮」かは文脈で判断。	concentration	

153

単語／発音	語義／フレーズ	同意表現
reasoning [ríːznɪŋ]	名 推論 by proper reasoning 正当な推論によって ＊ reason の動詞は「推論する」の意。	inference
attain [ətéɪn]	動 達成する；獲得する attain one's goal 目標を達成する	achieve
patriot [péɪtriət]	名 愛国者 an ardent patriot 熱烈な愛国者	nationalist
outbreak [áʊtbrèɪk]	名 勃発 outbreak of a civil war 内戦の勃発 ＊ break out「(戦争や火事が)起こる」からできた名詞。	occurrence
overtax [òʊvərtǽks]	動 重い負担をかける overtax one's brain 頭脳を酷使する	overload
segregation [sègrəgéɪʃən]	名 人種差別；分離, 隔離 lead to racial segregation 人種差別につながる ＊ ⇔ desegregation	discrimination
nomad [nóʊmæd]	名 放浪者；遊牧民 economic nomads 出稼ぎ労働者(経済的放浪者)	wanderer
mill [míl]	名 工場 a textile mill 繊維工場 ＊複合的に cotton や steal に続いていたら「工場」の意味。	factory
breakthrough [bréɪkθrùː]	名 大発見, 躍進；突破口 breakthroughs set to reshape medical care 医学治療をすっかり変えてしまう大発見(画期的療法)	discovery
mute [mjúːt]	形 ものが言えない；唖者の；無言の be mute with fear 恐怖で口が利けない	dumb
mechanical [məkǽnɪkl]	形 機械的な；力学的な maintain mechanical equipment 機械設備をメンテナンスする	automated
inhibit [ɪnhíbət]	動 抑制する；阻害する inhibit cancer cell growth がん細胞の増殖を抑制する	suppress

Track 139

単語／発音	語義／フレーズ	同意表現	難易度
discard [dɪskáːrd]	動 捨てる；廃棄する discard the empty bottles 空瓶を廃棄する ＊ℝ give up, abandon, relinquish との書き換えに気づくように。	dump	A
assurance [əʃúərəns]	名 保証；確信 quality assurance 品質保証	guarantee	
composition [kɑ́ːmpəzíʃən]	名 組み立て, 組成, 構造 study the composition of the chemical その化学物質の組成を調べる　＊もちろん「作文」の意味もある。	make-up	
dominate [dɑ́ːmənèɪt]	動 支配する dominate the colonies 植民地を支配する	control	B
tentative [téntətɪv]	形 一時的な reach a tentative agreement 暫定合意に達する	provisional	
localise [lóʊklàɪz]	動 局地的に限定する localised anaesthesia 局所麻酔 ＊ local anaesthesia とも言う。	focalise	
oxidise [ɑ́ːksədàɪz]	動 酸化する oxidise on exposure to air 空気に触れると酸化する	oxidate	C
dismiss [dɪsmís]	動 解雇する, 解散する dismiss an employee for his sexual harassment 性的嫌がらせで社員を解雇する　＊ fire よりも堅い意味。	fire	
hive [háɪv]	名 ミツバチの巣箱 keep bees in a hive 巣箱でミツバチを飼育する	beehive	
vertical [vɜ́ːrtɪkl]	形 垂直の；縦の a vertical cliff 切り立った崖 ＊⇔ horizontal「水平の」。	perpendicular	D
ponder [pɑ́ːndər]	動 熟考する ponder the state of the world 世界情勢を熟考する	contemplate	
eject [ɪdʒékt]	動 追い出す；噴出する；取り出す eject protesters from the building 抗議者を建物から追い出す	expel	

155

単語／発音	語義／フレーズ	同意表現
boulder [bóʊldər]	名 **大きな丸い岩** The boulder rolled down the mountain. 大岩は山を転がり落ちた。	rock
reorient [riɔ́:riənt]	動 **新しい方向に向ける；順応させる** reorient one's thinking about 〜 〜についての考え方を改める	readapt
fraction [frǽkʃən]	名 **小部分, 断片, 端数；分数** for a fraction of a second ほんの一瞬の間 ＊「分数」もこの単語。	portion
formulate [fɔ́:rmjəlèɪt]	動 **公式化する；明確に述べる** formulate one's ideas into a theory 自身の考えを公式化する	regularise
verify [vérəfàɪ]	動 **証明する** verify the hypothesis 仮説を証明する	attest
plane [pléɪn]	名 **面, 平面** a cutting plane 切断面	level
provoke [prəvóʊk]	動 **引き起こす；怒らせる, 挑発する** provoke criticism from certain quarters ある方面の人々から批判を引き起こす	arouse
flattering [flǽtərɪŋ]	形 **うれしがらせるような；お世辞の** flattering remarks うれしがらせるような発言 ＊ I'm flattered you say so.「そう言ってもらうと, 光栄だね。」	complimentary
army [á:rmi]	名 **大軍** an army of ants 大群のアリ ＊ an army of 〜 = a lot of 〜 = an array of 〜	a large number
precedent [présədənt]	名 **前例, 慣例** rely on legal precedent 判例に依拠する ＊ unprecedented「前例のない」も覚えよう！	antecedent
garbage [gá:rbɪdʒ]	名 **(生の)ごみ** take out the garbage ごみ出しをする ＊ garbage は, 本来は「生ごみ」。	rubbish
dizzy [dízi]	形 **目まいがする, ふらふらする** A balance disorder makes people feel dizzy. 平衡障害になると目まいがする。	giddy

Track 141

単語／発音	語義／フレーズ	同意表現	難易度
exhibit [ɪgzíbɪt]	動 明示する，提示する exhibit classic symptoms 典型的な症状を示す	show	A
monochrome [má:nəkróʊm]	形 単色の；白黒の monochrome landscape painting 単色（白黒）の風景画	one-coloured	
lunar [lú:nər]	形 月の lunar calendar 太陰暦	moony	
confirm [kənfə́:rm]	動 裏付ける，証明する New evidence confirmed his confession. 新たな証拠が彼の自白を裏付けた。 ＊これも類義の単語が多い。	verify	B
assimilate [əsíməlèɪt]	動 吸収する，同化する，消化する assimilate nutrients from the soil 土壌から栄養物を吸収する ＊表題の3つの意味と同意語を覚えるべき。	absorb	
surge [sə́:rdʒ]	動 押し寄せる；沸き上がる surge to the stage ステージに押し寄せる ＊もともとは「波が打ち寄せる」の意。	rush	
emit [ɪmít]	動 発散する，放出する emit a curious smell 不思議な匂いを発する ＊W2 give off と織り交ぜよう。	discharge	C
manufacturing [mænjəfǽktʃərɪŋ]	名 製造 the automobile manufacturing industry 自動車製造業界	production	
rusty [rʌ́sti]	形 下手になった，衰えた；さび付いた be rusty on English 英語が下手になった ＊このような状態になったら brush up「磨き直す」しかない。	out of practice	
restless [réstləs]	形 落ち着かない；静止しない have a restless night 不安な一夜を過ごす	uneasy	D
penetrate [pénətrèɪt]	動 染み透る；突き通す penetrate deeply into society 社会に深く浸透する ＊迷ったら「染み透る」を軸に，文脈で意味を決定したい。	permeate	
ambiguous [æmbíɡjuəs]	形 あいまいな，2つ以上の意味にとれる The prisoner's statement was ambiguous in places. その囚人の申し立ては所々あいまいだった。	vague	

157

単語／発音	語義／フレーズ	同意表現
charter [tʃάːrtər]	名 認可, 特許, 特権, 設立許可 The Royal College's charter was granted in 1967. ロイヤルカレッジの認可は1967年に認められた。	authorisation
urine [júərn]	名 尿 pass urine 放尿する	piss
trigger [trígər]	動 引き起こす；誘発させる trigger a chain reaction 連鎖反応を引き起こす	cause
soul [sóul]	名 人 an honest soul 正直な人 *L 「魂；感情」の意味で書き取りに対応できるように！	person
maternal [mətə́ːrnl]	形 母性の stimulate maternal instinct 母性本能を刺激する *⇔ paternal / fatherly「父性の；父親らしい」。	motherly
geometric [dʒìːəmétrɪk]	形 幾何学的な；幾何学の a geometric design on wallpaper 壁紙の幾何学的な模様	of geometry
handy [hǽndi]	形 便利な；器用な a handy tool 便利な道具 * come in handy「役に立つ」。	useful
bureaucracy [bjʊərάːkrəsi]	名 官僚制度；官僚 One disadvantage of bureaucracy is much paper work. 官僚主義の短所の1つは多量の事務仕事です。	a system of government
gene [dʒíːn]	名 遺伝子 a recessive gene 劣性遺伝子	any basic elements of heredity
abolish [əbάːlɪʃ]	動 廃止する abolish slavery 奴隷制度を廃止する *同意語が多く頻出。	repeal
self-sufficient [sélf-səfíʃənt]	形 自給自足の；自立心のある become self-sufficient in rice 米を自給できるようになる	independent
consecutive [kənsékjətɪv]	形 （間を置かず一定順序で）連続した eight consecutive wins 8連勝 * eight wins in a row とも言える。	successive

Track 143

単語／発音	語義／フレーズ	同意表現	難易度
delete [dɪlíːt]	動 削除する delete all reference すべての参考資料を削除する ＊同意句の cross out が会話なら出てきそう。	erase	A
financial [fənǽnʃəl]	形 財政上の，金融の a financial commitment 金銭上の債務	monetary	
rebel [rɪbél]	動 反抗する，謀反を起こす rebel against the government 政府に対して反乱を起こす	revolt	
regulate [régjəlèɪt]	動 規制する；調整する regulate smoking in public places 公共の場での喫煙を規制する　＊「規制する」と訳して駄目なら，「調整する」。	control	B
irresistible [ìrɪzístəbl]	形 抑えがたい；抗しがたい an irresistible desire 抑えがたい欲望 ＊ irresistible urge「抑えがたい衝動」もよく使う。	resistless	
burden [bə́ːrdn]	名 重荷，負担 minimise a tax burden 税負担を最小化する	load	
insulation [ìnsjəléɪʃən]	名 遮断，隔離，孤立，絶縁；絶縁物 insulation against noise 雑音の遮断 ＊「孤立」よりも「遮断，絶縁」の意味の方がやや頻出度は高い。	isolation	C
inherit [ɪnhérət]	動 相続する；（遺伝的に）受け継ぐ inherit a fortune from a relative 親戚から財産を相続する	take over	
molten [móʊltn]	形 溶けた molten rock 溶岩 ＊ molten lava（溶岩）とも言う。	melted	
negligence [néɡlɪdʒəns]	名 怠慢，不注意 an accident due to negligence 不注意による事故	neglect	D
shoot [ʃúːt]	名 芽；若い茎 bamboo shoots タケノコ	sprout	
outlook [áʊtlùk]	名 将来の見通し；見解；眺望 outlook for the world economy 世界経済の見通し ＊前後の文脈から決定しないと意味を外しやすい単語。	prospect	

159

Track 144

単語／発音	語義／フレーズ	同意表現
diminish [dɪmínɪʃ]	動 減る；減らす Our supplies are diminishing rapidly. 在庫が急速に減ってきている。　＊これも同意語(d で始まる)多数。	reduce
contemporary [kəntémpərèri]	形 同時代の；現代の contemporary historians 同時代の歴史家たち ＊「現代の；当代の」だけでなく「同時代の」も頻出。	concurrent
thrive [θráɪv]	動 栄える, 繁茂する, すくすく育つ thrive in business 事業で成功する ＊文明, 国, 動植物に使える。	flourish
integrate [íntəgrèɪt]	動 統合する integrate math into the curriculum 数学をカリキュラムに組み入れる	incorporate
parasite [pérəsàɪt]	名 寄生動植物 carry a parasite （体内に）寄生虫を持つ	infestant
runoff [rʌ́nɔ(ː)f]	名 (地中に吸収されず流れる)雨水, 流水 mountain snow runoff 山の雪解け水	overflow
novel [nάːvl]	形 目新しい, 新奇な introduce a novel technique 新たな技術を導入する	new
cram [krǽm]	動 ぎっしり詰め込む, 押し込む cram a bus with passengers 乗客をバスにぎゅうぎゅう詰めにする	stuff
spawn [spɔ́ːn]	動 引き起こす；産む spawn a number of problems 幾多の問題を引き起こす	produce
liner [láɪnər]	名 裏地 a coat with a silk liner シルクの裏地の付いたコート	lining
mandatory [mǽndətɔ̀ːri]	形 命令の；義務的な；必修の order a mandatory evacuation 強制避難命令を出す ＊⇔ elective「選択の」。	required
alternative [ɔːltə́ːrnətɪv]	名 (もう１つの)選択肢 a good alternative available now 今ある良い選択肢 ＊「二者択一の」と覚えるよりは,「代替の, 代わりの」。	option

単語／発音	語義／フレーズ	同意表現	難易度
barter [báːrtər]	動 物々交換する barter gold for guns 金を銃と交換する	exchange	A
economy [ɪkáːnəmi]	名 節約, 倹約 make economies in household spending 家計の出費を節約する	thrift	
stationery [stéɪʃənèri]	名 文房具；便箋 a stationery store 文房具店 ＊stationary「静止した」と区別して「e(イー)文房具」と覚える。	writing materials	
tardy [táːrdi]	形 のろい, 遅々とした tardy progress ゆっくりとした進展	late	B
leak [líːk]	動 漏らす leak a defence secret 防衛上の機密を漏らす	seep	
impact [ímpækt]	名 (強い)影響；衝突, 衝撃 the impact of recession on businesses 景気後退の企業に対する影響　＊「影響」の意味の方が盲点！	effect	
pesticide [péstəsàɪd]	名 殺虫剤, 農薬 spray pesticides on trees 木に殺虫剤をまく ＊pest「害虫」を cide「殺すもの」。	insecticide	C
akin [əkín]	形 類似した, 同族の be akin to one's father's opinion 父親の意見と類似している	similar	
friction [fríkʃən]	名 不和；摩擦 friction between labour and management 労使間の対立	discord	
exotic [ɪgzáːtɪk]	形 外来の；新種の；異国風の exotic species 外来種 ＊科学的な文章でない場合は「エキゾチック」の意味。	foreign	D
coverage [kávərɪdʒ]	名 取材範囲, 報道；適用範囲 newspaper coverage 新聞報道 ＊exclusive coverage「独占報道, 中継」も頻出。	reporting	
initially [ɪníʃəli]	副 初めのうちは；まず第一に though initially appealing 最初は魅力的だが ＊Rat first との同意関係は要注意。	at first	

単語／発音	語義／フレーズ	同意表現
acclaim [əkléɪm]	動 称賛する, 歓迎する Her techniques were widely acclaimed. 彼女の技術は広く称賛された。	praise
innate [ɪnéɪt]	形 生得の；固有の an innate ability to learn language 生来の言語獲得能力 ＊Ⓡ inborn, inherent, natural との言い換えに注意。	inborn
equivalent [ɪkwívələnt]	名 対応(するもの), 同等(のもの) The word has no equivalent in English. 英語にはその言葉に相当するものがありません。	counterpart
occupy [á:kjəpàɪ]	動 占める, 占有する；占領する occupy a high share of the world market 世界市場で高いシェアを占める	take up
bias [báɪəs]	名 偏見, 先入観 maintain a bias against big cities 大都市に対する偏見を持ち続ける	prejudice
surplus [sə́:rplʌs]	名 余り, 余剰, 黒字 surplus of the balance of trade 貿易収支の黒字 ＊⇔ trade deficit「貿易赤字」を暗記！	excess
artisan [á:rtəzən]	名 職人, 熟練工 a skilled and creative artisan 技術と創造性を持つ職工 ＊ artist の出現以前に主流を占めた仕事人たち。	craftsman
unmatched [ʌnmǽtʃd]	形 匹敵する者のない；釣り合わない be unmatched in the history of man 人類史上類を見ない　＊このままで最上級の意味！	peerless
pragmatic [prægmǽtɪk]	形 実用的な take a pragmatic approach 実際的なアプローチを取る	practical
audition [ɔ:díʃən]	名 オーディション have an audition for the part of Lady Macbeth マクベス夫人役のオーディションを受ける	try-out
millennium [mɪléniəm]	名 1000 年間 at the turn of a millennium 千年紀の変わり目に ＊単複の変化が, um → a 型なので注意。	a period of thousand years
commission [kəmíʃən]	動 委託する I was commissioned to paint the Lord Mayor's portrait. 私は市長の肖像画を描くことを依頼された。	contract

単語／発音	語義／フレーズ	同意表現	難易度
modest [mάːdəst]	形 適度の, 控えめな buy at a modest price そこそこの値段で買う	inexpensive	A
disproportionate [dìsprəpɔ́ːrʃənət]	形 不釣り合いな, 反比例の the disproportionate amount of money spent on war 軍事に使われる不釣り合いなほどの資金	imbalanced	
whereby [weərbáɪ]	関副 それによって；従って the process whereby DNA makes a copy of itself DNAがそれによって自己複製する過程	by which	
credit [krédɪt]	名 称賛, 功績, 手柄, 名声 the credit he deserves 彼にふさわしい称賛 ＊do someone credit「人の手柄, 功績とする」。	praise	B
repertoire [répərtwὰːr]	名 レパートリー, 才能の範囲 expand one's repertoire of skills 技術の幅を広げる	repertory	
intricate [íntrɪkət]	形 複雑な, 入り組んだ undo an intricate knot もつれた結び目をほどく	complex	
pop [pάːp]	動 ひょいと出る, ひょっこり現れる pop up from nowhere どこからともなく現れる	crop up	C
soak [sóʊk]	動 吸収する；浸す；びしょ濡れにする soak up water like a sponge スポンジのように水を吸う ＊ここは, soak up で「吸収する」。	seep	
packed [pǽkt]	形 満員の；いっぱい詰まった be packed like sardines 缶詰のイワシのように満員になっている ＊a packed lift「すし詰めのエレベーター」。	crowded	
timepiece [táɪmpìːs]	名 時計 a mechanical timepiece 機械仕掛けの時計	watch	D
exile [éɡzaɪl]	名 追放；亡命者 send a person into exile 人を国外に追放する ＊banishment or exile と唱えよう！	banishment	
periphery [pərífəri]	名 周囲, 周辺 centre and periphery 中心と周縁 ＊on the periphery of the town「その町の周辺部で」。	fringe	

単語／発音	語義／フレーズ	同意表現
generosity [dʒènərá:səti]	名 寛大さ，気前のよさ treat people with generosity and thoughtfulness 人を寛大さと思いやりをもって遇する	liberality
vigorous [vígərəs]	形 精力的な，力強い；精力旺盛な a vigorous election campaign 精力的な選挙運動	energetic
barely [béərli]	副 かろうじて〜する，ほとんど〜ない He barely passed the midterm. 彼は中間試験をかろうじてパスした。	only just
foremost [fɔ́:rmòust]	形 第一の，主要な the foremost British artist of this century 今世紀随一の英国人芸術家	leading
tag [tǽg]	動 くっついて行く tag around with someone 人の周りに付きまとう ＊名詞の「荷札」から意味を連想しよう。	trail
explore [ɪksplɔ́:r]	動 調査する；探検する explore every possible solution あらゆる可能な解決法を探る	research
makeup [méɪkʌ̀p]	名 組成，構成 alter the makeup of 〜 〜の構成を組み換える ＊文脈によっては，「化粧」や「再試験」の意味にも使える。	composition
hinterland [híntərlæ̀nd]	名 後背地；内陸地域 the hinterland far away from the seashore 海から遠く離れた奥地	back country
deforestation [di:fɔ́:rəstéɪʃən]	名 森林破壊(伐採) the problem of deforestation and desertification 森林破壊と砂漠化の問題	forest destruction
distribution [dìstrəbjú:ʃən]	名 流通；分布；配分；配置 the age distribution of population 年齢別人口分布	circulation
immunity [ɪmjú:nəti]	名 免疫；(危害などを)免れていること acquire immunity to a disease 病気に対する免疫を得る	insusceptibility
ideology [àɪdiá:lədʒi]	名 観念；思想 have a conservative ideology 保守的なイデオロギーを有する	doctrine

Track 149

単語／発音	語義／フレーズ	同意表現	難易度
credence [kríːdns]	名 信用；信頼 a letter of credence 信任状	confidence	A
senior [síːnjər]	形 上級の；年長の a senior partner in a law firm 法律事務所の上級弁護士	higher ranking	
urbanisation [əːrbənàɪzéɪʃən]	名 都市化 rapid and unplanned urbanisation 急速で無計画な都市化	metropolitanisation	
legislation [lèdʒɪsléɪʃən]	名 法律；立法，法律制定 new legislation on the sale of drugs 薬品販売に関する新たな法律	law	B
tripod [tráɪpɑːd]	名 三脚 set the camera on a tripod カメラを三脚にセットする	a three-legged rack	
recipient [rɪsípiənt]	名 受取人 a recipient of the Nobel Prize ノーベル賞受賞者	receiver	
pound [páʊnd]	動 強く打つ pound a nail with a hammer 釘を金づちで打つ	beat	C
scallop [skǽləp]	名 帆立貝 the eye of scallop 貝柱 ＊この場合の eye は「中心」。	bivalve	
bask [bǽsk]	動 (日光・熱などを)浴びる bask in the spring sunshine 春の日差しを浴びる	sun	
curator [kjʊ́ərèɪtər]	名 館長 a former curator of the museum 美術館の元館長 ＊「前館長」の場合は the former curator。	director	D
compliance [kəmpláɪəns]	名 従うこと；(法律などの)遵守 the company's compliance with international law その会社の国際法の遵守	conformity	
unfold [ʌnfóʊld]	動 広げる；開く；明らかにする unfold an umbrella 傘を広げる	open	

Track 150

単語／発音	語義／フレーズ	同意表現
contempt [kəntémpt]	名 軽蔑, 侮辱 contempt for authority 権威に対する軽蔑	scorn
menial [míːniəl]	形 つまらない；熟練を要しない a menial job つまらない仕事 ＊manual labour「肉体労働」と混同しないように！	unskilled
novelty [nάvlti]	名 珍しいもの, 目新しいもの；斬新さ An electric-powered car is still a novelty. 電気自動車はまだ珍しい。	freshness

IELTS必須英単語
Group C

Track 151

単語／発音	語彙／フレーズ	同意表現
deadly [dédli]	形 死に至る，致命的な a deadly combination of poverty and famine 貧困と飢饉の致命的組み合わせ	fatal
tide [táɪd]	名 潮の干満；満ち潮 the ebb and flow of the tide 潮の干満 ＊「満潮」は high tide。	ebb and flow
inhabit [ɪnhǽbət]	動 生息している，住んでいる inhabit the woods 森に生息している ＊ inhabitant「住民」も併せて覚えよう！	populate
glacier [gléɪʃər]	名 氷河 alpine glaciers 高山性氷河 ＊Ⓡ 準専門用語として頻出。	a large mass of ice from snow
remains [rɪméɪn]	名 遺跡 geological remains 地質学的遺跡 ＊本来「残り」の意だが，「化石」の意味もある。	relics
inherent [ɪnhíərənt]	形 固有の；生得の inherent viscosity 固有粘度	innate
collapse [kəlǽps]	名 崩壊 economic collapse 経済の崩壊 ＊Ⓦ「急落，暴落」で使える。	disintegration
manifestation [mæ̀nəfestéɪʃən]	名 現れ；兆候 a manifestation of discontent 不満の現れ	indication
cast [kǽst]	動 投げる；向ける cast doubt on the judgment その判断に疑いを投げかける ＊Ⓡ doubt was cast on 〜「〜に疑問が投げかけられた」。	throw
speculation [spèkjəléɪʃən]	名 投機；思索，熟考；推測 stock speculation 株式投機	gamble
flawed [flɔ́ːd]	形 間違いのある；欠点のある flawed data 誤りのあるデータ ＊Ⓛ 発音に注意。	faulty
eliminate [ɪlímənèɪt]	動 除去する，削除する eliminate iodine from the body ヨウ素を体内から取り除く	remove

168

Track 152

単語／発音	語彙／フレーズ	同意表現	難易度
compatible [kəmpǽtəbl]	形 矛盾しない；気が合う compatible with the facts 事実と矛盾しない	consistent	A
accelerate [əksélərèɪt]	動 (時期などを)早める；加速する accelerate the pace of global warming 地球温暖化のペースを早める	speed up	
shelf [ʃélf]	名 岩棚，岩礁；棚状のもの a continental shelf 大陸棚	ledge	
ground [gráʊnd]	動 地面に置く the grounded ice sheet 接地氷床	land	B
disintegrate [dɪsíntəgrèɪt]	動 崩壊する(させる) The planetoid disintegrated. その小惑星は崩壊した。	decay	
gauge [géɪdʒ]	名 計器；規格 a fuel gauge 燃料計 ＊いわゆる「ゲージ」。	meter	
tilt [tílt]	動 (バランスを)失わせる；傾ける tilt the balance of power 力の均衡を失わせる	disrupt	C
tap [tǽp]	動 (資源などを)利用する，開発する tap rich resources 豊富な資源を利用する ＊名詞「蛇口」という意もある。	exploit	
altimeter [æltímətər]	名 高度計 read a radio altimeter 電波高度計を読み取る ＊ altitude は「高度」。	height indicator	
transform [trænsfɔ́ːrm]	動 変える transform the country's economy 国の経済を変貌させる	change	D
synthetic [sɪnθétɪk]	形 合成の，本物でない；総合的な a synthetic fibre 合成繊維 ＊「(自然にできたものでなく)人工の」としても頻出。	compound	
replicate [répləkèɪt]	動 複製する replicate DNA DNA を複製する ＊ replica は「複製」。	copy	

Track 153

単語／発音	語彙／フレーズ	同意表現
diameter [daɪǽmətɚ]	名 直径 a crater 10 metres in diameter 直径10メートルのクレーター ＊半径は radius。	distance across
gland [glǽnd]	名 腺 the thyroid gland 甲状腺 ＊医学で，ある種の物質を分泌，排泄する細胞組織。	organ
comparable [kάːmpərəbl]	形 匹敵する；類似の comparable in size to the sun 太陽に匹敵する大きさの	equal
harvest [hάːrvəst]	動 (体内から)摘出する harvest cells 細胞を採取する	extract
equivalent [ɪkwívələnt]	形 同等の equivalent in amount 同量の ＊R 名詞「同等のもの」が頻出。	equal
substitute [sΛ́bstət(j)ùːt]	動 代わりに用いる substitute syrup for sugar 砂糖の代わりにシロップを使う ＊他動詞用法は注意！ 能動態では動作主を主語にする。	replace with
resistant [rɪzístənt]	形 耐える；抵抗する earthquake-resistant structure 耐震構造	tolerant
mimic [mímɪk]	動 真似る mimic a more dangerous animal より危険な動物をまねる ＊＝ copy	imitate
prediction [prɪdíkʃən]	名 予言(すること) an accurate prediction 正確な予測	forecast
creature [kríːtʃɚ]	名 生物 extraterrestrial creatures 地球外生物	living thing
envious [énviəs]	形 うらやんで an envious glance 羨望のまなざし ＊ envy「嫉妬, 妬み；妬む」も覚える。	jealous
adhesive [ædhíːsɪv]	形 粘着性のある adhesive tapes 接着テープ	sticky

Track 154

単語／発音	語彙／フレーズ	同意表現	難易度
secrete [sɪkríːt]	動 分泌する secrete a hormone ホルモンを分泌する ＊最後の e を取ると secret「秘密」になる。	release	A
tedious [tíːdiəs]	形 うんざりな a tedious meeting 退屈な会議	boring	
-proof [prúːf]	形（接尾）抵抗できる，負けない a bulletproof vest 防弾チョッキ ＊waterproof「防水の」も頻出。	resistant	
usher [ʌ́ʃər]	動 先導役を務める；案内する usher in a new era 新時代の先導役を務める	guide	B
universal [jùːnəvə́ːrsl]	形 普遍的な universal knowledge 万人に通じる知識 ＊「宇宙の」以外の意味の方が出やすい。	common	
diffusion [dɪfjúːʒən]	名 発散，普及 diffusion of knowledge 知識の普及	spreading	
extension [ɪksténʃən]	名 延長；拡張 ask for an extension on my paper レポートの締切延長をお願いする	prolongation	C
argue [áːrgjuː]	動 論じる；主張する argue persuasively against war 説得力をもって戦争反対を主張する	assert	
enhance [ɪnhǽns]	動 高める enhance performance 成果を高める	improve	
promotion [prəmóʊʃən]	名 昇進；促進，増進 get a promotion 昇進する	preferment	D
rote [róʊt]	名 機械的な手順 learn one's tables by rote 九九の表を丸暗記する ＊ここの tables は multiplication tables。	repetition	
outcome [áʊtkʌ̀m]	名 結果 a desirable outcome 望ましい結果 ＊ result, consequence とセットで覚える。	consequence	

単語／発音	語彙／フレーズ	同意表現
constitute [kɑ́:nstət(j)ù:t]	動 一部をなす，構成する find out what constitutes true addiction 真の中毒の原因は何なのかを知る	comprise
compile [kəmpáɪl]	動 収集する，編集する compile information 情報を集めてまとめる	collect
dynamic [daɪnǽmɪk]	形 精力的な a dynamic and ambitious person 精力的で野心的な人	energetic
reflective [rɪfléktɪv]	形 思慮深い；反射する in a reflective mood じっくり考えたい気分で	thoughtful
enthusiasm [ɪnθ(j)ú:ziæzm]	名 熱意；熱中 full of enthusiasm 熱意にあふれている ＊ⓢ be enthusiastic about 〜「〜に熱中している」を使いたい。	zeal
context [kɑ́:ntekst]	名 背景，状況；前後関係 historical contexts 歴史的背景	circumstances
accord [əkɔ́:rd]	動 与える；許可する accord the recognition he deserves 彼にふさわしい評価を与える	grant
concern [kənsə́:rn]	動 関心を持たせる；心配させる concern oneself with studying abroad 海外留学に関心を示す	interest
equip [ɪkwíp]	動 身につけさせる；素養を与える be equipped to handle a difficult situation 困難への対処力が備わっている	endow
cease [sí:s]	動 〜するのをやめる；終わる Passenger pigeons ceased to exist in 1914. リョコウバトは1914年に絶滅した。	stop
determinant [dɪtə́:rmənənt]	名 決定要素 a major determinant of desertification 砂漠化の第1の要因	factor
innovative [ínəvèɪtɪv]	形 革新的な，進取の気概に富む an innovative design 斬新な設計 ＊W2 若者が持つ innovative ideas「革新的なアイデア」。	novel

Track 156

単語／発音	語彙／フレーズ	同意表現	難易度
tackle [tǽkl]	動 取り組む tackle environmental problems 環境問題に取り組む ＊W2 tackle the problem は使える。	address	A
monitor [mάːnətər]	動 監視する monitor damage to the ozone layer オゾン層への害を監視する	watch	
nutritional [n(j)u(ː)tríʃənl]	形 栄養上の lessen nutritional value 栄養価を下げる	nutritive	
extinction [ɪkstíŋkʃən]	名 絶滅；消すこと be threatened with extinction 絶滅の危機にさらされている	demise	B
occur [əkə́ːr]	動 存在する，見いだされる；起こる Tortoises don't occur naturally on Mauritius. モーリシャスに亀は生息しない。　＊W2 自動詞。受動態にはできない。	exist	
attribute [ətríbjuːt]	動 〜のせいだとする attribute lung cancer to smoking 喫煙を肺がんの原因とする ＊名詞 attribute「性質」も注意！	ascribe	
sustenance [sʌ́stənəns]	名 (生命維持の)滋養物；維持 a certain sustenance to survive 生存のための若干の滋養分	nourishment	C
relative [rélətɪv]	名 親族，同類の動植物 a distant relative 遠い親戚	kin	
extract [ɪkstrǽkt]	動 抽出する；抜粋する extract caffeine from coffee beans コーヒー豆からカフェインを抽出する	distil	
mixture [míkstʃər]	名 調合薬；混合物 cough mixtures 咳止め調合薬 ＊[英]。	compound	D
utilise [júːtəlàɪz]	動 利用する utilise thermal energy 熱エネルギーを利用する	use	
facilitate [fəsílətèɪt]	動 容易にする facilitate the free flow of information 情報の自由な流れを容易にする	make easy	

単語／発音	語彙／フレーズ	同意表現
exposure [ɪkspóʊʒɚr]	名 さらされること prolonged exposure to the sun 長期間日光にさらされること	contact
withstand [wɪðstǽnd]	動 耐える withstand the attack from fungi 菌類からの攻撃に耐える	resist
specimen [spésəmən]	名 標本 a botanical specimen 植物標本 ＊R 生物学・地質学関係でよく見る単語。	sample
organ [ɔ́ːrɡən]	名 器官 digestive organs 消化器官 ＊脳も organ の一種。「組織, 機関」の意味もある。	apparatus
means [míːnz]	名 方法；財力 by any means 何としても（どんな手段でも） ＊単複同形。meaning は「意味」。	method
distinctive [dɪstíŋktɪv]	形 特有の, 特徴的な a distinctive shape 独特な形	unique
fluid [flúːɪd]	名 流動体《液体と気体の総称》；水分 Air is also a fluid. 空気もまた流動体です。	water
coating [kóʊtɪŋ]	名 塗装；被服物,（食物の）衣 waterproof coating 防水塗装	painting
wholesome [hóʊlsəm]	形 健康によい wholesome food 健康によい食べ物	healthy
distribute [dɪstríbjuːt]	動 配布する；分布する distribute leaflets ちらしを配る	pass out
onwards [ɑ́ːnwərdz]	副 前方へ, 先へ from the 1950s onwards 1950 年代以降 ＊W1 from 〜 onwards「〜以降」で使える。	forward
awareness [əwéərnəs]	名 意識；自覚すること raise the awareness of environmental issues 環境問題への意識を高める	consciousness

単語／発音	語彙／フレーズ	同意表現	難易度
provision [prəvíʒən]	名 用意, 対策；貯蔵品 make provision for emergencies 緊急時に備える ＊「供給, 提供」の意味もある。	preparation	A
exhaust [ɪgzɔ́ːst]	動 使い尽くす exhaust fossil fuel energy 化石燃料を使い尽くす ＊同意連語なら use up。	deplete	
finite [fáɪnaɪt]	形 有限な Human knowledge is finite. 人知は有限である。 ＊発音注意！	limited	
principle [prínsəpl]	名 原理, 原則 in principle 原則として	rule	B
invisible [ɪnvízəbl]	形 見えない invisible rays 目に見えない光線	unseeable	
contrary [kɑ́ːntrèri]	形 反対の a contrary position 反対の立場 ＊R opposite, conflicting との書き換えに注意！	opposite	
exercise [éksərsàɪz]	動 行使する；発揮する exercise the right to remain silent 黙秘権を行使する ＊ exercise rights「権利を行使する」で頻出。	use	C
deprive [dɪpráɪv]	動 (権利など)を奪う deprive children of all maternal contact 子と母親を全く接触させない ＊W2 deprive 人 of モノの使い方を覚える。	rob	
indispensable [ìndɪspénsəbl]	形 絶対必要な, 不可欠な the indispensable factors for good health 健康に不可欠な要素	essential	
stem [stém]	動 起因する, 派生する a feeling of hate that stems from envy 羨望に起因する憎悪	occur	D
accompany [əkʌ́mpəni]	動 伴う, 付随する；伴奏する a typhoon accompanied by heavy rains 集中豪雨を伴う台風 ＊「同時に起きる」の意味もある。	attend	
consistent [kənsístənt]	形 一貫した, 矛盾しない You aren't consistent with yourself. 君の言うことは一貫していない。	coherent	

Track 159

単語／発音	語彙／フレーズ	同意表現
underestimate [ʌ̀ndəréstəmèɪt]	動 過小評価する Never underestimate your opponent! 敵を決して見くびるな！　＊⇔「過大評価する」overestimate = exaggerate。	underrate
illusion [ɪlúːʒən]	名 幻覚，幻影，幻想 an optical illusion 目の錯覚	hallucination
disability [dìsəbíləti]	名 障害；身体障害 a mental disability 精神障害 ＊ the disabled「障害者」。	disorder
clientele [klàɪəntél]	名 (劇場，商店の)顧客 a regular clientele at a store 店の常連客	customer
stricken [stríkən]	形 打ちひしがれた a poverty-stricken area 貧困に打ちひしがれた地域	battered
autonomy [ɔːtáːnəmi]	名 自治(権)；自治体 achieve greater autonomy 今以上の自治権を獲得する ＊ auto- は「自動の；自身の」を表す接頭語。	independence
doomsday [dúːmzdèɪ]	名 この世の終わり(の)，最後の審判の日 a doomsday scenario この世が終わるという筋書き	Judgment Day
juvenile [dʒúːvənàɪl]	形 青少年の；未熟な juvenile crime 青少年犯罪 ＊ juvenile delinquency「青少年非行」もおなじみ。	young
indulge [ɪndʌ́ldʒ]	動 (趣味などに)ふける indulge in gambling ギャンブルに熱中する	be absorbed
earnest [ə́ːrnɪst]	形 真面目な；熱心な a reputation for being dreadfully earnest ひどく真面目だという評判	serious
mate [méɪt]	動 交尾させる，つがいになる a mating season 交尾期	pair
respiratory [résp ərətɔ̀ːri]	形 呼吸器官の；呼吸の a respiratory disease 呼吸器疾患	breathing

Track 160

単語／発音	語彙／フレーズ	同意表現	難易度
enduring [ɪndjúərɪŋ]	形 永久的な, 不朽の；辛抱強い establish an enduring peace 恒久的な平和を確立する ＊ lasting も同義語。	eternal	A
prowess [práʊəs]	名 能力；技術 great prowess as an athlete 運動選手としての偉大な能力 ＊R skill の堅めの言い換えで登場。	ability	
stimulus [stímjələs]	名 刺激；激励 act as a stimulus to exports 輸出品への刺激の役割を果たす ＊ stimuli は複数形。	incentive	
mould [móʊld]	動 (人格を)形成する；型に入れて作る mould one's character 人格を形成する ＊L 名詞「鋳型」は書き取りで出るかも。	shape	B
variable [véəriəbl]	形 変わりやすい, 不定の；気まぐれな variable temperatures 変わりやすい気温	fluctuating	
unpredictable [ʌ̀nprɪːdíktəbl]	形 予測できない unpredictable future 予測不能な未来	unforeseeable	
interact [ìntərǽkt]	動 相互作用する, 交流する interact with each other 互いに交流する ＊R 場合によっては少し柔らかく「やりとりをする」と訳したい。	interchange	C
-orientated [ɔ́ːriəntèɪtɪd]	形 ～志向の an exam-orientated school 試験志向の学校 ＊ -oriented も同じ。	-centred	
cub [kʌ́b]	名 (野生動物の)子 a fox cub キツネの子供	young	
cost [kɔ́(ː)st]	動 (損失・犠牲)を支払わせる That mistake will cost you your job. その失態で君は失職しますよ。　＊ cost A B「AにBを支払わせる」SVOO型。	destroy	D
pup [pʌ́p]	名 (犬などの)子 a sea otter pup ラッコの子供	puppy	
wag [wǽg]	動 振る, 揺り動かす a dog wagging its tail しっぽを振る犬	wave	

177

Track 161

単語／発音	語彙／フレーズ	同意表現
suckle [sʌ́kl]	動 (乳を)飲ませる, 飲む a cow suckling her calves 子牛に乳をやる牝牛 ＊ a suckling stage は「母乳を飲む時期」。	milk
kaleidoscope [kəláɪdəskòʊp]	名 絶えず変化する形；万華鏡 a behavioural kaleidoscope 絶え間ない行動の変化	
reciprocal [rɪsíprəkl]	形 相互の；対等の reciprocal rights and obligations 相互の権利と義務	mutual
equity [ékwəti]	名 公平；公明正大 treat people with equity and respect 人を公平と敬意をもって遇する	fairness
suppress [səprés]	動 抑える；鎮圧する suppress a desire 欲求を抑える	restrain
launch [lɔ́:ntʃ]	動 (事業などを)始める launch an investigation 捜査に乗り出す ＊発音注意！	start
bypass [báɪpæs]	動 迂回する；回避する bypass the town to the north その町を迂回して北へ向かう ＊「～を無視する」という意味もある。	detour
cross-section [krɔ́(:)s sékʃən]	名 断面(図)；横に切ること a cross-section of a plant stem 植物の茎の断面	
configuration [kənfìgjəréɪʃən]	名 形態；構成 the broad configuration of the economy 経済体制の一般的形態	layout
foster [fɔ́(:)stər]	動 育成する, 助長する foster good relations within the community 共同体内の良好な関係を育む	promote
periodic [pìəriɑ́:dɪk]	形 定期的な, 周期的な periodic check-ups 定期健診	regular
sensory [sénsəri]	形 感覚に関する, 知覚の sensory organs 感覚器官	of physical senses

Track 162

単語／発音	語彙／フレーズ	同意表現	難易度
interfere [ìntərfíər]	動 邪魔をする，干渉する interfere with children's performance at school 子供の学業を妨げる ＊ W2 interfere with 〜 の形で使う。	meddle	A
evaluate [ɪvǽljuèɪt]	動 価値を見きわめる，評価する evaluate the effectiveness of the drug その薬品の効果を見きわめる	assess	
phenomenal [fɪnɑ́:mənl]	形 並外れた；自然現象の a phenomenal success 驚異的な成功	extraordinary	
stride [stráɪd]	名 進歩，発展 make great strides 大きな進歩を遂げる	progress	B
auditory [ɔ́:dətɔ̀:ri]	形 耳の，聴覚の the visual and auditory sense 視覚と聴覚	hearing	
verbal [və́:rbl]	形 言葉による，口頭の verbal dexterity 言葉遣いの器用さ	oral	
perpetuate [pərpétʃuèɪt]	動 長引かせる perpetuate the confusion through inadvertence 怠慢により混乱を長引かせる ＊ perpetual「永久の」も覚える。	preserve	C
inequity [ɪnékwəti]	名 不公平；偏り overcome educational inequity 教育の不平等を克服する	unfairness	
administer [ədmínəstər]	動 治める，管理する administer the pension funds 年金基金を運営する	control	
gloomy [glú:mi]	形 憂鬱な；陰気な gloomy weather 陰鬱な天気	dreary	D
temper [témpər]	名 気性；一時的な気分 a short temper 短気な気性	mood	
muggy [mʌ́gi]	形 蒸し暑い；うっとうしい an unpleasantly muggy evening 不快に蒸し暑い夕暮れ	humid	

179

単語／発音	語彙／フレーズ	同意表現
riot [ráɪət]	名 暴動, 騒動 A riot broke out in the prison. 刑務所で暴動が起こった。 ＊発音に注意！	tumult
frequency [frí:kwənsi]	名 頻度；しばしば起こること the high frequency of accidents 事故の高い頻度	rate of occurrence
impair [ɪmpéər]	動 損なう, 害する impair one's ability to concentrate 集中力を損なう	damage
distract [dɪstrǽkt]	動 （注意や気を）散らす distract attention from the truth 真実から注意をそらす	divert
sceptical [sképtɪkl]	形 信じがたい；懐疑的な look highly sceptical 非常に信じがたい様子である ＊[英]。skeptical は[米]。	incredulous
moody [mú:di]	形 気分屋の；憂鬱な a moody person 気分屋の人	temperamental
disrupt [dɪsrʌ́pt]	動 崩壊させる；中断させる disrupt the balance of nature 自然のバランスを崩壊させる ＊R L 「崩壊させる」で頻出！	disturb
cope [kóʊp]	動 うまく処理する, 乗り切る cope with stress ストレスをうまく処理する	deal
establish [ɪstǽblɪʃ]	動 証明する, 立証する establish one's identity 身分を証明する ＊W2 a long-established way of ～ 「長く定着した～する方法」。	bear out
pepper [pépər]	動 散りばめる；コショウを振り掛ける His face is peppered with freckles. 彼の顔はソバカスだらけだ。	scatter
mounting [máʊntɪŋ]	形 次第に増える mounting pressure 次第にのしかかるプレッシャー	accumulative
perception [pərsépʃən]	名 認識, 理解（力）；知覚, 認知 public perception of risk リスクに対する一般人の認識 ＊「知覚」だと分かりにくいので, 「認識」で覚えよう。	recognition

Track 164

単語／発音	語彙／フレーズ	同意表現	難易度
rekindle [rɪkíndl]	動 再びかき立てる，再燃させる rekindle painful memories つらい記憶を再びかき立てる	reawaken	A
explosive [ɪksplóʊsɪv]	名 爆発物 those dogs that can detect explosives 爆発物を嗅ぎ分けられる犬	bomb	
complement [kɑ́:mpləmənt]	名 全数；乗組定員 a ship's full complement 船の乗組定員 ＊ℝ「補完するもの」という意味で頻出。	quota	
injury [índʒəri]	名 負傷，傷害；権利侵害 sustain serious injuries in the crash 衝突事故で重傷を負う ＊ sustain = suffer	wound	B
outstanding [àʊtstǽndɪŋ]	形 未解決の；未払いの pay outstanding bills 未払いの請求を支払う ＊ℝ「傑出した」というプラスの意味が頻出。	pending	
tactics [tǽktɪks]	名 戦術，作戦，かけひき delaying tactics 引き延ばし作戦	strategy	
dimension [dɪménʃən]	名 寸法；規模；次元 The dimensions of the box are 20 x10 x 4. その箱のサイズは 20 × 10 × 4 です。	size	C
contradict [kà:ntrədíkt]	動 反論する，否定する；矛盾する He contradicted everything she said. 彼は彼女の言葉すべてに反論した。	disagree with	
wisdom [wízdəm]	名 賢明さ；知恵 question the wisdom of doing so そうするのは賢明ではないと思う	sagacity	
unorthodox [ʌnɔ́:rθədà:ks]	形 正統的でない；伝統的でない unorthodox methods 正統ではない方法	unconventional	D
variable [véəriəbl]	名 変数；変わるもの with so many variables 非常に多くの変数を伴って ＊「要素」に近い意味で出ることも。		
duplicate [d(j)ú:plɪkèɪt]	動 繰り返す；複写する It is useless to duplicate the work already done. 済んだ仕事を繰り返すのは無駄だ。	repeat	

181

Track 165

単語／発音	語彙／フレーズ	同意表現
expend [ɪkspénd]	動 (労力などを)費やす，使い果たす expend all the energy on the scheme 全労力をその計画に費やす　＊金銭の場合は spend を使う。	consume
limb [lím]	名 手足の1本；脚 every joint and limb あらゆる関節と手足	leg
sprawl [sprɔ́ːl]	名 不規則な広がり，スプロール現象 urban sprawl 都市のスプロール現象 ＊ urban sprawl は都市が不規則に広がっていくこと。	spreading
doubt [dáʊt]	動 疑う doubt the truth of his statement 彼の供述の真実性を疑う ＊ⓇR suspect that SV は「SV ではないかと思う」。	mistrust
vanish [vǽnɪʃ]	動 消える vanish from sight 視界から見えなくなる ＊ banish「追放する」と混同しないように！	disappear
diversity [dəvə́ːrsəti]	名 多様性 ethnic diversity 民族の多様性 ＊ diverse, diversification も併せて記憶したい。	variety
induce [ɪnd(j)úːs]	動 誘発する，引き起こす induce a chemical reaction 化学変化を誘発する ＊ⓇR cause と同じ意味と考えれば OK。	cause
intimate [íntəmət]	形 親密な the intimate link between generations 世代間の親密なつながり　＊発音注意。語尾は [mət]。	close
bind [báɪnd]	動 結びつける，束縛する；とじる Good schools bind a community together. 良い学校は地域を結びつける。＊活用形とその発音に注意！	unite
apprentice [əpréntɪs]	名 徒弟，見習い a master and his apprentices 師匠と従弟たち	trainee
exclusively [ɪksklúːsɪvli]	副 もっぱら；独占的に available exclusively to women もっぱら女性だけが利用可能な	only
revive [rɪváɪv]	動 生き返らせる；生き返る，復活する revive and strengthen the economy 経済を再生し強化する	resurrect

Track 166

単語／発音	語彙／フレーズ	同意表現	難易度
medium [míːdiəm]	名 媒体；中間 a medium of advertisement 広告媒体 ＊media の単数形。意味は「メディア」と思えばよい。	intermediate	A
congestion [kəndʒéstʃən]	名 混雑 traffic congestion 交通渋滞　＊crowded は「場所・乗物が人で込み合った」, congested は「密集している」。	crowding	
fume [fjúːm]	名 (有害な)煙 exhaust fumes 排気ガス	harmful gas	
entail [intéil]	動 必然的に伴う, 要する；引き起こす entail a great risk 大きなリスクを伴う ＊W2 entail some drawbacks「欠点を伴う」。	necessitate	B
emission [imíʃən]	名 排気物質；放出(物) emission control 排気ガス規制 ＊「排出」だけでなく、「排出物」の意味もある。	emanation	
infection [infékʃən]	名 感染；伝染病 computer virus infection コンピュータウイルス感染	contagion	
anticipate [æntísəpèit]	動 予測する；期待する anticipate a bright future 明るい将来を予想する ＊predict も同義語。	expect	C
unbiased [ʌnbáiəsd]	形 公平な；偏りのない unbiased opinion 公平な意見 ＊bias は「偏見、偏り」。	impartial	
intending [inténdiŋ]	形 将来の, なるつもりの intending purchasers 購入見込み客	prospective	
formulation [fɔːrmjəléiʃən]	名 構築；公式化 formulation of a system システムの構築	construction	D
unprejudiced [ʌnprédʒədəsd]	形 偏見のない an unprejudiced view 公平な見方 ＊名詞「偏見」prejudice = bias。	impartial	
relevant [réləvənt]	形 直接的に関連する；適切な relevant evidence 関連性のある証拠 ＊Be relevant!「本題からそれないで！」。	related	

単語／発音	語彙／フレーズ	同意表現
emerge [ɪmə́:rdʒ]	動 現れる；出てくる Homelessness emerges as a social problem. ホームレスが社会問題として現れる。 ＊emerging countries「新興国」。	come out
exploratory [ɪksplɔ́:rətɔ̀:ri]	形 調査の，探検の；予備の be still in an exploratory stage まだ調査段階にある	investigative
light [láɪt]	名 観点，見方 in the light of international law 国際法の観点から ＊[英]。	view
rigorous [rɪ́gərəs]	形 厳格な，厳しい rigorous discipline 厳しいしつけ ＊strict, rigid と併せて覚える。	strict
serial [sɪ́əriəl]	形 連続の a serial number 通し番号	consecutive
alley [ǽli]	名 路地；小道 walk down the narrow alley 狭い路地を歩く	lane
dwelling [dwélɪŋ]	名 住居 ancient cave dwellings 古代の洞窟住居 ＊「〜に住む」dwell in = inhabit = populate。	house
confine [kənfáɪn]	動 制限する，限定する；閉じ込める confine our study to seven cases 我々の研究を7事例に制限する	restrict
predator [prédətər]	名 捕食動物；肉食動物 predator and prey 捕食動物と獲物 ＊natural predator は「天敵」。	carnivore
craft [krǽft]	名 技術；手工業 the carpenter's craft その大工の技術	skill
barbed [bá:rbd]	形 とげのある be injured by a barbed-wire fence フェンスの有刺鉄線で怪我をする ＊発音注意！	spiky
thorn [θɔ́:rn]	名 とげ a prick of a thorn とげによる刺し傷 ＊R 植物の話で頻出。	spine

Track 168

単語／発音	語彙／フレーズ	同意表現	難易度
ingenious [ɪndʒíːnjəs]	形 巧妙な；利口な use an ingenious method 巧妙な方法を用いる	clever	A
nip [níp]	動 摘み取る，かみ切る；つねる；妨げる nip a leaf 葉を摘み取る	pinch	
counterpart [káʊntərpɑ̀ːrt]	名 相対物，片割れ；同等のもの an export counterpart 輸出相手国 ＊W1 the male counterpart「その男性版」。	equivalent	
transmission [trænsmíʃən]	名 送信；伝達 worldwide data transmission 世界的なデータ送信	sending	B
pliable [pláɪəbl]	形 柔軟な a hat made of pliable leather 柔軟な皮製の帽子	flexible	
symmetrical [sɪmétrɪkl]	形 （左右）対称な；均整の取れた a symmetrical pattern 左右対称の図柄	proportionate	
pointer [pɔ́ɪntər]	名 ヒント，指針，助言 give someone a few pointers on 〜 〜について人に2，3助言をする	advice	C
sequential [sɪkwénʃəl]	形 連続して起こる，一連の sequential data processing 一連のデータ処理	consecutive	
beak [bíːk]	名 くちばし a bird with a long beak 長いくちばしの鳥	bill	
shortcoming [ʃɔ́ːrtkʌ̀mɪŋ]	名 欠点；欠陥 have a serious shortcoming 重大な欠陥がある	defect	D
industry [índəstri]	名 勤勉；産業，工業 demonstrate a great deal of industry in the job 業務で多大な勤勉さを示す　＊industrious は「勤勉な」。	diligence	
litter [lítər]	名 （散らかした）ごみ fines for those who drop litter ごみの投げ捨てをする者への罰金	waste	

185

Track 169

単語／発音	語彙／フレーズ	同意表現

ban
[bǽn]
動 禁止する
Mobile phones are banned at school.
携帯電話は学校への持ち込み禁止です。
prohibit

sewer
[súːər]
名 下水道
a sewer water treatment plant 下水処理工場
sewerage

drainage
[dréɪnɪdʒ]
名 排水；排水設備
a drainage ditch 排水溝
draining

blanket
[blǽŋkət]
形 全面的な, 包括的な；一律の
a blanket ban 全面的な禁止
＊「毛布」を思い浮かべれば「覆うもの」というイメージもわく。
comprehensive

resurrect
[rèzərékt]
動 復活させる；生き返る
resurrect the economy 経済を復興させる
revive

crackdown
[krǽkdàʊn]
名 取り締まり
crackdown on drunken driving 酒酔い運転の取り締まり
clampdown

leaver
[líːvər]
名 (中等学校の進学しない)卒業予定者
the early school-leaver rate 中途退学率
＊leave school は「(中等教育機関を)卒業する」の意味もある。
graduating senior

confer
[kənfə́ːr]
動 (学位を)与える, 贈る；協議する
confer an honorary degree on a famous writer
有名作家に名誉学位を与える
grant

loyalty
[lɔ́ɪəlti]
名 忠誠, 忠実, 誠実；忠誠心
pledge loyalty to the nation 国家への忠誠を誓う
faithfulness

egalitarian
[ɪgæ̀lətéəriən]
形 平等主義の
sexually egalitarian society 男女平等社会
equalitarian

seniority
[siːnjɔ́ːrəti]
名 年功, 先輩であること；年長
promotion by seniority 年功序列による昇進
longer service

mentor
[méntɔːr]
名 良き助言者；指導教官
look up to someone as a mentor
人を信頼できる助言者として仰ぐ
good adviser

単語／発音	語彙／フレーズ	同意表現	難易度
constructively [kənstrʌ́ktɪvli]	副 前向きに, 建設的に deal with drawbacks constructively 障害に前向きに対処する	positively	A
subcontractor [sʌ̀bkáːntræktər]	名 下請け業者 a nominated subcontractor 指定下請け業者	subcontracting company	
swift [swíft]	形 迅速な, 素早い；即座の take swift action against the squatters 不法占拠者に迅速な行動を取る	quick	
garment [gáːrmənt]	名 衣服；着物 work in the garment industry 服飾業界で働く	clothes	B
grant [grǽnt]	動 与える；(願いを)聞き入れる grant a privilege to students temporarily 学生に一時的に特権を与える	allow	
tangle [tǽŋgl]	動 絡まる, もつれる The rope became tangled in the wheels. ロープが車輪に絡まった。	entangle	
insatiable [ɪnséɪʃəbl]	形 飽くことを知らない, 貪欲な have an insatiable appetite for adventure 冒険に対する飽くなき欲求がある	voracious	C
intervene [ìntərvíːn]	動 介入する；仲裁する intervene in a dispute between Britain and Spain イギリスとスペインの紛争に介入する	interpose	
exaggerate [ɪgzǽdʒərèɪt]	動 誇張する, 大げさに言う；強調する The effect of the new drug was greatly exaggerated. 新薬の効果はひどく誇張されていた。　＊overestimateで代用可。	overstate	
capture [kǽptʃər]	動 捕える；(注意を)引きつける capture lions alive ライオンを生け捕りにする	catch	D
toddler [tɑ́ːdlər]	名 よちよち歩きの幼児 baby and toddler conditions 乳幼児の状況	young child	
therapeutic [θèrəpjúːtɪk]	形 癒す力のある；治療法の a therapeutic hot spring 治療効果のある温泉	healing	

単語／発音	語彙／フレーズ	同意表現
immortalise [ɪmɔ́ːrtlàɪz]	動 不朽の名声を与える；不滅にする immortalise someone's name 人の名に不朽の名声を与える	eternize
genuine [dʒénjuɪn]	形 誠実な, 真の；本物の show a genuine interest 真の興味を示す	sincere
common [kɑ́ːmən]	形 ありふれた, 一般的な；共通の the most common health problem 最もありふれた健康上の問題	usual
alleviate [əlíːvièɪt]	動 （苦痛などを）軽減する, 緩和する alleviate stomach pain 腹痛を和らげる ＊Ⓢ alleviate anxiety のように精神的な苦労にも使える。	ease
complaint [kəmpléɪnt]	名 不平, 不満；苦情 a noise complaint from neighbours 近隣住民からの騒音苦情	grievance
insomnia [ɪnsɑ́ːmniə]	名 不眠症 alleviate insomnia 不眠症を和らげる	sleeplessness
vessel [vésl]	名 血管；船 A blood vessel has burst on the left side of the brain. 脳の左側の血管が破裂した。	vein
consent [kənsént]	名 同意, 承諾；意見の一致 have parental consent when treating a child 子供を治療するとき親の同意を得る ＊品詞の別なく同一アクセント。	agreement
legitimate [lɪdʒítəmət]	形 正統な, 合法の；妥当な a legitimate heir to the throne 正当な王位継承者	lawful
interlink [ìntərlíŋk]	動 連結する；結びつける Two processes are closely interlinked with each other. 2つの工程は密接に結びついている。	interconnect
ulcer [ʌ́lsər]	名 潰瘍 develop into an ulcer 進行して潰瘍となる	ulceration
neurologist [n(j)ʊ́əroulədʒɪst]	名 神経科医 a clinical neurologist 臨床神経科医	

Track 172

単語／発音	語彙／フレーズ	同意表現	難易度
solicit [səlísit]	動 請い求める, 懇願する solicit opinions from the public 一般大衆から意見を募る	induce	A
distressing [dɪstrésɪŋ]	形 悲惨な, 苦しめる distressing circumstances 窮状	distressful	
polarise [póʊlərὰɪz]	動 分裂する, 二極化する；偏光させる polarise the world 世界を二極化させる	dichotomize	
evoke [ɪvóʊk]	動 呼び起こす；引き起こす evoke a sense of anxiety 不安感を呼び起こす	inspire	B
aggravate [ǽgrəvèɪt]	動 さらに悪化させる；さらに深刻にする Do not aggravate the problem. 問題を悪化させるな。	worsen	
drowsiness [dráʊzɪnəs]	名 眠気；ものうさ feel a sudden drowsiness 突然眠気を催す	sleepiness	
rationale [rǽʃənǽl]	名 理論的根拠；原理的説明 the rationale for imposing protectional tariff on imports 輸入品に関税を課す理論的根拠　＊⑤ 根拠を聞かれる。	logical ground	C
designate [dézɪgnèɪt]	動 指名する, 指定する；明示する designate a small island as a world heritage site ある小島を世界遺産に指定する	appoint	
alert [ələ́:rt]	形 油断のない, 用心深い；機敏な remain alert to every sound and movement どんな音や動きにも用心深いままである	careful	
persevere [pə̀:rsəvíər]	動 辛抱する；耐える persevere in efforts 辛抱して努力する	persist	D
perk [pə́:rk]	名 特別手当 one of the perks of my last job 前職の特別手当の 1 つ	special allowance	
offence [əféns]	名 違反 a minor offence 軽犯罪 ＊[英]。[米]では offense。	violation	

189

Track 173

単語／発音	語彙／フレーズ	同意表現
address [ədrés]	動 (問題などに)取り組む, 焦点を当てる address the issue of poverty 貧困問題に取り組む ＊W2 address the issue を使えるように。	deal with
gear [gíər]	動 適合させる be geared to the US market アメリカ市場向けである ＊W2 be geared to 名詞 の形で使う。	adjust
vapour [véɪpər]	名 蒸気 water vapour 水蒸気	haze
condense [kəndéns]	動 短縮する；濃縮する, 凝縮する condense the whole chapter into three paragraphs 章全体を三段落に短縮する	abridge
atomise [ǽtəmàɪz]	動 (液体を)霧化する；細分化する a nozzle to atomise liquid 液体を霧化するノズル ＊ atomiser「噴霧器」。	nebulise
shoot [ʃúːt]	動 (写真・映画を)撮影する；撃つ The movie was shot in black and white. 映画は白黒で撮影された。 ＊この「撮影する」は頻出。	film
revere [rɪvíər]	動 崇拝する be revered as a national hero 国民的英雄として崇拝されている	adore
aptitude [ǽptət(j)ùːd]	名 適性；才能 an academic aptitude test 学力適性テスト	competence
intact [ɪntǽkt]	形 損なわれていない intact nature 手付かずの自然 ＊ undamaged, flawless, perfect と一緒に覚える。	unspoiled
monotonous [mənáːtənəs]	形 単調な monotonous and repetitive work 単調で繰り返しの多い作業	humdrum
proceeds [próʊsiːd]	名 売上高, 収益 the proceeds of the day その日の売上金	yield
orphanage [ɔ́ːrfənɪdʒ]	名 孤児院 adopt someone from an orphanage 人を孤児院から養子にもらう	orphan asylum

Track 174

単語／発音	語彙／フレーズ	同意表現	難易度
advocate [ǽdvəkət]	名 擁護者, 支持者；弁護士 a powerful advocate of women's rights 女性権利の強力な擁護者　＊名詞・動詞で発音が変わる。	proponent	A
drag [drǽg]	動 引きずる, 引っ張る drag a heavy suitcase 重いスーツケースを引きずり回す	haul	
forthcoming [fɔːrθkʌ́miŋ]	形 じきに来る予定の a forthcoming book 近刊書	upcoming	
roam [róum]	動 うろつく roam around foreign countries 外国を放浪する	drift	B
wander [wɑ́:ndər]	動 歩き回る wander around the city 街をぶらつく	ramble	
breed [brí:d]	名 品種；系統 a mixed-breed dog 雑種犬 ＊動詞「繁殖させる, 飼育する」も頻出。	variety	
sparsely [spɑ́:rsli]	副 まばらに, ちらほらと a sparsely populated area 過疎地	thinly	C
trait [tréɪt]	名 特質 physical traits 身体的特徴 ＊ feature, characteristic と一緒に覚える。	feature	
burrow [bə́:rou]	名 (動物の)巣穴 hide in a burrow 巣穴に隠れる	den	
offspring [ɔ́(:)fsprìŋ]	名 子孫 pass on 〜 to offspring 〜を子孫に伝える	descendent	D
decompose [dì:kəmpóuz]	動 分解する；腐敗する decompose at high temperatures 高温で分解する	break down	
scrub [skrʌ́b]	動 (ゴシゴシと)洗う scrub a bathtub 浴槽をゴシゴシと洗う	scour	

Track 175

単語／発音	語彙／フレーズ	同意表現
erosion [ɪróʊʒən]	名 浸食；腐食 soil erosion 土壌の浸食 ＊L 書き取りで出てもいいようにスペリングを覚える。	denudation
output [áʊtpʊ̀t]	名 生産高 the annual output 年間生産量 ＊「作品」という意味もある。	yield
exploitation [èksplɔɪtéɪʃən]	名 利用，搾取；開発 exploitation of intellectual property 知的財産の活用	utilisation
mining [máɪnɪŋ]	名 採掘 the coal-mining industry 石炭産業	digging
confront [kənfrʌ́nt]	動 直面する confront a difficult situation 困難な状況に直面する	face
yield [jíːld]	動 産出する yield a desired result 望ましい結果をもたらす	produce
plough [pláʊ]	名（農具の）すき a snow plough 雪かき機 ＊[英]。[米]では plow。	spade
irrigation [ìrəgéɪʃən]	名 灌漑 an irrigation channel 用水路 ＊R 川などから水を引くこと。農業の話で出てくる。	watering
contaminate [kəntǽmənèɪt]	動 汚染する contaminate drinking water 飲料水を汚染する	pollute
enlightened [ɪnláɪtnd]	形 啓蒙された；ものの分かった an enlightened people 文明開化した民族	educated
residue [rézɪd(j)ùː]	名 残り industrial residues 産業廃棄物 ＊打ち上げ花火の近くでは falling residue に注意！	remainder
lethal [líːθl]	形 致死の a lethal disease 命に関わる病気	deadly

Track 176

単語／発音	語彙／フレーズ	同意表現	難易度
rotate [róʊteɪt]	動 回転する rotate on an axis 軸を中心に回転する	revolve	A
focal [fóʊkl]	形 焦点の；とても重要な a focal point 焦点	of a focus	
defined [dɪfáɪnd]	形 明確な a defined border 明確な境界線	definite	
frown [fráʊn]	動 眉をひそめる, 難色を示す frown on cosmetic surgery 美容整形手術に難色を示す	lower	B
irritation [ìrətéɪʃən]	名 苛立たせること；苛立ち, 立腹 The heavy traffic is a constant source of irritation. 渋滞は常に苛立ちの原因です。	annoyance	
haunt [hɔ́ːnt]	動（幽霊・不吉な思いなどが）付きまとう a haunted house 幽霊屋敷 ＊考えや思い出の場合も使う。	obsess	
nuisance [n(j)úːsəns]	名 迷惑 nuisance e-mail 迷惑メール ＊i は発音しない。	trouble	C
superficial [sùːpərfíʃəl]	形 表面的な superficial knowledge うわべだけの知識	surficial	
originate [ərídʒənèɪt]	動 由来する originate from the same cause 同じ起源に由来する ＊ begin に置き換えられる。	derive	
subconscious [sʌbkáːnʃəs]	形 潜在意識の subconscious desire 意識下の欲望	subliminal	D
chunk [tʃʌ́ŋk]	名 塊 a large chunk of rock 大きな岩の塊 ＊単語は chunk（意味の塊）で覚えれば使えるようになる。	lump	
bond [báːnd]	名 絆, 結び付き bonds of friendship 友情の絆	link	

193

単語／発音	語彙／フレーズ	同意表現
clue [klúː]	名 手掛かり，ヒント a clue to the solution 解明の糸口	hint
venture [véntʃər]	動 危険を冒して進む venture into an unexplored field 未開拓の分野に進出する	embark
synthesise [sínθəsàɪz]	動 合成する；総合する synthesise the parts into a whole 部分から全体を作り上げる	combine
innumerable [ɪn(j)úːmərəbl]	形 数え切れない innumerable stars of the Milky Way 天の川の無数の星	countless
reagent [riéɪdʒənt]	名 試薬 diagnostic reagent 診断試薬	chemical agent
cleave [klíːv]	動 割る；切り裂く cleave wood for the fire 焚き火用に薪を割る	split
hybrid [háɪbrɪd]	名 交配種 a hybrid between a horse and a donkey 馬とロバの交配種	crossbreed
petal [pétl]	名 花びら a piece of a petal 1枚の花びら	corolla
scented [séntɪd]	形 よい香りのする；香水をつけた a scented candle よい香りのするろうそく	perfumed
tolerance [tάːlərəns]	名 許容，寛大；忍耐，我慢 religious tolerance 信仰の自由	permissiveness
susceptible [səséptəbl]	形 影響を受けやすい be susceptible to diseases 病気にかかりやすい ＊⇔ immune	vulnerable
premium [príːmiəm]	名 割増；景品 premium price プレミアム価格	extra

Track 178

単語／発音	語彙／フレーズ	同意表現	難易度
prune [prúːn]	動 刈り取る prune a branch 枝を切り取る	clip	A
succulent [sʌ́kjələnt]	形 (果肉などが) 水気の多い succulent plants 多肉植物	juicy	
tint [tínt]	名 色合い tint control 色合い調整	colour shade	
hamper [hǽmpər]	動 妨げる hamper economic development 経済発展を妨げる ＊impede も一緒に覚えたい。	hinder	B
lush [lʌ́ʃ]	形 (植物が) 青々とした lush fertile land 緑の多い豊かな土地 ＊感じとしてプラスの意味。	exuberant	
barren [bǽrən]	形 不毛な；実を結ばない a barren desert area 不毛の砂漠地帯 ＊出るとすれば土地に関して。	infertile	
despondency [dɪspɑ́ːndənsi]	名 落胆, 失望 fall into despondency 意気消沈する	disheartenment	C
horrifying [hɔ́ːrəfàɪɪŋ]	形 (光景などが) 恐ろしい a horrifying plane crash 恐ろしい飛行機墜落事故	frightful	
degradation [dègrədéɪʃən]	名 (品格・質・価値の) 低下；劣化 environmental degradation 環境の悪化	debasement	
destabilise [diːstéɪbəlàɪz]	動 不安定にする；動揺させる destabilise society 社会を揺るがす	unsettle	D
crumble [krʌ́mbl]	動 砕ける, 崩れる crumble to the ground 地面に崩れ落ちる	fall apart	
revert [rɪvə́ːrt]	動 (元の状態に) 戻る revert to the previous stage 前段階に戻る	return	

単語／発音	語彙／フレーズ	同意表現
flee [flíː]	動 逃れる flee from the reality 現実から逃れる	run away
frightening [fráɪtnɪŋ]	形 恐ろしい, ぞっとするような a frightening crime 恐ろしい犯罪	terrifying
ramification [ræməfɪkéɪʃən]	名 (好ましくない)結果；分岐 environmental ramifications 環境に与える悪影響	consequence
mortality [mɔːrtǽləti]	名 死亡率, 死亡数；死ぬ運命 mortality from lung cancer 肺がんによる死亡率	fatality
toll [tóʊl]	名 犠牲者数, 犠牲；料金, 通行料 the death toll 死亡者数 ＊R 「犠牲；通行料」どちらも頻出。toll free は「通話料無料」。	casualties
halt [hɔ́ːlt]	動 中止させる halt global warming 地球温暖化に歯止めをかける	stop
boundless [báʊndləs]	形 無限の；広大な boundless universe 無限の宇宙	limitless
artifice [ɑ́ːrtəfɪs]	名 策略 get what one wants by artifice 策略によって欲しいものを得る	ruse
delusion [dɪlúːʒən]	名 妄想；惑わし a delusion of persecution 被害妄想	illusion
vigilant [vídʒələnt]	形 油断のない, 用心深い vigilant eyes 油断のない目	watchful
mite [máɪt]	名 ダニ；ごく小さいもの mite allergen ダニアレルギー起因物質	tick
paediatric [pìːdiǽtrɪk]	形 小児科の a paediatric hospital 小児科病院	of the medical care of children

Track 180

単語／発音	語彙／フレーズ	同意表現	難易度
mucus [mjúːkəs]	名 粘液 mucus membrane 粘膜	slime	A
proximity [prɑːksíməti]	名 近接 advantage of the proximity to the city centre 街の中心に近接しているという利点	closeness	
enigma [ənígmə]	名 謎；謎めいた言葉 solve an enigma of life 生命の謎を解く ＊puzzle も同義語。	mystery	
antiseptic [æntiséptɪk]	形 防腐の, 消毒作用のある antiseptic properties of salt 塩の持つ殺菌作用の性質 ＊名詞では「防腐剤, 消毒剤」。	disinfectant	B
literacy [lítərəsi]	名 読み書きの能力；教養 a high literacy rate in Japan 日本の高い識字率	reading and writing ability	
wryly [ráɪli]	副 皮肉っぽく answer wryly 皮肉っぽく答える ＊発音注意！	cynically	
amorphous [əmɔ́ːrfəs]	形 不定形の amorphous shapes of jellyfish クラゲの不定形な姿	shapeless	C
skew [skjúː]	動 ゆがめる be skewed by a prejudice 先入観によってゆがめられた	distort	
disparity [dɪspérəti]	名 相違, 不等 disparity between theory and reality 理論と現実の相違	inequality	
reckon [rékən]	動 計算する；考える reckon the loss and gain 損得を計算する ＊[英]では think と同じ意味で I reckon that SV と使う。	calculate	D
watertight [wɔ́ːtərtàɪt]	形 水も漏らさぬ, 完璧な a watertight defence 水も漏らさぬ防御 ＊もちろん「防水の」という意味もある。	perfect	
genetically [dʒənétɪkəli]	副 遺伝子上で Genetically Modified foods (GM foods) 遺伝子組み換え食品	in genes	

Track 181

単語／発音	語彙／フレーズ	同意表現
transgenic [trænsdʒénɪk]	形 遺伝子組み換えの create transgenic animals 遺伝子導入動物を生み出す	genetically modified
ravage [rǽvɪdʒ]	動 荒廃させる a region ravaged by famine 飢饉により荒廃させられた地域	devastate
insecticide [ɪnséktəsàɪd]	名 殺虫剤 spray an insecticide on plants 植物に殺虫剤をまく ＊-cide は「殺し」を表す接尾辞。	pesticide
resurgence [rɪsə́ːrdʒəns]	名 復活，再起 resurgence in popularity 人気の復活	revitalisation
prescribe [prɪskráɪb]	動 規定する；処方する the sentence that federal law prescribes 連邦法が規定する判決	stipulate
dose [dóʊs]	名 (薬の)一服，服用量 a lethal dose of poison 致死量の毒	dosage
elicit [ɪlísət]	動 (情報・結論を)引き出す，聞き出す elicit a confession 自白を引き出す	draw out
restoration [rèstəréɪʃən]	名 回復；復元 restoration of peace 平和の回復 ＊restoration of buildings のように「修復」も頻出。	reconstruction
inflammation [ìnfləméɪʃən]	名 炎症；発火 reduce inflammation 炎症を抑える	flare
arthritis [ɑːθráɪtɪs]	名 関節炎 a patient with rheumatic arthritis リウマチ性関節炎の患者	joint inflammation
degenerative [dɪdʒénərəɪtɪv]	形 徐々に悪化する；堕落しつつある a degenerative disease 退行性疾患	gradually worsening
intoxicated [ɪntɑ́ːksəkèɪtɪd]	形 酩酊した；熱狂した；中毒した intoxicated driving 酒酔い運転	drunk

単語／発音	語彙／フレーズ	同意表現	難易度
recoil [rɪkɔ́ɪl]	動 たじろぐ，ひるむ recoil in horror 恐ろしくなってひるむ	wince	A
bleak [blíːk]	形 荒涼とした a bleak desert 荒涼とした砂漠	stark	
topographical [tàpəgrǽfɪkl]	形 地形の，地勢上の a topographical feature 地形の特徴	geographical	
geyser [gáɪzər]	名 間欠泉 geyser eruption 間欠泉噴出	blowhole	B
geothermal [dʒìːouθə́ːrml]	形 地熱の geothermal energy 地熱エネルギー	geothermic	
maverick [mǽvərɪk]	名 異端者；一匹オオカミ an internet maverick ネット界の異端児	rebel	
veer [víər]	動 進行方向を変える veer off course コースからそれる	swerve	C
laconic [ləkɑ́ːnɪk]	形 簡潔な laconic explanation 簡潔な説明	terse	
oblique [əblíːk]	形 傾いた in an oblique direction 斜め方向に	inclined	
coin [kɔ́ɪn]	動 造語する coin a term 用語を新しく作り出す	create	D
detour [díːtuər]	名 回り道，迂回 make a small detour 少し回り道をする ＊発音に注意。	roundabout	
tun [tʌ́n]	名 大だる the whole tun of wine 大だるいっぱいのワイン	cask	

単語／発音	語彙／フレーズ	同意表現
traverse [trəvə́ːrs]	動 横断する traverse the Pacific Ocean 太平洋を横断する ＊ traverse the desert「砂漠を横切る」も頻出。	cross
abate [əbéɪt]	動 減らす；(痛みなどを) 和らげる abate a tax 減税する	decrease
convoy [káːnvɔɪ]	名 船団, 車両隊；護送 a convoy of merchant ships 商船隊	fleet
squander [skwáːndər]	動 浪費する, 乱費する squander one's inheritance in gambling 賭事に遺産を浪費する	waste
crude [krúːd]	形 加工されていない；生の crude oil 原油 ＊「大まかな」の意味でも出る。	raw
inhale [ɪnhéɪl]	動 吸い込む inhale cigarette smoke タバコの煙を吸い込む	breathe in
effluent [éfluənt]	形 流れ出る effluent wastewater 流出廃水	outflowing
crockery [kráːkəri]	名 瀬戸物, 陶器類 microwave-safe crockery 電子レンジでも使える瀬戸物 ＊[英]。[米]では earthenware。	dinnerware
cutlery [kʌ́tləri]	名 (ナイフ・フォークなどの) 食卓食器類 stainless-steel cutlery ステンレス製の食器類	silverware
virtually [vɚ́ːrtʃuəli]	副 ほぼ；事実上 virtually the same ほとんど同じ	nearly
isotope [áɪsətòʊp]	名 同位元素 isotope analysis 同位体分析	
moon [múːn]	名 衛星 the moons of Jupiter 木星の衛星	satellite

単語／発音	語彙／フレーズ	同意表現	難易度
vent [vént]	名 穴；通気孔 a smoke vent 排煙口	blowhole	A
surmise [sərmáɪz]	動 推量する surmise the mind of ～ ～の胸中を推し量る	suppose	
host [hóust]	名 多数 a host of ～ 多数の～	horde	
spew [spjú:]	動 吐き出す；噴出する spew carbon dioxide into the atmosphere 二酸化炭素を大気中に排出する	belch out	B
seep [sí:p]	動 染み込む；染み出る seep into the ground 地面に染み込む	infiltrate	
creep [krí:p]	動 忍び寄る；はう creep up on a victim 犠牲者に忍び寄る ＊creepy は「気味悪い」。	stalk	
reassurance [rìəʃúərəns]	名 安心 create a sense of reassurance 安心感を生む	ease	C
cylindrical [səlíndrɪkl]	形 円筒形の cylindrical structure 円柱構造	tubular	
fidelity [fɪdéləti]	名 忠誠；忠実 fidelity to the country 国への忠誠	faithfulness	
longitude [lá:ndʒət(j)ù:d]	名 経度 find the latitude and longitude of a site 現場の経緯度を見出す　＊⇔ latitude		D
convict [kənvíkt]	動 (人に)有罪判決を下す be convicted of murder 殺人罪で有罪の判決を受ける ＊名詞「罪人、既決囚」。	find guilty	
initiate [ɪníʃièɪt]	動 開始する initiate a dialogue with students 学生たちとの対話を始める ＊begin, start と置き換え可。	start	

Track 185

単語／発音	語彙／フレーズ	同意表現
transoceanic [trænsòuʃiǽnɪk]	形 大洋横断の a transoceanic submarine cable 大洋横断海底ケーブル ＊trans- は「〜の向こう側へ」を表す接頭辞。	across-the-ocean
discrete [dɪskríːt]	形 個別の，ばらばらの four discrete stages in a process ある過程における4つの個別的段階	distinct
requisite [rékwəzɪt]	名 必要条件 requisite for life 生活必需品	requirement
integrity [ɪntégrəti]	名 誠実；高潔；完全性 a woman of high integrity 非常に誠実な女性	soundness
ponderous [pɑ́ːndərəs]	形 重たい；扱いにくい a ponderous volume ずっしりと重たい書物	unwieldy
discursive [dɪskə́ːrsɪv]	形 とりとめのない；広範囲にわたる a discursive conversation とりとめのない会話	excursive
erudite [érjədàɪt]	形 学識のある，博学な an erudite discussion among scholars 学者の間での博学な議論	learned
alliteration [əlìtəréɪʃən]	名 頭韻 the use of alliteration in poetry 詩の中での頭韻の使用	head rhyme
colloquial [kəlóukwiəl]	形 口語の a colloquial expression 口語表現	spoken
hilarity [hɪlǽrəti]	名 浮かれ騒ぎ turn into hilarity 浮かれ騒ぎの状態になる ＊形容詞 hilarious の方がさらに頻出。	amusement
inflict [ɪnflíkt]	動 押し付ける；苦しめる inflict a heavy tax on people 人々に重い税金をかける	impose
legion [líːdʒən]	名 軍団；多数 legions of worldwide fans 世界中のたくさんのファン	host

単語／発音	語彙／フレーズ	同意表現	難易度
statute [stǽtʃuːt]	名 法律, 制定法, 成立法；規制 consumer-protection statute 消費者保護法	law	A
clamour [klǽmər]	動 うるさく要求する；やかましく叫ぶ clamour for his resignation 彼の辞任を強く要求する	demand	
anarchy [ǽnərki]	名 無政府状態；無秩序, 混乱 This country is collapsing into anarchy. この国は無政府状態に陥っている。	lawlessness	
courtesy [kə́ːrtəsi]	形（バス・車・電話が）無料の a courtesy bus（送迎などの）無料バス ＊名詞だと「礼儀；厚意」。	free	B
recount [rikáunt]	動 詳しく話す recount the story of 〜 〜の話を詳述する	enlarge on	
miraculously [mərǽkjələsli]	副 奇跡的に miraculously escape injury 奇跡的に怪我をせずに済む	by a miracle	
concussion [kɑːnkʌ́ʃən]	名 振動；衝撃 have a concussion of the brain 脳震とうを起こす	commotion	C
deteriorate [dɪtíəriərèɪt]	動 悪化する；堕落する His condition has deteriorated in the ICU. 集中治療室で彼の容態は悪化した。 ＊自動詞でも他動詞でも使える。	degrade	
detachment [dɪtǽtʃmənt]	名 超然としていること, 無関心；分離 detachment from the outside world 外界からの超脱	aloofness	
debris [dəbríː]	名 がれき, 破片, 残骸 be buried under debris がれきの下敷きになる ＊発音注意！	rubble	D
obesity [oʊbíːsəti]	名 肥満 prevent obesity in children 児童の肥満を防ぐ ＊obese は「肥満の」。	fatness	
solace [sɑ́ːləs]	名 慰め seek solace in religion 宗教に慰めを求める ＊consolation は「慰め」。consolation match は「敗者復活戦」。	comfort	

203

単語／発音	語彙／フレーズ	同意表現
disabuse [dìsəbjúːz]	動 （迷い・誤解を）解く；解放する disabuse a person of superstition 迷信を取り除く	disillusion
culprit [kʌ́lprɪt]	名 容疑者；被告人 turn the culprit over to the police 容疑者を警察に引き渡す ＊turn over「引き渡す」。	suspect
threshold [θréʃhoʊld]	名 出発点；敷居 at the threshold of their careers 彼らのキャリアの出発点に	start
morbid [mɔ́ːrbɪd]	形 病的な；不健全な have a morbid fear of ～ ～を病的に恐れている	pathological
predispose [prìːdɪspóʊz]	動 （病気などに）かかりやすくする be genetically predisposed to ～ 遺伝的に～にかかりやすい ＊predisposition「傾向, 性質」。	susceptible
modification [màːdəfɪkéɪʃən]	名 変更；調整 make a slight modification to the design 設計に若干の修正を加える　＊change の類義語。	adjustment
claim [kléɪm]	動 （事故などが人命を）奪う Traffic accidents claim many lives annually. 交通事故が毎年多くの人命を奪う。＊もちろん「主張する」の意味あり。	take
hitherto [híðərtùː]	副 これまでは hitherto unused land これまで使われていなかった土地	so far
budding [bʌ́dɪŋ]	形 新進の support a budding artist 新進の芸術家を支援する ＊bud は「芽, つぼみ」。	up-and-coming
prospective [prəspéktɪv]	形 将来の；見込みのある a prospective candidate for president 将来の大統領候補	coming
-oriented [-ɔ́ːrièntɪd]	形 ～本位の, ～志向の, ～重視の profit-oriented organisations 利益本位の団体 ＊-orientated と同じ。	conscious
heterogeneous [hètəroʊdʒíːniəs]	形 異質のものからなる, 混成の a heterogeneous society of today 今日の混成社会 ＊⇔ homogeneous「同質の；均一の」。	diverse

単語／発音	語彙／フレーズ	同意表現	難易度
profuse [prəfjúːs]	形 夥しい，豊富な；物惜しみしない Profuse sweating is a symptom of heat exhaustion. 夥しい発汗は熱中症の症状です。	plentiful	A
tingling [tíŋglɪŋ]	形 ちくちくする a tingling pain ちくちくする痛み	stinging	
intensify [ɪnténsəfàɪ]	動 激しくする；増強する Increasing demand intensified competition. 高まる需要が競争を激化させた。	escalate	
disorientated [dɪsɔ́ːrièntɪd]	形 混乱して，方向が分からなくなって feel surprised and disorientated 驚き，うろたえている ＊disoriented も同じ。	confused	B
catastrophic [kæ̀təstrɑ́ːfɪk]	形 壊滅的な a catastrophic disaster 壊滅的な災害 ＊名詞は catastrophe「大災害」。	disastrous	
devastate [dévəstèɪt]	動 荒廃させる；打ちのめす The hurricane devastated many people. そのハリケーンが多くの人々を打ちのめした。	destroy	
benign [bənáɪn]	形 害のない；親切な a benign tumour 良性の腫瘍	harmless	C
overwhelming [òʊvərwélmɪŋ]	形 圧倒的な，とてもかなわない win overwhelming support 圧倒的な支持を得る	very powerful	
immemorial [ìməmɔ́ːriəl]	形 太古の，遠い昔の way back to time immemorial 太古の時代にさかのぼって ＊way は副詞で back に掛かり，「はるかに」。	ancient	
bequeath [bɪkwíːð]	動 遺譲する；遺す bequeath money to one's son 息子にお金を遺す ＊R pass down との書き換えに注意。	leave	D
permeate [pə́ːrmièɪt]	動 浸透する，染み込む；行き渡る Water permeates the soil. 水は地面に染み込む。 ＊他動詞で「〜に広がる」。	seep	
plateau [plætóʊ]	名 停滞(安定)期；高原・台地 reach a plateau 停滞期に達する ＊自動詞で「(主語の)進歩が止まる」でも使われる。	period of little change	

Track 189

単語／発音	語彙／フレーズ	同意表現
meteorologist [mìːtiərάːlədʒɪst]	名 気象学者 weather reports by meteorologists 気象学者の気象情報	weather forecaster
surge [sə́ːrdʒ]	名 高まり，急激な増加；うねり a surge in the oil price 原油価格の急騰 ＊W1 グラフ説明で使える。	explosion
lucrative [lúːkrətɪv]	形 儲かる a lucrative business 儲かる商売	profitable
fete [féɪt]	動 歓迎する；敬意を表する be feted everywhere 至る所で歓迎された ＊発音注意！	welcome
provided [prəváɪdɪd]	接 もし〜ならば provided the weather is clear もし天気さえ良ければ ＊動詞と間違えないこと。	only if
relish [rélɪʃ]	動 楽しむ；味わう relish a good joke 面白い冗談を楽しむ	enjoy
literati [lìtərάːti]	名 知識人；知識階級 the middle class literati 中産階級の知識人	intellectual
mythology [mɪθάːlədʒi]	名 神話 Greek mythology ギリシャ神話	myths
redemption [rɪdémpʃən]	名 救済 God's redemption 神による救済	salvation
bode [bóʊd]	動 前兆となる，予示する This bodes well (ill) for you. これは，あなたにとって良い(悪い)兆候だ。	portend
low-profile [lóʊ-próʊfaɪl]	形 控えめな；目立たない a low-profile attitude 控えめな態度 ＊profile は「注目度；横顔」という意味もある。	quiet
bizarre [bɪzάːr]	形 奇妙な；風変わりな bizarre deep-sea creatures 奇妙な深海生物 ＊odd, funny も覚えよう。	strange

Track 190

単語／発音	語彙／フレーズ	同意表現	難易度
wed [wéd]	動 固執させる；堅く結びつける be wedded to old customs 古い慣習に固執する ＊be wedded to 〜 ＝ stick to 〜「〜に拘る」。	stick	A
proportionally [prəpɔ́ːrʃənli]	副 比例して，釣り合って proportionally dependent 互いに均等に依存して	in proportion to	
pharmaceutical [fɑ̀ːrməs(j)úːtɪkl]	形 製薬の the pharmaceutical industry 製薬業	of pharmacy	
cripple [krípl]	動 駄目にする；体を不自由にさせる High interest rates crippled industry. 高金利が産業を駄目にした。	damage	B
maize [méɪz]	名 トウモロコシ；トウモロコシの実 maize growers トウモロコシ栽培者	corn	
utopia [juːtóʊpiə]	名 理想郷，理想的場所 a vision of a utopia 理想郷という幻想	paradise	
palatable [pǽlətəbl]	形 味のよい，口に合う harmless and palatable to vertebrates 脊椎動物にとって無害でおいしい	tasty	C
strain [stréɪn]	名 負担，重圧；緊張 serious strains on the global environment 地球環境への深刻な負担	pressure	
operate [ɑ́ːpərèɪt]	動 操業する，運営する；運転する The firm operates from the south of England. その会社は英国南部で操業中だ。	do business	
form [fɔ́ːrm]	名 学年；学級 in the sixth form 6年生で ＊[英]だが，やや古い用語。	grade	D
vulnerable [vʌ́lnərəbl]	形 弱点がある，傷つきやすい especially vulnerable to attack 攻撃に特に弱い ＊R 単純な weak との書き換えに注意！	weak	
buffer [bʌ́fər]	動 衝撃を和らげる，緩和する buffer the effects of inflation インフレの影響を和らげる ＊鎮痛剤×××リンという薬がありますね。	lessen	

207

Track 191

単語／発音	語彙／フレーズ	同意表現
menace [ménəs]	名 脅威, 脅威を与えるもの menace to crops 作物への脅威	threat
tense [téns]	形 緊張した；ぴんと張った She sounded tense. 彼女は緊張しているようだった。	strained
spasm [spǽzm]	名 けいれん, ひきつけ；発作 a muscle spasm 筋肉のけいれん	cramp
strip [stríp]	名 （土地・布・板の）細長い1片 cut a strip of paper 6 cm wide 細長い紙片を6センチ幅に切る	narrow piece
lenticular [lentíkjələr]	形 レンズ状の；レンズの lenticular clouds レンズ型の雲	lentoid
mains [méɪn]	名 （水道・ガスの）本管；電気幹線 turn off the water at the mains 水道の本管を止める	the chief pipe
rear [ríər]	動 育てる；飼育する rear six children 6人の子供を育てる ＊フレーズなら bring up。	raise
poultry [póʊltri]	名 家禽（飼い鳥類）；鶏肉 rear sheep and poultry 羊と家禽を飼育する ＊食用に飼っている鳥のこと。	farmyard birds
tender [téndər]	形 （傷などが）触ると痛む, 敏感な His injured leg is still tender. 彼の負傷した足はまだ痛む。 ＊本来の「傷つきやすい；柔らかい」から連想したい。	painful
fertilise [fə́ːrtəlàɪz]	動 （動植物を）受精（受胎）させる a fertilised egg 受精卵 ＊ fertile「（土地が）肥えた」を覚える。	inseminate
deadstock [dédstɑ́ːk]	名 農機具；売れ残り品 livestock and deadstock 家畜と農機具	farm machines
repercussion [rìːpərkʌ́ʃən]	名 影響, 余波；反響 serious repercussions on the economy 経済体制への深刻な影響	consequence

Track 192

単語／発音	語彙／フレーズ	同意表現	難易度
outlay [áutlèɪ]	名 費用，支出 an advertising outlay 広告宣伝費 ＊他の類義語 spending, expenditure。	expense	A
decoy [díːkɔɪ]	名 おとり，（鳥などを）おびき寄せる手段 a decoy duck おとりのカモ ＊ decoy cameras は「ダミー防犯カメラ」のこと。	lure	
perimeter [pərímətər]	名 境界；周囲 a huge perimeter wall of the jail 刑務所の巨大な外壁	boundary	
glazing [gléɪzɪŋ]	名 （窓用の）ガラス double glazing to keep out the cold 寒さを締め出す二重ガラス	pane	B
hinge [híndʒ]	名 蝶番；要点 doors with hinges 蝶番の付いたドア	movable joint	
adjacent [ədʒéɪsnt]	形 近隣の，付近の cooperation among adjacent nations 近隣諸国間の協力 ＊ neighbouring も近い意味。	adjoining	
self-esteem [sélf-ɪstíːm]	名 自尊心 enhance self-esteem 自尊心を高める ＊ conceit「うぬぼれ」。	pride	C
preoccupation [priːɑːkjəpéɪʃən]	名 夢中にさせるもの；先入観 Art is his sole preoccupation. 芸術が唯一，彼を夢中にさせるものだ。	obsession	
excusable [ɪkskjúːzəbl]	形 許される，無理もない an excusable mistake under the circumstances その状況下では無理もない誤り	forgivable	
dilute [daɪlúːt]	動 薄める，弱める dilute strong bleach with water 強い漂白剤を水で薄める	thin out	D
enquire [ɪnkwáɪər]	動 尋ねる；調査する enquire of a shop assistant about the price 価格について販売員に尋ねる　＊[英]。	ask	
refresher [rɪfréʃər]	名 再教育；気分を刷新するもの（人） take a refresher course every five years 5年ごとに再教育講座を受ける	re-education	

単語／発音	語彙／フレーズ	同意表現
procrastination [prəkræstɪnéɪʃən]	名 先送り, ぐずぐず先延ばしすること avoid procrastination in business ビジネスではぐずぐず先延ばしすることを避ける	delay
outskirts [áʊtskɚːrts]	名 (町, 都市の)外れ, 郊外 live in the outskirts of London ロンドン郊外に住む	outlying areas
jury [dʒʊ́əri]	名 陪審員団；審査員団 sit on a jury 陪審員を務める	juror
wilderness [wíldɚrnəs]	名 未開拓の大自然, 荒野 the arctic wilderness 北極の未開の大自然 ＊発音注意!	wilds
self-contained [sélf-kəntéɪnd]	形 自給自足の self-contained community 自給自足のコミュニティ	independent
cutting-edge [kʌ́tɪŋ-èdʒ]	形 最先端の cutting-edge technology 最先端の技術	state of the art
consignment [kənsáɪnmənt]	名 委託；委託販売品 sell one's belongings at a consignment store 中古品委託販売店で持物を売る	delivery
sturdy [stɚ́ːrdi]	形 丈夫な, 頑丈な a small but sturdy car 小さいけど頑丈な車	strong
typify [típəfàɪ]	動 ～を代表する, ～の典型となる He typified politicians in the times. 彼はその時代を代表する政治家だった。	symbolise
fungus [fʌ́ŋgəs]	名 菌類, きのこ a type of fungus 菌類の一種 ＊複数は fungi。	
extraterrestrial [èkstrətəréstriəl]	形 地球外の extraterrestrial life 地球外生命 ＊略すと ET。	alien
unmanned [ʌnmǽnd]	形 無人の, 自動操縦の unmanned exploration 無人探査 ＊乗り物に人が乗っていないことを表す。	automatic

Track 194

単語／発音	語彙／フレーズ	同意表現	難易度
inaugurate [ɪnɔ́ːgjərèɪt]	動 〜の落成式を行う，〜を始める inaugurate the museum 博物館の落成式を行う ＊officially openということ。inauguralは「初開催の」の意味もある。	launch	A
majesty [mǽdʒəsti]	名 陛下，王，皇帝 Her Majesty the Queen 女王陛下	Royal Highness	
case [kéɪs]	名 真実；事例；事件 If that's the case, もしそれが事実なら,	fact	
stick [stík]	動 執着する；離れずついて行く stick to one's own idea 自身の意見に執着する ＊stick in my mind は「頭に残る」。	cling	B
constraint [kənstréɪnt]	名 制限，制約；強制 government constraints on the industry その業界への政府の締め付け	restriction	
unsound [ʌnsáʊnd]	形 不十分な；信用できない be regarded as unsound 不十分とみなされる ＊形容詞のsound（信頼できる）は頻出。	inaccurate	
sundries [sʌ́ndriz]	名 雑費，雑貨 filled with sundries 様々なものでいっぱい	odds and ends	C
anecdotal [æ̀nɪkdóʊtl]	形 必ずしも信頼できない；逸話的な an anecdotal story without hard evidence 確証のない不確かな話	unreliable	
elastic [ɪlǽstɪk]	形 弾力のある；伸縮自在の an elastic bandage 伸縮性の包帯	flexible	
overrun [òʊvərrʌ́n]	動 超過する，群がる，侵略する overrun the time limit 時間制限を超過する	exceed	D
sanitation [sæ̀nətéɪʃən]	名 公衆衛生 food sanitation 食品衛生 ＊hygieneも同義。	cleanliness	
illiterate [ɪlítərət]	形 無学の；読み書きのできない musically illiterate 音楽については無知な ＊名詞「読み書きができない人」。	uneducated	

211

Track 195

単語／発音	語彙／フレーズ	同意表現
weave [wíːv]	動 機をおる weave on a loom 織機でおる	knit
reimburse [rìːɪmbə́ːrs]	動 払い戻す, 返金する reimburse expenses 費用を払い戻す	refund
nomadic [noʊmǽdɪk]	形 遊牧の；放浪生活の a nomadic hunter-gatherer さまよえる狩猟採集民	wandering
dissertation [dìsərtéɪʃən]	名 学位論文 complete the doctoral dissertation 博士論文を書き上げる	thesis
insight [ínsàɪt]	名 洞察(力), 見識 insight into the problem その問題への洞察	observation
devise [dɪváɪz]	動 考案する；工夫する devise a new system to control traffic 交通制御の新システムを考案する	invent
dent [dént]	動 へこませる, 傷つける dent a wing of a car 車のフェンダーをへこませる ＊ fender は[英]。	depress
filthy [fílθi]	形 汚れた, 不潔な a filthy kitchen 汚れた台所	dirty
itinerary [aɪtínərèri]	名 旅程 a provisional itinerary 暫定的な旅程	route
invaluable [ɪnvǽljuəbl]	形 非常に貴重な serve an invaluable role 非常に貴重な役割を果たす ＊ valuable とほぼ同じ。	priceless
storey [stɔ́ːri]	名 階 a two-storey house 2 階建ての家 ＊[米]では story と書く。	story
CV(curriculum vitae) [kəríkjələm váɪtiː]	名 履歴書 submit a CV 履歴書を提出する ＊[英]。[米]では通常 resume。	resume

単語／発音	語彙／フレーズ	同意表現	難易度
ethos [íːθɑːs]	名 精神；特性；気質 the ethos of the Olympics オリンピック精神	spirit	A
offshoot [ɔ́(ː)fʃùːt]	名 派生物, 分派；横枝 offshoot of the group その団体の分派	spin-off	
quote [kwóut]	名 (略式)見積額 get a quote 見積もりをもらう ＊動詞だと「値をつける；引用する」の意味がある。	estimate	
vice versa [váɪsi vəːrsə]	副 反対に；逆もまた同様 〜 and vice versa その反対も正しい	on the contrary	B
clone [klóun]	名 クローン, 複製品 a clone of the computer そのコンピュータの複製品	reproduction	
jargon [dʒɑ́ːrɡən]	名 専門用語；訳の分からない言葉 business jargon ビジネス用語 ＊terminology も集合的に「専門用語」の意味。	lingo	
conservation [kɑ̀ːnsərvéɪʃən]	名 保護, 管理, 保存 wildlife conservation 野生生物の保護	protection	C
detergent [dɪtə́ːrdʒənt]	名 洗剤 dishwashing detergent 食器洗い用洗剤 ＊動詞 deterge「ぬぐい去る」。	soap	
simmer [símər]	動 とろとろ煮える simmer on low heat 弱火で煮る	boil	
lather [lǽðər]	動 泡立つ rub until it lathers 泡立つまでこする ＊名詞も lather「泡」。	bubble	D
inlet [ínlət]	名 入り江, 注入口 a narrow inlet 細い入り江 ＊outlet は「出口, 排水口」。	estuary	
fir [fə́ːr]	名 モミ；モミ材 collection of fir leaves モミの葉を集めたもの		

Track 197

単語／発音	語彙／フレーズ	同意表現
cedar [síːdər]	名 シーダー, ヒマラヤスギ a giant cedar tree 巨大なヒマラヤスギの木	
fierce [fíərs]	形 獰猛な, 荒々しい a fierce tiger 獰猛なトラ	violent
solitary [sɑ́lətèri]	形 孤独を好む, 単独行動する take a solitary walk ひとりで散歩する ＊Sそのまま使えるフレーズ。	lonely
retractable [rɪtræktəbl]	形 収納できる；取り消しできる a knife with a retractable blade 刃先収納式ナイフ	stowaway
distributor [dɪstríbjətər]	名 販売業者, 販売代理店 a wholesale liquor distributor 酒類卸販売業者	dealer
foyer [fɔ́ɪər]	名 ロビー, 待合室 the foyer of the theatre 劇場のロビー	lobby
dubbed [dʌ́bd]	形 （映画など）吹替えの a movie dubbed into Japanese 日本語に吹き替えられた映画 ＊ dubbing「ダビング」を思い出して！	
turnout [tə́ːrnàut]	名 参加者数, 生産高 have a large turnout 出席者が多い	attendance
civil engineering [sívl èndʒəníərɪŋ]	名 土木工学 civil engineering machinery 土木機械 ＊Rこれが出たら建設に関係する。「市民の…」ではない。	
standing [stændɪŋ]	形 動かない, 流れない standing water よどんだ水 ＊ standings は「順位表」。	still
negotiate [nəɡóuʃièɪt]	動 交渉する negotiate a business deal 商取引について交渉する	talk
custody [kʌ́stədi]	名 保護；保護権；管理, 保管 custody of a child 子供の養育権	guardianship

Track 198

単語／発音	語彙／フレーズ	同意表現	難易度
certify [sə́ːrtəfàɪ]	動 証明する, 認証する certify the accounts as correct 鑑定書を正確だと証明する	verify	A
hard-wearing [háːrd-wéərɪŋ]	形 丈夫な, 長持ちする a hard-wearing leather jacket 丈夫な革ジャン	durable	
colourfast [kʌ́lərfæ̀st]	形 変色(退色)しない a colourfast ink 変色しないインク	resistance to discolourment	
aboriginal [æ̀bərídʒənl]	形 先住の, 土着の aboriginal people in America アメリカの先住民	indigenous	B
accredited [əkrédɪtɪd]	形 認可された, 公認の an accredited high school （大学進学基準としての）認可高校	official	
replenish [rɪplénɪʃ]	動 補給する, 補充する replenish our stock of food 食料の在庫を補充する	refill	
muddle [mʌ́dl]	動 混乱させる, ごちゃ混ぜにする muddle one's mind 考えを混乱させる	confuse	C
viral [váɪrəl]	形 ウイルス性の, ウイルスの viral infections ウイルス感染	virus-caused	
undermine [ʌ̀ndərmáɪn]	動 害する, 衰えさせる Smoking undermines your health. 喫煙は健康を害する。	weaken	
phase [féɪz]	名 段階, 局面 enter the final phase 最終段階に入る	stage	D
slumber [slʌ́mbər]	名 眠り, まどろみ fall into a slumber 眠りに落ちる	sleep	
paralyse [pǽrəlàɪz]	動 麻痺させる Legs are paralysed. 脚が麻痺している。	disable	

Track 199

単語／発音	語彙／フレーズ	同意表現
resort [rɪzɔ́ːrt]	名（困難を切り抜ける）手段 as a last resort 最後の手段として	recourse
wean [wíːn]	動（習慣から）引き離す；離乳させる wean someone off smoking 喫煙の習慣から引き離す	gradually stop
marshal [máːrʃəl]	動案内する, 先導する；整列させる Guests are marshalled. ゲストは案内された。	usher
detective [dɪtéktɪv]	名刑事；探偵 a private detective 私立探偵	investigator
en-suite [àːn swíːt]	形（寝室と）ひと揃いになっている a bedroom with the bathroom en-suite バスルームとひと続きになった寝室	a suite of
communal [kəmjúːnl]	形共有の, 共同使用の a communal kitchen in the dorm 寮の共同キッチン	shared
radius [réɪdiəs]	名半径 within a radius of 50 miles 半径 50 マイル以内の ＊⇔ diameter「直径」。	semidiameter
hatch [hǽtʃ]	動孵化する a hatching egg かえろうとしている卵	incubate
immunisation [ìmjənaɪzéɪʃən]	名予防接種 an immunisation against influenza インフルエンザの予防接種	vaccination
nil [níl]	名ゼロ, 零点 three goals to nil 3 対 0 ＊主にスポーツで使う。nought, naught も「0」を表す。	zero
agrarian [əgréəriən]	形農業の；土地の agrarian society in the middle ages 中世の農業社会	farming
term [tɔ́ːrm]	名条件, 条項 the terms of a contract 契約条件 ＊「用語；期間；間柄」の意味も重要。	condition

Track 200

単語／発音	語彙／フレーズ	同意表現	難易度
enclosure [ɪnklóʊz]	名 囲われた土地；同封(物) a wildlife enclosure 野生生物保護区	premise	A
voice [vɔ́ɪs]	動 表明する voice opinions 意見を述べる	express	
incorporate [ɪnkɔ́ːrpərèɪt]	動 組み込む，合体させる incorporate his suggestion into our work 彼の提案を業務に組み入れる	integrate	
plagiarise [pléɪdʒəràɪz]	動 盗作する；盗用する plagiarise articles of other authors 他の作者の記事を盗む ＊ Plagiarism will not be tolerated. 「盗作は許されない」。	copy	B
deduce [dɪd(j)úːs]	動 推論する；演繹する deduce from the evidence 証拠から推論する	reason	
life-size [láɪf-sàɪz]	形 等身大の，実物大の a life-size statue 等身大の像		
meteorite [míːtiəràɪt]	名 隕石 the impact of a meteorite 隕石の衝突 ＊ meteor「流星；隕石」。	meteor	C
vertebrate [vɝːrtəbrət]	名 脊椎動物 a large land vertebrate 陸上の大型脊椎動物 ＊ invertebrate は「無脊椎動物」。	a creature with a backbone	
pervasive [pərvéɪsɪv]	形 普及している a pervasive influence 広範囲にわたる影響	widespread	
implicit [ɪmplísɪt]	形 暗に含んでいる an implicit agreement 暗黙の了解	implied	D
feeble [fíːbl]	形 弱い old and feeble 年老いて，か弱い	weak	
pretentious [prɪténʃəs]	形 これ見よがしの hate his pretentious manner 彼のこれ見よがしな態度を嫌う	ostentatious	

単語／発音	語彙／フレーズ	同意表現
anonymous [ənáːnəməs]	形 匿名の，無名の；特徴のない an anonymous donation 匿名の寄付	unnamed
fortnight [fɔ́ːrtnàɪt]	名 2 週間 once a fortnight 2 週間に 1 度	two weeks
imperceptible [ìmpərséptəbl]	形 知覚できないほど微小な imperceptible changes 気づかないほど微小な変化	undetectable
resolute [rézəlùːt]	形 断固とした a resolute will 揺るがぬ決意	determined
vulgar [vʌ́lgər]	形 無作法な vulgar expressions and behaviour 無作法な言動	impolite
invigorating [ɪnvígərèɪtɪŋ]	形 爽快にさせる invigorating mountain air 爽快な山の空気	refreshing
mundane [mʌndéɪn]	形 平凡でつまらない a mundane routine つまらない日課 ＊ordinary, everyday, normal も同義語。	boring
touchstone [tʌ́tʃstòʊn]	名 基準，試金石 a touchstone for an assessment 査定の基準	standard
hype [háɪp]	名 （誇大な）宣伝，売り込み a media hype マスコミの煽り宣伝	publicity
lexical [léksɪkl]	形 語彙の a lexical element of English 英語の語彙的要素 ＊S 採点基準の Lexical Resource「語彙力」でおなじみ。	relating to the words
heyday [héɪdèɪ]	名 絶頂，最盛期 short heyday of athletes 運動選手の短い絶頂期	peak
instalments [ɪnstɔ́ːlmənt]	名 分割（金） pay for the car in monthly instalments 車代を月賦で支払う	partial payment

Track 202

単語／発音	語彙／フレーズ	同意表現	難易度
predecessor [prédəsèsər]	名 前任者 take over the job from the predecessor 前任者から業務を引き継ぐ	precursor	A
shade [ʃéɪd]	名 わずかな違い；ニュアンス a word with several shades of meaning いくつかの微妙に異なる意味を持つ単語	nuance	
nurture [nə́:rtʃər]	名 養育 Nature or nurture? 生まれか育ちか？	upbringing	
thereby [ðèərbáɪ]	副 それによって overslept and was thereby late for school 寝坊して，そのせいで遅刻した	as a result	B
balk [bɔ́:k]	動 しりごみする，ためらう balk at an extreme idea 過激な考え方にしりごみする ＊野球のボークもこれ。	hesitate	
lunatic [lú:nətɪk]	形 実にばかげた lunatic ideas とてもばかげた考え	crazy	
discrepancy [dɪskrépənsi]	名 食い違い，不一致 a discrepancy between spelling and pronunciation 綴りと発音の不一致	divergence	C
remnant [rémnənt]	名 残されたもの remnants of the past 過去の遺物	remains	
surrender [səréndər]	動 降伏する surrender to the police 警察に自首する	capitulate	
plausible [plɔ́:zəbl]	形 もっともらしい a plausible excuse もっともらしい言い訳 ＊発音注意！	specious	D
lobbying [lá:bɪŋ]	名 ロビー活動，陳情運動 grass-roots lobbying 草の根レベルのロビー活動	petition	
impartial [ɪmpá:rʃəl]	形 公平な impartial judgment 公正な判断	unprejudiced	

Track 203

単語／発音	語彙／フレーズ	同意表現
constituent [kənstítʃuənt]	名 構成要素 a constituent of food 食物の成分	component
impetus [ímpətəs]	名 刺激；誘因 give an impetus to trade 貿易を促進する ＊アクセント注意！	incentive
dwindling [dwíndlɪŋ]	形 徐々に減少する a dwindling birth rate 低下する出生率	decreasing
amass [əmǽs]	動 蓄積する；集める amass a large fortune 巨万の富を蓄える	accumulate
soluble [sá:ljəbl]	形 溶解性の a water-soluble substance 水溶性物質	dissoluble
hollow [há:lou]	名 空洞 a tree hollow 樹洞	cavity
disdain [dɪsdéɪn]	動 軽蔑する, 見下す disdain worldly fame 世俗的名声を蔑視する	scorn
unparalleled [ʌnpérəleld]	形 比類なき unparalleled opportunity またとない機会	unequalled
despise [dɪspáɪz]	動 軽蔑する；嫌悪する despise a liar 嘘つきを軽蔑する	disdain
ultrasonic [ʌltrəsá:nɪk]	形 超音波の ultrasonic cleaning 超音波洗浄	supersonic
pant [pǽnt]	動 あえぐ；息切れする pant for air あえぎながら呼吸する	gasp
mutate [mju:téɪt]	動 変異する；変化する mutate into a new form 新しい型に変異する	change

Track 204

単語／発音	語彙／フレーズ	同意表現	難易度
fairground [féərgràund]	名 催し物会場 fairground attractions 催事会場のアトラクション	exhibition ground	A
tuck [tʌk]	動 (裾などを)押し込む, まくり上げる tuck up one's sleeves 袖をまくり上げる	insert	
shudder [ʃʌ́dər]	動 身震いする shudder with cold 寒さで震える	shiver	
empirical [empírɪkl]	形 経験的な empirical knowledge 経験的知識	experimental	B
scour [skáuər]	動 ゴシゴシ磨く scour the floor 床をゴシゴシ磨く	scrub	
ignite [ɪgnáɪt]	動 点火する；刺激する ignite a debate over 〜 〜にまつわる論争に火をつける	fire up	
inverted [ɪnvə́ːrtɪd]	形 逆転した an inverted triangle 逆三角形	upside-down	C
prototype [próutoutàɪp]	名 原型 the prototype of the modern bicycle 現代の自転車の原型	epitome	
elusive [ɪlúːsɪv]	形 捉えどころのない；捕まえにくい elusive words 捉えどころのない言葉	subtle	
elapse [ɪlǽps]	動 (時が)経過する A month elapsed. 1ヵ月が経過した。	go by	D
uptake [ʌ́ptèɪk]	名 (体内への)摂取 nutrient uptake 栄養摂取	intake	
wring [ríŋ]	動 絞る wring a towel タオルを絞る	squeeze	

Track 205

単語／発音	語彙／フレーズ	同意表現
swivel [swívl]	動 旋回する, 回す swivel one's chair around to face the student 椅子を回して生徒の方を向く	pivot
capsize [kæpsáɪz]	動 転覆させる[する] a capsized ship 転覆した船	overturn
haul [hɔ́:l]	動 引っ張る haul ~ out of … …から~を引きずり出す	draw
grossly [gróʊsli]	副 ひどく；下品に grossly inappropriate（言動などが）ひどく不適切な ＊ grossly はネガティブな場合に使う。	terribly
feat [fí:t]	名 偉業；功績 accomplish a feat 偉業を達成する	exploit
numeration [n(j)ù:məréɪʃən]	名 数え方, 計算；計算法 the decimal numeration system 十進法	count
suffice [səfáɪs]	動 十分である；満足させる A phone call will suffice. 1回電話すれば十分です。	do
hindrance [híndrəns]	名 妨害, 邪魔；障害物 hindrance to others' sleep 人の睡眠の妨害	interference
stun [stʌ́n]	動（驚きで）唖然とさせる；失神させる be stunned by the view from the summit 頂上からの眺めに唖然とする	amaze
hypnosis [hɪpnóʊsɪs]	名 催眠術 group hypnosis 集団催眠 ＊ hypnotic「眠気を起こさせる」の方が頻出。	mesmerism
whim [wím]	名 気まぐれ out of a whim 気まぐれから	caprice
gimmick [gímɪk]	名 策略；からくり a marketing gimmick マーケティングの仕掛け	device

Track 206

単語／発音	語彙／フレーズ	同意表現	難易度
entice [ɪntáɪs]	動 誘惑する, 気を引く entice a new audience into the theatre 新たな観客を劇場に呼び込む	tempt	A
redundant [rɪdʌ́ndənt]	形 冗長な redundant expression 冗長表現 ＊［英］「（従業員が）過剰な, 不要な」。	tautological	
affiliation [əfìliéɪʃən]	名 提携, 協力関係 capital affiliation 資本提携	tie-up	
incongruous [ɪnkɑ́ːŋgruəs]	形 不調和な, 釣り合わない incongruous with our technological age この技術の時代に不釣り合いな	inappropriate	B
manipulative [mənípjəlèɪtɪv]	形 巧みに操作する manipulative activity 操作活動	controlling	
publicise [pʌ́bləsàɪz]	動 公表する；宣伝する publicise scandals 不祥事を公表する	announce	
infirmity [ɪnfə́ːrməti]	名 虚弱 the infirmities of old age 老化による衰弱	frailty	C
tout [táʊt]	動 しつこく売り込む tout a new product 新製品を売り込む	hard-sell	
retard [rɪtɑ́ːrd]	動 遅らせる retard the progress of ～ ～の進行を遅らせる	delay	
extravagance [ɪkstrǽvəgəns]	名 浪費, 濫費 cut out all his extravagance 彼の浪費をやめさせる ＊Ⓢ be dressed extravagantly「豪華に着飾っている」。	prodigality	D
sheer [ʃíər]	形 全くの；純然たる sheer luck 全くの幸運	pure	
glossy [glɑ́ːsi]	形 光沢のある glossy paper 光沢紙	shiny	

単語／発音	語彙／フレーズ	同意表現
skyrocketing [skáɪrɑ̀:kətɪŋ]	形 とどまる所を知らない skyrocketing prices 高騰する価格 ＊W1 the rate skyrocketed「レートは急上昇した」。	spiralling
crusade [kru:séɪd]	名 改革運動；十字軍 a crusade against crime 犯罪防止運動	campaign
taunt [tɔ́:nt]	動 嘲（あざけ）る taunt someone with cowardice 人を卑怯だと嘲る	twit
shove [ʃʌ́v]	動 グイッと押す shove ～ to the side ～を脇に押しやる	thrust
refrain [rɪfréɪn]	動 差し控える refrain from drinking alcohol 飲酒を控える	abstain
disseminate [dɪsémənèɪt]	動 (思想などを)広める disseminate one's views 自分の考えを広める	spread
curious [kjúəriəs]	形 好奇心が強い；好奇心をそそる be curious about his whereabouts 彼の行方に好奇心を抱く ＊S natural curiosity「生まれ持った興味」。	inquisitive
hail [héɪl]	動 歓迎する be hailed as a hero 英雄として迎えられる	applaud
drip [drɪ́p]	動 滴る The sweat was dripping. 汗が滴っていた。	drop
petition [pətíʃən]	名 請願 court petition 裁判所への申し立て	appeal
overlook [òʊvərlʊ́k]	動 見落とす，見過ごす overlook a fault 過失に目をつぶる ＊「見下ろす」の意味もある。	disregard
unravelled [ʌnrǽvld]	形 ほぐされた an unravelled string ほぐされた糸	disentangled

Track 207

単語／発音	語彙／フレーズ	同意表現	難易度
illegible [ɪlédʒəbl]	形 判読しにくい，読みにくい illegible handwriting 読みにくい手書き文字 ＊⇔ legible	hardly readable	A
eradicate [ɪrǽdəkèɪt]	動 根絶する，撲滅する eradicate malaria マラリアを撲滅する	exterminate	
deterrent [dɪtə́:rənt]	名 抑止するもの nuclear deterrent 核兵器所有による戦争の抑止 ＊W2 use ~ as a deterrent「~を抑止力として使う」	inhibition	
regime [rəʒí:m]	名 政権 current regime 現政権	administration	B
terminal [tə́:rmənl]	形 末期の terminal illness 末期疾患	final	
oblige [əbláɪdʒ]	動 余儀なくさせる；義務づける A serious injury obliged him to give up his work. 彼は重傷で退職を余儀なくされた。	compel	
simultaneously [sìməltéɪniəsli]	副 同時に occur simultaneously with ~ ~と同時に発生する	coincidentally	C
sway [swéɪ]	動 揺れる；揺らす sway from side to side 横揺れする	swing	
bankrupt [bǽŋkrʌpt]	形 破産した；(必要なものを)欠いている Many companies went bankrupt in the recession. 不景気で多くの会社が破産した。	broke	
impulsively [ɪmpʌ́lsɪvli]	副 衝動的に act impulsively 衝動的に行動する ＊W2「衝動的に買う」で使える。buy on impulse も同じ。	impetuously	D
disposable [dɪspóʊzəbl]	形 使い捨ての；自由に使える disposable plastic cups 使い捨てのプラスチックカップ ＊ recyclable は「何度でも使える」。	expendable	
condemn [kəndém]	動 非難する，責める condemn someone's failure 人の失敗を非難する	blame	

Track 209

単語／発音	語彙／フレーズ	同意表現
compulsion [kəmpʌ́lʃən]	名 衝動 irresistible compulsion 抑えがたい衝動	impulse
embed [ɪmbéd]	動 埋め込む；はめ込む a crown embedded with jewels 宝石が埋め込まれた王冠	plough in
quay [kíː]	名 岸壁，波止場 a quay crane 岸壁クレーン ＊発音注意！	wharf
sequel [síːkwəl]	名 続編：続き a sequel to the hit movie ヒットした映画の続編	continuation
affectionately [əfékʃənətli]	副 愛情を込めて ruffle one's son's hair affectionately 愛情を込めて息子の髪をくしゃくしゃにする	dearly
demolish [dɪmɑ́ːlɪʃ]	動 破壊する；廃止する demolish an old building 古い建物を解体する ＊R 同義語として dismantle も覚えたい。	destroy
contour [kɑ́ːntʊər]	名 輪郭；外形 the contour of the mountains 山々の輪郭	silhouette
till [tíl]	名 レジ pay at the till レジで払う ＊[英]（[米] cash register）。	cash register
expiry [ɪkspáɪri]	名（契約や期限などの）終了，満了 extension of the expiry date 有効期限終了期日の延長	expiration
horticulture [hɔ́ːrtəkʌ̀ltʃər]	名 園芸 the horticulture department 園芸科	gardening
broaden [brɔ́ːdn]	動（視野などを）広げる broaden one's horizons 視野を広げる ＊「視野」なら horizons（複数）。	extend
malicious [məlíʃəs]	形 悪意のある malicious intention 悪意	ill-intentioned

単語／発音	語彙／フレーズ	同意表現	難易度
gleaming [glíːmɪŋ]	形 キラリと光る gleaming eyes キラリと光る目	glittering	A
stark [stáːrk]	形 全くの；ありのままの stark reality ありのままの現実	bare	
blackout [blǽkàut]	名 停電；消灯；失神 a sudden power blackout 突然の停電	power failure	
consolidate [kənsάːlədèɪt]	動 強固にする consolidate relations 関係を強固にする	solidify	B
hectic [héktɪk]	形 非常に忙しい a hectic day 慌ただしい1日 ＊S My life has been hectic recently.「最近忙しい」。	very busy	
bustle [bʌ́sl]	名 慌ただしい動き；活気 a bustle of a big city 都会の喧騒	fuss	
lure [juə]	動 誘い出す lure someone to 〜 人を〜へと誘う ＊釣りで使うルアー（疑似餌）のこと。	tempt	C
transcend [trænsénd]	動 超越する transcend barriers of 〜 〜の壁を乗り越える	exceed	
milestone [máɪlstòun]	名 画期的事件 a milestone in the history of South Africa 南アフリカの歴史における画期的事件	landmark event	
absurdity [əbsə́ːrdəti]	名 不合理，不条理；ばかげていること the absurdity of war 戦争の不合理さ	irrationality	D
rendering [réndərɪŋ]	名 表現；解釈 sensitive rendering 繊細な表現	rendition	
clash [klǽʃ]	名 衝突；対立 military clashes 軍事衝突	collision	

Track 211

単語／発音	語彙／フレーズ	同意表現
token [tóukən]	名 しるし；商品引換券 as a token of our appreciation 我々からの感謝のしるしとして	sign
pledge [plédʒ]	名 誓約 a policy pledge 公約	oath
confidential [kà:nfədénʃəl]	形 内密の；信用のおける disclose confidential documents 機密文書を暴く	secret
breach [brí:tʃ]	名 違反 be guilty of a breach of the law 法律違反の罪を犯す	violation
disclose [dɪsklóuz]	動 暴露する；明らかにする disclose a secret 秘密を暴露する	expose
sip [síp]	動 少しずつ飲む sip a glass of rum 1杯のラム酒をちびちびと飲む	sup
prerequisite [prì:rékwəzɪt]	名 必須[前提]条件 prerequisite for the course 科目の受講条件	requirement
addictive [ədíktɪv]	形 中毒性の Tobacco is a highly addictive drug. タバコは中毒性の高い薬物だ。	habit-forming
censorship [sénsərʃìp]	名 検閲 government censorship during war 政府による戦時中の検閲	blue pencil
clarify [klérəfài]	動 明らかにする clarify the meaning of the term 用語の意味を明らかにする	elucidate
coherent [kouhíərənt]	形 首尾一貫した a coherent argument 首尾一貫した主張 ＊W2 アイデアの筋が通っていること。	logical
cohesive [kouhí:sɪv]	形 粘着性のある；団結した cohesive strength 結合力 ＊W2 文と文とのつながりがいいこと。	adhesive

Track 212

単語／発音	語彙／フレーズ	同意表現	難易度
considerate [kənsídərət]	形 思いやりのある；思慮深い considerate care 思いやりのある世話 ＊considerable「かなりの」との混同に注意！	thoughtful	A
inaudible [ɪnɔ́:dəbl]	形 聞き取れない inaudible to the human ear 人間の耳には聞き取れない	unhearable	
intelligibility [ɪntèlɪdʒəbíləti]	名 分かりやすさ sentence intelligibility 文の明瞭度	comprehensibility	
interrupt [ìntərʌ́pt]	動 中断する interrupt a conversation 会話に割って入る	disrupt	B
pointed [pɔ́ɪntɪd]	形 とがった pointed beaks とがったくちばし	acuate	
real-life [rí:jəllàɪf]	形 実在の a real-life figure 実在の人物	actual	
stocky [stá:ki]	形 ずんぐりした a stocky build ずんぐりした体格 ＊この場合 build は「体格」。	tubby	C
texture [tékstʃər]	名 質感；生地；組織 delicate texture 繊細な質感 ＊「舌触り」を表すことも。	feel	
fluctuate [flʌ́ktʃuèɪt]	動 変動する；動揺する Prices fluctuate according to the season. 物価は季節によって変動する。　＊W1 使えるようにして！	waver	
marginal [má:rdʒɪnl]	形 周辺的な a marginal position 周辺的な地位	peripheral	D
plunge [plʌ́ndʒ]	動 急落する Stock markets plunged at the news of the earthquake. 地震の報せで株価が急落した。　＊W1 名詞も同じ。	plummet	
dump [dʌ́mp]	動 投げ捨てる，処分する dump ～ into a trash can ～をごみ箱に捨てる	dispose of	

Track 213

単語／発音	語彙／フレーズ	同意表現
dune [d(j)úːn]	名 砂丘 coastal dunes 海岸砂丘	sand hill
envision [ɪnvíʒən]	動 （将来などを）想像する，思い描く envision a future 未来を心に描く ＊envisage, imagine と併せて覚える。	visualise
grind [gráɪnd]	動 すりつぶす grind rice to powder 米を挽いて粉にする ＊grind - ground - ground と変化する。	mill
implement [ímpləmènt]	動 実行する，施行する implement a new idea 新しいアイデアを実行する ＊名詞なら tool の意。	execute
outstrip [àʊtstrɪ́p]	動 〜をしのぐ；追い越す outstrip the reality 現実を上回る	surpass
foliage [fóʊliɪdʒ]	名 葉 a foliage plant 観葉植物	leaf
reside [rɪzáɪd]	動 住む，居住する；駐在する He has resided abroad for many years. 彼は長年海外に居住していた。	live
circumference [sərkʌ́mfərns]	名 外周，円周 the ratio of the circumference of a circle 円周率	perimeter
grid [gríd]	名 碁盤目；格子 in a grid 碁盤の目状に	trellis
wart [wɔ́ːrt]	名 イボ a wart caused by a virus ウイルスによるイボ	verruca
flinch [flíntʃ]	動 たじろぐ without flinching たじろがずに	wince
trance [trǽns]	名 意識朦朧状態 a hypnotic trance 催眠術によるトランス状態	twilight state

Track 214

単語／発音	語彙／フレーズ	同意表現	難易度
charter [tʃɑ́ːrtər]	動 （乗物などを）借り上げる；認可する a chartered plane チャーター機	hire	A
duration [d(j)uréɪʃən]	名 継続期間；持続 the duration of effect 効果持続時間	period	
evacuate [ɪvǽkjuèɪt]	動 避難させる；立ち退く evacuate residents from their homes 住民を自宅から避難させる	remove	
extinguish [ɪkstíŋgwɪʃ]	動 （火や灯りを）消す extinguish a fire 消火する ＊ a fire extinguisher「消火器」。	quench	B
divulge [daɪvʌ́ldʒ]	動 （秘密などを）漏らす，暴露する divulge his whereabouts 彼の所在を漏らす	disclose	
comply [kəmpláɪ]	動 （要求・規則などに）従う，応じる comply with regulations 規則に従う ＊いわゆる compliance「法令遵守」の動詞形。	follow	
shoplift [ʃɑ́ːplìft]	動 万引きする shoplift 〜 from the store 店から〜を万引きする	derrick	C
discern [dɪsə́ːrn]	動 識別する；見分ける discern good from evil 善悪を見分ける	distinguish	
delegate [délɪgət]	名 使節；代表（者） delegates from the UN 国連からの使節	representative	
casualties [kǽʒuəlti]	名 死傷者，犠牲者 civilian casualties in this war この戦争での民間人の犠牲者	victim	D
famine [fǽmɪn]	名 飢饉 death toll from famine 飢饉による死者数	dearth	
wholesale [hóʊlsèɪl]	名 卸売り a wholesale price 卸売価格	wholesaling	

Track 215

単語／発音	語彙／フレーズ	同意表現
revenue [révən(j)ùː]	名 歳入 tax revenue 税収	comings in
recession [riséʃən]	名 不景気 an economic recession 経済不況	depression
ridge [rídʒ]	名 尾根 mountain ridges 山の尾根	hump
free-range [fríː-réɪndʒ]	形 (家畜などが)放し飼いの free-range hens' eggs 放し飼いの鶏の卵	range-fed
asylum [əsáɪləm]	名 (政治犯などの)庇護；保護施設 appeal for political asylum 政治的亡命を懇願する	refuge
capital [kǽpətl]	形 極めて重要な；大文字の a capital mistake 致命的過失 ＊capital punishment は「極刑, 死刑」。	crucial
verdict [vɜ́ːrdɪkt]	名 判決 a guilty verdict 有罪判決	sentence
prosecute [prɑ́səkjùːt]	動 訴追する；起訴する prosecute a defendant 被告人を訴追する	indict
solicitor [səlísətər]	名 事務弁護士 an official solicitor 公認事務弁護士	proctor
barrister [bǽərəstər]	名 法廷弁護士 barristers and judges in the court 法廷の弁護士と判事	counsel
defendant [dɪféndənt]	名 被告(人) find the defendant guilty 被告人を有罪とする	accused person
loophole [lúːphòʊl]	名 (制度の)抜け穴 a legal loophole 法の抜け穴	chink

Track 216

単語／発音	語彙／フレーズ	同意表現	難易度
holistic [hoʊlístɪk]	形 全体論的な holistic perspective 全体論的視野	organismic	A
insolvency [ɪnsá:lvənsi]	名 破産状態 bank insolvency 銀行破綻	bankruptcy	
languish [læŋgwɪʃ]	動 衰える languish in illness 病気で弱る	fade	
concur [kənkə́:r]	動 同意する，是認する concur with her idea 彼女の意見と一致している	agree	B
proactive [proʊæktɪv]	形 先を見越した a proactive measure 未然防止策	prevenient	
verge [və́:rdʒ]	名 瀬戸際，寸前；端，ふち on the verge of divorce まさに離婚の瀬戸際で	brink	
laden [léɪdn]	形 どっさりと積み込んだ；意気消沈した a person laden with prejudices 偏見に満ちた人物 ＊doom-laden は「悲運を暗示する」。	loaded	C
ration [ræʃən]	名 (配給) 食料；割当量 decrease the food ration 食糧の配給を減らす ＊発音注意！	distribution	
impart [ɪmpá:rt]	動 知らせる，伝える；与える impart vital information 重要な情報を伝える ＊目的語は knowledge や information。	disseminate	
prone [próʊn]	形 傾向がある，しがちな be prone to illness 病気がちである	likely	D
synchronisation [síŋkrənàɪzéɪʃən]	名 同時に動くこと be in synchronisation with ～ ～と同期[同調]している ＊映画関係で頻出。	simultaneity	
exert [ɪgzə́:rt]	動 力を及ぼす；発揮する exert pressure on the government 政府に圧力を及ぼす ＊名詞 exertion「努力；力の発揮」。	apply	

233

Track 217

単語／発音	語彙／フレーズ	同意表現
notoriety [nòutəráiəti]	名 悪名高さ gain international notoriety 国際的な悪評を得る ＊形容詞 notorious「悪名高い」。	ill fame
sanction [sǽŋkʃən]	名 制裁；認可；拘束力 UN economic sanctions 国連による経済制裁 ＊語義にプラスとマイナス両方あり。	punishment
allergic [ələ́ːrdʒɪk]	形 アレルギーがある Many Japanese are allergic to pollen. 多くの日本人が花粉アレルギーです。　＊allergic to pollen で2語をいっきに暗記。	intolerant
peer [píər]	動 じっと見る；目を凝らす peer closely at the photograph 写真をじっと見る ＊通常，前置詞は at。	gaze
reign [réin]	動 支配する，統治する reign over the territory of ～ ～の領土を支配する ＊rein（手綱），rain（雨）と同音。	rule
annihilate [ənáiəlèit]	動 全滅させる annihilate the whole city 都市を全滅させる ＊発音も注意。h を読まない。	ruin
obsolete [àːbsəlíːt]	形 時代遅れの，すたれた become obsolete overnight 一夜にして時代遅れになる	outdated
strife [stráif]	名 争い，闘争 economic and political strife 経済的・政治的対立 ＊動詞 strive「奮闘する」。	conflict
ratify [rǽtəfài]	動 批准する ratify the treaty 条約を批准する	approve
bibliography [bìbliáːgrəfi]	名 参考文献目録 A bibliography enables us to follow up other studies. 参考文献目録によって他の研究をたどっていくことができる。	reference
inventory [ínvəntɔ̀ːri]	名 在庫目録 the real-time inventory management system リアルタイム在庫管理システム	stock list
campaign [kæmpéin]	名 組織運動，選挙運動，軍事行動 the Burma campaign in WWII 第二次世界大戦におけるビルマ作戦　＊選挙関係以外なら，この意味が重要。	movement

234

Track 218

単語／発音	語彙／フレーズ	同意表現	難易度
vicinity [vɪsínəti]	名 付近 city and its vicinity 街とその周辺 ＊a nearby area と同意。	neighbourhood	A
destine [déstɪn]	動 運命づける be destined to enter the church 牧師になる運命である ＊名詞は「destiny」。	doom	
soothe [súːð]	動 なだめる, 鎮める, 和らげる soothe a sore throat 喉の痛みを和らげる ＊⑤ have a soothing effect「鎮静効果がある」。	calm	
assess [əsés]	動 査定する, 評価する；税金を課す His impact is too enormous to assess. 彼の影響は大き過ぎて評価するのが難しい。	estimate	B
ripple [rípl]	名 さざ波；小じわ ripple effect 波及効果	ruffle	
heredity [hərédəti]	名 遺伝(形質)；遺伝傾向；相続 the effects of heredity and environment 遺伝と環境の影響	inheritance	
scan [skǽn]	動 精査する, 細かく調べる scan ～ for any evidence of … …の痕跡がないか～を詳しく調べる　＊「ざっと目を通す」意もある。	scrutinise	C
thesis [θíːsɪs]	名 命題；テーマ；論文 prove the thesis 命題を証明する	proposition	
top-notch [tɑ́ːpnɑ́ːtʃ]	形 一流の；最高の offer top-notch services 一流のサービスを提供する	first-rate	
secular [sékjələr]	形 非宗教的な；世俗的な secular politics 政教分離の政治	profane	D
regional [ríːdʒənl]	形 地域の；局地的な regional variations in pronunciation 地域による発音の違い	local	
satire [sǽtaɪər]	名 風刺, 皮肉 aim satire at someone 人に当てつけを言う	irony	

Track 219

単語／発音	語彙／フレーズ	同意表現
opt [ɑ́:pt]	動 選ぶ opt for stability over change 変化よりも安定を選ぶ ＊ opt to V「Vすることを選ぶ」。option は「選択肢」。	choose
imaginary [imǽdʒənèri]	形 仮想の，想像上の，架空の The earth's axis is an imaginary line. 地軸は仮想の線である。　＊ imaginative writer「想像力の豊かな作家」。	unreal
evaporate [ɪvǽpərèɪt]	動 蒸発する；消えうせる Most of the liquid has evaporated. ほとんどの液体は蒸発してしまった。	vaporise
testimony [téstəmòuni]	名 証言，証拠；証書 take testimony from a witness 証人から証言を得る	proof
gradation [greɪdéɪʃən]	名 段階的変化；色の推移 discern gradations of polarization 偏光の段階的変化を見分ける	process
illiteracy [ɪlítərəsi]	名 文字が読めないこと illiteracy rates 非識字率 ＊⇔ literacy	illiterateness
combustible [kəmbʌ́stəbl]	形 可燃性の，燃えやすい；興奮しやすい combustible materials 可燃物 ＊名詞 combustion。	inflammable
stiffen [stífən]	動（態度・決心を）固くする；凝る Conversely, punishment only stiffened his resolve. 罰は逆に彼の決意を固くした。	strengthen
grazing [gréɪzɪŋ]	名 放牧；牧草地；牧草 the field of grass for grazing 放牧用の草地	pasturage
premiere [prɪmíər]	名 初演 see a movie before the premiere 映画を封切り前に見る	first performance
appreciation [əprì:ʃiéɪʃən]	名（正しい）理解，鑑賞；感謝；批評 a deep appreciation of poetry 詩についての深い鑑賞力（理解）	understanding
rubble [rʌ́bl]	名 瓦礫 piles of rubble 瓦礫の山 ＊ debris の方が頻出。	debris

単語／発音	語彙／フレーズ	同意表現	難易度
infirmary [ɪnfə́ːrməri]	名 病院, 診療室 a well-equipped infirmary 設備の整った診療所	clinic	A
bogus [bóʊɡəs]	形 にせの, いんちきの She was fooled by his bogus identity card. 彼女は彼のにせの身分証明書によって騙された。	false	
philanthropic [fìlənθrɑ́ːpɪk]	形 慈善の, 博愛の a philanthropic organisation 慈善団体	benevolent	
deplore [dɪplɔ́ːr]	動 遺憾に思う, 非難する deplore the Russian invasion ロシアの侵略を非難する	regret	B
preamble [príːæmbl]	名 前置き, 前文, 序文 begin without preamble 前置きなしに話を切り出す	preface	
cereal [síəriəl]	名 穀物 Wheat and barley are cereals. 小麦と大麦は穀物です。 ＊ breakfast cereals「穀物食品」。	grain	
simulate [símjəlèɪt]	動 模擬演習する；ふりをする simulate flight situations 飛行状況を模擬演習する	imitate	C
intrigue [ɪntríːɡ]	動 興味を起こさせる, 引き付ける be intrigued by the innovative design 斬新な設計に興味をそそられる	fascinate	
defiance [dɪfáɪəns]	名 挑戦的態度, 反抗, 無視 Queen Margaret's defiance against Scottish Parliament マーガレット王女のスコットランド議会に対する反抗	resistance	
outermost [áʊtərmòʊst]	形 最外の, 一番外れの an outermost layer of ~ ~の最外層 ＊⇔ innermost	outmost	D
hypothesise [haɪpɑ́ːθəsàɪz]	動 仮定する；仮説を立てる hypothesise that birds navigate by the stars 鳥は星座に従って移動すると仮定する	assume	
saturate [sǽtʃərèɪt]	動 飽和状態にする；いっぱいにする；完全に浸す saturate the domestic market 国内市場を飽和状態にする ＊ saturation point「飽和点」。	flood	

Track 220

Track 221

単語／発音	語彙／フレーズ	同意表現
outgrowth [àʊtgròʊθ]	名 当然の結果, 自然の成り行き as a natural outgrowth of 〜 〜の当然の結果として ＊ consequence や outcome がより頻出。	consequence
outset [áʊtsèt]	名 初め, 発端 at the outset of the 20th century 20世紀初頭に ＊ at the outset「最初の時点で」。	beginning
conquer [ká:ŋkər]	動 征服する, 克服する the drive to conquer difficulties 困難を克服しようとする衝動 ＊ concur「同意する」と混同しないように。	overcome
foreign [fá:rən]	形 異質の, なじみのない potentially harmful foreign objects 潜在的に有害な異質の物体	alien
allocate [ǽləkèɪt]	動 割り当てる；分配する allocate a room to each student 各生徒に部屋を割り当てる ＊ W2 allocate the budget「予算を分配する」。	assign
plague [pléɪg]	名 疫病, 伝染病 catch the plague from animals 動物を介して疫病にかかる	epidemic
perch [pə́:rtʃ]	名 止まり木 be on the perch 止まり木に止まっている	roost
prosperity [prɑ:spérəti]	名 繁栄；(金銭上の)成功 prosperity and stability of the world 世界の繁栄と安定 ＊ 動詞 prosper「繁栄する」は thrive, flourish が同義語。	success
aspiring [əspáɪərrɪŋ]	形 野心に燃える, 意欲的な an aspiring ballet dancer 野心に燃えるバレエダンサー	ambitious
startle [stá:rtl]	動 びっくりさせる, 跳び上がらせる startle the world 世間を仰天させる ＊ startling, astonishing は surprising の同義語。	surprise
mediocre [mì:dióʊkər]	形 平凡な, 二流の live a mediocre life 平凡な人生を送る ＊「まあまあ」という感じ。	average
stagnate [stǽgneɪt]	動 停滞する, 成長が止まる；よどむ stagnate in one place for a long time いつまでも1カ所にとどまる ＊ stagflation「不況下のインフレ」。	become sluggish

単語／発音	語彙／フレーズ	同意表現	難易度
layman [léɪmən]	名 一般人，素人 explain the concept in layman's terms 概念を素人でも分かる言葉で平たく説明する　＊layman も laywoman もある。	amateur	A
subsist [səbsíst]	動 生き残る subsist on ～ as food ～を食べて生きる ＊subsistence「生存最低生活」。	survive	
immobilise [ɪmóʊbəlàɪz]	動 （患部を）固定する；動けなくする immobilise a broken arm 骨折した腕を固定する	disable	
credentials [krədénʃəl]	名 資格証明書，信用証明物；信任状 credentials for the job その仕事にふさわしい資格証明	qualifications	B
fetch [fétʃ]	動 行って取って来る；～で売れる Fetch me some bread from the shop. パンをお店で買って来てよ。　＊go-getter は「やり手」。	go and get	
consume [kəns(j)úːm]	動 摂取する，食べる；消費する consume a good deal of sugar in drinks 飲料からかなりの糖分を摂取する　＊「食べる」という意味は盲点。	ingest	
fusion [fjúːʒən]	名 融合，溶解；混合；核融合 a perfect fusion of image and sound 映像と音声の完璧な融合　＊動詞の fuse も頻出。	blend	C
tangible [tǽndʒəbl]	形 確実な，明白な；触れて分かる tangible benefits from investment 投資からの確実な利益	actual	
embark [ɪmbáːrk]	動 乗り出す；乗船する embark on a new business 新しい事業に乗り出す ＊bark はもともと「バーク船」という「船」。	launch	
hurl [hə́ːrl]	動 強く放る，投げつける hurl a brick through the window 窓からレンガを放り投げる	throw	D
afford [əfɔ́ːrd]	動 与える afford women the right to vote 女性に選挙権を与える ＊こっちの意味が盲点。	give	
subsidise [sʌ́bsədàɪz]	動 助成金を出す；援助する subsidise small businesses 中小企業を助成する ＊W2 S 「政府の補助金」はアイデアとして使いやすい。	fund	

単語／発音	語彙／フレーズ	同意表現
harass [hərǽs]	動 悩ます, 困らせる；攻撃する complain of being sexually harassed at work 職場で性的な嫌がらせを受けたことを訴える	annoy
arbitrary [ɑ́ːrbətrèri]	形 恣意的な；任意の；気ままな arbitrary employer decisions 雇用主の自分勝手な決定	capricious
articulate [ɑːrtíkjələt]	形 考えをはっきり述べられる；(理路)整然とした a bright and articulate student 利口で考えをしっかりと言える生徒	eloquent
peck [pék]	動 (くちばしで)つつく peck grains on the ground 地面の穀物をついばむ ＊ pecking order「序列」。	pick
piety [páɪəti]	名 孝行；敬虔さ, 信心 filial piety 子供としての孝行(親孝行)	piousness
discharge [dɪstʃɑ́ːrdʒ]	動 排出する, 降ろす, 免除する discharge toxic chemicals into the river 毒性化学物質を川に排出する　＊「退院する」ときも使える。	release
pollute [pəlúːt]	動 汚染する pollute the river with waste 廃棄物で川を汚染する	contaminate
larva [lɑ́ːrvə]	名 幼虫 a mosquito larva 蚊の幼虫 ＊複数形は larvae。	young worm
obscene [ɑːbsíːn]	形 卑猥な make an obscene gesture 卑猥な身ぶりをする	filthy
render [réndər]	動 〜の状態にする；〜を与える render the patent invalid 特許を無効にする ＊ give か使役の make の意味。	make
exclusive [ɪksklúːsɪv]	形 排他的な；それだけに限られた mutually exclusive options 互いに両立しない選択肢 ＊ an exclusive interview「独占インタビュー」。	only
circulation [sə̀ːrkjəléɪʃən]	名 発行部数 the circulation of that weekly magazine その週刊誌の発行部数　＊「循環」以外なら, この意味が狙い目。	distribution

Track 224

単語／発音	語彙／フレーズ	同意表現	難易度
prestigious [prestíːdʒəs]	形 名声のある，一流の；有名な enter a prestigious university 名門大学に入る	esteemed	A
freight [fréɪt]	名 輸送貨物；貨物運送 a freight train 貨物列車	cargo	
terminology [tə̀ːrmənáːlədʒi]	名 用語 be just a matter of terminology （本質と関係ない）用語の問題にすぎない	vocabulary	
catastrophe [kətǽstrəfi]	名 大異変，大災害，大惨事 Early warnings prevent another major catastrophe. 早期警告が次の大惨事を防ぐ。	disaster	B
count [káʊnt]	動 価値がある，重要である It is the result that counts. 結果こそ大切です。	matter	
equilibrium [ìːkwəlíbriəm]	名 釣り合い，平衡；（心の）平静 achieve an equilibrium between demand and supply 需要と供給の均衡を達成する	balance	
orderly [ɔ́ːrdərli]	形 整然とした form an orderly line 整然とした列を作る ＊類義語 neat「こぎれいな；きちんとした」。	tidy	C
spell [spél]	名 まじない，呪文，魔法 cast a spell on 〜 〜に魔法をかける ＊「期間」の意もある。動詞だと mean（意味する）が同義語。	charm	
outrageous [aʊtréɪdʒəs]	形 法外な；とんでもない charge an outrageous fee 法外な料金を吹っかける	exorbitant	
lyric [lírɪk]	名 歌詞；抒情詩 learn lyrics by heart 歌詞を暗記する	words	D
ore [ɔ́ːr]	名 鉱石 iron ore industry 鉄鉱業	mineral	
sluggish [slʌ́gɪʃ]	形 不景気な；怠惰な；のろい sluggish global economy 停滞する世界経済	stagnant	

241

単語／発音	語彙／フレーズ	同意表現
renounce [rɪnáuns]	動 破棄する；拒否する renounce nuclear weapons 核兵器を破棄する	relinquish
excavate [ékskəvèɪt]	動 発掘する excavate pottery and weapons from the burial site 陶器や武器を埋葬地から発掘する	unearth
exempt [ɪgzémpt]	形 免除された；〜がない be exempt from the placement test クラス分けテストを免除された	excused
versatility [vɚ̀ːrsətíləti]	名 多芸多才 functional versatility 機能の多様性 ＊俗に言う「引き出しが多いこと」。	resourcefulness
underlie [ʌ̀ndɚrláɪ]	動 背後にある；基礎となる a principle that underlies the party's policies その政党方針の基礎となる原理	build
regenerate [rɪdʒénərèɪt]	動 再生する regenerate damaged tissues 傷ついた組織を再生する	reproduce
peril [pérəl]	名 危険, 危難 put one's life in peril 命を危険にさらす	danger
forage [fɔ́ːrɪdʒ]	動 (食べ物を)探し回る, あさる forage for food in the cupboard 棚の食料をあさる ＊名詞は「飼料；かいば」。	hunt
probation [proʊbéɪʃən]	名 仮採用；執行猶予, 保護観察 work on probation as a teacher 先生として仮採用で働く	trial
flux [flʌks]	名 流動；変化 Events are in a state of flux. 事象は絶えず変化している。	flow
famished [fǽmɪʃt]	形 非常に空腹である I'm famished. 私はおなかがペコペコです。	starving
fugitive [fjúːdʒətɪv]	名 逃亡者；避難民 a fugitive from justice 司法の裁きを逃れた者	escapee

Track 226

単語／発音	語彙／フレーズ	同意表現	難易度
dough [dóu]	名（パイなどの）生地 Doughs are made from a variety of flours. 生地は様々な穀物粉で作られる。　＊発音注意！	paste	A
overhang [óuvərhæŋ]	名突出部, 張り出し overhang of the cliff 崖の張り出したところ	projection	
prodigious [prədídʒəs]	形巨大な, 並外れた；驚異的な, 素晴らしい a prodigious sum of money 莫大な金 ＊名詞の prodigy とともに頻出。	enormous	
velocity [vəlá:səti]	名速度 supersonic velocity 超音速 ＊rate「速度」は頻出。	speed	B
inmate [ínmèɪt]	名囚人 a death-row inmate 死刑囚	prisoner	
deplete [dɪplí:t]	動激減させる；使い果たす severely deplete salmon populations 鮭の数を激減させる　＊ozone depletion「オゾン層枯渇」。	exhaust	
repel [rɪpél]	動追い払う, 寄せ付けない repel enemy forces 敵の軍を撃退する ＊形容詞 repellent「寄せ付けない」。	repulse	C
elude [ɪlú:d]	動避ける, すり抜ける elude capture by predators 捕食動物に捕まるのを避ける	avoid	
mural [mjúərəl]	名壁画 decorate a wall with a mural 壁を壁画で飾る ＊形容詞だと,「壁の」。	wall painting	
asteroid [ǽstərɔ̀ɪd]	名小惑星 asteroids in our solar system 太陽系の小惑星 ＊Ⓡ the asteroid belt（小惑星帯）は火星と木星の間にある。	minor planet	D
homogeneous [hòumədʒí:niəs]	形同種の, 同質の；均一の a homogeneous country 単一民族国家 ＊homogenous も同じ。⇔ heterogeneous「異質の」。	uniform	
elliptical [ɪlíptɪkl]	形楕円の an elliptical shape of depression 楕円形のへこみ ＊= oval で決まり。	oval	

243

Track 227

単語／発音	語彙／フレーズ	同意表現
emancipation [ɪmænsəpéɪʃən]	名 解放, 釈放, 自由 emancipation from unfair domination 不当な支配からの解放　＊〜 proclamation「開放宣言」。	liberation
faction [fǽkʃən]	名 派閥, 徒党 There were various factions within the party. 党内には様々な派閥があった。　＊= camp「同志」。	sect
deliberate [dɪlíbərət]	動 熟慮する, 審議する deliberate on the sentence 判決に関して熟慮する ＊R deliberately「故意に」は頻出。	ponder
offset [ɔ́(:)fsèt]	動 相殺する；埋め合わせる advantages offsetting disadvantages 短所を補う長所	compensate
oath [óʊθ]	名 誓約 declare on oath that 〜 宣誓した上で〜と断言する	pledge
mitigate [mítəgèɪt]	動（怒り・苦痛などを）和らげる mitigate the pain of a patient 患者の苦痛を和らげる	relieve
pluck [plʌ́k]	動 むしり取る pluck a chicken 鶏の羽をむしる	pick
brittle [brítl]	形（硬いが）もろい brittle like glass ガラスのように硬いがもろい	fragile
cavity [kǽvəti]	名 穴, 空洞 hide the necklace in a cavity in the wall 壁の穴にネックレスを隠す　＊「虫歯」の意味もある。	cavern
tentacle [téntəkl]	名 触手, 触角 octopus tentacle タコの脚	feeler
analogy [ənǽlədʒi]	名 類推, 類似, たとえ explain the complicated theory with an analogy 複雑な理論をたとえで説明する	comparison
hibernation [hàɪbərnéɪʃən]	名 冬眠 go into hibernation 冬眠する ＊ metabolism「新陳代謝」。	winter sleep

Track 228

単語／発音	語彙／フレーズ	同意表現	難易度
vow [váʊ]	動 誓う，誓約する vow revenge on ～ ～への復讐を誓う	swear	A
aesthetic [esθétɪk]	形 美的な；美的感覚のある an acute aesthetic sensibility of an artist 芸術家の鋭い美的感覚　＊発音注意！	artistic	
ingestion [ɪndʒéstʃən]	名 摂取 ingestion of a large amount of ～ ～の大量摂取 ＊= eating	consumption	
dormant [dɔ́ːrmənt]	形 休止状態の lie dormant for many months 何カ月も休止状態のままでいる　＊火山関係や種子か。	inactive	B
imperative [ɪmpérətɪv]	形 命令的な；必須の in an imperative tone 命令的な口調で	dominant	
trickle [tríkl]	動 少しずつ流れる；徐々に伝わる trickle out of the tap （水が）蛇口から少しずつ漏れる	dribble	
comprehensive [kɑ̀mprɪhénsɪv]	形 包括的な，広範囲な a comprehensive census 包括的国勢調査 ＊CTBT「包括的核実験禁止条約」のC。	inclusive	C
abide [əbáɪd]	動 遵守する abide by the international agreements 国際的な同意事項を遵守する　＊abide by ～の形が頻出。	observe	
adverse [ǽdvəːrs]	形 不都合な；不利な；敵意に満ちた the most adverse effect on Northern Ireland 北アイルランドに対する最も不利な影響　＊マイナスの意味の単語。	negative	
swat [swɑ́ːt]	動 ピシャリと打つ swat someone on the back 人の背中をたたく	blow sharply	D
sedimentary [sèdəméntəri]	形 堆積（物）の；沈殿物の sedimentary rocks 堆積岩 ＊igneous rock「火成岩」。	accumulated	
precipitate [prɪsípɪtèɪt]	動 （雨・雪を）降らせる；引き起こす Water precipitates many chemical compounds. 水は多くの化学物質を降らせる。　＊precipitation「降雨；降雪」。	drop	

245

Track 229

単語/発音	語彙/フレーズ	同意表現
depression [dɪpréʃən]	名 不景気；へこみ；憂鬱 the Great Depression of the 1930's 1930年代の大恐慌 ＊精神, 景気, 物体の「へこみ」。	recession
rodent [róʊdnt]	名 (ネズミ・リスなどの)げっ歯類 rodent pellets 殺鼠剤	gnawer
nominal [nά:mənl]	形 ほんの少しの work for a nominal salary 名ばかりのわずかな給料で働く ＊「名ばかりの」と覚えよう！	small
perplex [pərpléks]	動 当惑させる be perplexed with difficult problems 難問で困っている	puzzle
scale [skéɪl]	動 よじ登る scale a castle wall 城壁をよじ登る ＊「はしご」の意味から派生。	climb
withhold [wɪðhóʊld]	動 与えずにおく；保留する withhold important evidence 重要な証拠を与えずにおく ＊ suspend と組み合わせて。	suspend
eclipse [ɪklíps]	名 日食, 月食 a total eclipse of the sun 皆既日食 ＊ solar や lunar を付けて意味を識別。	blocking
staple [stéɪpl]	名 主要なもの；必需品 staples of the diets 主食	necessity
endow [ɪndáʊ]	動 (才能などを)授ける；遺贈する She was endowed with great beauty. 彼女は類まれな美貌を授かった。 ＊ give 系で同意語が非常に多い。	give
authentic [ɔ:θéntɪk]	形 本物の, 純粋な, 信頼できる show authentic certificates and documents 本物の証明書と文書を提示する ＊～information なら「信頼できる情報」。	genuine
retract [rɪtrǽkt]	動 撤回する, 取り消す；引っ込める retract one's words 前言を撤回する	withdraw
probe [próʊb]	名 調査, 探査；無人観測宇宙船 initiate one's own probe 独自の調査に着手する	exploration

Track 230

単語／発音	語彙／フレーズ	同意表現	難易度
infrastructure [ínfrəstrʌ̀ktʃər]	名 インフラ(文明社会の基本となる設備), 構造基盤；下部構造 improve urban infrastructure 都市生活基盤を整備する ＊必要な「施設」をまとめる単語。	social foundation	A
anchor [ǽŋkər]	動 固定する；錨で留める anchor climbers to each other by a rope 登山者を互いにロープで固定する	fix	
awkward [ɔ́:kwərd]	形 気まずい；ぎこちない；不器用な Children tend to ask awkward questions. 子供は気まずい質問をしがちです。　＊「不器用な」の clumsy と同意。	embarrassing	
suffrage [sʌ́frɪdʒ]	名 選挙権, 参政権 women's suffrage movement 女性参政権運動 ＊®「参政権」は頻出。	vote	B
disguise [dɪsgáɪz]	動 変装する, 姿を変える, 隠す The burglars were heavily disguised. 強盗は十分に変装していた。	camouflage	
celestial [səléstʃəl]	形 天の, 空の a celestial body 天体 ＊⇔ terrestrial「陸上の；地球上の」。	heavenly	
plaintiff [pléɪntɪf]	名 原告, 申立人 plaintiff versus defendant 原告対被告 ＊⇔ defendant「被告」。	suitor	C
impede [ɪmpí:d]	動 邪魔する；遅らせる impede a good relationship 良好な関係を妨げる ＊= hamper	hinder	
apprehensive [æ̀prɪhénsɪv]	形 懸念する；恐れる be apprehensive about the safety of the victims 犠牲者の安否を懸念する	anxious	
pier [píər]	名 桟橋, 埠頭 come alongside the pier 桟橋に接岸する	wharf	D
meticulous [mətíkjələs]	形 細かいことに気を配る, 細心な meticulous physical examination 細部にわたる身体検査	fastidious	
merger [mə́:rdʒər]	名 合併 municipal merger 市町村合併 ＊ Merger and Acquisition「吸収合併」。日本語では逆。	amalgamation	

Track 231

単語／発音	語彙／フレーズ	同意表現
underscore [ʌ̀ndərskɔ́ːr]	動 強調する；明白にする underscore an important point 要点を強調する	emphasise
apply [əpláɪ]	動 （薬・ペンキなどを）塗る；適用する apply ointment to a cut 切り傷に軟膏を塗る ＊ apply paint「ペンキを塗る」。	paint
insulate [ínsəlèɪt]	動 隔離する, 孤立させる, 絶縁する insulate politics from religion 宗教から政治を分離する	isolate
verse [vɔ́ːrs]	名 韻文, 詩歌 narrative in verse 韻文の物語 ＊ rhyme は名詞だと「韻」, 動詞だと「韻を踏む」。	poetry
beam [bíːm]	名 梁（はり）, 横柱 a frame of concrete columns and iron beams コンクリートの柱と鉄の梁でできたフレーム	girder
antiquated [ǽntəkwèɪtɪd]	形 時代遅れの；古風な change an antiquated educational system 時代遅れの教育システムを変える	outdated
avid [ǽvɪd]	形 熱心な, 渇望している an avid reader 熱心な読書家	keen
substantially [səbstǽnʃəli]	副 相当に, かなり, 十分に；大体 The costs increased substantially. 経費は大幅に増大した。 ＊マイナスのときにも使える。	considerably
breadbasket [brédbæ̀skət]	名 穀倉地帯 East Anglia is now the breadbasket of England. 今や英国東部は英国の穀倉地帯です。＊ granary は「穀物倉庫」。	granary
dictate [díkteɪt]	動 決定する；命令する Your job usually dictates where you live. 仕事で通常住む場所が決まる。　＊意味は文脈から！	determine
feasible [fíːzəbl]	形 実現可能な, 実行可能な；適した only one feasible solution to the problem その問題の実現可能な唯一の解決法　＊＝viable	possible
dehydrated [diːháɪdreɪtɪd]	形 脱水症状の；乾燥させた get seriously dehydrated 重度の脱水症状になる ＊ stay hydrated は「水分補給した状態でいる」こと。	of dehydration

Track 232

単語／発音	語彙／フレーズ	同意表現	難易度
concede [kənsíːd]	動 (負けなどを)認める concede defeat reluctantly 嫌々ながら敗北を認める ＊「負けなどを認める」と覚えよう！	admit	A
toxic [tɑ́ksɪk]	形 有毒な；中毒の dumping of toxic waste 毒性廃棄物の投棄 ＊＝ venomous	poisonous	
receptor [rɪséptər]	名 感受器官 activate a receptor 受容体を活性化する	sensory organ	
trample [trǽmpl]	動 踏みつける trample on someone's human right 人の人権を踏みにじる　＊＝ stamp	tread	B
buoyancy [bɔ́ɪənsi]	名 浮力 Coconuts drift on ocean currents by their buoyancy. ココナッツの実は浮力によって海流に乗って漂う。	flotation	
alien [éɪliən]	形 異質の；なじみのない Unkindness was alien to his gentle nature. 不親切は彼の優しい性質にとって異質のものだった。	foreign	
spinal [spáɪnl]	形 脊柱の，背骨の damage to the spinal cord 脊髄損傷 ＊ spinal column「脊柱；背骨」。	relating to the spine	C
disposal [dɪspóʊzl]	名 処分の自由，自由に使えること；処分 a car at his disposal 彼が自由に使える車	availability	
unprecedented [ʌnprésədəntɪd]	形 前例のない，先例のない unprecedented business opportunity 空前のビジネスチャンス	unheard-of	D
metabolise [mətǽbəlàɪz]	動 (新陳)代謝する metabolise fat into energy 脂肪をエネルギーに代謝する	change food into energy	
influx [ínflʌks]	名 流入，流れ込み，殺到 influx of Asian immigrants アジア系移民の流入 ＊移民の「流入」は頻出。	inflow	
unwarranted [ʌnwɔ́ːrəntɪd]	形 不当な，正当性を欠く make an unwarranted assumption 不当な推定を行う	unjustified	

249

Track 233

単語／発音	語彙／フレーズ	同意表現

scrutinise
[skrúːtənàɪz]
動 細かく調べる
scrutinise entry visas 入国ビザを念入りに調べる
＊= examine

fully examine

cumbersome
[kʌ́mbərsəm]
形 厄介な, かさばる
a cumbersome process 厄介な手順
＊後ろが some なので形容詞。

involved

boon
[búːn]
名 恵み, 恩恵, 利益
It's been a real boon to have a car this week.
今週手元に車があるので本当に助かっています。

blessing

liability
[làɪəbíləti]
名 法的責任；負債
accept liability for damages 損害賠償の責任を負う
＊形容詞 liable から意味を連想！

responsibility

intuitive
[ɪntʃúːətɪv]
形 直感の, 直感的な
make an intuitive judgement 直感的な判断を下す

instinctive

unadorned
[ʌnədɔ́ːrnd]
形 装飾のない；質素な
unadorned face 地のままの顔
＊動詞 adorn「飾る」より頻出。

plain

vaccinate
[væksənèɪt]
動 ワクチンを投与する
vaccinate a child against measles
子供にはしかの予防接種をする　＊vaccine「ワクチン」。

inoculate

legislative
[lédʒɪslèɪtɪv]
形 立法上の；立法府の
a legislative committee 立法委員会

lawmaking

meteor
[míːtiər]
名 流星；隕石
a shower of meteors 流星群
＊meteorite「（落下した）隕石」。

shooting star

preliminary
[prɪlímənèri]
形 準備の, 予備の
conduct preliminary research 予備調査をする
＊preliminary list「科目予備リスト」。

preparatory

weathering
[wéðərɪŋ]
名 風化作用
be resistant to weathering and erosion
風化や浸食に強い

weather action

dispatch
[dɪspǽtʃ]
動 送り出す, 発送する
dispatch letters asking for financial help 財政援助を求める手紙を発送する　＊「派遣する」場合も使える。

send

単語/発音	語彙/フレーズ	同意表現	難易度
caulk [kɔ́ːk]	動 隙間を詰める caulk the area around the sink 流しの周辺の隙間に詰め物をする	insulate	A
daydream [déɪdrìːm]	名 白昼夢, 楽しい空想 be lost in a daydream 空想に耽っている	reverie	
overthrow [òuvərθróu]	動 (政府などを)転覆させる overthrow the present regime 現政権を打倒する	subvert	
account [əkáunt]	動 (ある割合を)占める;説明する account for the majority of the elderly citizens 高齢市民の大多数を占める ＊W1 account for ＋数字。	occupy	B
repeal [rɪpíːl]	動 廃止する, 破棄する, 撤回する repeal laws that limit free speech 言論の自由を制限する法律を廃止する	annul	
supplant [səplǽnt]	動 取って代わる be supplanted by the next generation 次世代に取って代わられる	supersede	
seedling [síːdlɪŋ]	名 苗木, 若木 transplanting of rice seedlings 稲の苗の移植(田植え) ＊ -ling「〜に関わりのあるもの」。	sapling	C
toil [tɔ́ɪl]	動 せっせと働く;苦労して進む toil to make a living 生計を立てるためにせっせと働く	labour	
nuance [n(j)úːɑːns]	名 (表現・色などの)微妙な差異 pick up the small nuances 微妙なニュアンスを感じ取る	shade	
chronological [krɑ̀ːnəláːdʒɪkl]	形 年代順の, 発生順の in a chronological order 年代(日付)順に	sequential	D
outweigh [àutwéɪ]	動 〜を上回る;〜より重い outweigh the cost of 〜 〜の費用を上回る ＊W2 課題文でおなじみ。力関係を表すときに使う。	surpass	
sober [sóubər]	形 節度のある, まじめな;酔っていない live a sober life まじめな生活を送る	serious	

Track 235

単語／発音	語彙／フレーズ	同意表現
shed [ʃéd]	動 流す；脱ぎ捨てる shed tears 涙を流す ＊〜 skin / blood「脱皮する；血を流す」。	spill
paramount [pérəmàunt]	形 最高の；卓越した matter of paramount importance 最も重要な事柄	predominant
ordinance [ɔ́ːrdənəns]	名 法令，条例；布告 pollution control ordinance 公害防止条例 ＊＝ law	regulation
drought [dráut]	名 干ばつ，日照り The reservoir dried up during the drought. 貯水池は干ばつ中に涸れた。　＊発音注意！	dry spell
esteem [ɪstíːm]	名 尊敬；尊重 hold him in great esteem 彼を非常に尊敬する ＊ self-esteem は「自尊心」。	respect
crater [kréɪtər]	名 火口，（おわん型の）へこみ the craters on the moon 月面のクレーター（へこみ） ＊地質学や火山関係で出てきそう。	bowl
encompass [ɪnkʌ́mpəs]	動 含む；取り囲む The group encompasses all ages. そのグループにはあらゆる年齢の者が含まれている。	surround
improvisation [ɪmprɑ̀ːvəzéɪʃən]	名 即興，機転；（ジャズの）即興演奏 take an attitude of improvisation 臨機応変の態度を取る ＊全セクションでかなり頻出なのが「即興」。	resource
counterfeit [káuntərfɪt]	形 ニセの counterfeit bills ニセ札 ＊類義語：fake, false, sham。	bogus
perish [pérɪʃ]	動 死ぬ；滅びる；腐敗する perish in the war 戦死する ＊ perishable「腐りやすい」も頻出。	die
teem [tíːm]	動 〜でいっぱいである lakes teeming with life 生命で満ちあふれている湖 ＊ team とスペリングを混同しないこと。	be filled with
locomotion [lòukəumóuʃən]	名 運動（力），移動 organs of locomotion 運動器官	movement

単語／発音	語彙／フレーズ	同意表現	難易度
thaw [θɔ́:]	動 解凍する thaw food at room temperature 冷凍食品を室温で解凍する	melt	A
stationary [stéɪʃənèri]	形 静止した；定置型の be in stationary orbit 静止軌道にある ＊stationery「文房具；便箋」。	still	
postulate [pá:stʃəlèɪt]	動 （自明のこととして）仮定する；前提とする；主張する postulate the existence of 〜 〜の存在を仮定する ＊得意な単語と組み合わせて暗記！	posit	
appraise [əpréɪz]	動 評価する，査定する appraise the employees' job performance 職員の業務実勢を査定する	evaluate	B
manoeuvre [mənú:və]	動 操る，動かす；作戦行動をとらせる manoeuvre behind the scenes 裏工作をする ＊名詞だと「策略」。	operate	
pose [póuz]	動 引き起こす；提示する pose a danger to others 他人に危険をもたらす ＊ pose a question「疑問を投げかける」。	cause	
algae [ǽldʒi:ə]	名 (複)藻類；藻 Algae capture the Sun's energy by photosynthesis. 藻類は光合成によって太陽エネルギーを獲得する。		C
crucial [krú:ʃəl]	形 決定的な，重大な a crucial decision 重大な決定 ＊very important ということ。	critical	
terrestrial [təréstriəl]	形 地球の，地上波の digital terrestrial broadcasting 地上波デジタル放送 ＊「陸地の」の意味もある。⇔ celestial「天の，空の」。	earthly	
harness [há:rnəs]	動 （自然の力を）利用する harness the sun as a source of heat and power 熱と電力の資源として太陽を利用する	exploit	D
bewilder [bɪwíldər]	動 当惑させる，狼狽させる She was bewildered by her husband's sudden fury. 彼女は夫の突然の激怒に当惑した。	puzzle	
reliant [rɪláɪənt]	形 当てにしている，頼っている be reliant on someone for everything 何もかも誰かに依存している　＊reliable「信頼できる」と区別。	dependent	

Track 237

単語／発音	語彙／フレーズ	同意表現
polygon [pɑ́:lɪgɑ̀:n]	名 多角形 a dental polygon mirror 歯科用多面ミラー ＊poly- は「多」を意味する。	polygonal shape
spur [spə́:r]	動 刺激する；駆り立てる spur the economy 経済を刺激する	stimulate
whereabouts [wéərəbàuts]	名 行方 discover his whereabouts 彼の所在を突き止める ＊通常複数形で使う。	dwelling place
preservative [prɪzə́:rvətɪv]	名 保存料，防腐剤 preservative against mould かび止め	antiseptic
eerie [íəri]	形 不気味な；ぞっとする an eerie silence 不気味な静けさ ＊類義語 weird, strange。	uncanny
preeminent [prɪémənənt]	形 きわめて優秀な，抜群の preeminent economic power in the world 世界で秀でた経済大国	outstanding
decay [dɪkéɪ]	名 腐敗，腐朽，崩壊，虫歯 radioactive decay 核崩壊	decomposition
ruin [rú:ɪn]	動 台無しにする，破滅させる ruin someone's efforts 人の努力を台無しにする	devastate
markedly [má:rkɪdli]	副 著しく，際立って differ markedly in appearance 外見が明らかに異なる ＊L 発音注意！	notably
representation [rèprɪ:zentéɪʃən]	名 代表，議員団；表現 taxation without representation 代表なき課税 ＊tion で終わっていても，代表者。	representative
latently [léɪtəntli]	副 潜在的に cells latently infected with HIV 潜在的に HIV に感染した細胞	potentially
succinct [səksíŋkt]	形 簡潔な give a succinct explanation 簡潔な説明をする	concise

Track 238

単語／発音	語彙／フレーズ	同意表現	難易度
exorbitant [ɪgzɔ́ːrbətnt]	形 法外な charge exorbitant prices 法外な価格を請求する ＊＝ out of sight	outrageous	A
jolt [dʒóʊlt]	動 衝撃を与える；急激に揺する jolt someone into action 人を駆り立てて行動に移らせる	jar	
forsake [fərséɪk]	動 見捨てる, 縁を絶つ；諦める forsake all one's high principles すべての節操を捨てる	abandon	
precursor [prɪkə́ːrsər]	名 前身, 先駆者, 前任者 Ragtime is a precursor of jazz. ラグタイムはジャズの先駆者である。	predecessor	B
knack [næk]	名 コツ a knack for making money 金儲けのコツ ＊発音・スペリング注意！	know-how	
mock [máːk]	動 からかって真似る；あざける, ばかにする mock someone's accent 人のなまりを真似てからかう ＊「からかう」＋「真似る」。	ridicule	
whirl [wə́ːrl]	動 ぐるぐる回る；渦巻く whirl around in the wind 風に舞う ＊ whirlpool「(風・水の)渦」。	swirl	C
ascribe [əskráɪb]	動 〜のせいとする, 〜のおかげとする ascribe his success to the help from his friends 彼の成功を友達の助力のおかげとする	attribute	
spark [spáːrk]	動 刺激する；(刺激して)引き起こす spark a controversy 物議を醸す	set off	
incubate [ɪ́ŋkjəbèɪt]	動 孵化させる；(細菌などを)培養する incubate eggs in the nest 巣で卵を抱いてかえす ＊ incubator は「孵化器(卵を人工的にかえすための装置)」。	brood	D
composite [kəmpάːzɪt]	形 合成の；混合の a composite picture 合成写真	compound	
dampen [dǽmpən]	動 湿らせる dampen thick paper moderately 厚紙を適度に湿らせる	moisten	

255

Track 239

単語／発音	語彙／フレーズ	同意表現
pigment [pígmənt]	名 色素；顔料 pigment melanin in dark skin 浅黒い肌のメラニン色素	colour
empathy [émpəθi]	名 感情移入；共感 have empathy with others 他人に共感する	emotional involvement
expertise [èkspərtíːz]	名 専門的な知識, 技術, 能力 require a high level of expertise in psychiatry 精神医学の高度な専門知識を要求する	special knowledge
compulsory [kəmpʌ́lsəri]	形 義務的な；強制的な；必修の complete compulsory education 義務教育を終える ＊W2 教育関連の課題で使える。	mandatory
primate [práɪmeɪt]	名 霊長類の動物；サル目 non-human primates 人間以外の霊長類	
kiln [kíln]	名 かま；炉 a gas-fired kiln ガスがま	furnace
tantalise [tǽntəlàɪz]	動 じらす；からかう be tantalised by someone's behaviour 人の行動にじらされる	tease
radiant [réɪdiənt]	形 きらきら輝く have a radiant look 晴れやかな表情をしている	glittering
filmy [fílmi]	形 薄もやのような；薄い膜状の a filmy layer of dust ほこりの薄い層	diaphanous misty
cipher [sáɪfər]	動 暗号で記す, 暗号化する cipher the important documents 重要書類を暗号化する	code
conifer [káːnəfər]	名 針葉樹 forest of conifer trees 針葉樹林 ＊ hard wood「広葉樹」。	needle-leaved tree
jumble [dʒʌ́mbl]	動 ごちゃ混ぜにする get all jumbled together あらゆるものをごちゃごちゃにする	mix

単語／発音	語彙／フレーズ	同意表現	難易度
save [séɪv]	接前 ～を除いて save that ～ ～ということを除いて	except	A
mimetic [mɪmétɪk]	形 模倣の；見せかけの a mimetic word 擬態語	imitative	
voracious [vɔːréɪʃəs]	形 旺盛な；がつがつした a voracious appetite 旺盛な食欲	insatiable	
humility [hjuːmíləti]	名 謙虚さ；謙遜 have an attitude of humility 謙虚な態度を取る	humbleness	B
tranquillity [trænkwíləti]	名 静けさ tranquillity of society 社会の平穏	quietness	
unsung [ʌnsʌ́ŋ]	形 （不当に）世に知られていない an unsung hero 世に知られていない英雄	obscure	
eruption [ɪrʌ́pʃən]	名 噴出；発疹 eruptions of volcanic gases and ashes 火山性ガスや灰の噴出	spout	C
conspiracy [kənspírəsi]	名 陰謀 conspiracy to assassinate the President 大統領暗殺の陰謀	intrigue	
turbulent [tə́ːrbjələnt]	形 激動の；（風波が）荒れ狂う the turbulent times of the French Revolution フランス革命という激動の時代	tempestuous	
imbibe [ɪmbáɪb]	動 飲む；吸い込む imbibe democratic principles 民主主義の原則を吸収する	drink	D
opaque [oʊpéɪk]	形 不透明の a window with opaque glass くもりガラスの窓	obscure	
bipedal [báɪpèdəl]	形 二足動物の；二足を持つ a bipedal dinosaur 二足歩行の恐竜	two-footed	

Track 241

単語／発音	語彙／フレーズ	同意表現
vault [vɔ́:lt]	名 丸天井, アーチ型屋根；金庫室 a barrel vault かまぼこ型天井	dome
shy [ʃáɪ]	動 しりごみする；引き下がる shy away from any publicity 人前に出たがらない	recoil
proliferation [prəlìfəréɪʃən]	名 増殖；激増 proliferation of cancer cells がん細胞の増殖	rapid multiplication
hydrosphere [háɪdrousfìər]	名 水圏；水界 The hydrosphere covers 70 percent of the Earth's surface. 水圏（すいけん）は地球の表面の 70%を占めている。	watery layer
ledge [lédʒ]	名 岩棚 topple off a ledge 岩棚から転落する	rock shelf
engraving [ɪngréɪvɪŋ]	名 版画；彫刻；印刷物 a wood engraving print 木版画	etching
edifice [édəfɪs]	名 大建造物 a splendid and magnificent edifice 豪華壮麗な大建造物	large building
optimal [á:ptəml]	形 最適な；最善の determine optimal selling price 最適な販売価格を決める	optimum
pertinent [pə́:rtənənt]	形 適切な；関連する have plenty of pertinent knowledge 関連知識が豊富である	appropriate
afflict [əflíkt]	動 苦しめる, 悩ます be afflicted by epidemics 伝染病に苦しめられる	annoy
culture [kʌ́ltʃər]	名 栽培；培養；養殖 the culture of crops 作物の栽培	cultivation
clump [klʌ́mp]	名 かたまり；集団 a clump of trees 木の茂み	cluster

単語／発音	語彙／フレーズ	同意表現	難易度
figural [fígjərəl]	形 人物像の；図形の a figural sculpture 人物像の彫刻 ＊ figurine は「小さな像」。	figurative	A
discourse [dískɔːrs]	名 講話, 談話 give a discourse on peace 平和について講演する	lecture	A
abbreviate [əbríːvièɪt]	動 （言葉などを）短縮する；省略する European Union is abbreviated to EU. 欧州連合は EU と短縮される。	shorten	A
flare [fléər]	名 ゆらめく炎；赤々と輝く光 take a photo with a flare of flashlight フラッシュの光で写真を撮る	flame	B
girder [gə́ːrdər]	名 桁（けた），大梁（はり） a concrete bridge girder コンクリートの橋桁	beam	B
cardiac [káːrdiæk]	形 心臓の cardiac arrest 心臓停止 ＊ cardi- は「心臓」を表す接頭辞。	relating to the heart	C
decipher [dɪsáɪfər]	動 解読する；判読する decipher hieroglyphics 象形文字を解読する	decode	C
cramped [kræmpt]	形 すし詰めの；窮屈な a cramped jail cell 窮屈な牢屋 ＊ packed が同義語として頻出。	packed	C
gait [géɪt]	名 足取り；足並み walk with a rolling gait 千鳥足で歩く	step	D
asymmetrical [èɪsəmétrɪkl]	形 非対称の；不均整の a modern asymmetrical building 現代的な非対称建築物	non-symmetric	D
flick [flík]	名 軽くひと打ちすること；（ピシッ）という音 with a flick of the whip 鞭をひと振りして	flip	D
pupa [pjúːpə]	名 さなぎ emerge from a pupa さなぎから羽化する	chrysalis	D

単語／発音	語彙／フレーズ	同意表現
airborne [éərbɔ̀ːrn]	形 空気で運ばれる；空輸の airborne infectious disease 空気感染病	conveyed by or through air
engulf [ɪngʌ́lf]	動 巻き込む, のみ込む be engulfed by a tsunami 津波にのまれる	suck in
venomous [vénəməs]	形 有毒な bite by a venomous snake 毒ヘビによる咬み傷 ＊同義語として toxic も併せて覚える。	poisonous
corpse [kɔ́ːrps]	名 死体 abandonment of a corpse 死体遺棄 ＊人の死体のこと。「動物の死骸」は carcass。	remains
avert [əvə́ːrt]	動 そむける, そらす；避ける avert my eyes from the horrible sight 恐ろしい光景から目をそらす	turn away
transition [trænzíʃən]	名 移行, 推移, 変遷；変わり目 transition between the old system and the new one 旧システムから新システムへの移行	passage
signature [sígnətʃər]	名 特徴；痕跡 reveal a signature of 〜 〜の特徴を明らかにする	distinction
advent [ǽdvent]	名 到来, 出現；開始 the advent of new technology 新たなテクノロジーの到来	arrival
adjunct [ǽdʒʌŋkt]	名 付属品；付加物 be used as an adjunct to a computer コンピュータの付属品として使用される	supplement
equivocal [ɪkwívəkl]	形 はっきりしない；両義にとれる have an equivocal attitude はっきりしない態度をとる	ambiguous
conducive [kɑːnd(j)úːsɪv]	形 助けになる, 貢献する be conducive to economic prosperity 経済的繁栄に貢献する	contributory
convection [kənvékʃən]	名 対流；還流；伝達 circulate hot air by convection 対流で暖気を循環させる	movement in a gas or liquid

単語／発音	語彙／フレーズ	同意表現	難易度
uncanny [ʌnkǽni]	形 異様な；並外れて鋭い an uncanny coincidence 無気味なほどの偶然の一致	weird	A
diverge [daɪvə́ːrdʒ]	動 分岐する，分かれる diverge from a common ancestor 共通の祖先から分かれる	branch	
submerge [səbmə́ːrdʒ]	動 水浸しにする，沈める；覆い隠す Floodwater submerged the fields. 洪水で畑が水没した。 ＊L submerged の と続くと d の音がほぼ消える。	immerse	
prop [prάːp]	名 支え；支柱，つっぱり an emotional prop 精神的支え	strut	B
scarcity [skéərsəti]	名 不足，欠乏 a serious scarcity of resources 深刻な資源の欠乏	shortage	
dietary [dáɪətèri]	形 食事の；食餌療法の establish good dietary habits 良い食習慣を確立する	alimentary	
expanse [ɪkspǽns]	名 広がり；広々とした場所 boundless expanse of ocean 果てしない海の広がり	area	C
deductive [dɪdʌ́ktɪv]	形 演繹的な；推論の by deductive inference 演繹的推論によって	involving inferences from general principles	
refuse [réfjːs]	名 くず，がらくた，廃物 disposal of refuse 廃棄物の処理 ＊発音・アクセントに注意！	waste	
wobble [wάːbl]	動 ふらつく，よろよろする；動揺する The planet wobbles as it spins. その惑星は回転中にふらつく。	shake	D
blueprint [blúːprìnt]	名 詳細な計画，青写真 blueprint for success 成功への青写真	detailed plan	
per capita [pərkǽpətə]	形 1人当たりの per-capita GDP 1人当たりの国内総生産	capitated	

Track 245

単語／発音	語彙／フレーズ	同意表現
haphazard [hæphǽzərd]	形 無計画の；でたらめの a haphazard plan of action 行き当たりばったりの行動計画	random
aquatic [əkwɑ́:tɪk]	形 水生の；水の aquatic plants and animals 水生の動植物	water-dwelling
marvel [mɑ́:rvl]	名 驚くべきこと, 不思議なこと the marvels of nature 自然の驚異 ＊形容詞 marvellous「不思議な；素晴らしい」。	wonder
crouch [kráutʃ]	動 身を低くする, しゃがむ crouch down because of a stomach-ache 腹痛でうずくまる　＊ crouched position は「かがんだ体勢」。	squat
divert [daɪvə́:rt]	動 方向を変える, そらす divert public attention from the scandal そのスキャンダルから世間の注目をそらす	distract
cetacean [sɪtéɪʃən]	名 クジラ目の動物 dolphins and other cetaceans イルカや他のクジラ目動物	Cetacea
deflect [dɪflékt]	動 そらす；片寄らせる deflect foreign pressure 外国からの圧力をそらす	turn away
gale [géɪl]	名 強風 warnings for gales 強風注意報	strong wind
waggle [wǽgl]	動 （尾を）振る waggle the tail furiously 激しく尾を振る	wag
ferment [fərmént]	動 発酵させる ferment sugars into alcohol 糖を発酵させてアルコールに変える	leaven
adorn [ədɔ́:rn]	動 飾る；美観を添える adorn the table with flowers テーブルを花で飾る	decorate
crash [kræʃ]	形 応急的な, 一気に行う a crash course 集中特訓講座	intensive

単語／発音	語彙／フレーズ	同意表現	難易度
prodigy [prá:dədʒi]	名 天才児；驚異 be known as a child prodigy 神童として知られる ＊形容詞 prodigious「並外れた」も覚える。	wonder child	A
contagious [kəntéɪdʒəs]	形 伝染性の；うつりやすい a highly contagious disease 伝染性の高い病気	infectious	
surveillance [sərvéɪləns]	名 監視, 監督, 見張り be watched by surveillance cameras 監視カメラで見張られる	supervision	
pillar [pílər]	名 柱 an important pillar of the reform 改革の重要な柱	column	B
acuity [əkjú:əti]	名 鋭さ improve visual acuity 視覚の鋭さ(視力)を改善する ＊形容詞 acute「鋭い」。	sharpness	
outing [áutɪŋ]	名 小旅行 go on a company outing 社員旅行に行く	excursion	
frigid [frídʒɪd]	形 極寒の；冷淡な unexpectedly frigid winter 予想外に冷え込む冬	icy	C
decode [di:kóud]	動 解読する, 暗号を解く decode the entire human genome ヒトゲノム全体を解読する ＊⇔ encode「暗号化する」。	decipher	
nook [núk]	名 隅；人目につかないところ search every nook and cranny 隅から隅までくまなく捜す	corner	
covert [kávə:rt]	形 ひそかな, 目立たない make a covert agreement 暗黙の合意に至る	secret	D
demise [dɪmáɪz]	名 死, 逝去；消滅 her tragic demise 彼女の悲劇的な死 ＊「消滅, 絶滅」の意味が頻出。	death	
condolence [kəndóʊləns]	名 お悔やみ Let me offer my condolences to you. お悔やみを申し上げます。	commiserations	

Track 246

Track 247

単語／発音	語彙／フレーズ	同意表現
propulsion [prəpʌ́lʃən]	名 推進力；噴射 propulsion to escape from gravity 重力を振り切るための推進力	thrust
gorge [gɔ́ːrdʒ]	動 むさぼり食う gorge oneself 満腹になるまでたらふく食べる	devour
lurk [lə́ːrk]	動 待ち伏せする lurk in the shadows 物陰に潜む	ambush
vascular [vǽskjələr]	形 脈管の；導管の a vascular disease of the heart 心臓血管症	of vessels
intrusive [ɪntrúːsɪv]	形 侵入的な；押し付けがましい exhibit intrusive behaviour 押し付けがましい態度を示す	obtrusive
capillary [kǽpəlèri]	形 毛管の；毛細血管の soak water up by capillary action 毛管現象によって水を吸い上げる	relating to capillaries
pounce [páʊns]	動 急に襲いかかる pounce on ~ like a savage beast 〜に猛獣のように飛びかかる	strike
inscribe [ɪnskráɪb]	動 刻む；銘記する inscribe one's name on a rock 岩に名前を刻む	engrave
relic [rélɪk]	名 遺物；遺品；遺跡 relics from the past 過去の遺物	antiquities
attest [ətést]	動 (真実性などを)証明する attest to his innocence 彼の無実を証明する	certify
deputy [dépjəti]	名 代理(人)；補佐官 a deputy chairman 議長代理	surrogate
rebellion [rɪbéljən]	名 反乱，謀反 put down the rebellion against the government 政府に対する反乱を鎮圧する	uprising

Track 248

単語／発音	語彙／フレーズ	同意表現	難易度
rhetoric [rétərɪk]	名 修辞法；特別な効果を狙った表現；美辞麗句；大げさな言い回し exhaust one's rhetoric 美辞の限りを尽くす	oratory	A
conceit [kənsíːt]	名 うぬぼれ；自尊心 be full of conceit うぬぼれが強い	vanity	
rally [ræli]	動 （再）結集する；回復する rally under the national flag 国旗のもとに集結する	muster	
appendix [əpéndɪks]	名 付録；補遺；虫垂 a map as an appendix to the guide book ガイドブック付録の地図　＊ appendicitis「虫垂（ちゅうすい）炎」。	supplement	B
endorse [ɪndɔ́ːrs]	動 是認する，支持する；（小切手などに）裏書する officially endorse the decision 決定を正式に承認する	approve	
fiscal [fískl]	形 財政上の，会計の；国庫の improve fiscal deficits 財政赤字を改善する	financial	
infringe [ɪnfríndʒ]	動 （法律・契約などを）破る；侵害する infringe basic human rights 基本的人権を侵害する	impinge	C
allure [əljúə(r)]	動 魅了する；そそのかして～させる be allured by the advertisement 広告にそそのかされる	tempt	
augment [ɔːgmént]	動 増加させる augment the competitiveness 競争力を増加させる ＊アクセント注意！	increase	
enzyme [énzaɪm]	名 酵素 an enzyme necessary for digesting 消化に必要な酵素	ferment	D
affirmative [əfə́ːrmətɪv]	形 肯定的な，賛成の；断定的な an affirmative vote 賛成票 ＊名詞 affirmation「肯定」。	positive	
ardour [άːrdər]	名 情熱；熱心 awake one's ardour for study 学習意欲を呼び起こす	passion	

265

Track 249

単語／発音	語彙／フレーズ	同意表現
apathy [ǽpəθi]	名 冷淡；無関心 apathy of the young for an election 若者の間での選挙への無関心　＊形容詞 apathetic。	indifference
narcotic [nɑːrkάtɪk]	名 麻薬 addiction to narcotics 麻薬中毒	drug
admonish [ədmάnɪʃ]	動 勧告する，忠告する；警告する admonish students against smoking 学生にタバコを吸わないよう忠告する	advise
captivity [kæptívəti]	名 監禁状態；束縛 be released from captivity 監禁状態から解放される	incarceration
detain [dɪtéɪn]	動 引き留める，待たせる；勾留する arrest and detain a suspect 容疑者を逮捕，勾留する	confine
curtail [kərtéɪl]	動 （予定より）短縮する；削減する the need to curtail the use of nuclear weapons 核兵器使用を削減する必要性	cut back
agenda [ədʒéndə]	名 協議事項；議事；予定表 set the agenda for the meeting 会議の協議事項を設定する	subject for discussion
antipathy [æntípəθi]	名 嫌悪，反感；反発 a strong antipathy to spiders クモに対する強い嫌悪感	aversion
appease [əpíːz]	動 なだめる；鎮める；譲歩する appease public criticism 市民の批判を鎮める	pacify
besiege [bɪsíːdʒ]	動 包囲する；取り囲む；攻める besiege a fortress 要塞を包囲する	beleaguer
ambivalence [æmbívələns]	名 矛盾する感情；両面価値 an ambivalence between love and hate 愛憎の矛盾する感情（葛藤）	contradiction
veterinarian [vètərənéəriən]	名 獣医 have a veterinarian look at the puppy 子犬を獣医師に診てもらう	veterinary surgeon

Track 250

単語／発音	語彙／フレーズ	同意表現	難易度
arbitrate [á:rbətrèɪt]	動 仲裁する，調停する arbitrate the dispute between the two 両者の争議を仲裁する	mediate	A
lapse [lǽps]	名 時の経過；過失；失策；堕落 temporary lapse of memory 短期的な記憶の欠落 ＊time-lapse video は建設現場や風景変化のコマ送り映像。	elapse	
relentless [rɪléntləs]	形 情け容赦のない，無慈悲な relentless military attack 情け容赦のない軍事攻撃	ruthless	
introvert [íntrəvə̀:rt]	名 内向的な人；はにかみ屋 a pathological introvert 病的に内向的な人 ＊⇔ extrovert	inhibited person	B
subdue [səbd(j)ú:]	動 鎮圧する；征服する；抑制する subdue a riot 暴動を鎮圧する	repress	
hierarchy [háɪərá:rki]	名 階層制度；職階級；支配層 without a clear hierarchy 明確な上下関係のない	rank	
assent [əsént]	動 同意する；承諾する assent to a proposal 提案に同意する	agree	C
conflicting [kə̀nflíktɪŋ]	形 矛盾する；対立する reconcile two conflicting views 対立する 2 つの意見を調停する ＊R opposing と書き換えられる。	contradictory	
fend [fénd]	動 扶養する；世話をする fend for oneself 自力で生活する ＊自動詞用法は for を伴う。	take care of	
saline [séɪlaɪn]	形 塩分を含んだ；塩辛い physiological saline solution 生理食塩水	salty	D
basin [béɪsn]	名 (川の)流域；水ばち；洗面器；盆地 the Amazon river basin アマゾン川流域	watershed	
clinch [klíntʃ]	動 (問題・議論などに)けりをつける clinch a deal 取引をまとめる ＊確定させること。	settle	

267

単語／発音	語彙／フレーズ	同意表現
embellish [ɪmbélɪʃ]	動 (飾って)美しくする；飾る embellish a room with flowers 部屋を花で飾る	decorate
crumple [krʌ́mpl]	動 捻じ曲げる；しわくちゃにする crumple the paper in one's fist 紙を拳の中でくしゃくしゃにする	rumple
inexorable [ɪnéksərəbl]	形 情け容赦のない inexorable forces of nature 自然の情け容赦のない猛威	relentless

IELTS必須英単語
Group D

単語／発音	語義／フレーズ	同意表現
calamitous [kəlǽmətəs]	形 災難をもたらす；悲惨な calamitous rise in sea level 災難をもたらす海面の上昇	disastrous
discipline [dísəplən]	名 学問分野, 学科 biology as a discipline 学問分野としての生物 ＊「規律」の意味もある。interdisciplinary は「多分野にまたがった」。	field
dire [dáɪər]	形 悲惨な；不吉な dire consequences 悲惨な結果	terrible
subsidence [səbsáɪdns]	名 沈下, 陥没；倒壊 land subsidence 地盤沈下	settling
buttress [bʌ́trəs]	動 支える buttress the ice sheet 氷床を支える ＊名詞「支え」の意味もある。	support
buckle [bʌ́kl]	動 曲がる；崩れる buckle under the weight 重みで曲がる	bend
excrete [ɪkskríːt]	動 排出する(される) excrete the salts from the body 体外に塩分を排出する	discharge
solvent [sáːlvənt]	名 溶媒, 溶剤 chemical solvents 化学溶剤	flux
envisage [ɪnvízɪdʒ]	動 予想する；心に描く envisage a positive future 前向きな未来を予想する ＊ imagine, envision とも同義語。発音に注意！	foresee
surrogate [sʌ́ːrəgèɪt]	形 代理の a surrogate mother 代理母	substitute
globule [gláːbjuːl]	名 小球体；血球 fat globules 脂肪球	small drop
channel [tʃǽnl]	動 向ける, 集中する channel one's energy into study エネルギーを学習に向ける ＊名詞「水路」。	direct

Track 253

単語／発音	語義／フレーズ	同意表現	難易度
intrinsic [ɪntrínsɪk]	形 固有の，本来備わっている the intrinsic value of music 音楽の本来の価値 ＊⇔ extrinsic	inherent	A
extrinsic [ekstrínsɪk]	形 外的な，付帯的な extrinsic factors 外因的要素	external	
reiterate [ríːtərèɪt]	動 繰り返し言う reiterate the argument その主張を何度も繰り返し言う	repeat	
exponential [èkspounénʃəl]	形 急激な，幾何級数的な grow at an exponential rate 急激な割合で増大する	precipitous	B
dignity [dígnəti]	名 威厳 retreat with dignity 威厳をもって引き下がる	stateliness	
indigenous [ɪndídʒənəs]	形 先住の，固有の；生まれつきの The Maori are indigenous people of New Zealand. マオリ族はニュージーランドの先住民です。	native	
confectionery [kənfékʃənèri]	名 菓子類；菓子製造 a box of confectionery 菓子折り	sweets	C
viable [váɪəbl]	形 実行可能な；成功しそうな financially viable 財政的に実行可能な ＊R feasible とともに possible の同義語として覚える。	possible	
immerse [ɪmə́ːrs]	動 浸す，沈める；埋める immerse beans in the chemical solvent 豆を化学溶剤に浸す	soak	
kelp [kélp]	名 海藻，海藻灰 harvest kelp to make a fertilizer 肥料を作るために海藻を収穫する	seaweed	D
swell [swél]	名 うねり，大波；隆起 surge with swells うねりとともに押し寄せる	roller	
propagation [prɑ̀ːpəgéɪʃən]	名 繁殖，増殖；伝播 propagation of seaweeds 海藻の繁殖 ＊動詞は propagate。	reproduction	

単語／発音	語義／フレーズ	同意表現
spore [spɔ́ːr]	名 胞子，芽胞 A spore is a tiny seedlike cell. 胞子は小さな種に似た細胞です。	sporule
dehydration [diːhaɪdréɪʃən]	名 脱水；脱水症状 severe dehydration ひどい脱水症状 ＊de- は「分離；除去」。	desiccation
apportion [əpɔ́ːrʃən]	動 配分する，振り分ける apportion housework equally between partners パートナーに等しく家事を振り分ける	divide out
revelation [rèvəléɪʃən]	名 (意外な)新事実；暴露 a startling revelation 驚くべき新事実	disclosure
autonomous [ɔːtɑ́nəməs]	形 自治の；自律性の an autonomous province 自治州	self-governing
analogous [ənǽləgəs]	形 類似した，相似の Sleep is in some way analogous to death. 睡眠は幾分か死に類似している。	similar
extrapolation [ɪkstræpəléɪʃən]	名 (既知事実からの)推定 extrapolation from the evidence その証拠からの推定	inference
engrossed [ɪŋgróʊst]	形 夢中である，没頭して become engrossed in conversation 会話に夢中になる	absorbed
exuberant [ɪgz(j)úːbərənt]	形 元気にあふれた in an exuberant mood 元気にあふれた気分で	buoyant
manoeuvre [mənúːvər]	名 策略；大演習 many cunning manoeuvres 多くの狡猾な策略	trick
window [wíndoʊ]	名 (限られた)期間 a window of opportunity 束の間のチャンス	moment
predatory [prédətɔ̀ːri]	形 捕食性の；肉食性の a predatory animal 捕食動物 ＊predatory nature は「捕食の性質」。	predacious

単語／発音	語義／フレーズ	同意表現	難易度
cognitive [káːgnətɪv]	形 認識の a child's cognitive development 子供の認知発達 ＊R cognitive skills「認識能力」は頻出。	perceptual	A
bout [báʊt]	名（病気や活動の）一期間 a long bout of asthma 長期間にわたる喘息の病	spell	
predicate [prédəkət]	動 根拠を置く be predicated on an assumption 仮定に基づく	base	
fluorescent [flʊərésnt]	形 蛍光を発する，蛍光性の a fluorescent light 蛍光灯		B
murky [mə́ːrki]	形 陰気な；濁っている murky weather 陰気な天候	gloomy	
brew [brúː]	動（嵐，陰謀などが）起こる There's trouble brewing in the neighbourhood. 近所でトラブル発生中。	occur	
invoke [ɪnvóʊk]	動（法の力）に訴える；切望する invoke a veto 拒否権に訴える	resort	C
vex [véks]	動 苛立たせる，怒らせる；困らせる His behaviour vexed her. 彼の行動が彼女を苛立たせた。 ＊形容詞 vexing「イライラさせる」。	annoy	
depletion [dɪplíːʃən]	名 枯渇 depletion of natural resources 天然資源の枯渇	exhaustion	
alienate [éɪliənèɪt]	動 遠ざける，疎外する His radical comments alienated conservative voters. 彼の過激な言葉が保守的な有権者を遠ざけた。	estrange	D
inductive [ɪndʌ́ktɪv]	形 帰納的な；誘導の an inductive method 帰納法〔具体から一般法則を導く〕 ＊a deductive method「演繹法」も併せて覚えたい。	recursive	
antidote [ǽntɪdòʊt]	名 解毒剤；対応策 an antidote for snakebite 毒ヘビ用の解毒薬	antitoxin	

Track 256

単語／発音	語義／フレーズ	同意表現
tenacious [tənéɪʃəs]	形 不屈の, 粘り強い；断固たる a tenacious negotiator 粘り強い交渉人	**p**ersistent
tapered [téɪpərd]	形 先細の tapered trousers 先細のズボン	**n**arrowing
hard-wired [há:rd wáɪərd]	形 固有で変わりにくい；PCに内蔵の hard-wired character 固有の気質 ＊「生まれつき備わっている」という意味でも出る。	**b**uilt-in
incinerate [ɪnsínərèɪt]	動 焼却処分する incinerate waste ごみを焼却する	**b**urn
flounder [fláʊndər]	動 もがく, あがく, しどろもどろになる flounder helplessly どうしようもなく, しどろもどろになる	**s**truggle
attribute [ǽtrəbjù:t]	名 特質；性質, 属性 a human attribute of reason 理性という人間の特質 ＊動詞 attribute A to B「AをBのせいにする」も重要。	**p**roperty
permanency [pə́:rmənənsi]	名 永続性, 永久不変 Spoken words lack permanency. 話し言葉は永続性に欠ける。 ＊「終身雇用」は permanent / lifetime employment。	**p**erpetuity
deduction [dɪdʌ́kʃən]	名 控除, 差し引き the deduction of tax 税の控除	**s**ubtraction
frequent [frí:kwənt]	動 頻繁に行く, よく出入りする the hotel frequented by British tourists イギリス人旅行者がよく行くホテル	**g**o **o**ften
anaesthetic [æ̀nəsθétɪk]	名 麻酔薬 Surgery is carried out under an anaesthetic. 手術は麻酔をかけて行われる。	**n**arcotic
migraine [máɪɡrèɪn]	名 偏頭痛 suffer from severe migraine ひどい偏頭痛に苦しむ	**h**emicrania
bronchitis [brɑ:ŋkáɪtəs]	名 気管支炎 be afflicted with bronchitis 気管支炎で苦しむ	**r**espiratory **t**ract **c**omplications

Track 257

単語／発音	語義／フレーズ	同意表現	難易度
extremities [ɪkstréməṭis]	名 四肢；手足 paralysis of the extremities 四肢の麻痺	four limbs	A
consistency [kɑːnsístənsi]	名 密度, 濃度；一貫性 the consistency of thick milk 濃いミルクのような密度 ＊W1 rose consistently「一貫して上昇した」。	thickness	
vested [véstɪd]	形 既得の vested interests 既得権益	acquired	
fallow [fǽloʊ]	形 休閑中の fallow farmland 休閑中の農地	idle	B
exacerbate [ɪgzǽsərbèɪt]	動 悪化させる；苛立たせる exacerbate the conflict 対立を悪化させる	aggravate	
awry [əráɪ]	副 間違って；ゆがんで when things go awry 物事がうまくいかないとき ＊ go awry をフレーズで覚える。	amiss	
assay [ǽseɪ]	名（鉱物・薬品などの）分析 DNA assay DNA 分析	analysis	C
permutation [pə̀ːrmjʊtéɪʃən]	名 置換 data permutation データ置換	substitution	
antiquity [æntíkwəṭi]	名 古代, 太古 date back to antiquity 古代まで遡る	ancientry	
wreak [ríːk]	動（破壊・損害を）もたらす, 加える wreak enormous damage on the county of Devon デボン州に甚大な被害をもたらす	inflict	D
havoc [hǽvək]	名 大惨事 play havoc with 〜 〜をめちゃめちゃにする	catastrophe	
tertiary [tə́ːrʃièri]	形 第三の the primary, secondary and tertiary industry 第一次, 第二次および第三次産業	third	

Track 258

単語／発音	語義／フレーズ	同意表現
appreciable [əpríːʃəbl]	形 かなりの；はっきり感知できる an appreciable change in Earth's climate はっきり分かるほどの気候変化	considerable
paraphernalia [pèrəfərnéɪliə]	名 装備, 設備；手回り品 buy camping paraphernalia online キャンプ装備をネットで買う	equipment
homeopathy [hòumiáːpəθi]	名 ホメオパシー（同種・同毒療法） a practitioner of homeopathy ホメオパシー医	
venom [vénəm]	名 毒 snake venom ヘビの毒 ＊「毒」は poison, toxin, venom の3つを覚える。	poison
placebo [pləsíːbou]	名 プラシーボ（偽薬） a placebo effect プラシーボ効果 ＊治療というよりも気休めのための薬のこと。	fake drug
moraine [məréɪn]	名 氷堆石（氷河による堆石） boulder-rich moraine 巨礫の多い氷堆石	
forensic [fərénzɪk]	形 法医学の；犯罪科学の find forensic evidence 法医学的な証拠を発見する	medicolegal
annotation [ænətéɪʃən]	名 注釈 an edition with detailed annotations 詳しい注釈付きの版	note
whilst [wáɪlst]	接 〜する間；〜である一方 I had my bag stolen whilst I was snoozing. 居眠りしている間に鞄を盗まれた。	while
custodial [kʌstóʊdiəl]	形 拘留の；保護（者）の, 後見の a custodial sentence 拘置判決	detention
substantial [səbstǽnʃəl]	形 しっかりした；相当な, かなりの a substantial house しっかりした家屋 ＊類義語 significant。	considerable
acquisitive [əkwízətɪv]	形 貪欲な an acquisitive nature of humans 人間の貪欲な性格	greedy

単語／発音	語義／フレーズ	同意表現	難易度
collate [kəléɪt]	動 集めて分析する；照合する collate information from across Britain イギリス全土の情報を照合する	collect	A
cardio- [káːrdioʊ-]	連結 心臓 a cardiovascular disease 心臓血管疾患 ＊cardiac は「心臓の」。	heart	A
subsidy [sʌ́bsədi]	名（政府からの）補助金，助成金 offer a subsidy to low-income families 低所得の家庭に補助金を交付する	aid	A
composter [káːmpoʊstər]	名 生ごみ処理機 natural composters 自然の生ごみ処理機	disposer	B
annum [ǽnəm]	名 年 two percent interest per annum 1年につき2%の利子 ＊形容詞 annual「年間の」。	year	B
matinee [mǽtəneɪ]	名 昼の公演 the matinee on Sunday 日曜の昼公演	afternoon performance	B
endoscope [éndəskòʊp]	名 内視鏡 examination with an endoscope 内視鏡検査	gastroscope	C
fertility [fərtíləti]	名 繁殖力があること；肥沃さ a low fertility rate 低い繁殖率	productivity	C
staggering [stǽgərɪŋ]	形（数量が）信じがたいほどの，膨大な a staggering amount of data in the computer コンピュータ内の膨大なデータ	surprising	C
puerile [pjʊ́ərəl]	形 幼稚な a puerile excuse 幼稚な言い訳	childish	D
rickety [ríkɪti]	形 壊れそうな，ガタガタの a rickety old car 壊れそうな古い車	broken-down	D
revulsion [rɪvʌ́lʃən]	名 嫌悪，反感 a revulsion against the war 反戦感情	repugnance	D

単語／発音	語義／フレーズ	同意表現
flustered [flʌ́stərd]	形 狼狽した flustered and unsettled 狼狽して落ち着かない	unnerved
elucidate [ɪlúːsədèɪt]	動 解明する；はっきり説明する elucidate the true nature of the universe 宇宙の本質を明らかにする	illuminate
transient [trǽnziənt]	形 一時的な a transient effect 一時的効果	transitory
viscous [vískəs]	形 粘性のある, 粘性の高い viscous fluid 粘り気のある液体	tacky
granular [grǽnjələr]	形 粒状の granular powder 顆粒状の粉末	grained
punchline [pʌ́ntʃlàɪn]	名 (ジョークの)落ち a catchy punchline 受けそうな落ち	tagline
reflex [ríːfleks]	名 反射(作用)；反射能力 conditional reflex 条件反射	reaction
pedigree [pédɪgrìː]	名 血統 a dog with a pedigree 血統書付きの犬	bloodline
ludicrous [lúːdəkrəs]	形 ばからしい a ludicrous failure ばかげた失敗	ridiculous
incongruity [ìnkəngrúːəti]	名 不一致；不調和 resolve the incongruity 不一致を解消する	disaccord
perverse [pərvə́ːrs]	形 つむじ曲がりの, ひねくれた a perverse sense of humour ひねくれたユーモアのセンス	perverted
repatriate [riːpǽtrièɪt]	動 (本国へ)送還する repatriate a prisoner of war 戦争捕虜を本国送還する	extradite

Track 261

単語／発音	語義／フレーズ	同意表現	難易度
accrue [əkrúː]	動 （利益などを）獲得する accrue the wealth 富を獲得する ＊金銭的な利益を増やすことを表す。	accumulate	A
perennial [pəréniəl]	形 永続する；多年生の perennial plants 多年生植物	everlasting	
vegetative [védʒətèɪtɪv]	形 植物人間状態の；植物の a vegetative state 植物人間状態	comatose	
quota [kwóʊtə]	名 割当量 a sales quota 販売ノルマ	ration	B
intermodal [ìntərmóʊdl]	形 協同一貫輸送の international intermodal transport 国際協同一貫輸送		
referendum [rèfəréndəm]	名 住民投票 a national referendum 国民投票	plebiscite	
morale [məræl]	名 やる気, 士気 a morale booster 士気を鼓舞するもの	motivation	C
retrenchment [rɪtréntʃmənt]	名 削減 budget retrenchment 予算削減	downsizing	
contingent [kəntíndʒənt]	形 偶然の, 不慮の；依存する a contingent event 不慮の出来事	incidental	
remuneration [rɪmjùːnəréɪʃən]	名 報酬 directors' remuneration 役員報酬	salary	D
regimen [rédʒəmən]	名 養生法 a meal regimen 食事療法	remedy	
emblazon [ɪmbléɪzn]	動 （紋章で）飾る a cap emblazoned with the name of the team チーム名で飾られた帽子	adorn	

Track 262

単語／発音	語義／フレーズ	同意表現
dispense [dɪspéns]	動 施す；分配する dispense justice 正義を施す	administer
grapple [grǽpl]	動 取り組む grapple with difficult issues 難問に取り組む	tackle
recalcitrant [rɪkǽlsɪtrənt]	形 反抗的な a recalcitrant student 反抗的な学生	disobedient
inundate [ínʌndèɪt]	動 水浸しにする；殺到する be inundated with complaints 不満の声が殺到する	flooded
euthanasia [jùːθənéɪʒə]	名 安楽死 legalise euthanasia 安楽死を合法化する	mercy killing
excruciate [ɪkskrúːʃièɪt]	動 ひどく苦しめる be excruciated by a pain 痛みにひどく苦しめられる	torment
obsolescence [àːbsəlésns]	名 退化, 衰退；すたれること products with built-in obsolescence 意図的に老朽化する製品	retrogression
hygiene [háɪdʒiːn]	名 衛生 public hygiene 公衆衛生	sanitation
efficacy [éfɪkəsi]	名 有効性, 効果 treatment efficacy 治療効果	effectiveness
delinquency [dɪlíŋkwənsi]	名 非行；過失；怠慢 juvenile delinquency 少年の非行	misbehaviour
stag [stǽg]	形 男性だけの a stag party（花婿用の）男性だけのパーティー	men only
forge [fɔ́ːrdʒ]	動 偽造する forge paper money 紙幣を偽造する ＊「（関係を）築く；前進する」の意味もある。	counterfeit

Track 263

単語／発音	語義／フレーズ	同意表現	難易度
tiered [tíərd]	形 層(段)になった tiered seating 段になった客席	stair-like	A
superannuation [sùːpərænjuéɪʃən]	名 老齢退職；老齢者年金 a superannuation plan 老齢年金制度	retirement	
refurbishment [rɪfəːrbɪʃmənt]	名 改修 refurbishment work 改修作業	revamping	
ambience [ǽmbiəns]	名 雰囲気；環境 an international ambience in a big city 大都市の国際的な雰囲気	atmosphere	B
preponderance [prɪpɑ́ːndərəns]	名 優勢 by a preponderance of evidence 優位な証拠によって	prevalence	
quibble [kwíbl]	動 屁理屈を言う quibble over trivialities ささいなことに屁理屈を言う	split hairs	
scruffy [skrʌ́fi]	形 みすぼらしい scruffy neighbourhood みすぼらしい地区	shabby	C
plummet [plʌ́mət]	動 急落する Stock prices have plummeted. 株価が急落した。 ＊W1 plunge と同様に名詞でも動詞でも使える。	plunge	
collude [kəlúːd]	動 共謀する；結託する collude with drug traffickers 麻薬の売人と共謀する	conspire	
contravene [kɑ̀ːntrəvíːn]	動 違反する；反論する contravene a law 法律に違反する	infringe	D
corporal [kɔ́ːrpərəl]	形 肉体の corporal punishment 体罰	bodily	
deport [dɪpɔ́ːrt]	動 国外追放する deport illegal immigrants 不法入国者を国外追放する	exile	

281

Track 264

単語／発音	語義／フレーズ	同意表現
expedient [ɪkspíːdiənt]	名 (急場しのぎの)方法，手段；方便 as a temporary expedient その場の間に合わせに	crisis measures
assiduous [əsídʒuəs]	形 勤勉な；根気強い an assiduous worker 勤勉な労働者	diligent
despondent [dɪspɑ́ːndənt]	形 意気消沈した；元気のない a despondent look 意気消沈した顔つき	dejected
atrophy [ǽtrəfi]	名 (身体器官の)萎縮；(機能の)退化 the gene causing muscular atrophy 筋萎縮を引き起こす遺伝子	withering
consanguinity [kɑ̀ːnsæŋgwínəti]	名 血縁関係；密接な結びつき consanguinity of the third degree 三親等の血縁関係	blood relationship
vanguard [vǽngɑ̀ːrd]	名 前衛 vanguard technology 先端技術	forefront
auspicious [ɔːspíʃəs]	形 幸先のよい；吉兆の choose an auspicious day for the wedding 結婚式のための吉日を選ぶ	propitious
clout [kláʊt]	名 影響力；勢力 political clout 政治的影響力	influence
sufferance [sʌ́fərəns]	名 忍耐(力) beyond sufferance 我慢できない	endurance
meritocracy [mèrɪtɑ́ːkrəsi]	名 実力主義；能力主義社会 the rise of meritocracy in society 社会における能力主義の高まり	merit system
anomaly [ənɑ́ːməli]	名 異常 climate anomalies caused by global warming 地球温暖化による気象異常	abnormality
mercenary [mə́ːrsənèri]	形 金目当ての a mercenary soldier 傭兵	money-oriented

Track 265

単語／発音	語義／フレーズ	同意表現	難易度
spurious [spjúəriəs]	形 偽りの，にせの spurious coins 偽造貨幣	fake	A
decrepit [dɪkrépət]	形 よぼよぼの；おんぼろの a decrepit old man よぼよぼの老人	feeble	
dilapidate [dɪlǽpədèɪt]	動 荒廃させる；破損させる be dilapidated by neglect 放置によって荒れ果てた	ruin	
preside [prɪzáɪd]	動 議長を務める；統括する preside at a summit サミットで議長を務める ＊「管理する；統括する」意味でも使う。	chair	B
tendon [téndən]	名 腱 tendon Achilles アキレス腱 ＊tendonitis「腱鞘炎」。	sinew	
marsupial [mɑːrsúːpiəl]	名 有袋類 the marsupium organ of a marsupial 育児嚢という有袋動物の器官　＊胸に pouch「小物入れの袋」がある。	pouched mammal	
germination [dʒèːrmənéɪʃən]	名 発芽 the germination of the bean 豆の発芽 ＊germ には「胚芽；萌芽」もある。	sprouting	C
smother [smʌ́ðər]	動 抑える；もみ消す；窒息させる smother a laugh 笑いを抑える	suppress	
paradigm [pérədàɪm]	名 方法論，パラダイム；実例 break out the old paradigm 古い方法論を打ち破る ＊「模範；範例」という意味もある。	theoretical framework	
kinetic [kənétɪk]	形 運動の kinetic energy of a moving object 移動物体の運動エネルギー	motional	D
pronounced [prənáʊnst]	形 はっきりした cause a pronounced change はっきりした変化をもたらす	clear	
mint [mínt]	動 造幣する；鋳造する mint a gold coin 金貨を鋳造する ＊「王立造幣局」Royal Mint。	coin	

Track 266

単語／発音	語義／フレーズ	同意表現
incubation [ìnkjəbéɪʃən]	名 抱卵, 孵化；培養 duration of incubation 抱卵期間	hatching
precarious [prɪkéəriəs]	形 不安定な make a precarious living 不安定な暮らしをする	unstable
parole [pəróul]	名 仮釈放；仮出所；釈放宣誓 life sentence without parole 仮釈放なしの終身刑	conditional permission to leave
sterilise [stérəlàɪz]	動 殺菌する, 消毒する sterilise 〜 by boiling 〜を煮沸消毒する	disinfect
obsess [əbsés]	動 とりつく be obsessed about details 些細なことにこだわる ＊ obsession 妄想；執念；強迫観念。	haunt
subduction [səbdʌ́kt ʃən]	名 (地質学の)沈み込み subduction of oceanic plate 海洋プレートの沈み込み	subsidence
exploit [ɪksplɔ́ɪt]	動 搾取する；最大限に活用する exploit children as cheap labour 低賃金労働者として子供を搾取する ＊プラスとマイナスの意味がある。	abuse
enigmatic [ənɪgmǽtɪk]	形 謎めいた an enigmatic smile 謎めいた微笑	mysterious
ingrain [ɪŋgréɪn]	動 (習慣・信念などを)深く根付かせる be ingrained in culture 文化に根差している	instil
scorching [skɔ́ːrtʃɪŋ]	形 焼けつくような under the scorching sun 炎天下で	searing
masonry [méɪsnri]	名 レンガ工事, 石造り建築；壁田のレンガ masonry walls 石造りの壁	
varsity [váːrsəti]	名 大学代表チーム a varsity track and field team 学校の陸上競技代表チーム ＊ e ではなくて a。	first team

単語／発音	語義／フレーズ	同意表現	難易度
torso [tɔ́ːrsou]	名 胴体 have a long torso and short legs 胴長短足である	trunk	A
intoxication [ɪntàːksɪkéɪʃən]	名 中毒；酩酊，夢中 food intoxication 食中毒	poisoning	
stethoscope [stéθəskòup]	名 聴診器 apply a stethoscope to a patient's chest 患者の胸に聴診器を当てる	auscultator	
igneous [ígnɪəs]	形 火成の igneous rocks 火成岩 ＊sedimentary rocks「堆積岩」。	volcanic	B
nocturnal [nɑːktə́ːrnl]	形 夜行性の nocturnal mammals 夜行性の哺乳類	night	
coalesce [kòuəlés]	動 合体する，合同する Their ideas coalesced to form a policy. 彼らの意見は合体し，1つの方針となった。	combine	
divergence [daɪvə́ːrdʒəns]	名 相違；分岐 divergence between the US and Europe 合衆国とヨーロッパの相違　＊di- は「分かれること」。	difference	C
pulmonary [pʌ́lmənèri]	形 肺の；肺病の a pulmonary tumour 肺腫瘍	pneumonic	
illicit [ɪlísɪt]	形 違法な illicit drugs 違法薬物	illegal	
optimisation [ɑ̀ːptəmàɪzéɪʃən]	名 最適化；最大利用 facilitate the optimisation 最適化を促進する	exploitation	D
slab [slǽb]	名 平板 a slab of chocolate 板チョコ ＊南極にあるのは slabs of ice。	piece	
itinerant [aɪtínərənt]	形 巡回する；放浪の an itinerant library 巡回図書館 ＊名詞「旅芸人；行商人；巡回布教師」にも注目。	wandering	

285

単語／発音	語義／フレーズ	同意表現
rabies [réɪbiːz]	名 狂犬病，恐水病 anti-rabies vaccination 抗狂犬病ワクチン ＊複数形ではない。不可算。	lyssa
pueblo [pwéblou]	名 先住民の集団住居；プエブロ族；先住民の部落 a Pueblo-style building プエブロ様式の建物	
proprietary [prəpráɪətèri]	形 所有者の；私有の proprietary rights 所有権	private
shroud [ʃráud]	動 覆い隠す，包む be shrouded in mystery 神秘に包まれている	cover
entity [éntəti]	名 実体，実在するもの exist as a separate entity 別個の実体として存在する	being
posterity [pɑːstérəti]	名 後世，後代の人々；子孫 hand down to posterity 後世に伝える	descendant
leukaemia [luːkíːmiə]	名 白血病 increase leukaemia risk 白血病の危険を高める	leucosis
pollination [pɑ̀lənéɪʃən]	名 授粉 pollination of flowers by insects 昆虫による花の授粉 ＊ pollen「花粉」。	pollinisation
secede [sɪsíːd]	動 脱退する secede from a party 離党する	withdraw
catalyse [kǽtəlàɪz]	動 触媒作用を及ぼす；促進する catalyse an increase in investment 投資の増加に触媒作用を及ぼす	accelerate
burgeon [bə́ːrdʒən]	動 急激に発展する，急増する Cotton mills burgeoned in the town. 紡績工場がその町に急増した。　＊「新芽を出す」からきた単語。	develop quickly
silt [sílt]	名 沈泥 silt build-up 沈泥の堆積	sediment

単語／発音	語義／フレーズ	同意表現	難易度
profusion [prəfjúːʒən]	名 豊富；夥(おびただ)しい数量 a profusion of information 大量の情報 ＊ a profusion of ～「夥しい数／量の～」。	abundance	A
myriad [míriəd]	形 無数の myriad stars in the night sky 夜空の無数の星	innumerable	
embryo [émbriòu]	名 胎芽；胚芽 An egg contains the embryo of a chicken. 鶏卵は鶏の胎芽を含んでいる。	fetus	
prosaic [prouzéɪɪk]	形 平凡な, 退屈な, つまらない live a prosaic life 平凡な生活を送る	humdrum	B
sabbatical [səbǽtɪkl]	形 研究休暇の；安息(年)の a professor on sabbatical leave 研究休暇中の教授 ＊ on leave「(軍人や公務員の)休暇中で」。	sabbatic	
confiscate [ká:nfɪskèɪt]	動 没収する Due to his tax evasion, his property was confiscated. 脱税のために, 彼の財産は没収された。	impound	
turmoil [tə́ːrmɔɪl]	名 混乱, 騒乱, 不安 trigger political turmoil 政治的な混乱を引き起こす ＊W2 政治関連の課題で使えそう。	chaos	C
gradient [gréɪdiənt]	名 勾配；傾斜 compensate the gradient 勾配を補正する	inclination	
façade [fəsáːd]	名 正面；外見 the impressive façade of a new hotel 新しいホテルの印象的な正面	frontage	
glaze [gléɪz]	名 (陶器の)上薬(うわぐすり)；光沢 glaze for pottery 陶磁器用の上薬	glost	D
amenable [əmíːnəbl]	形 (忠告などに)従順な；(法則などに)かなう a person amenable to reason 道理に従順な(道理の分かる)人	obedient	
tributary [tríbjətèri]	名 支流 be divided into three tributaries 3本の支流に分かれる	affluent	

Track 270

単語／発音	語義／フレーズ	同意表現
squirt [skwə́:rt]	動 噴出する；ほとばしる squirt out of the nozzle ノズルから噴出する	**s**pout
despoiler [dɪspɔ́ɪlər]	名 荒らす者；略奪者 a greedy despoiler 強欲な略奪者	**l**ooter
labyrinth [lǽbərɪnθ]	名 迷宮；迷路 a labyrinth of streets 迷路のように入り組んだ街路	**m**aze
tenement [ténəmənt]	名 長屋；安アパート a tenement in a slum スラム街の安アパート	**a**partment
stringent [stríndʒənt]	形 厳格な；厳しい under stringent conditions 厳しい条件下で ＊rigid, rigorous も同義語。	**s**trict
portend [pɔːrténd]	動 前兆となる；〜を予告する portend a catastrophe 大惨事の前兆となる	**f**oretell
malleable [mǽliəbl]	形 展性の；従順な；影響されやすい children's malleable minds 子供の影響されやすい心	**p**liable
viscosity [vɪskɑ́:səti]	名 粘着性 reduce viscosity of oil オイルの粘度を低下させる	**s**tickiness
continuum [kəntínjuəm]	名 連続(体)；少しずつの変化 an evolutionary continuum （生物の）進化の連続体	**c**ontinuous **b**ody
irrevocable [ɪrévəkəbl]	形 取り返しのつかない；くつがえらない suffer irrevocable loss 取り返しのつかない損失を被る	**i**rretrievable
concert [kɑ́:nsəːrt]	動 協定する；一致団結する concert an alliance with the company その会社と同盟を協定する	**c**ollaborate
sewerage [sú:ərɪdʒ]	名 下水設備 water supply and sewerage systems 上下水道システム ＊「下水」は drainage。	**d**rains

Track 271

単語／発音	語義／フレーズ	同意表現	難易度
consort [kənsɔ́:rt]	動 付き合う；一致する Don't consort with bad friends. 悪い仲間と付き合うな。	assort	A
congenial [kəndʒí:njəl]	形 性分に合う；快適な；同じ性質の create a congenial atmosphere 打ち解けた雰囲気を作り出す	agreeable	
deference [défərəns]	名 敬意；服従 deference to authority 権力に対する服従	respect	
crippling [kríplɪŋ]	形 壊滅的な；ひどく有害な have a crippling effect on the economy 経済に壊滅的な打撃を与える	devastating	B
sobriquet [sóubrəkèɪ]	名 あだ名，異名 a self-given sobriquet 自分で付けたあだ名 ＊発音注意！	nickname	
pseudo [s(j)ú:dou]	形 にせの，偽りの，見せかけの a pseudo-experience device 疑似体験装置	false	
excite [ɪksáɪt]	動 活発化させる；扇動する excite the molecules 分子運動を活発化させる	energise	C
morphology [mɔ:rfá:lədʒi]	名 形態学；形態 major differences in morphology 形態上の大きな相違 ＊生物の構成を研究する分野。		
galvanise [gǽlvənàɪz]	動 電気を通す galvanised barbed wire 電流を通した有刺鉄線	electrify	
metamorphosis [mètəmɔ́:rfəsɪs]	名 変形；変態 insects that undergo complete metamorphosis 完全変態をする昆虫	transformation	D
blast [blǽst]	動 騒々しく鳴らす；爆発する（させる） blast the trumpet トランペットを鳴り響かせる	blare	
squeamish [skwí:mɪʃ]	形 吐き気を起こさせる；気分が悪くなる feel slightly squeamish ちょっと気分が悪くなる	nauseous	

Track 272

単語／発音	語義／フレーズ	同意表現
rugged [rʌ́gɪd]	形 起伏の多い a rugged mountainous area 起伏の多い山岳地帯	rough
encroach [ɪnkróʊtʃ]	動 侵食する；侵害する encroach on someone's rights 人の権利を侵害する	impinge
topography [təpɑ́grəfi]	名 地形；地勢 ocean floor topography 海底地形	land form
align [əláɪn]	動 提携する；一直線に並べる, 整列させる align oneself with a certain party 特定の政党と提携する ＊名詞 alignment「整列すること」。	ally
hiss [hís]	動 シューッと音を出す air hissing from a tire タイヤからシューッと漏れる空気	whish
feign [féɪn]	動 ふりをする feign illness 病気のふりをする	pretend
terrain [təréɪn]	名 地域；地形 hilly terrain 丘陵地帯	topography
aggregate [ǽgrɪgət]	名 総計, 合計；集合体 the aggregate of goals from the two football matches そのサッカーの 2 試合の得点合計	total
coercive [koʊə́ːrsɪv]	形 強制的な, 威圧的な resort to coercive measures 強制的な手段に訴える ＊動詞は coerce = force。	imperative
toxin [tɑ́ːksn]	名 毒素 neutralize a toxin 毒素を中和する ＊ venom も一緒に覚える。	poison
quantum [kwɑ́ntəm]	名 量子；量；特定量 a quantum theory in physics 物理学における量子論	
circumvent [sə̀ːrkəmvént]	動 回避する, 抜け道を見つける；迂回する circumvent the law 法律の抜け道を見つける	evade

単語／発音	語義／フレーズ	同意表現	難易度
destitute [déstət(j)ùːt]	形 極貧の be forced to live a destitute life 赤貧生活を余儀なくされる	impoverished	A
subterranean [sÀbtəréɪniən]	形 地下の；隠れた a subterranean shopping mall 地下商店街	underground	
adobe [ədóʊbi]	名 日干しレンガ a stone and adobe house 岩と日干しレンガでできた家	sun-dried brick	
thatch [θǽtʃ]	動 （ワラなどで屋根などを）葺く thatch a roof with straw ワラで屋根を葺く		B
lathe [léɪð]	名 旋盤；ろくろ a skilled lathe worker 熟練旋盤工	turning machine	
fault [fɔ́ːlt]	動 断層を起こす layer faulted to the surface 地表に向けて断層の起こった地層	produce a geologic fault	
theorem [θíːərəm]	名 定理；原理, 法則 energy conservation theorem エネルギー保存の法則	axiom	C
protrude [prətrúːd]	動 突き出る protrude outward from the surface 表面から外側に突き出る	stick out	
cursory [kə́ːrsəri]	形 大まかな；早まった a cursory inspection 大まかな（粗略な）調査	perfunctory	
siege [síːdʒ]	名 包囲攻撃 a castle under siege 包囲攻撃された城	beleaguerment	D
rogue [róʊg]	形 群れを離れた a rogue wolf はぐれオオカミ	lone	
seam [síːm]	名 シーム《2つの地層間の岩石・石炭などの薄い層》 coal seam gas 炭層ガス	middle layer	

単語／発音	語義／フレーズ	同意表現
delineate [dɪlínièɪt]	動 輪郭を描く；描写する delineate a picture of the future 将来像を描く	outline
prospector [prá:spektər]	名 試掘者，探鉱者 a gold prospector 金の探鉱者 ＊金などの鉱物や油田を探し求める人。	
dislodge [dɪslá:dʒ]	動 取り除く；移動させる dislodge the enemy from a fort 砦から敵を取り除く	remove
leaven [lévn]	動 発酵させる leaven bread with yeast イーストでパンを発酵させる	ferment
pinnacle [pínəkl]	名 絶頂；頂点；小尖塔 the pinnacle of happiness 幸福の絶頂	peak
recur [rɪkə́:r]	動 再び浮かぶ；再発する recur after initial treatment 初期治療後に再発する	reappear
collateral [kəlǽtərəl]	名 見返り担保；付随事実 collateral for a loan 借り入れに対する担保	security
traffic [trǽfɪk]	名 売買，取引 traffic in humans 人身売買	trade
hoard [hɔ́:rd]	動 貯蔵する hoard money in preparation for 〜 〜に備えてお金を貯める	lay away
delicacy [délɪkəsi]	名 珍味，ごちそう taste a delicacy in the region その地域の珍味を味わう	dainty
thwart [θwɔ́:rt]	動 挫折させる；妨げる thwart computer viruses コンピュータウイルスを妨げる	frustrate
jurisdiction [dʒùərɪsdíkʃən]	名 支配権；司法権 exclusive territorial jurisdiction 独占的領有支配権	legal power

単語／発音	語義／フレーズ	同意表現	難易度
brush [bráʃ]	動 無視する；払いのける brush aside repeated warnings 度重なる警告を無視する	ignore	A
indict [ɪndáɪt]	動 起訴する；非難する sufficient evidence to indict 起訴するのに十分な証拠 ＊スペリングと発音に注意！	accuse	
deposition [dèpəzíʃən]	名 堆積；沈殿 sediment deposition 土砂の堆積	sedimentation	
optometrist [ɑːptɑ́ːmətrɪst]	名 視力検査師 get one's eyes checked by an optometrist 視力検査師に目を検査してもらう	oculist	B
molar [móʊlər]	名 臼歯；奥歯 have a sore molar 奥歯が痛む	grinder	
dermal [dɚ́ːməl]	形 皮膚の；表皮の dermal tissue restoration 皮膚組織の修復	cutaneous	
blight [bláɪt]	名 荒廃；無秩序化 urban blight 都市の荒廃	devastation	C
kernel [kɚ́ːrnl]	名 仁；実；核心 the kernel of the question 問題の核心	centre	
epicentre [épəsèntər]	名 地震の中心, 震央 locate the epicentre of an earthquake 地震の震源地を探す	centre of an earthquake	
repellent [rɪpélənt]	形 寄せつけない；反発する a water repellent material 撥水剤	repulsive	D
levy [lévi]	動 (税金などを)取り立てる；課す levy a heavy tax 重い税金を課する	impose	
tract [trǽkt]	名 (陸・海の)広がり, 地域, 水域 vast tracts of forest 広大な森林地帯	area	

Track 276

単語／発音	語義／フレーズ	同意表現
allot [əlάːt]	動 割り当てる；分配する allot equal time to each speaker 各演説者に平等な時間を割り当てる	distribute
seclusion [sɪklúːʒən]	名 隔離；隠遁；閑居 live a life of seclusion 隠遁生活を送る	reclusion
glossary [ɡlάːsəri]	名 （専門的な）用語解説；語彙集 glossary at the back of the book 巻末の用語集 ＊grocery「食料；雑貨」との誤解に注意。	lexicon
scapegoating [skéɪpɡòʊtɪŋ]	名 責任転嫁 escape blame by scapegoating 責任転嫁により責めを逃れる	buck-passing
extort [ɪkstɔ́ːrt]	動 ゆすり取る，だまし取る extort ransom money 身代金をゆすり取る	squeeze
deploy [dɪplɔ́ɪ]	動 （軍隊を）展開する；（人員などを）配備する deploy troops and weapons 部隊と武器を配備する	position
manifest [mǽnəfèst]	動 明らかにする；表す manifest the opposition to the act その法案に対し反対を表明する　＊manifesto「声明文」も覚えよう。	display
assassinate [əsǽsənèɪt]	動 暗殺する a plot to assassinate the President 大統領暗殺の陰謀	murder
dismantle [dɪsmǽntl]	動 解体する；分解する dismantle the run-down theatre 寂れた劇場を解体する	take apart
convene [kənvíːn]	動 招集する；召還する convene an urgent meeting 緊急会議を招集する	convoke
smuggle [smʌ́ɡl]	動 密輸する smuggle and sell illegal drugs 違法薬物を密輸, 販売する	bootleg
jeopardy [dʒépərdi]	名 危険（にさらされていること） be put in serious jeopardy 重大な危険にさらされる ＊S put 〜 in jeopardy の形で使う。	danger

単語／発音	語義／フレーズ	同意表現	難易度
scavenger [skǽvɪndʒər]	名 掃除動物 scavengers of the bottom of the ocean 海底の掃除動物 ＊ハイエナのように死体やごみを食べる動物。	animal feeding on refuse	A
stalemate [stéɪlmèɪt]	名 行き詰まり；手詰まり；膠着状態 stalemate in the Middle East peace process 中東和平交渉の停滞	deadlock	
pivotal [pívətl]	形 重要な，中心的な，軸となる play a pivotal role 中心的な役割を担う	crucial	
incandescent [ìnkəndésnt]	形 白熱光を発する；眩しい an incandescent light bulb 白熱電球	candent	B
scruple [skrúːpl]	名 ためらい；疑念 lie without scruples ためらいなく嘘をつく	hesitation	
contingency [kəntíndʒənsi]	名 予期せぬ緊急事態；偶発 prepare for all possible contingencies あらゆる不測の事態に備える	eventuality	
crustacean [krʌstéɪʃən]	名 （カニ・エビなどの）甲殻類 feed on crustacean plankton 甲殻類プランクトンを餌にする	shellfish	C

IELTS必須英熟語

Track 278

熟語	語義／例文	同意表現／コメント
a large [great, enormous] amount of ~	大[多]量の~ a large amount of expenditure 多額の支出	不加算名詞や金額で使う。
a large [great] number of ~	非常に多くの~ a large number of nations 非常に多くの国	可算名詞で使う。 ちなみに the number of ~ は「~の数」の意。
a man of ~	~な人 a man of few words 寡黙な人	
a matter of course	当然のこと It is taken as a matter of course. それは当然のことと考えられている。	
a pair of ~	1組[1対]の~ a pair of shoes 1足の靴	後ろは複数形。
A rather than B [rather A than B]	BよりもむしろA I prefer to play tennis rather than to watch it. 私はテニスを見るより、やる方が好きだ。	
a sheet of ~	1枚の~ a sheet of paper 1枚の紙	紙などの場合、単位は複数形。 two sheets of paper 「2枚の紙」。
a variety of ~	さまざまな~ a variety of opinions 様々な意見	後ろの名詞は常に複数形。不加算名詞はだめ。 various kinds of work 「様々な種類の仕事」とする。
a week from today	来週の今日 There will be no class a week from today. 来週の今日は授業が休みだ。	= this day week / today week
absent oneself from ~	~を休む、~を欠席する She wanted to absent herself from the class. 彼女は授業を休みたかった。	= be absent from ~
according to ~	~によると、~に従って according to their survey 彼らの調査によると	= in accordance with ~
account for ~	~を占める；~(の理由)を説明する Books account for 30% of the total expenses. 本は支出の30％を占める。	W1 円グラフで全体に占める割合を書くときに使おう！

Track 279

熟語	語義／例文	同意表現／コメント
accuse 人 of ～	～のことで人を訴える[非難する] I'll accuse him of fraud. 私は彼を詐欺で訴えるでしょう。	
act on [upon] ～	～に基づいて行動する；～に作用する act on instinct 本能のままに行動する	
add A to B	A を B に加える add chemicals to water 薬品を水に加える	
after all	結局 After all we found the plan failed. 結局，我々はその計画が失敗だったと分かった。	[S] エピソードを話すときに便利。I initially thought ～, but after all I found …「最初は～と思ったが，結局…だと分かった」。
against one's will	～の意志に反して I was forced to do it against my will. 私の意志に反して，それをするよう強制された。	
agree with ～	～に同意する I agree with his proposal. 私は彼の提案に同意します。	[W2] 使い方に注意！agree with the idea.「そのアイデアに賛成する」，agree that SV「SV に賛成する」。
aim at ～	～を目指す，～を狙う They aim at a new market in Asia. 彼らはアジアでの新しい市場を狙っている。	be aimed at ～「～を対象にしている」も覚えたい。The product is aimed at children aged under 5.「その製品は5歳未満の子供を対象にしている。」
all along	初めから；当初から；ずっと It was planned all along. それは初めから計画されていた。	
all but ～	ほとんど；～以外全部 The meeting was all but over. その会議はほとんど終わっていた。	= almost この but は「～を除いて」の意。
all of a sudden	突然 All of a sudden he began to laugh. 彼は突然笑い出した。	= all at once
all the same	それでもやはり All the same you should review a procedure. それでもやはり，あなたは方法を見直すべきだ。	= just the same
all the time	いつも，その間ずっと I studied English all the time during summer. 夏の間ずっと英語の勉強をしていた。	= continuously

Track 280

熟語	語義／例文	同意表現／コメント
all the way	(途中)ずっと；はるばる；最後まで I support you all the way. 最後まであなたを応援する。	= completely
allow for ~	~を考慮に入れる，~を斟酌する allow for the delay 遅れることを考慮しておく	
amount to ~	~に達する；~に等しい Our work amounted to nothing. 我々の仕事は何もしていないに等しかった。	
and [but] yet	しかし，それにもかかわらず I was sick. And yet I passed the exam. 私は具合が悪かった。にもかかわらず試験に合格した。	
~ and so forth [on]	~など The police officer asked me my name, my address, and so forth. 警察官は私に名前，住所などを尋ねた。	= and the like [W2] 無用な羅列は避ける。
answer for ~	~に対して責任を持つ The government has a lot to answer for in this regard. このことに関して政府には大いに責任がある。	= be responsible for ~
anything but ~	決して~ではない The city is anything but safe. その都市は決して安全ではない。	= far from ~ この but は「~を除く」の意味。
apart from ~	~は別にして；~から離れて Apart from 2000, the figure continuously rose. 2000年を除き，その数字は継続的に伸びた。	= aside from / except for ~ [W1] 例外を書くときに便利！
apologize to A for B	BのことでAに謝る I have to apologise to you for being late. 私は遅れたことを，あなたに謝らなければならない。	[S] apologize to 人。to を忘れないように！
appeal to ~	~(人の心)に訴える，~にとって魅力的に映る The toy appeals to young children. そのおもちゃは小さな子供にとって魅力的だ。	[W2] 使い方に注意！「(主語が)魅力的だ」ということ。
apply for [to] ~	~に応募する，~に申し込む apply for a college grant 大学の奨学金に応募する	
apply A to B	AをBに適用する apply psychology to business issues 心理学をビジネスの問題に適用する	

Track 281

熟語	語義／例文	同意表現／コメント
approve of ~	~をよいと認める，~に賛成する My boss approved of my leaving early. 上司は私が早退することを認めた。	⇔ disapprove of ~
arrange for ~	~の手配[準備]をする arrange for my own lunch 自分の昼食を準備する	
as far as ~	~である限り，~の範囲では As far as I am concerned, I have no objection. 私に関する限り，異論はありません。	= if limiting to ~ [S] as far as I know「私が知る限り」は使いやすい。
as a matter of fact	実際のところ As a matter of fact, it's not true. 実際のところ，それは真実ではない。	= in fact
as a result	結果として As a result, our proposal was accepted. 結果として，我々の提案は受け入れられた。	= in consequence
as a rule	概して，普通は As a rule doctors earn a lot. 概して医者は高給取りだ。	= in general
as a token of ~	~の印に；~の記念として as a token of my gratitude 感謝の印として	= in token of ~
as a whole	概して；全体として the country as a whole 国全体として	
as follows	次の通り What I thought is as follows. 私が思ったことは次の通りです。	as follows の s はもともと三単現の s なので抜かさないように。
as for ~	~に関して，~について（言うと） as for the costs 費用に関しては	= as to ~ / with regard to ~ [W1] 次の項目の説明に移るときに文頭で使う。
as good as ~	ほとんど~も同然 The work is as good as finished. その作業は終わったも同然だ。	
as is often the case with ~	~にはよくあることだが as is often the case with teenagers ティーンエージャーにはよくあることだが	= as is common [usual] with ~

301

熟語	語義／例文	同意表現／コメント
as it were	いわば London is, as it were, my second home. ロンドンは、いわば、第2の故郷だ。	文中に挿入して使うことも多い。
as regards [to] ～	～に関しては、～については as regards the result 結果に関しては	= as far as ～ is concerned
as such	それ自体での；そういうものとしての There isn't a garage as such. それ自体での車庫はない。	肯定文では「そのようなものとして」、否定文では「それ自体での」の意。
as the saying goes	ことわざにもあるように As the saying goes, time is money. ことわざにもあるように、時は金なりだ。	saying は「ことわざ」。
as to ～	～に関して、～について（言うと） I have no complaint as to my pay. 私の給料に関しては全く文句はありません。	= about ～ / as for ～
as usual	いつものように the same as usual いつもと同じように	ⓢ be busier than usual のように比較級でも使える。
～ as well	同様に～、～もまた The test result changes as well. そのテスト結果もまた変わります。	
as yet	今までのところ、まだ This singer is unknown as yet. この歌手は今のところ知られていない。	
ascribe A to B	A を B のせいにする He ascribed his failure to bad luck. 彼は失敗を不運のせいにした。	= attribute A to B
ask a favour of ～	～にお願いする[頼む] May I ask a favour of you? あなたにお願いがあるのですが。	= ask ～ a favour
ask for ～	～を求める、～を要求する The student asked for advice from his professor. その学生は彼の教授にアドバイスを求めた。	ⓢ ask for help も言いやすい。
at [on] short notice	即座に、急に、すぐに I had to leave for Boston at short notice. 私は即座にボストンに向かわなければならなかった。	= at a moment's notice

Track 283

熟語	語義／例文	同意表現／コメント
at a glance	一目で；すぐに I recognised her at a glance. 私は一目で彼女だと分かった。	= at first glance
at a loss	（どうしていいか）途方に暮れて，困って I was at a loss for words 私は何と言っていいか途方に暮れていた。	= (all) at sea / at one's wit's [wits'] end
at a time	一度に；同時に You should focus on one problem at a time. あなたは一度に1つの問題に専念すべきだ。	= at the same time
at all times	いつも You are courteous at all times. あなたはいつも礼儀正しい。	= always
at an end	終わって；尽きて The war was finally at an end. 戦争はついに終わった。	= over
at any cost	ぜひ；どんな犠牲を払っても I want to pass the exam at any cost. 何が何でも，その試験に合格したい。	= at all events / at any price
at any moment [minute]	今にも It may rain at any moment. 今にも雨が降るかもしれない。	
at any rate	とにかく，いずれにせよ At any rate, I will try. とにかくやってみます。	= at all events / in any event [case]
at any time	どんなときでも Please contact me at any time. いつでも連絡してください。	= at any moment / whenever 〜
at best	よくても，せいぜい She will get 6.0 on IELTS at best. 彼女の **IELTS** はせいぜい 6.0 だろう。	
at ease	くつろいで I feel at ease. 私はくつろいでいます。	⇔ ill at ease 「落ち着かない」。
at face value	額面通りに，真に take everything at face value すべてを額面通りに受け取る	

Track 284

熟語	語義／例文	同意表現／コメント
at first	最初は At first, I studied hard. 最初は，一生懸命勉強した。	W2 = initially。firstly「まず初めに」とは異なる意味。
at first hand	直接に I've seen a koala at first hand. 私はコアラを直接（自分の目で）見たことがある。	
at first sight	一見したところでは；一目で For her, it was love at first sight. 彼女にとって，それは一目惚れだった。	
at hand	（時間的に・空間的に）すぐ近くに keep a dictionary at hand 辞書を手近に置いておく	
at heart	心底は，根は He looks strict, although kind at heart. 彼は厳しく見えるが根は親切だ。	
at issue	論争中の，懸案となっている the point at issue 論争点	
at large	捕まらないで，自由で；概して The criminal is still at large. 犯人はまだ捕まっていない。	= free
at last	ついに At last we achieved our goal. ついに我々は目標を達成した。	= finally S エピソードの最後を話すときに入れるとよい。
at least	少なくとも Study English at least an hour a day. 少なくとも1日1時間は英語の勉強をしなさい。	⇔ at most「最大で」。
at leisure	暇なときに；ゆっくりと Let's discuss the matter at leisure. 時間があるときに，その件について話し合おう。	
at length	詳細に；ついに Please describe the reason at length. 理由を詳細に説明してください。	= in detail
at once	すぐに I recognised her at once. 私はすぐに彼女だと分かった。	= immediately / in no time

Track 285

熟語	語義／例文	同意表現／コメント
at one's best	最高の状態で，(花などが)盛りで He seems to be at his best. 彼は最高の状態のようだ。	= at one's height
at one's convenience	都合のいいときに Please ring me up at your convenience. あなたの都合のいいときに電話をください。	
at ones wits' [wit's] end	途方に暮れて，困って He was at his wits' end with the problem. 彼はその問題をどう解くべきか，途方に暮れた。	= at a loss
at present	現在は My friend is staying in Sydney at present. 私の友人は今シドニーに滞在している。	= now
at random	でたらめに，雑然と，無作為に The subjects for this experiment were selected at random. この実験の被験者は無作為に選ばれた。	⇔ in order
at the age of ~	~の年齢で，~歳のときに His father died at the age of 80. 彼の父親は80歳の年齢で亡くなった。	= when a person is ~ years old
at the back of ~	~の後ろで coffee shop at the back of the grocery store スーパーの裏側にある喫茶店	⇔ in the front of ~
at the cost [price / expense] of ~	~を犠牲にして Many people work at the cost of their health. 多くの人が健康を犠牲にして働いている。	= at one's cost
at the mercy of ~	~のなすがままに be at the mercy of the weather 天候のなすがままである	
at the minute	今現在，現時点で What are you doing at the minute? あなたは今現在何しているの？	
at the risk of ~	~の危険を冒して Many refugees crossed the border at the risk of their life. 多くの難民が命の危険を冒して国境を越えた。	
at the same time	同時に Two events begin at the same time. 2つのイベントが同時に始まります。	[S] 文頭につなぎの言葉として使いたい。

Track 286

熟語	語義／例文	同意表現／コメント
at the sight of ~	~を見て He cried at the sight of a picture of his late father. 彼は亡父の写真を見て泣いた。	
at the top of one's voice [lungs]	声をかぎりに sing at the top of one's voice 声を張り上げて歌う	
at this [that] rate	この[その]調子だと，これ[それ]が続けば The company will be bankrupt at this rate. その会社はこの調子だと破産するだろう。	
at will	意のままに The dictator manipulated the military at will. 独裁者は軍部を意のままに操った。	
at work	仕事中で；活動中で He is at work at present. 彼は現在仕事中です。	= on duty
attribute A to B	AをBのせいにする He attributes his failure to lack of effort. 彼は失敗を努力不足のせいにする。	= ascribe A to B W2 to の後は名詞！
avail oneself of ~	~(機会など)を利用する I will avail myself of every opportunity. 私はあらゆる機会を利用するだろう。	= take advantage of ~
above all	何よりもまず，とりわけ I recommend cheese cakes above all other desserts. 私はデザートの中でもとりわけチーズケーキをお勧めします。	= among other things
be (all) Greek to ~	~にはさっぱり分からない This textbook is all Greek to me. この教科書は，私にはさっぱり分からない。	
be (just) about to ~	(まさに)~しようとしている，~するところである The show was about to start. ショーが始まるところだった。	S I was just about to V の形が使いやすい。
be a match for ~	~と対等である；~の競争相手である He is a match for you in tennis. テニスでは，彼はあなたと対等(互角)である。	
be above ~ing	~することはしない；~することを恥じる He is above telling a lie. 彼は嘘をつくことはしない。	

306

Track 287

熟語	語義／例文	同意表現／コメント
be absorbed in ～	～に没頭する, ～に夢中になる She is absorbed in reading mystery novels. 彼女は推理小説を読むのに夢中です。	= be intent on ～ / be into ～ ⑤で使いたい。
be abundant in ～	～が豊富である This fruit is abundant in nutrients. この果物は栄養が豊富である。	= be rich in ～
be accustomed to ～ [～ing]	～に［～することに］慣れている He is accustomed to driving long distances. 彼は長距離運転に慣れている。	= be used to ～［…ing］。to の後は名詞。used to V「かつて～した」と混同しないように。
be acquainted with ～	～と知り合いである；～を知っている I am well acquainted with him. 私は彼のことをよく知っている。	= be familiar with ～
be adept at ～	～が上手だ She is adept at teaching English. 彼女は英語を教えるのが上手だ。	
be afraid of ～	～を恐れている Many people in Japan are afraid of earthquakes. 日本の多くの人が地震を恐れている。	= be scared of ～
be against ～	～に反対である I'm against the plan. 私はその計画に反対です。	⇔ be for ～ ⑤ 話し言葉では disagree with ～ より自然。
be all ears	熱心に耳を傾ける He was all ears for the speech. 彼はそのスピーチに熱心に耳を傾けていた。	
be anxious about ～	～を心配している All parents are anxious about their children. すべての両親は子供のことを心配している。	= be worried about ～
be anxious for ～	～を切望している Everyone is anxious for his well-being. 皆が彼の幸せを願っている。	
be anxious to ～	～することを切望する, ～したいと切に思う I'm anxious to see her again. 私は彼女にもう一度会いたいと切に願う。	= be impatient to ～
be apt to ～	～しがちである, ～する傾向がある She is apt to make careless mistakes. 彼女はうっかりミスをしがちである。	= be inclined [likely / prone / liable] to ～ = tend to ～

307

Track 288

熟語	語義／例文	同意表現／コメント
be ashamed of ～	～を恥じている He is ashamed of his son for having shoplifted at a store. 彼は息子が店で万引きしたことを恥じている。	
be at home in [with] ～	～に精通している He is at home in archaeology. 彼は考古学に精通している。	
be attached to ～	～に愛情を持っている，慕っている The boy is attached to his uncle. その少年は叔父を慕っている。	
be aware of ～	～に気づいている，～を知っている Are you aware of his true intention? あなたは彼の真意に気づいていますか？	= be conscious of ～
be based on[upon] ～	～に基づいている This movie is based on a true story. この映画は実話に基づいている。	
be bent on ～	～に熱心である The owner is bent on gain. そのオーナーは金儲けに熱心である。	
be bound by ～	～に束縛される，～に縛られている Human behaviour is bound by laws and regulations. 人間の行動は法律や規則に束縛される。	= be restricted by ～
be caught in ～	（雨・風など）～にあう He was caught in a shower on his way home. 彼は帰る途中，にわか雨にあった。	
be certain [sure] of ～	～を確信している He is certain of getting the first prize. 彼は1位を取れることを確信している。	sure は人を主語にするのが普通。It is sure ～とはしない！
be characteristic of ～	～の特徴[に特有のもの]である Positive thinking is characteristic of that coach. プラス思考が，あのコーチの特徴である。	= be typical of ～
be compelled to ～	～せざるを得ない He was compelled to give false testimony. 彼は嘘の証言をせざるを得なかった。	= be forced [obliged] to ～
be composed of ～	～から成り立っている This orchestra is composed of 50 violinists. このオーケストラは50人のバイオリニストから成り立っている。	= consist of ～ / be made up of ～

Track 289

熟語	語義／例文	同意表現／コメント
be concerned about ～	～を心配している She is concerned about her son's future. 彼女は息子の将来を心配している。	= be worried [anxious] about ～
be conditioned to ～	～に［～することに］慣れている Japanese people are conditioned to use chopsticks. 日本人は箸を使うことに慣れている。	= adjust (oneself) to ～ be conditioned by ～「～に左右［支配］される」。
be confident of ～	～を確信している The entrepreneur is confident of success. その起業家は成功を確信している。	
be connected with ～	～と関係している，～と関係がある He is connected with the murderer. 彼はその殺人犯と関係がある。	= be related to [with] ～ / be concerned with ～
be conscious of ～	～に気づいている She was conscious of the harsh reality. 彼女は厳しい現実に気づいていた。	= be aware of ～
be considerate of ～	～に対して思いやりがある We should be considerate of the elderly. 私たちは高齢者に対して思いやりを持つべきだ。	
be content to ～	喜んで［進んで］～する He will be content to accept the offer. 彼はその申し出を喜んで受け入れるだろう。	
be content with ～	～に満足している I am content with a quiet life. 私は平穏な生活に満足している。	= be satisfied [contented] with ～
be crowded with ～	～で混雑している The concert hall was crowded with young fans. そのコンサートホールは若者のファンで混雑していた。	crowded は「人が多い」congested は「密集している」。
be curious about ～	～を知りたいと思う I'm curious about what you think about the issue. 私はその問題に関する君の考えを知りたいと思う。	[S] be interested in ～ だけではなく、これも使えるように！
be cut out for ～	～に向いて［適して］いる I'm cut out for office work. 私はオフィスワークに向いている。	= be fit for ～

309

Track 290

熟語	語義／例文	同意表現／コメント
be derived from ～	～に由来する These words are derived from ancient Greek mythology. これらの言葉は古代ギリシャ神話に由来する。	= derive from ～
be determined to ～	～することを（固く）決心している He is determined to become a lawyer. 彼は弁護士になることを決心している。	
be different from ～	～と違っている This swimsuit is different from the one I ordered online. この水着は私がオンラインで注文したものと違っている。	= differ from ～
be disappointed at [with / in] ～	～に失望している I am disappointed at the result. 私は結果に失望している。	
be dressed in ～	～を身につけている She is always dressed in a pair of blue jeans. 彼女はいつも青いジーパンを身につけている。	= wear ～
be due to ～	～のせいである；～のためである Severe damage was due to the hurricane. 大きな被害はハリケーンのせいであった。	be due to the fact that SV の形でもよく使う。
be dying to ～	～したくてたまらない I'm dying to see you just one more time. 私は君にもう一度会いたくてたまらない。	be dying for ～は「～がほしくてたまらない」。
be eager for ～	～を熱望している The team is eager for victories. そのチームは勝利を熱望している。	⑤ be eager to V「～することを熱望している」も使いたい。
be endowed with ～	～を授けられている，～に恵まれている The boy is endowed with genius. その男の子は才能に恵まれている。	
be engaged in ～	～に従事している They are engaged in antiwar demonstration. 彼らは反戦デモに従事している。	= engage oneself in ～
be entitled to ～	～する権利がある Only students are entitled to get a discount on all new items. 学生だけが新商品の割引を受ける権利がある。	= have the right to ～
be envious of ～	～をうらやむ Every colleague is envious of his success. すべての同僚が彼の成功をうらやんでいる。	envy は名詞だと「うらやみ，ねたみ」。

熟語	語義／例文	同意表現／コメント
be equal to ~	~をこなすことができる；~に等しい She is equal to the job. 彼女はその仕事をこなすことができる。	= be able to deal with
be equipped with ~	~を備え付けている，~が装備されている The school is equipped with a computer room. その学校にはコンピュータ室が備わっている。	
be equivalent to ~	~に相当する，~に等しい 1 pound is roughly equivalent to 453.6 grams. 1パウンドはほぼ453.6グラムに相当する。	= be equal to ~
be expected to ~	~すると思われている，~するはずである。 The rock singer was expected to perform in London. そのロック歌手はロンドンで演奏するはずであった。	
be faced with [by] ~	~に直面している Many workers are faced with stressful situations. 多くの労働者がストレスを感じる状況に直面している。	= be confronted with [by] ~ W2 be faced with many problems「多くの問題に直面している」が使えそう。
be familiar to ~	~になじみがある，~によく知られている Sumo wrestling is familiar to Japanese people. 相撲は日本人になじみがある。	A is familiar to B は「AはBに知られている」，A is familiar with B は「AはBを知っている」。
be famous for	~で有名である Kyoto is famous for many old shrines and temples. 京都は多くの古い寺や神社があることで有名です。	= be well-known [noted] for ~
be fed up with ~	~にうんざりしている I'm fed up with your excuses. 私は君の言い訳にうんざりしている。	= be tired of ~ / be sick of ~
be filled with ~	~でいっぱいである Her closet is filled with luxury clothing. 彼女のクローゼットは高級な衣服でいっぱいである。	= be full of ~ / be teeming with ~
be fit to ~	~するのにふさわしい，~するのに適している You are fit to take on the job. あなたはその仕事を引き受けるのに適している。	= be cut out for ~
be fond of ~	~を好む She is fond of decorating a room with flowers. 彼女は部屋を花で飾ることを好む。	= like ~ S like の代わりに使いたい。

Track 292

熟語	語義／例文	同意表現／コメント
be forced to 〜	〜せざるを得ない I was forced to pretend to be dead. 私は死んだふりをせざるを得なかった。	= be compelled to 〜
be free from 〜	〜を免れている，〜がない The city is free from pollution. この都市には汚染がない。	
be free to 〜	自由に〜する，自由に〜してよい You are free to come anytime. あなたはいつでも自由に来ていいですよ。	
be gifted with 〜	〜（才能など）に恵まれている She is gifted with artistic talent. 彼女は画才に恵まれている。	= be endowed with 〜
be grateful to A for B	B について A に感謝する I am grateful to you for your help. 私はあなたの力添えについてあなたに感謝します。	
be hard on 〜	〜につらく当たる He is hard on his colleagues. 彼は同僚たちにつらく当たる。	
be ignorant of 〜	〜を知らない She is ignorant of the world. 彼女は世間知らずだ。	
be ill at ease	落ち着かない，不安である，気づまりである I'm ill at ease in the new surroundings. 私は新しい環境で落ち着かない。	
be impressed with [by] 〜	〜に感銘を受ける I was impressed with your emotional speech. 私はあなたの感動的なスピーチに感銘を受けた。	= be moved [touched] by 〜
be in charge of 〜	〜を管理［担当］している I was in charge of recruitment. 私は採用を担当していた。	ⓢ 自分の仕事を説明するときに便利！
be in danger	危険な状態にある His life is in danger. 彼の生命は危険な状態にある。	
be in danger of 〜ing	〜する恐れがある，〜する危険がある The building is in danger of collapsing soon. その建物はじきに倒壊する恐れがある。	

熟語	語義／例文	同意表現／コメント
be in demand	需要がある Their skills are in demand from many companies. 彼らの技術は多くの会社から需要がある。	
be in favour of 〜	〜に賛成である His party is in favour of legalising euthanasia. 彼の党は安楽死の合法化に賛成である。	= support 〜
be in good health	健康である Her granny is in good health for her age. 彼女のおばあちゃんは年の割に健康です。	⇔ be in bad [poor] health
be in the habit of 〜 ing	〜する習慣[癖]がある The boss is in the habit of seeing the good in his staff. その上司は部下の長所を見る習慣がある。	[S] 自分の習慣を言うときに使おう！
be incapable of 〜 ing	〜することができない I'm incapable of calculating without a calculator. 私は電卓を使わずに計算することができない。	⇔ be capable of 〜 ing
be inclined to 〜	〜する傾向がある；〜したい気がする She is inclined to act exaggeratedly. 彼女はおおげさに振る舞う傾向がある。	= be apt to 〜
be independent of 〜	〜から独立している He is financially independent of his parents. 彼は経済的に両親から独立している。	⇔ be dependent on
be indifferent to 〜	〜に無関心である I am indifferent to others' opinions. 私は他人の意見に無関心である。	
be indispensable to 〜	〜にとって不可欠である Student loan system is indispensable to those who struggle financially. 学費ローンのシステムは，経済的に苦しい立場の人々にとって不可欠である。	= be essential to 〜 [W2] 形式主語でなければ to の後は不定詞ではなく名詞！
be inferior to 〜	〜より劣る His score is inferior to his opponent. 彼のスコアは対戦相手より劣る。	⇔ be superior to 〜
be involved in 〜	〜に巻き込まれる；〜に関わる I don't want to be involved in the trouble. 私はその揉め事に巻き込まれたくありません。	

熟語	語義／例文	同意表現／コメント
be jealous of ~	~を妬む, ~をうらやむ I'm so jealous of my beautiful friend. 私はきれいな友人がとてもうらやましい。	= be envious of ~
be keen on ~	~に熱中している The boy is keen on listening to techno music. その男の子はテクノ音楽を聴くことに熱中している。	= be absorbed in ~ S 自分の興味を言うときに便利！
be keen to ~	~するのに乗り気である Airlines will be keen to lease more aircraft. 航空会社はより多くの飛行機をリースするのに乗り気である。	
be lacking in ~	~が[に]欠けている His paper on international affairs is lacking in concreteness. 彼の国際情勢に関する論文は具体性に欠ける。	= lack ~ / be wanting in ~
be liable to ~	~しそうである, ~しやすい She is liable to trust others easily. 彼女は他人を簡単に信用しやすい。	= be apt [likely] to ~
be likely to ~	~しそうである, ~する可能性が高い He is likely to catch the bus on time. 彼は時間通りにバスに間に合いそうである。	= It is likely that
be made from ~	~から作られる Wine is made from grapes. ワインはブドウから作られる。	素材の形が変わっているときに使う。
be made of ~	~で作られる This desk is made of wood. この机は木材で作られる。	素材がそのまま残っているときに使う。
be made up of ~	~からなる This city is made up of 15 districts. この町は15の地区からなっている。	= consist of ~ / be composed of ~
be nothing like ~	~とはまるで違う He is nothing like he used to be. 彼は昔の彼とはまるで違う。	
be obliged to ~	~する義務がある, ~せざるを得ない Everyone is obliged to obey the rule. すべての人がルールに従わざるを得ない。	
be occupied with ~	~で忙しい；~に従事している I am occupied with routine work. 私は日常の作業で忙しい。	S このフレーズはそのまま使える。

熟語	語義／例文	同意表現／コメント
be of service [help] to ~	~の役に立つ We want to be of service to the needy. 私たちは貧しい人の役に立ちたい。	
be of the opinion that ~	~という意見を持っている, ~という意見である I am of the opinion that he will win the championship. 彼が優勝するという意見である。	
be on good [bad] terms with ~	~とは仲が良い[悪い] I am on good terms with my boss. 私は上司と良い関係である。	
be on the books	(人・名前が)登録されている He is on the books of the football club. 彼はそのサッカークラブに登録されている。	
be on the increase	増えていく, 増加しつつある Child obesity rate seems to be on the increase. 子供の肥満の割合が増加しつつあるようだ。	W2 増加傾向を説明するときに使えそう。
be on the point of ~ ing	まさに~しようとしている When I was on the point of giving up, 私がまさに諦めようとしていたときに,	= be about to ~
be on the rise	上昇中である The number of people with drinking problems are on the rise. 飲酒問題を抱えている人の数は上昇中である。	
be on the verge of ~	今にも~しようとしている；~の寸前である She was on the verge of suicide. 彼女は今にも自殺しそうだった。	= be on the brink of ~
be open to ~	~を受けやすい His radical opinion is open to attack. 彼の過激な意見は攻撃を受けやすい。	
be particular about ~	~について好みがうるさい He is particular about food. 彼は食べ物について好みがうるさい。	
be peculiar to ~	~に特有である This custom is peculiar to Japan. この習慣は日本に特有である。	
be poor at ~	~が苦手である I'm really poor at Math. 私は本当に数学が苦手です。	⇔ be good at ~ poor には「悪い」という意味もある。

Track 296

熟語	語義／例文	同意表現／コメント
be popular with [among] ～	～に人気がある，～に評判がよい This type of online game is popular among teens. このタイプのオンラインゲームは10代に人気がある。	ⓢ among までセットで覚えると使いやすい。
be possessed of ～	～を所有している His family is possessed of an enormous fortune. 彼の一族は莫大な財産を所有している。	
be proud of ～	～を誇りにする I am proud of you for saving my children. 私の子供を救ってくれて私はあなたを誇りに思う。	＝ take pride in ～ / pride oneself on ～
be ready for ～	～の準備ができている He is ready for the final exam tomorrow. 彼は明日の期末試験に向けての準備ができている。	
be reluctant to ～	いやいや～する，～したがらない Jennifer is reluctant to eat raw fish. ジェニファーは生魚を食べたがらない。	＝ be unwilling to ～
be representative of ～	～の典型を示す；～を代表する The buildings of this style are representative of ancient architecture. この様式の建物は，古代建築の典型を示している。	
be responsible for ～	～の原因である；～に責任がある Cigarette smoking is responsible for lung cancer. 喫煙は肺がんの原因である。	プラスのことにも使える。
be satisfied with ～	～に満足している Everyone is satisfied with the decision a judge has made. 全員が裁判官が下した判決に満足している。	＝ be content with ～
be second to none	誰にも劣らない Bob is second to none in his Biology class. ボブは生物学のクラスでは誰にも劣らない。	be second only to ～「～に次いで2位」も覚えたい。
be sensible of ～	～に気づいている We are sensible of the difficulties ahead. 我々は先にある困難に気づいている。	

熟語	語義／例文	同意表現／コメント
be sensitive to ~	~に敏感である This species is sensitive to changes in the environment. この種は環境の変化に敏感である。	
be short of ~	~が不足している They are short of capital. 彼らは資金が不足している。	
be specific to ~	~に特有[独特]である This symptom is specific to lung cancer. この症状は肺がんに特有である。	= be peculiar to ~
be strict with ~	~に厳しい My parents were strict with money. 私の両親はお金に厳しかった。	
be subject to ~	~（の影響を）を受けやすい；~にさらされる Japan is subject to typhoons. 日本は台風の影響を受けやすい。	「~に従う」の意味も覚えたい。
be suitable for ~	~に適している This jigsaw puzzle is suitable for children aged 4-5. このジグソーパズルは4～5歳の子供に適している。	= be fit for ~
be superior to ~	~より優れている Your design is superior to mine in use of colours. 君のデザインは色使いの面で私のものより優れている。	⇔ be inferior to ~
be sure to ~	必ず~する He will be sure to get his work done by tomorrow. 彼は明日までに必ず仕事を終わらせるだろう。	She is sure to win. はこのことを言った人が彼女の勝利を信じている。She is sure of winning. は彼女自身が勝利を信じている。
be through with ~	~と縁を切る；~を終える I am through with alcohol. 私はアルコールと縁を切っている。	
be tired of ~	~にうんざりしている Students are tired of wearing school uniforms every day. 生徒たちは毎日制服を着ることにうんざりしている。	= be fed up with ~ / be sick of ~ 「~で疲れている」は be tired from ~。
be to blame (for ~)	（~について）非難されるべきである，（~について）責任がある He is to blame for the traffic collision that happened last night. 彼には昨夜起きた交通事故の責任がある。	= be responsible for ~

Track 298

熟語	語義／例文	同意表現／コメント
be true of ～	～に当てはまる The same is true of Japan and Canada. 同じことが日本とカナダに当てはまる。	= apply to ～ / hold good for ～
be under way	進行中である The annual school meeting is under way. 年に一度の学校集会が進行中である。	= be in progress
be up to ～	～次第である；～の責任である；～の義務である It's all up to you whether to move out or not. 出て行くかどうかは、すべてあなた次第です。	「最大で～」も頻出。up to three people「最大 3 人」
be well off	裕福である、暮らし向きがよい Jack's family seems to be well off. ジャックの家族は裕福そうである。	be well off for ～「～を十分に持っている」も覚えたい。
be wide of the mark	的外れである Your sales forecast turned out to be wide of the mark. あなたの売上予測は的外れだった。	= be beside the mark
be willing to ～	～するのをいとわない、進んで（喜んで）～する He is willing to donate a large amount of money to the children's hospital. 彼は進んで小児病院に多額の寄付をする。	[S] I'm more than willing to ～「本当に喜んで～する」という表現もある。
be worn out	疲れ果てる She is really worn out after working the night shift. 彼女は夜勤の後で本当に疲れ果てている。	= be exhausted / be used up / be done up
be worried about ～	～を心配している I'm worried about feeling pain after surgery. 私は術後の痛みを心配している。	= be concerned about ～
be worthy of ～	～に値する Her deeds are worthy of respect. 彼女の行為は尊敬に値する。	
be wrong with ～	～の調子が悪い、故障している I feel like something is wrong with my new cell phone. 新しい携帯電話の調子が悪いような気がする。	= ～ be in bad shape
be yet [still] to ～	まだ～していない The missing boy is yet to come home safely. その行方不明の少年は、まだ無事に帰宅していない。	

熟語	語義／例文	同意表現／コメント
bear [keep] ~ in mind	~を心に留めておく，~を覚えておく You should keep this formula in mind. あなたはこの公式を覚えておくべきだ。	
bear fruit	実を結ぶ；実がなる Your hard work will bear fruit for sure. あなたの努力は必ず実を結ぶでしょう。	= pay off
beat around [about] the bush	遠回しに言う The criminal kept beating around the bush when questioned by a police officer. 犯人は警察官に尋問された際，(論点には触れず)遠回しに話し続けた。	
because of ~	~のために because of the following reasons 次の理由のために	= due to ~
become of ~	~はどうなるのだろうか What will become of his wife and children if he is killed in the war? もし彼が戦死したら彼の妻と子供たちはどうなるのだろうか。	
before long	やがて，間もなく You will recover from jet lag before long. あなたは時差ボケから間もなく回復するでしょう。	= soon
behave oneself	行儀よくする A male teacher told his pupils to behave themselves. 男性教師が生徒に行儀よくするように言った。	= shape up
behind one's back	陰で Don't make fun of him behind his back. 陰で彼のことをばかにするな。	
behind the times	時代遅れの I think your business strategies seem behind the times. 君の経営戦略は時代遅れのように感じるよ。	⇔ ahead of the times
believe in ~	~(の存在)を信じる；~の正当性を信じる Naomi believes in ghosts. ナオミは幽霊の存在を信じている。	

熟語	語義／例文	同意表現／コメント
believe it or not	信じられないかもしれないが Believe it or not, I won the lottery. 信じられないかもしれないが，私は宝くじに当たりました。	
belong to ~	~に属する He once belonged to a famous baseball team. 彼はかつて有名な野球チームに属していた。	The bag belongs to him. のように物を主語で使うこともある。
beside oneself (with ~)	(~で)我を忘れて；逆上して She was beside herself with grief. 彼女は悲しみで我を忘れていた。	
Besides ~	~に加えて，~だけでなく Besides skiing, she likes snowboarding. 彼女はスキーに加えて，スノーボードも好きだ。	= In addition to ~
between ourselves	ここだけの話だが，内緒にして Between ourselves, he was convicted of theft. ここだけの話だが，彼には窃盗の前科があります。	= between you and me
between you and me	内緒の話ですが，ここだけの話だが Between you and me, he broke up with his long-term girlfriend. 内緒の話ですが，彼は長年交際していた恋人と別れました。	= between ourselves
beyond [above] words	言葉では言い表せないほど be terribly shocked beyond words 言葉では言い表せないほどひどくショックを受けている	
beyond description	言葉で表現できないほど The night view from the top floor is beautiful beyond description. 最上階からの夜景は言葉で表現できないほど美しい。	
blame A for B	BのことでAを責める Why do you blame me for it? 何でそのことで僕を責めるんだ？	⑤ I was blamed for ~ と受動態でも使える。
blow up	爆発する；(嵐などが)起こる The gas tank suddenly blew up. ガスタンクが突然爆発した。	
boast of ~	~を自慢する He boasts of his education. 彼は学歴を自慢している。	= be boastful about
bound for ~	(列車などが)~行きの Which train is bound for Paris? パリ行きはどちらの電車ですか。	電車内の放送でおなじみ。

Track 301

熟語	語義／例文	同意表現／コメント
break away (from 〜)	(〜と)関係を断つ，(〜から)離脱する You should break away from the past. あなたは過去との関係を断つべきだ。	= break up with
break down (〜)	故障する；崩壊する Because of heavy rain, my car broke down. 大雨のせいで車が故障した。	
break into 〜	〜に押し入る；急に〜し始める A burglar broke into his house. 彼の家に泥棒が押し入った。	
break out	(戦争・災害などが)突然起こる A civil war broke out. 内乱が起こった。	「(主語が)起きる」という自動詞の使い方。
break the ice	話を切り出す It is hard to break the ice. 話を切り出しにくい。	イベントの最初にはicebreak(場を和ますもの)も大切。
bring 〜 to light	〜を明るみに出す，〜を暴露する Investigations brought the new fact to light. 調査が新たな事実を明るみに出した。	
bring 〜 to one's senses	〜を正気に返らせる The experience brought him to his senses. この経験が彼を正気に返らせた。	
bring A home to B	B に A を痛感させる I want to bring the importance home to her. 私は彼女に，その重要性を痛感させたい。	
bring about 〜	〜をもたらす；〜を引き起こす The new drug may bring about mental illness. その新薬は精神疾患を引き起こすかもしれない。	= lead to 〜 / result in 〜 / cause 〜
bring oneself to 〜	〜する気になる He could not bring himself to tell the truth. 彼は真実を言う気になれなかった。	
bring out 〜	〜を出版する，〜を世に出す The author will bring out a new non-fiction novel. その作家は新しいノンフィクション小説を出版するでしょう。	= publish
bring up 〜	〜を育てる；〜(問題など)を持ち出す She was brought up in Hawaii. 彼女はハワイで育てられた。	= raise / rear

Track 302

熟語	語義／例文	同意表現／コメント
brush up ～	～(外国語など)をやり直す；～に磨きをかける I have to brush up my English and Chinese. 私は英語と中国語をやり直さなければならない。	
burn down	焼け落ちる Somebody set fire to the church, and it was burned down completely. 誰かが教会に火をつけ、教会は完全に焼け落ちた。	
burst into ～	(部屋等に)乱入する；(突然)～し出す He burst into the room without knocking. 彼はノックしないで部屋に乱入した。	burst into tears 「突然泣き出す」も覚えたい。
by [for] choice	進んで, 選ぶとすれば He lives as a homeless person by choice. 彼は進んでホームレスとして生活している。	
by [in] contrast	対照的に She likes online shopping by contrast with her friend. 彼女は友人とは対照的にオンラインショッピングが好きだ。	W1 つなぎ言葉として使う!
by [in] virtue of ～	～によって, ～のおかげで He rose to fame by virtue of winning a singing competition. 彼は歌唱大会で優勝したことによって名声をあげた。	= because of ～
by accident	偶然, たまたま The famous photo that won the Pulitzer Prize was taken by accident. ピューリッツァー賞を受賞したその有名な写真は偶然撮られた。	= by chance / accidentally
by air	飛行機で Carol has never travelled by air. キャロルは飛行機で旅行したことがありません。	= by plane 冠詞は不要。
by all means	何としても, ぜひとも I want to study abroad by all means. 私は何としても留学したい。	= at all costs
by and large	概して, 一般に By and large, your argument is to the point. 概して, 君の主張は的を射ている。	= on the whole
by birth	生まれつき, 生まれは He is a French noble by birth. 彼は生まれはフランス貴族である。	= by nature
by chance	たまたま, 偶然 Dr. Moore discovered a new cell by chance. ムーア先生は偶然, 新しい細胞を発見した。	= by accident chance には「偶然」の意味もある。

熟語	語義／例文	同意表現／コメント
by comparison	それにひきかえ，比較すると Your handwriting is very neat by comparison to hers. 君の筆跡は，彼女のものと比較するととてもきれいだ。	
by degrees	次第に，徐々に My physical condition deteriorated by degrees. 私の体調は徐々に悪化した。	= little by little / gradually
by far	ずばぬけて，ずっと He is by far the best professor that I've ever had in my school. これまで授業を受けた教授の中で，彼はずばぬけて一番だ。	最上級を修飾するときに使う。
by halves	中途半端に Emma is always doing things by halves. エマはいつも物事を中途半端にしている。	
by means of ～	～（の手段）によって give a presentation by means of PowerPoint パワーポイントによってプレゼンを行う	
by nature	生まれながらの；本来；生まれは He is blind by nature. 彼は生まれながらの盲目です。	= by birth
by no means ～	決して～でない It is by no means easy to meet your expectations. 君の期待に応えることは決して容易でない。	= not ～ at all
by oneself	1人で；独力で Young men should travel around the world by themselves. 若者は世界中を1人で旅するべきだ。	= alone
by the time ～	～するころ（まで）には Dinner will be ready by the time you come home. あなたが帰宅する頃には，夕食の準備ができています。	期限を表す。until（～までずっと）との違いに注意！
by the way	ところで By the way, have you had lunch already? ところで，もう昼ごはんは食べましたか。	= incidentally
by way of ～	～経由で We went to London by way of Hong Kong. 私たちは香港経由でロンドンに行った。	
call for ～	～を必要とする；～を呼び求める I heard someone call for help in debris. 私は瓦礫の下から誰かが助けを求めているのが聞こえた。	

Track 304

熟語	語義／例文	同意表現／コメント
call it a day	その日の仕事を終える，切り上げる It's getting dark outside. Let's call it a day. 暗くなってきたし，このへんで切り上げましょう。	
call off ～	～を中止する They called off their engagement. 彼らは婚約を解消(中止)した。	
call on ～	～を訪ねる I called on my parents for the first time in a while. 私は久しぶりに両親を訪ねた。	= visit ～ on の後は人。場所なら at を使う。
call up	～に電話をかける Please call up my doctor. 私の主治医に電話をかけてください。	
calm down (～)	～を静める；静まる You should calm down your mind. 君は気持ちを静めるべきだよ。	⑤ calm の発音に注意！
can afford to ～	～する(経済的)余裕がある He can afford to buy a new Ferrari car. 彼はフェラーリの新車を購入する余裕がある。	
cannot help ～ ing	～せずにはいられない I cannot help feeling angry. 私は怒りを感じずにはいられない。	= cannot but ～ 「思わず～してしまう」に近い意味。ここの help は「避ける」の意味。
care for ～	～の世話をする Melissa cares for her mother in law. メリッサは義母の世話をする。	= take care of ～ / look after ～ / attend to ～
carry out ～	～を実行する，～を果たす We will carry out a survey of stress management. 我々はストレス管理の調査を実行するでしょう。	= fulfil ～
catch [get] a glimpse of ～	～をちらりと見る I could catch a glimpse of a shooting star. 私は流れ星をちらりと見ることができた。	
catch [seize, hold] ～ by the arm	～の腕をつかむ A police officer caught him by the arm. 警察官が彼の腕をつかんだ。	
catch on	流行する，人気が出る；理解する This type of sneakers catches on now. このタイプのスニーカーが今流行している。	

熟語	語義／例文	同意表現／コメント
catch sight of ～	～を見かける, ～を見つける I caught sight of a big hole in my favourite sweater. 私はお気に入りのセーターに大きな穴を見つけた。	⇔ lose sight of ～
catch up with ～	～に追いつく He worked hard in practice to catch up with his teammates. 彼はチームメートに追いつくために一生懸命練習した。	= overtake ～ [S] catch up「追いつく」だけでも使える。I tried to catch up.
catch 人 ～ ing	人が～しているところを見つける I caught them bullying my friend. 私は彼らが私の友人をいじめているところを見つけた。	
change into ～	～に変わる, ～になる She changed into another person by cosmetic surgery. 彼女は整形手術によって別人になった。	[W1] 地図では be changed into ～「(主語が) ～に変えられる」が便利。
charge 人 with ～	人を～で告発する, 非難する The police charged him with assault. 警察は彼を暴行容疑で告発した。	= accuse 人 of ～
check into ～	(記帳して)～(ホテル・会議など)に入る We checked into the hotel at noon. 私たちは正午にホテルに入った。	
classify A into B	A を B に分類する The researcher classified these results into 5 patterns. その研究者はこれらの結果を5つのパターンに分類した。	
clear A of B	A から B を取り除く We clear the beach of garbage every day. 私たちは毎日ビーチからゴミを取り除く。	= rid A of B
clear one's throat	せきばらいをする He cleared his throat very often during his presentation. 彼はプレゼンの間, 頻繁に咳払いをした。	
close [near] at hand	(時が)近づいて；手近に, すぐ近くに Monica's 21st birthday is close at hand. モニカの21歳の誕生日が近づいている。	
close to ～	～の近くに[で] His university is close to the airport. 彼の大学は空港の近くにある。	
come about	起こる Natural disasters come about suddenly. 自然災害は突然起こる。	= take place / happen / occur

Track 306

熟語	語義／例文	同意表現／コメント
come across [upon] ~	~に偶然出くわす I came across my old friend. 私は古い友人に偶然出くわした。	= run across ~ bump into ~ という言い方もある。
come before ~	~より優先する, ~より重要である Those in need should come before anyone else. 誰よりも困っている人を優先するべきだ。	
come by ~	~を手に入れる He came by wealth as a result of hard work. 彼は努力の結果, 富を手に入れた。	= get ~
come home (to ~)	(~にとって)(危険・事実などが)痛切に感じられる Your advice comes home to my heart. あなたの助言が痛切に感じられる。	
come into being	生まれる, 出現する The Internet came into being many decades ago. インターネットは何十年も前に生まれた。	= come into existence
come into effect	実施される The new school rule will come into effect soon. 学校の新規則はまもなく実施される。	
come into existence	生まれ出る, 生じる Please explain why religion came into existence. なぜ宗教が生まれ出たのかを説明してください。	= come into being
come into view	見えてくる Several meteor showers come into view. 複数の流星群が見えてくる。	= come in sight
come near [close] (to) ~ ing	危うく~する, 今にも~しそうである We came near to being killed. 我々は危うく殺されるところだった。	to の後は不定詞ではなく名詞！
come off ~	落ちる；(ボタンなどが)~から取れる He came off his bike when it skidded. 自転車がスリップして彼は落下した。	
come out	出版(発表)される；(月などが)現れる His latest album comes out in the summer. 彼の最新アルバムが夏に発表される。	
come to one's senses [oneself]	意識を取り戻す He waited for Sarah to come to her senses. 彼はサラが意識を取り戻すのを待った。	

Track 307

熟語	語義／例文	同意表現／コメント
come to [reach] the conclusion that ～	～という結論に達する We came to the conclusion that the game should be postponed. 我々は試合は延期すべきだという結論に達した。	
come to ～	～するようになる Soon he came to love her. やがて彼は彼女を愛するようになった。	= get to ～ W2 become to ～ という表現はないので注意！
come to an end	終わる All the best things come to an end. 良いことにもすべて終わりはくるもの。	= end
come to light	明らかになる, 明るみに出る That evidence did not come to light. その証拠は明らかにならなかった。	
come true	実現する Soon, his dream will come true. 間もなく, 彼の夢は実現するだろう。	= be realised / be materialised
come up	(事が)発生する, 起こる, 生じる I'll let you know if something comes up. 何か起こったら知らせるよ。	= happen
come up with ～	～を思いつく I came up with a new idea. 私は新しいアイデアを思いついた。	= hit on [upon] ～ S そのまま使えそうなフレーズ。
command a fine view	見晴らしがよい His room commands a fine view. 彼の部屋は見晴らしがよい。	
complain to A about [of] B	AにBについて不平を言う The customer complained to the shop assistant about the product. その客は商品について店員に文句を言った。	「不満を言う」は complain を使う。claim ではない。
concentrate (A) on B	(Aを)Bに集中する I will concentrate all my efforts on doing well on IELTS. 私はすべての努力をIELTSで好成績を取ることに集中する。	= focus on B
congratulate A on B	BのことでAを祝う I congratulate you all on your success. 私は諸君の成功について諸君全員にお祝いを申し上げます。	
consent to ～	～に同意する He reluctantly consented to his son's decision. 彼は息子の決心に渋々と同意した。	= agree to ～

327

Track 308

熟語	語義／例文	同意表現／コメント
consist in ~	~にある Happiness consists in how careful you are of small joy. 幸福はどれだけ深く小さな喜びに気を配っているかにある。	= lie in ~
consist of ~	~からなる A week consists of seven days. 1週間は7日で成り立っている。	= be composed of ~ / be comprised of / be made (up) of ~
contrary to ~	~に反して contrary to popular belief 一般的な考えに反して	= as opposed to 名詞
cope with ~	~に対処する He teaches himself how to cope with life. 彼は人生に対処する方法を独習する。	= deal with ~ / manage
correspond with ~	~と一致する；~と文通する His account of events does not correspond with hers. 彼の経緯報告は、彼女のそれと一致しない。	
count for much with	非常に重要である，大変価値がある His help counted for much with her. 彼の援助は、彼女にとって非常に重要だった。	⇔ matter little
count on ~	~に頼る；~次第である Please count on me if you need any help. 助けが必要なときは私に頼ってください。	= depend [rely] on ~
cry for ~	~を求めて叫ぶ(泣く) A bullied kid is crying for help. いじめられている子供が助けを求めて叫んでいる。	
cure A of B	AのBを治す His doctor cured him of migraine. 彼の主治医が彼の偏頭痛を治した。	
cut down ~	~を切り詰める(削減する)；~を切り倒す The new mayor decided to cut down the city's annual budget. 新市長は市の年間予算を切り詰めることを決めた。	
cut in	話をさえぎる，邪魔をする，割り込む He suddenly cut in when we were talking. 私たちが話していると彼が突然割り込んできた。	
day after day	くる日もくる日も He has to struggle with serious disease day after day. 彼はくる日もくる日も重病と闘わなければならない。	= day in day out

熟語	語義／例文	同意表現／コメント
deal with 〜	〜に対処する，〜を処理する I had to deal with difficult situations. 私は困難な状況に対処しなければならなかった。	= handle
dedicate oneself to 〜	〜に専念する Later she dedicated herself to charity. その後，彼女は慈善事業に専念した。	= devote oneself to 〜
depend on A for B	（援助など）BのことでAに頼る I always depend on him for a history assignment. 私はいつも歴史の宿題のことで彼に頼る。	= turn to A for B
deprive A of B	AからBを奪う War deprives people of their humanity. 戦争は人々から人間性を奪う。	W2 受動態 be deprived of B「Bを奪われる」も使える。
devote A to B	AをBに捧げる Devote all of your time to your studies. 研究にすべての時間を捧げなさい。	to の後は不定詞ではなく名詞！
devote oneself to 〜	〜に専念する，〜に身を捧げる Ron devoted himself to writing novels. ロンは小説の執筆に専念した。	= be devoted to 〜
die of 〜	〜（病気・老衰・飢えなど）で死ぬ Many people die of lung cancer every year. 毎年多くの人が肺がんで死ぬ。	die from overwork from は「過労」などの間接的原因の場合。
die out	絶滅（死滅・消滅）する Passenger pigeons died out in 1914. リョコウバトは1914年に絶滅した。	= become extinct / be exterminated
differ from 〜	〜と異なる Our company regulations differ from theirs. 私たちの社則は彼らのものとは異なる。	= be different from 〜 W2 品詞に注意！be 動詞は不要。
differ in 〜	〜の点で異なる，〜が違う These two advertisements differ in colour. これらの2つの広告は色使いが違う。	
direct A to B	AにBへの道を教える An old lady directed me to the post office. 老婦人が私に郵便局への道を教えてくれた。	
discourage 人 from 〜 ing	人が〜するのを思いとどまらせる Parents discourage their kids from going out late at night. 親は子供が夜遅くに出歩くのを思いとどまらせる。	

熟語	語義／例文	同意表現／コメント
dispose of ～	～を処理する、捨てる The factory disposed of waste illegally. その工場は違法に廃棄物を処理した。	
distinguish A from B	AとBを区別する It is difficult to distinguish an authentic designer handbag from a replica. 本物のデザイナーバッグとレプリカを区別するのは難しい。	= distinguish between A and B / tell A from B
do away with ～	～を廃止する、～を捨てる My school did away with the old curriculum. 私の学校は古いカリキュラムを廃止した。	= abolish ～
do good to ～ [～ good]	～にとってよい、～のためになる You should do good to those in need. あなたは困っている人々のためになるべきだ。	= be good for ～ / benefit ～ ⇔ do harm to ～
do harm to ～ [～ harm]	～に害を与える Secondhand smoke may do harm to non-smokers. 副流煙は非喫煙者に害を与えるかもしれない。	⇔ do good to ～
do more harm than good	有害無益である Taking too many supplements does more harm than good. サプリメントの摂り過ぎは有害無益である。	
do with ～	～を扱う、～を処理する The shop manager did with customers' complaints. 店の経営者が客の苦情を処理した。	to do with ～ は「～と関係がある」。
do without ～	～なしで済ます I cannot do without a heater this winter. この冬はヒーターなしで済ませられない。	= dispense with ～
do 人 a favour	人の願いを聞き入れる Will you do me a favour? お願いがあるのですが。	favour の直訳は「親切な行為」。
don't fail to ～	必ず～する Don't fail to call me tonight. 今夜必ず電話してね。	R fail to ～ は肯定文だと「～できない」の意味。
don't forget to ～	忘れずに～する He doesn't forget to brush his teeth before going to bed. 彼は寝る前に忘れずに歯磨きする。	= remember to ～
doubt if [whether] ～	～かどうか疑問に思う I doubt if it is true. 私はそれが本当かどうか疑う。	R doubt that ～ は否定的に「～ではないように思う」。

Track 311

熟語	語義／例文	同意表現／コメント
dozens of ～	何十もの～，多数の～ Jill collects dozens of antique goods for a hobby. ジルは趣味で多数の骨董品を集めている。	= several tens of ～
draw [catch] attention to ～	(～に)注意を引く His comment helped draw attention to the environmental issue. 彼のコメントが環境問題に注目を引きつける一助となった。	draw a conclusion は「結論に達する」。
draw out ～	～を引き出す He drew out the money from the bank. 彼は銀行からお金を引き出した。	
dream of ～	～を夢みる I never dreamed of such a thing. 私にはそんなことは思いも寄らなかった。	
dress oneself	服を着る Her child can dress herself even though she's only 2 years old. 彼女の子供はまだ2歳なのに，服を着ることができる。	= get dressed
drive out (～)	～を追い出す；車で出掛ける Bad money drives out good. 悪貨は良貨を駆逐する。	
drop ～ a line	～に一筆書き送る I'll drop you a line when I get to London. ロンドンに着いたら，あなたに一筆書き送ります。	= write to ～
drop in (on 人/at 場所)	(～に)立ち寄る I often drop in at the cafeteria on my way to morning class. 私はよく朝の授業に行く途中にカフェテリアに立ち寄る。	= look [stop] in ～
drop out (of ～)	(～から)脱落する；手を引く She dropped out of college. 彼女は大学を中退した。	
due to ～	～のために，～のせいで The train was delayed this morning due to an earthquake. 地震のために今朝電車が遅れた。	= because of ～ / owing to ～
each other	お互い We have known each other since childhood. 私たちは子供の頃からお互いを知っている。	= one another
eat up ～	～を食べ尽くす A group of lions ate up a zebra. ライオンの群れがシマウマを食べ尽くした。	= gobble up ～

Track 312

熟語	語義／例文	同意表現／コメント
end in ~	（結局）〜に終わる Her debut performance ended in success. 彼女の初舞台は成功に終わった。	= result in ~
end up ~ ing	結局〜することになる，結局〜するはめになる He ended up quitting the company. 彼は結局会社を辞めることになってしまった。	ⓢ エピソードのオチを言うときに使おう！
end up with ~	（結局は）〜で終わる The party ended up with his speech. パーティーは彼のスピーチで終わった。	
enjoy oneself	楽しく過ごす I really enjoyed myself at the concert. 私はコンサートではとても楽しく過ごした。	= have a good time
enter into ~	〜（話・仕事など）を始める They entered into a discussion about the issue. 彼らはその問題について議論を始めた。	= begin
equip A with B	A に B を備え付ける We need to equip our office with computers. 我々はオフィスにコンピュータを備え付けねばならない。	be equipped with 〜 「〜が備え付けられている」も使いたい。
every inch	全く，どこから見ても She is now every inch a mature woman. 彼女は今やどこから見ても成熟した女性だ。	= every bit
every other ~	〜おきに Write on every other line. 1行おきに書きなさい。	
every other day	1日おきに The tennis player practises every other day. そのテニス選手は1日おきに練習する。	= every second day
every three days	2日おきに，3日ごとに I go to the library every three days. 私は2日おきに図書館へ行く。	= every third day
except for ~	〜を除けば Josh likes watching all the sports except for golf. ジョシュはゴルフを除けば，すべてのスポーツ観戦が好きだ。	= other than ~
excuse 人 for ~ ing	人の〜を許す Please excuse me for breaking school rules. 私の校則違反をどうか許してください。	= pardon 人 for ~ ing

Track 313

熟語	語義／例文	同意表現／コメント
expect A of [from] B	BにAを期待する We cannot expect much of him. 彼に多くは期待できない。	
expose A to B	AをBにさらす Don't expose photos to the sun. 写真を日光にさらすな。	be exposed to 〜「〜に触れる, さらされる」の方が使いやすい。
face to face	直接会って, 面と向かって I have to apologise to you face to face. 私はあなたに直接会ってお詫びしなければならない。	W2 face-to-face communication のように形容詞ならハイフンでつなぐ。
fade away	（次第に）消え失せる The drum faded away. 太鼓の音は次第に遠のいていった。	
fall in love with 〜	〜に恋をする She's falling in love with a young actor. 彼女は若い俳優に恋をしている。	= lose one's heart to 〜
fall into 〜	〜に陥る；（急に）〜になる They fell into serious financial difficulty. 彼らは深刻な財政難に陥った。	
fall off (〜)	（〜から）落ちる；減少する He fell off the horse. 彼は馬から落ちた。	
fall on 〜	〜に当たる My birthday this year falls on Sunday. 今年の私の誕生日は日曜日に当たる。	
fall out with 〜	〜とけんかをする, 仲たがいする She often falls out with her neighbours. 彼女はよく隣人とけんかをする。	
fall [come] short of 〜	〜に及ばない；〜が不足する Sales this month have fallen short of expectations. 今月の売り上げは予想に及ばなかった。	⇔ come up to
far from 〜	決して〜ではない Rebecca is far from a beautiful woman. レベッカは決して美女ではない。	= anything but 〜 / by no means 〜 R 出てきたら否定語と考えよう！
feel at ease	落ち着く, 安心する A doctor made his patient feel at ease. 医者が彼の患者を落ち着かせた。	= feel relaxed

333

Track 314

熟語	語義／例文	同意表現／コメント
feel for 〜	〜に同情する I feel for my friend who lost her only child. 私はひとりっ子を亡くした友人に同情する。	= sympathise with 〜
feel free to 〜	遠慮なく〜する, 自由に〜してよい Feel free to contact me. 気軽に連絡してください。	手紙やメールの最後に書くおなじみのフレーズ。
feel ill at ease	気づまりである, 落ち着かない I feel ill at ease in an unfamiliar town. 私は見知らぬ町にいると落ち着かない。	⇔ feel at ease
figure out 〜	〜を理解する I figured out how to install the program on my PC. 私はそのプログラムのインストール方法を理解した。	= make out 〜 / understand 〜
fill in 〜	（必要事項を）〜に書き込む, 〜を埋める Students filled in the questionnaire sheets. 生徒たちはアンケート用紙を埋めた。	= fill out 〜
fill out 〜	（書類など）〜に書き込む, 必要事項を記入する He filled out the online application form. 彼はオンライン上で申請用紙に必要事項を記入した。	= fill in 〜
fill up (〜)	満杯になる；〜を満たす Fill up the tank, please. 満タンにしてください。	
find fault with 〜	〜のあらを探す He always finds fault with others' ideas. 彼はいつも他人のアイデアのあらを探す。	= try to find a flaw in 〜
find out 〜	〜を発見する, 〜に気がつく Paul finally found out his lost dog's whereabouts. ポールはついに迷子になった飼い犬の居所を発見した。	= discover 〜
first of all	第一に First of all, let me apologise for being late. 第一に, 遅刻したことをお詫びさせてください。	= to begin with W2 firstly の方がフォーマル。
for [with] all 〜	〜にもかかわらず For all her popularity, her latest movie wasn't a big hit. 彼女の人気にもかかわらず, 彼女の最新映画はヒットしなかった。	= in spite of 〜
for a change (of air)	気分転換に, たまには I go to the gym for a change. 私は気分転換にジムに通っている。	= for a switch

熟語	語義／例文	同意表現／コメント
for a rainy day	まさかの時に備えて Let's keep food in the storeroom for a rainy day. まさかの時に備えて，物置に食べ物を保管しよう。	= against a rainy day
for a while	しばらくの間 Alex will leave here for a while. アレックスはしばらくの間ここを離れます。	= for a short time
for certain [sure]	はっきりと，確かに I don't know for certain where she works. 私は彼女がどこで働いているのかはっきりと分からない。	= certainly [surely]
for ever	永久に The child has to live with chronic disease for ever. その子は永久に慢性の病気と共に生きなければならない。	= for good [英]では for と ever を離すのも可。
for fear of ～ing	～しないように I must work hard for fear of failing. 私は落第しないように猛勉強しなければならない。	= in order not to ～ [S] for fear that SV も使える。
for good	永久に He quit smoking and drinking alcohol for good. 彼はタバコと酒を永久にやめた。	= for ever
for instance	例えば In developed countries, in Sweden and Canada for instance, 先進国，例えばスウェーデンやカナダでは，	= for example [W2] 例を書く前につなぎ言葉として入れる。
for lack [want] of ～	～が不足して，～がなくて The flower died for lack of water. その花は水がなくて枯れた。	
for nothing	ただで；無駄に They help war orphans for nothing. 彼らは無償で(ただで)戦争孤児を助ける。	= for free / in vain
for one thing ～ and for another ～	1つには～で，また1つには～である For one thing, I am busy and for another, I have no money. 私は(理由として)1つには忙しいし，また1つには金もない。	
for one's age	年の割には He's mature for his age. 彼は年の割にはませている。	[R]「～の割には」の for は頻出。
for one's part	自分としては For my part, I like jasmine tea rather than green tea. 私としては，緑茶よりもジャスミン茶が好きです。	= as far as one is concerned

335

熟語	語義／例文	同意表現／コメント
for oneself	独力で The climber reached the summit for himself. その登山家は独力で登頂した。	= by oneself
for or against	～に賛成かそれとも反対か Are you for or against his idea? あなたは彼の案に賛成ですか，それとも反対ですか。	
for sure [certain]	確かに，きっと，必ず I'll email you tomorrow for sure. 私は明日あなたに必ずメールします。	= surely [certainly]
for the first time	初めて Kyle saw the pyramids in Egypt for the first time. カイルはエジプトで初めてピラミッドを見た。	= first [S] for the first time in 10 years「10年ぶりに」も使えるように！
for the life of 人	どうしても I cannot do it for the life of me. 私はそれはどうしてもできない。	
for the most part	大部分は，たいてい The group of tourists are, for the most part, from China. その観光客グループの大部分は中国から来ている。	= mostly
for the purpose of ～ing	～する目的で，～するために Many tourists go to New York for the purpose of seeing a Broadway musical. 多くの観客がブロードウェイのミュージカルを鑑賞する目的で，ニューヨークへ行く。	= with the view of ～ing purpose で使う前置詞は for。 for different purposes「様々な目的のために」。
for the sake of ～	～のために Refugees fled from their countries for the sake of freedom. 難民は自由を求めて自国から逃げ出した。	= for the benefit [good] of ～
for the time being	しばらくの間，差し当たり I'll be in the hospital for the time being. 私はしばらくの間，入院します。	= for the present
force A on B	A を B に押しつける Don't force your kindness on others. あなたの親切を人に押し売りするな。	= impose ～ on 人
forget ～ing	～したことを忘れる I'll never forget seeing you. 私はあなたに会ったことを決して忘れないだろう。	動名詞は過去のニュアンス。「(もうすでに)～したことを忘れる」。

Track 317

熟語	語義／例文	同意表現／コメント
forget to ~	~するのを忘れる Don't forget to see him tomorrow. 明日彼に会うのを忘れるな。	不定詞は未来のニュアンス。「(これから)~するのを忘れる」。
forgive A for B	Bに対してAを許す A mother forgave her kid for telling a lie. 母親は子供に対して、嘘をついたことを許した。	= excuse A for B
from ~ point of view	~の観点[見地]から You should look at it from a customer's point of view. 君たちは客の観点からそれを見るべきだ。	
from A to Z	何から何まで He knows this neighbourhood from A to Z. 彼はこの界隈のことを何から何まで知っている。	= from first to last
from now on	今後は I'll never make the same mistakes from now on. 私は今後決して同じ間違いを犯しません。	= after this
from time to time	時々 She goes for a drink with her friends from time to time. 彼女は友人と時々飲みに出掛ける。	= once in a while / at times / now and then
get [become] acquainted with ~	~と知り合いになる Rachel got acquainted with her last night. レイチェルは昨夜彼女と知り合いになった。	= get to know ~ acquaintance「知人」も覚える。
get [put] A across to B	AをBに分からせる He couldn't get his jokes across to the students. 彼はジョークを学生に分からせることができなかった。	
get [rise] to one's feet	立ち上がる He got to his feet and looked around the room. 彼は立ち上がって部屋を見渡した。	= stand up
get [stand] in the way of ~	~の邪魔をする I don't want anyone to get in the way of my lifestyle. 私は自分の生き方を誰にも邪魔されたくない。	道の中に立つ=邪魔になる と連想で覚える。
get A ready for B	BのためにAを準備する Did you get everything ready for tomorrow? 明日の準備はすべてできたかい？	
get along with ~	~とうまくやっていく；暮らしていく John does not get along with Peter. ジョンはピーターとウマが合わない。	⑤ 周りの人との関係を言うときに便利。

熟語	語義／例文	同意表現／コメント
get at ～	～を意味する；～に達する I can't understand what you're trying to get at. 私はあなたが何を言いたいのか分かりません。	
get ～ back on track	再び～を軌道に乗せる I finally got my studies back on track. 私はようやく勉強を再び軌道に乗せた。	
get down to ～	(仕事など)～に(本気で)取り掛かる Let's get down to business. さあ本題に取り掛かろう。	= set to ～
get in contact with ～	～に連絡をとる；～と接触する He got in contact with his friends from college. 彼は大学時代の友達に連絡を取った。	= get in touch with ～
get into ～	～の中へ入る；～(ある状態)になる He got into financial difficulties. 彼は財政難に陥った。	
get lost	(道に)迷う；途方に暮れる A gentleman helped me when I got lost. 私が道に迷ったとき、紳士が助けてくれた。	= lose one's way lose は「失う」。lose one's way で「迷う」。
get married (to ～)	(～と)結婚する He got married to his high school sweetheart. 彼は高校時代の恋人と結婚した。	= marry ～ ⑤ 前置詞は to を使う。
get nowhere	何の成果もない、うまくいかない、どうにもならない The negotiations got nowhere. その交渉は何の成果もなかった。	
get on one's nerves	～の癇[神経]に障る Her looseness sometimes gets on my nerves. 彼女のだらしなさが時々私の癇に障る。	= irritate ～
get out of ～	～から出る；～から降りる Get out of here! ここから出て行け！	
get over ～	～を克服する I have to get over altitude sickness. 私は高山病を克服しなければならない。	= overcome ～
get rid of ～	～を取り除く This ointment gets rid of pimples. この軟膏はニキビを取り除いてくれます。	= clear ～ ® remove との書き換えにも気づくように！

Track 319

熟語	語義／例文	同意表現／コメント
get the better of ~	~に打ち勝つ I want to get the better of him in the sociology exam. 私は社会学の試験で彼に打ち勝ちたい。	= beat ~
get through with ~	~を片付ける, ~をやり遂げる I got through with my term paper at 11pm. 私は11時に期末レポートをやり遂げた。	= have done with ~
get to ~	~に到着する She got to the small country in Africa after a long trip. 彼女は長旅の末にアフリカの小国に到着した。	= arrive at [in] ~ / reach ~
get [bring] ~ under control	~を抑えつける, ~をコントロールする The government got the riot under control. 政府は暴動を抑えつけた。	
get used [accustomed] to ~ [~ ing]	~に[~することに]慣れる He got used to living in China. 彼は中国で生活するのに慣れました。	getは「~になる」というニュアンス。be動詞だと状態を表す。
give away ~	寄付する；~を(ただで)やる He gave away all his money to charity. 彼はすべての金を慈善事業に寄付した。	
give birth to ~	~を生む, ~を生み出す；~を産む She gave birth to twins. 彼女は双子を出産した。	= yield
give in to ~	~に屈する He gave in to temptation. 彼は誘惑に負けた。	= yield to ~ / submit to ~
give off ~	~を放出する, ~を発する Sulphur gases were given off by the volcano. 硫黄ガスが火山から放出された。	= discharge ~ / emit ~
give rise to ~	~を引き起こす This issue will give rise to a conflict of opinions. この問題は意見の対立を引き起こすだろう。	= bring about ~ R causeだと思って読めばOK。
give the green light to	(着手, 実施などの)許可を与える The government gave the green light to the new project. 政府は新プロジェクト実施に許可を与えた。	
give up (~)	(~を)やめる；あきらめる He gave up smoking on his doctor's advice. 彼は医者の勧めで喫煙をやめた。	= quit / abandon

Track 320

熟語	語義／例文	同意表現／コメント
give way to ~	(~に)譲歩する, 屈する；道を譲る He reluctantly gave way to their demands. 彼は嫌々ながら彼らの要求に屈した。	= yield (to ~)
give 人 a hand	人を手伝う Let me give you a hand with those books. それらの本を運ぶのを手伝いますよ。	= help 人
give 人 a ride [lift]	人を車に乗せる Can you give me a ride to the station? 駅まで乗せて行ってもらえますか。	
give 人 up for [as] dead [lost]	人を死んだものと諦める He gave his runaway son up for dead. 彼は家出息子を死んだものと諦めた。	
go bad	腐る Milk will go bad unless bacteria are removed. バクテリアを除去しないと牛乳は腐る。	= spoil / decay / rot goには「~の状態になる」という意味がある。
go bankrupt	破産する About 80% of the companies go bankrupt in 10 years. 企業の約80％は10年で倒産する。	= go into bankruptcy / fail
go by	経過する；通り過ぎる Time goes by slowly here. ここでは時間がゆっくりと流れる。	
go Dutch	割り勘にする, 自分の分は自分で払う Students usually go Dutch when eating out. 学生は通常外食のとき割り勘です。	= split the bill
go from bad to worse	ますます悪くなる The situation went from bad to worse. その事態はますます悪化した。	
go on ~ing [with ~]	~し[~を]続ける He went on talking endlessly about himself. 彼は自身について話し続けた。	= keep on ~ing
go on to ~	続けて~する；次に移る He played Bach, and went on to play Chopin. 彼はバッハを弾き, 続けてショパンを弾いた。	
go out	交際する；消える；流行らなくなる She and I have been going out for 6 months now. 私と彼女は付き合って6カ月です。	= go together

熟語	語義／例文	同意表現／コメント
go over ~	を見直す；繰り返す；~をよく調べる You should go over notes for tomorrow's midterm. あなたは明日の中間テストに備えてノートを見直すべきだ。	= check ~ / repeat ~ / review ~
go so far as to ~	~さえもする，~しさえする His father went so far as to hit him. 彼の父親は彼を殴りさえした。	
go through ~	~を経験する；~を通過する You have no idea what I went through to get this. 私がこれを入手するためにどんなことを経験したか君には分かるまい。	= pass through ~
go through with ~	~をやり遂げる I will go through with this whatever you may say. 君が何と言おうと私はこれをやり遂げる。	= carry through ~
go with ~	~に調和する，~に似合う Fish goes with white wine. 魚は白ワインに合う。	
go wrong	~が故障する；(計画が)失敗する Something went wrong with the printer. プリンタのどこかが故障した。	= fail
graduate from ~	~を卒業する Which university did you graduate from? あなたはどちらの大学を卒業されましたか。	ⓢ from を忘れないように！
half the size of ~	~の半分の大きさ The Atlantic Ocean is about half the size of the Pacific. 大西洋は太平洋のほぼ半分の大きさです。	= half as large as ~
hand down	[通例 be ~ ed]伝わる；遺伝する That story was handed down by word of mouth. その話は口伝で伝えられた。	= pass on [down] ~
hand [turn] in ~	~を提出する He handed in his resignation to the director. 彼は重役に辞表を提出した。	= submit ~
hand in hand	手を取り合って；協力して Doctors and nurses work hand in hand. 医師と看護師は協力して働く。	
hang up	電話を切る Don't hang up, but hold on. 電話を切らず，そのままで待って。	

熟語	語義／例文	同意表現／コメント
have [get] one's own way	自分の思い通りにする，勝手に振る舞う My elder brother always has his own way. 私の兄はいつも自分の思い通りにする。	= do as one likes
have [make] an impact on ～	～に影響[衝撃]を与える His father's absence had a great impact on him. 父親の不在が彼に多大な影響を与えた。	= have an effect [influence] on ～
have ～ in mind	～のことを思って[意図して]いる That's exactly what I have had in mind. それは，まさに私が思っていたことです。	= bear ～ in mind
have ～ to oneself	専用の～を持っている She has a car to herself. 彼女は自分専用の車を持っている。	
have a good [great] command of ～	～が自由に使える，～が堪能である She has a good command of English. 彼女は英語が堪能である。	
have a narrow escape	～を間一髪で[危うく]逃れる His firm had a narrow escape from bankruptcy. 彼の会社は危うく倒産を逃れた。	= narrowly survive
have a sweet tooth	甘いものが大好きである My mother has had a sweet tooth. 私の母は甘いものが大好きです。	= like sweets
have a weakness for ～	～が大好きである，～が大好物である He has a weakness for chocolate. 彼はチョコレートが大好きである。	
have an effect on ～	～に効果[影響]を与える Her advice had no effect on him. 彼女の忠告は彼に何の効果も与えなかった。	= have an influence on ～ / tell on ～
have an eye for ～	～を見る目がある，～に眼識がある He has an eye for people. 彼は人を見る目がある。	
have an influence on ～	～に影響を与える The eruption had a great influence on the area. 噴火が地域に多大な影響を与えた。	= influence ～
have difficulty (in) ～ ing	～するのに苦労する He had difficulty understanding the content. 彼は内容を理解するのに苦労した。	= have trouble (in) ～ ing [S] It is difficult to V と同様に，使える場面が多い。

Track 323

熟語	語義／例文	同意表現／コメント
have every [good] reason to ~	~するのも当然だ He has every reason to be angry. 彼が怒るのも当然だ。	= It is natural that SV
have faith [confidence] in ~	~を信用する I have a lot of faith in my mentor. 私は指導教官を本当に信用しています。	= believe in ~
have had enough of ~	~はもうたくさんだ，~はもう十分である I have had enough of art museums. 私は美術館はもうたくさんだ。	= be tired of ~
have little [a lot, a great deal] to do with ~	~とほとんど関係がない[大いに関係がある] Knowledge has little to do with wisdom. 知識は英知とほとんど関係がない。	= be little related to ~ little は「ほとんど~ない」を表す否定語。
have little [a lot, nothing] in common	共通点がほとんどない[多い，ない] We have little in common. 私たちには共通点がほとんどない。	
have no choice but to ~	~するよりほかに仕方がない We have no choice but to accept his proposal. 我々は彼の提案を受け入れるしかない。	= have no alternative but to ~ / be forced to ~
have no idea (~)	(~が)全く分からない I have no idea as to what to do next. 私は次に何をやるべきかが全く分からない。	= not understand ~ at all ⑤ この例文はそのまま使える。as to を続けるのは通常，後に wh- 語があるとき。
have no say	言う権利が全くない We have no say in the decision. 我々はその決定について言う権利が全くない。	= have no right to say
have nothing to do with ~	~と少しも関係がない Some say luck has nothing to do with success. 運は成功と全く関係がないという人もいる。	= be entirely unrelated to ~
have one's own way in	自分の思い通りにする，自分勝手にする She has her own way in everything. 彼女は何でも自分の思い通りにする。	
have [say] one's say	言いたいことを言う，意見を述べる Has everyone had his say? 皆さん，言いたいことを言いましたか。	= speak one's mind
have only to ~	ただ~さえすればよい You have only to follow the instructions. あなたは説明書に従いさえすればいい。	= All 人 have to do is (to) ~

343

Track 324

熟語	語義／例文	同意表現／コメント
have second thoughts	二の足を踏む，決心がつかない He was having second thoughts about marrying her. 彼は彼女との結婚に二の足を踏んでいた。	= think again
have some bearing on ～	～と多少関係がある Luck has some bearing on success. 運は成功と多少関係がある。	= have something to do with ～
have something [a lot] to do with ～	～と何らかの[大いに]関係がある He has something to do with the group. 彼はそのグループと何か関係がある。	
have something to live for	生きがいを持つ People need to have something to live for. 人は生きがいを持つことが必要だ。	⇔ have nothing to live for
have the right to ～	～する権利がある You do have the right to appeal. 君には実際抗議する権利があるよ。	= be entitled to ～
have [exchange] words with ～	～と口論する He had words with his mother on the bus. 彼はバスの中で母親と口論した。	= get an argument with ～
head for ～	～へ向かう Where are you heading for? あなたはどこへ向かっているの？	= go to [toward] ～ / leave for ～
hear from ～	～から便りがある Let me hear from you. お便りをください。	= get word [a letter] from
hear of ～	～の消息[うわさ]を聞く，～のことを聞く Have you heard of her recently? あなたは最近彼女の消息を聞いていますか。	
help 人 with ～	人の～を手伝う I helped him with his homework. 私は彼の宿題を手伝った。	「～を助ける」では help の直後には人。事柄の場合は with をつける。
help oneself to ～	～を自由に取って食べる[飲む] Please help yourself to more. お代わりは自由に取って食べてください。	"Be my guest."「自由にお使い[お召し上がり]ください。」
hit on [upon] ～	～をふと思いつく I hit on a good idea. 私はいいアイデアを思いついた。	= ～ occur to 人

熟語	語義／例文	同意表現／コメント
hold on	電話を切らないでおく；がんばる Hold on a second. 電話を切らないで、しばらくお待ちください。	⇔ hang up
hold one's breath	かたずをのむ，息を殺す I held my breath while watching the match. 私はかたずをのんで試合を見守った。	= catch one's breath
hold one's tongue	黙る Hold your tongue. お前は黙ってろ。	= shut one's mouth
hold onto ~	~にしがみ[すがり]つく，~を離さない She held onto her husband for support. 彼女は支えを求めて夫にしがみついた。	cling to ~
hold out	もつ，続く；もちこたえる The company cannot hold out any longer. その会社はもうもたない。	= hold one's own / last (out)
hold the line	電話を切らずにそのまま待つ Hold the line, please. 電話を切らないでください。	= hold on
hold true (for [of, with] ~)	(~に)当てはまる，適用できる This rule holds true for any case. この規則はどの事例にも当てはまる。	= be true of ~
hold up (~)	~を(持ち)上げる；耐える Students vigorously held up their fists. 学生たちは力強くこぶしを突き上げた。	= raise / lift
hope [wish] for ~	~を望む They waited and hoped for the best. 彼らは事がうまくいくのをじっと望んだ。	= be desirous of ~
How come ~ ?	どうして[なぜ] ~なのか How come you are so clever? あなたはなんでそんなに抜け目がないの？	= Why ~ ?
impose A on B	AをBに課す[押しつける] The government imposed a new tax on farmers. 政府は農家に新税を課した。	= burden B with A W2 政府関連の課題で使えそうな例文。
in a panic	慌てふためいて Due to the stock market crash, investors are in a panic. 株の暴落で投資家は慌てふためいている。	= in confusion

Track 326

熟語	語義／例文	同意表現／コメント
in [with] regard to ～	～に関して Radical changes were made in regard to regulations. 規制に関して根本的な変更がなされた。	＝ as to ～
in a hurry	急いで, 慌てて；簡単には They left in such a hurry that they forgot their tickets. 彼らは非常に慌てて出発したので切符を忘れた。	＝ in haste
in a low voice	低い声で, 小声で He muttered in a low voice. 彼は小声でぶつぶつ言った。	＝ in a whisper
in a minute [second]	すぐに, 間もなく I'll be there in a minute. 私はすぐにそちらへ行きます。	＝ in a short while
in a sense	ある意味で Your decision was right in a sense. ある意味で君の決断は正しかった。	＝ in a way
in a word	ひと言で言えば, 要するに In a word he has blundered. ひと言で言えば, 彼はしくじった。	＝ in short ／ in brief ／ to be brief
in accordance with ～	～に従って, ～の通りに In accordance with the instructions the experiment was conducted. 指示に従って実験は行われた。	＝ according to accordance は「一致, 調和」。動詞 accord は「一致する(させる)」。
in addition (to ～)	(～に)加えて In addition to his regular profession, he is also known as a singer. 本職に加えて, 彼は歌手としても知られている。	＝ besides ～ ／ on top of ～ [W2] Body で次のアイデアに移るときに使える。furthermore, moreover も合わせて覚える。
in advance	前もって, あらかじめ；前金で I'll let you know that in advance. 私はそれについては前もってあなたに知らせるよ。	＝ beforehand
in case of ～	～の場合には；～する場合に備えて In case of fire, call 999. 火事の際には999番に電話を。	＝ in the event of

熟語	語義／例文	同意表現／コメント
in common (with ～)	(～と)共通して They have nothing in common with each other. 彼らにはお互いに共通点が何もない。	[S] have a lot in common「共通点が多い」も使えそう。
in comparison with ～	～と比べて In comparison with other novels of his, this one is boring. 彼の他の小説と比べて、これは退屈だ。	= compared with [to] ～
in consequence	その結果, したがって In consequence more than 100 people were injured. その結果100人以上が負傷した。	= consequently
in contrast (with [to] ～)	(～とは)対照的に The building stands out in contrast with its surroundings. その建物は周囲とは対照的に目立ちます。	= unlike ～ /as opposed to ～
in detail	詳しく, 詳細に The instructor explained the process in detail. その講師は手順を詳しく説明した。	= at length
in earnest	熱心に[な], 真剣に[な]；本格的に[な] He worked on the project in earnest. 彼はその企画に熱心に取り組んだ。	= earnestly
in effect	実際には, 事実上；有効な In effect, the result was not what we had expected. 実際, 結果は我々が期待したものではなかった。	= in fact
in exchange for [of] ～	～と引き換えに；～の代わりに I was assigned to clean the whole house in exchange for 100 dollars. 私は100ドルと引き換えに家中の掃除を命じられた。	= in return for ～
in fact	(ところが)実は；実際 In fact, I have seen him in person. 実は, 私は彼に直に会ったことがあるよ。	= as a matter of fact [S] 例を言うときのつなぎ言葉として使おう！
in fashion	流行して This type of hat is in fashion this year. この型の帽子は今年流行しています。	⇔ out of fashion fashion は「流行；方法」の意味を覚える。
in favour of ～	～に賛成して；～の利益となるように Are you in favour of the plan? あなたはその計画に賛成ですか。	= in support of
in full	全部, 省略せず Please choose to pay in full or pay in monthly instalments. 全額払うか, 月賦で払うか選んでください。	= completely

熟語	語義／例文	同意表現／コメント
in general	一般的に Students in general do not have enough faith in themselves. 生徒は一般的に, 自分に十分な信念を持っていない。	= as a rule / at large
in harmony with ～	～と仲良く［調和して］ I want to work in harmony with the environment. 私は自然と調和して働きたい。	= in accord with ～
in haste	急いで I always have breakfast in haste. 私はいつも朝食を急いで食べる。	= in a hurry
in honour of ～	～に敬意を表して, ～のために The monument was erected in honour of a prominent poet. その記念碑は著名な詩人に敬意を表して建てられた。	= out of respect for ～
in line (with ～)	(～と)調和して；並んで Japan acted in line with England. 日本は英国と行動をともにした。	
in need (of ～)	(～を)必要として He was badly in need of money. 彼はとても金を必要としていた。	= in want of
in nine cases out of ten	十中八九, 間違いなく They will win in nine cases out of ten. 彼らは十中八九勝つだろう。	= ten to one
in no time	すぐに, 間もなく He recovered from the cold in no time. 彼はすぐに風邪から回復した。	= soon / at once
in obedience to ～	～に従って I attended court in obedience to the summons. 私は召喚に応じて出廷した。	
in one's company	～と一緒にいる［と］ I feel comfortable in his company. 私は彼と一緒だと気が楽だ。	
in one's place	～の代わりに My boss made me attend the party in his place. 上司は自分の代わりに私をパーティーに出席させた。	= in place of ～
in one's teens	10代で She got married in her teens. 彼女は10代で結婚した。	in one's 20's なら「20代で」。

熟語	語義／例文	同意表現／コメント
in oneself	それ自体［自身］ Knowledge is not an end in itself. 知識それ自体が目的なのではない。	
in order	秩序立てて，整然と You should put your ideas in order. あなたは考えを整理するべきだ。	⇔ at random
in other words	言い換えれば；すなわち He never does his homework. In other words, he is lazy. 彼は宿題をやらない。言い換えれば，怠け者だ。	＝ that is (to say)
in part	1つには，ある程度 The problem stems in part from lack of money. その問題は1つには資金不足からきている。	＝ partly
in particular	特に I'm fond of seafood, crabs in particular. 私はシーフードの中でも特にカニが好きです。	＝ particularly ⑤ 具体例を広げるときに便利。
in practice	実際に（は），実際上 The idea did not work in practice. その考えは実際にはうまくいかなかった。	＝ in reality
in proportion to [with] 〜	（〜に）比例して，釣り合って Their earnings are in proportion to their ability. 彼らの稼ぎは能力に比例する。	＝ in line with
in prospect	見込まれて，予想して A good result is in prospect. 良い結果が予想される。	
in public	人前で，公然と Don't put on makeup in public. 人前で化粧をするな。	＝ in the presence of others / to the view ⇔ in private
in return for 〜	〜のお礼に I bought a drink in return for his help. 私は手伝いのお礼として彼に一杯おごった。	W2 文頭でつなぎ言葉としても使える。
in search of 〜	〜を求めて，〜を探して Many people come to Japan in search of employment. 多くの人が仕事を求めて日本に来る。	＝ in quest of 〜
in short [brief]	要するに In short, the project was not successful. 要するに，そのプロジェクトは成功しなかった。	＝ to make a long story short / to sum up ⑤ まとめを言うときに便利。

Track 330

熟語	語義／例文	同意表現／コメント
in short supply	不足して Good teachers are in short supply. いい先生が不足している。	= scarce
in spite of 〜	〜にもかかわらず He worked hard in spite of his illness. 彼は病気にもかかわらず懸命に働いた。	= despite 〜 / in spite of + 名詞 / although + SV なので使い方に注意。
in spite of oneself	思わず，意に反して I began to laugh in spite of myself. 私は思わず笑い出した。	= despite oneself
in succession	連続して，次々に He won the tournament three years in succession. 彼は3年連続でトーナメントに優勝した。	= in a row
in terms of 〜	〜の点から；〜の立場で He sees everything in terms of money. 彼は何事もお金中心に見る。	= in the light of 〜 W2 話題を絞るときに使おう！
in the air	(噂などが)広まって；空中に There is a rumour in the air that they will get married soon. 彼らはすぐに結婚するという噂が広まっている。	= in the wind
in the course of time	やがて，そのうち The nation will recover from the depression in the course of time. その国はやがて不景気から回復するだろう。	= in due course / before long
in the dark	暗がりで；秘密に Cats can see in the dark. 猫は暗がりでも目が見える。	
in the end	結局は，最後には Everything went well in the end. 最後はすべてがうまくいった。	= in the long run / at last
in the face of 〜	〜に直面して；〜にもかかわらず He is strong in the face of criticism. 彼は批判に直面しても強い。	= in spite of
in the first place	まず，第一に You have to set goals in the first place. あなたはまず目標を決めなければならない。	= first of all / to begin with
in the future	将来(に)，今後 I look forward to seeing you in the near future. 私は近い将来あなたにお会いできるのが楽しみです。	⇔ in the past

熟語	語義／例文	同意表現／コメント
in the light of ~	~を考慮して[すると] I agree in the light of the current situation. 現状を考慮すると私は賛成です。	= in view of ~ 「~に照らし合わせて」と考えればよい。
in the long run	結局は, 長い目で見れば This will benefit the country in the long run. このことは長い目で見れば国に利益をもたらすだろう。	= in the end
in the main	大部分, 概して The project was in the main successful. プロジェクトは大部分は成功だった。	= mainly
in the meantime	その一方で；その間に, とかくするうちに In the meantime, the rate in France decreased. 一方で, フランスのレートは減少した。	= meanwhile [W1] 別の項目を説明する際のつなぎ言葉として使える。
in the name of ~	~の名のもとに；~という名目で The war was started in the name of God. その戦争は神の名のもとに始まった。	= on the pretext of
in the negative	否定的に[な]；拒否して He shook his head in the negative. 彼は否定的に首を横に振った。	⇔ in the affirmative
in the presence of ~	~の(面)前で, ~がいる前で Parents should never quarrel in the presence of their children. 親は子供の前で口げんかすべきではない。	⇔ in the absence of ~
in the process of ~	~の過程[途中]で The church is in the process of restoration. その教会は修復の途中だ。	= in the course of ~
in the way	邪魔になって This box stands in the way. この箱が邪魔だ。	stand in the way of ~「~の邪魔をする」と覚えると使いやすい。
in the world	一体全体 Why in the world did you not tell me the truth? あなたは一体何で私に本当のことを言わなかったんだ？	= on earth 疑問文で使う。
in time for ~	~に間に合って My brother came home in time for dinner. 兄は夕食に間に合って帰宅した。	⇔ late for ~ on time は「時間通りに」。
in turn	今度は, 次に, 順番に If you love others, you will be loved in turn. あなたが他者を愛すれば, 今度は自分が愛されるだろう。	

熟語	語義／例文	同意表現／コメント
in vain	無駄に, 効果なく He tried to stop smoking in vain. 彼は禁煙しようとしたが効果がなかった。	= to no avail
in view of	～に照らして, ～を考慮して I disagree in view of the recent economic downturn. 最近の景気の停滞を考慮して, 私は反対だ。	= in the light of ～
in youth	若い頃 Heavy work in youth is quiet rest in old age. 若いときの苦労は買ってでもせよ。	= in early life
indulge in ～	～にふける Never indulge in gambling. ギャンブルにふけってはならない。	= devote oneself to ～
inform A of B	A に B を知らせる I did not inform him of my decision. 私は彼に私の決定を伝えなかった。	= let A know about B [S] 堅い表現なので話し言葉としては使わない。tell で十分。
inside out	裏返しにして He wore his clothes inside out. 彼は服を裏返しに着ていた。	
insist on ～	～を主張する My boss always insists on paying for my drinks. 私の上司はいつも, 私の飲み物の代金を払うと主張する。	= assert
instead of ～	～の代わりに I stayed home instead of going out. 私は外出する代わりに家にいた。	= in place of
It goes without saying that ～	～は言うまでもない It goes without saying that time is money. 時は金なりとは言うまでもない。	
jump at ～	(よく考えずに)～に飛びつく；～に飛びかかる I would jump at such a proposal. 私はそんな申し出なら思わず飛びつくよ。	
just around the corner	もう間もなく；目と鼻の先 Spring is just around the corner. もうすぐ春です。	
just in case	万一に備えて I made a copy of all the data just in case. 万一に備えて, 私はすべてのデータのコピーを取った。	in case of 名詞, in case that SV の 2 つの使い方も覚えよう。

Track 333

熟語	語義／例文	同意表現／コメント
keep [get] in touch with ～	～と連絡をとる，～と接触を保つ I keep in touch with friends from school. 私は学校の友達と連絡を保っている。	= continue to communicate with ～
keep ～ to oneself	～を秘密にしておく I kept my dream to myself for a long time. 私は長い間，自分の夢を秘密にしていた。	= keep ～ under one's hat
keep abreast of [with] ～	～に遅れないでついていく Young girls keep abreast of the latest fashion trends. 若い女の子は最近のファッションの流行についていく。	= keep up with ～
keep an eye on ～	～に目を離さずにいる Parents should keep an eye on social media accounts of their children. 親は子供のソーシャルメディアのアカウントから目を離さずにいるべきだ。	= watch over ～ ⑤「～に目を保つ」と考えれば意味は分かるが，意識しないと使えない。I always keep my eye on ～ の形で使おう！
keep away from ～	～を避ける；～から離れている Keep away from drinking too much alcohol. 酒の飲み過ぎを避けなさい。	= keep out of ～ / keep off ～
keep company with ～	～と付き合う，～と交際する You should not keep company with such people. あなたはそんな人たちと付き合うべきではない。	= associate with ～
keep early [good] hours	早寝早起きする To keep early hours makes us healthy. 早寝早起きは私たちを健康にする。	⇔ keep late hours
keep good [perfect] time	（時計が）正確である My new watch keeps good time. 私の新しい時計は正確です。	= be on time
keep on ～ ing	～し続ける She kept on studying English for ten years. 彼女は10年間，英語を勉強し続けた。	= continue to ～
keep one's word	約束を守る You should always keep your word. あなたはいつも約束を守るべきだ。	= be as good as one's word
keep to ～	～を守る，～に従う I managed to keep to a schedule. 私は何とかスケジュールを守った。	= abide by ～ schedule の発音に注意！

353

Track 334

熟語	語義／例文	同意表現／コメント
keep up with ～	～に(遅れないで)ついていく He strived to keep up with his classmates. 彼はクラスメートについていくために努力をした。	= keep pace with ～
keep 人 company	人と一緒にいる, 人に付き合う Thank you for keeping me company. 私と一緒に付き合ってくれてありがとう。	
kill time	時間[暇]をつぶす Shopping may be a good way to kill time at the airport. 買い物は空港で時間をつぶすいい方法かもしれない。	= burn away time
know ～ by name	～の名前は知っている I know her by name. 彼女の名前は知っている。	
know a good deal about ～	～について多く知っている He knows a good deal about computers. 彼はコンピュータについて多くのことを知っている。	= know a lot about ～
know better than to ～	～するほどばかではない I know better than to do such a thing. 私はそんなことをするほどばかではない。	= be wise enough not to ～
know one's way around [about] ～	～の地理に明るい He seemed to know his way around the area. 彼はその地域の地理に明るいようだった。	= be knowledgeable about ～
lay aside ～	～を取っておく, ～を(横に)置く I will lay aside funds for the future. 私は将来のための資金を取っておくでしょう。	= set aside ～ / put aside [by] / preserve
lay off ～	～を(一時)解雇する The company decided to lay off some employees. その会社は一部の従業員を一時解雇することに決めた。	
learn ～ by heart	～を暗記する Students need to learn vocabulary by heart. 生徒は語彙を暗記しなければならない。	= memorise ～
leave A for B	A を出て B へ(向けて)出発する He will leave Japan for London. 彼は日本を出てロンドンに行く。	
leave ～ behind	～を置き忘れる Don't leave your umbrella behind. 傘を忘れないようにしなさい。	= forget to take [bring] ～

Track 335

熟語	語義／例文	同意表現／コメント
leave A to B	AをBに任せる We should leave web design to experts. 我々はウェブデザインを専門家に任せるべきだ。	= commit A to B
leave nothing to be desired	全く申し分ない His work leaves nothing to be desired. 彼の仕事は全く申し分がない。	= leave no room for improvement
leave out ~	~を省く Don't leave out the details. 詳細を省くな。	= exclude
lend [give] ~ a hand	~に手を貸す，~の手助けをする He lent us a hand with the project. 彼はプロジェクトで私たちを手伝ってくれた。	= help ~
let ~ down	~をがっかりさせる；~を降ろす His action let the whole team down. 彼の行動はチーム全体をがっかりさせた。	= disappoint ~ / take ~ down
let alone ~	~は言うまでもなく I don't like grilled fish, let alone raw fish. 私は焼き魚が好きではない。生魚は言うまでもない。	= not to mention
let go of ~	~を離す My mother told me not to let go of her hand. 母は私に手を離すことがないように言った。	= release ~
let out ~	（秘密など）~を漏らす，~をうっかりしゃべる I don't want to let out the secret of this wonderful place. 私はこの素晴らしい場所の秘密を漏らしたくない。	= reveal ~
let up	（雨などが）やむ The rain has let up. 雨が上がった。	
lie in ~	~にある，~に存在する The problem may lie in lack of planning. 問題は計画不足にあるかもしれない。	= exist in ~ / consist in ~
like a bolt from the blue	晴天のへきれきのように The news hit me like a bolt from the blue. その知らせは晴天のへきれきのように私を襲った。	= out of the blue
limit A to B	AをBに制限する，AをB内にとどめる We should limit the use of these substances to medical purposes. 我々はこれらの物質の使用を医療目的に限るべきだ。	= confine A to B

355

熟語	語義／例文	同意表現／コメント
live from hand to mouth	その日暮らしをする The majority of immigrants live from hand to mouth. 移民の多くはその日暮らしをしている。	= live from day to day
live on ~	~を常食とする, ~で暮らす Some plants live on insects. 一部の植物は虫を常食とする。	= subsist on ~ R 生物の話題では頻出。
live up to ~	~(期待など)に添う；~(主義など)に基づいて行動する He will live up to our demands. 彼は我々の要望に応えるだろう。	= do as well as 人 was expected to
long [yearn] for ~	~を熱望[切望]する We all long for peace. 私たちはみんな平和を熱望している。	= hanker for ~
look on [upon] A as B	A を B とみなす His students look on him as a great teacher. 彼の生徒は彼を偉大な先生とみなしている。	= regard A as B / think of A as B
look [watch] out for ~	~に用心する, ~に注意する Look out for fire. 火に用心しなさい。	= be on one's guard against ~ / be careful of ~
look ~ in the face	~の顔をまともに見る I'm ashamed to look you in the face. 私は君の顔をまともに見るのが恥ずかしい。	
look after ~	~の世話をする Many young mothers stay home to look after their children. 多くの若い母親たちは子供の世話をするために家にいる。	= take care of ~
look back on [upon] ~	~を思い出す, ~を回顧する I sometimes look back on my school days. 私は時々, 学生時代を思い出す。	= remember ~
look down on [upon] ~	~を軽蔑する We should not look down on others even in our hearts. 私たちはたとえ心の中でも他人を軽蔑するべきではない。	= despise ~ ⇔ look up to ~
look for ~	~を探す We've been looking for that car. 私たちはその車を探していたんだよ。	= seek ~
look forward to ~	~を楽しみにする, ~を期待する I'm looking forward to seeing you. 私はあなたにお目にかかれるのを楽しみにしています。	to の後は名詞か ing がくる。不定詞ではないので注意!

熟語	語義／例文	同意表現／コメント
look into ~	~を調べる We want you to look into the problem. 私たちはあなたにその問題を調べてほしい。	= go into ~ / inquire into ~
look over ~	~にざっと目を通す，~を調べる Ask someone else to look over the documents. 誰か他の人に書類に目を通すように頼みなさい。	= run over ~
look to ~	~に目を向ける[注意する]；~当てにする Look to your health. 健康に気をつけなさい。	= turn to ~
look up ~	（辞書などで）~を調べる Look up the word in your dictionary. 辞書でその言葉を調べてごらん。	The economy has looked up. のように「（主語が）上向く」という意味もある。
look up to ~	~を尊敬する I look up to my boss as a leader. 私はリーダーとして上司を尊敬している。	= admire ~ ⇔ look down on ~
lose (one's) face	面目を失う The government will lose face if they fail to pass this bill. この法案を成立できなければ，政府は面目を失うだろう。	⇔ save (one's) face
lose no time (in) ~ing	すぐに~する We should lose no time leaving here. 我々は一刻も早くここを立ち去らねばならない。	
lose one's temper	かんしゃくを起こす Losing your temper rarely works. 短気は損気。	= fly into a rage
lose one's way	道に迷う We suddenly lost our way in the forest. 私たちは突然，森で道に迷った。	= lose oneself
lose sight of ~	~を見失う Don't lose sight of the original object! 当初の目的を忘れるな。	
major in ~	~を専攻する I am planning to major in psychology. 私は心理学を専攻するつもりだ。	= specialise in ~ ⑤ Part1 で聞かれることも多い。
make (both) ends meet	収支内でやり繰りする，収支を合わせる It is hard to make both ends meet on his income alone. 彼の収入だけでやり繰りするのは難しい。	

Track 338

熟語	語義／例文	同意表現／コメント
make [earn] one's living	生計を立てる Many people made their living by manual work. 多くの人は肉体労働で生計を立てていた。	= earn one's bread and butter
make [pull] a face	しかめ面をする He made a face when he saw the test results. 試験の結果を見たとき，彼はしかめ面をした。	= frown
make a choice	選択する Make a choice between the two. その2つから選択しなさい。	= choose
make a contribution to ～	～に貢献[寄与]する Many celebrities make a contribution to charity. 多くの有名人がチャリティーに貢献する。	= contribute to ～
make a difference	重要である It makes a difference whether or not you come tonight. あなたが今夜来るかどうかは重要だ。	= matter
make a fool of oneself	ばかなまねをする I made a fool of myself in public. 私は人前でばかなことをした。	= do something foolish / make an ass of oneself
make A from B	B(原料)からAを作る We make sake from rice in Japan. 日本では米から酒をつくる。	
make A into B	AをBにする We make rice into sake in Japan. 日本では米を酒にする。	
make a noise [noises]	(騒)音を立てる；騒ぎ立てる Don't make a noise when you eat soup. スープを飲むとき音を立てるな。	
make a point of ～ing	必ず～することにしている He makes a point of surfing the Internet before breakfast. 彼は朝食前に必ずネットサーフィンすることにしている。	= make it a rule to ～
make allowance(s) for ～	～を考慮に入れる We must make allowance for her situation. 我々は彼女の状況を考慮に入れなければならない。	= allow for ～
make an appointment (with ～)	(～と会う)約束をする I made an appointment to see the doctor. 私は診察の予約をした。	

熟語	語義／例文	同意表現／コメント
make an effort (to ～)	(～するため)努力する We will make an effort to meet your request. 我々はあなたのご要望に応えられるように努力します。	
make believe ～	～のふりをする He made believe that he was a lawyer. 彼は弁護士のふりをした。	= pretend a make-believe world は「架空の世界」。
make do with ～	～で間に合わせる，～で済ます We had to make do with what was available. 私たちは手に入るもので間に合わせなければならなかった。	= manage with ～
make for ～	～に役立つ；～へ向かって行く Disarmament is sure to make for peace. 軍縮は必ず平和に貢献する。	
make friends with ～	～と友達になる，～と親しくなる I made friends with many local residents. 私は多くの地元住民と友達になった。	= become friends with ～ ⑤ 旅行先のエピソードとして使えそうな例文。
make fun of ～	～をからかう Don't make fun of others because of accent. なまりのせいで他人をからかってはならない。	= make a fool of ～ / pull one's leg
make good	成功する；(損害など)～をつぐなう He will make good in the future. 彼は将来成功するだろう。	= succeed
make it a rule to ～	～することにしている；～する習慣である I make it a rule to study every morning. 私は毎朝勉強することにしている。	= make a point of ～ ing
make money	金儲けをする This film is making a lot of money in the US. この映画はアメリカで大金を儲けている。	= earn money make には「(お金を)稼ぐ」という意味がある。
make much of ～	～を重視する，～を尊重する They didn't make much of your opinion. 彼らはあなたの意見を重視しなかった。	⇔ make little of ～
make no difference	どうでもよい，重要ではない It makes no difference whether you agree or not. あなたが同意しようがしまいがどうでもよい。	= count for nothing
make one's way (to ～)	(～に)進む[行く] I made my way to a conference room. 私は会議室に向かって行った。	= advance

熟語	語義／例文	同意表現／コメント
make oneself at home	くつろぐ Make yourself at home, will you? くつろいでくださいね。	= make oneself comfortable
make oneself heard	自分の声を聞かせる It was so noisy that I could not make myself heard. うるさ過ぎて私の声は聞きとってもらえなかった。	
make oneself understood	〜自身(の考え)を理解してもらう I could not make myself understood in English. 私は英語で自分の考えを理解してもらえなかった。	
make out 〜	〜を理解する I couldn't make out what he said. 私は彼が言ったことが理解できなかった。	= understand
make progress (in 〜)	(〜において)進歩する[進む] Our country made great progress in controlling inflation. 我が国はインフレ対策で大いに進歩した。	= advance
make room for 〜	〜のために場所を空ける The old school was torn down to make room for a new building. その古い学校は新しい建物の場所を空けるために取り壊された。	
make sense (of 〜)	筋が通っている；道理にかなう；〜を理解する It doesn't make sense to me. それは私には筋が通っていないように思える。	= add up
make sure that 〜 [wh- 〜][of 〜]	〜であることを[〜を]確かめる I wanted to make sure that we were safe. 私は我々が安全であることを確かめたかった。	= confirm that SV
make the most of 〜	〜をできるだけ利用する You should make the most of the lectures. あなたは授業をできるだけ利用すべきだ。	= get the most out of 〜
make up 〜	〜を構成する；〜を補う Alcohol made up roughly 10% of the sales. アルコール類は売り上げの約10％を占めた。	W1 円グラフの説明でaccount for 〜 と同様に「〜を占める」で使える。
make up for 〜	〜を補う，〜の埋め合わせをする You have to make up for the missed class. あなたは欠席した授業を補わなければならない。	= compensate for 〜
make up one's mind to 〜	〜する決心をする I made up my mind to study abroad. 私は留学する決心をした。	= decide to 〜

Track 341

熟語	語義／例文	同意表現／コメント
make use of 〜	〜を利用する Students are eligible to make use of the sports facilities. 生徒はスポーツ施設を利用する資格がある。	= take advantage of 〜
make way for 〜	〜に道を譲る，〜に道をあける We should make way for the next generation. 私たちは次の世代に道を譲るべきだ。	= give way to 〜
meet the demands	要求を満たす，要求に応じる This school meets the demands of students by offering a wide range of courses. この学校は，幅広いコースを提供することで生徒の要求を満たす。	= satisfy[fill] the demand(s) [L] meet や satisfy の後に demand や needs が入ることを予想できるように！
mistake A for B	A を B と間違える My friend mistook me for my brother on the phone. 友人は電話で私と兄を間違えた。	= take A for B
more often than not	たいてい；しばしば He arrives late for school more often than not. 彼はたいてい学校に遅れてくる。	= (as) often as not
more or less	多少，およそ，多かれ少なかれ They are more or less similar to modern humans. 彼らは現生人類に多少似ている。	= to a greater or lesser extent [W1] more or less the same 「ほとんど同じ」でも使える。
more than 人 can help	しないで済む以上の，必要以上に，なるべく Don't spend more than you can help. 必要以上にお金を使うな。	
move to 〜	〜に引っ越す She plans to move to her hometown. 彼女は故郷に引っ越す予定だ。	= migrate to 〜
name 〜 A after B	B にちなんで〜に A と名付ける They named their son Charlie after Scottish midfielder Charlie Adam. 彼らは息子をスコットランドのミッドフィルダー，チャーリー・アダムにちなんでチャーリーと名付けた。	after 〜 は「〜にちなんで，〜の名をとって」の意味。
next to impossible	ほとんど不可能で It is next to impossible to live without electric appliances. 電化製品なしで生活することはほとんど不可能だ。	= almost impossible

Track 342

熟語	語義／例文	同意表現／コメント
next to nothing	ないも同然だ；ただに等しい His contribution is next to nothing. 彼の貢献はないも同然だ。	= almost nothing ⑤ この例文は本人には言えないけれど、IELTS本試験で言うならOK。
no less than ~	～も（多く） I spent no less than five hours preparing a speech. 私はスピーチを準備するのに5時間も費やした。	= as many as ~
no longer ~	もはや～ない The conventional way of data analysis is no longer useful. 従来のデータ分析の方法はもはや役に立たない。	= not ~ any longer
no more than ~	たった～, わずかに～, ただ～にすぎない We have no more than ten staff members. 私たちには10人しかスタッフがいない。	= only
none of one's business	余計なお世話 That's none of your business. 大きなお世話だ。	
none the less for ~	～にもかかわらずやはり I love him none the less for his faults. 彼には欠点があるけれど、それでも私は彼を愛している。	
nothing but ~	～にすぎない, ～だけ He is nothing but a lazy man. 彼は怠け者にすぎない。	= only ~ but は「除く」。「～を除いて何者でもない」という意味。
now and then	時々 She goes to a party now and then. 彼女は時々パーティーに行く。	= at times / on occasion(s)
object to ~	～に反対する They strongly object to the proposed plan. 彼らは提案された計画に強く反対している。	= oppose oneself to ~ to の後は名詞。
of great interest	大変面白い The theme of the seminar was of great interest to me. そのセミナーのテーマは大変面白かった。	= very interesting 〈of + 名詞〉は形容詞の役割。
of great use	非常に役に立つ Our experiences will be of great use in the near future. 私たちの経験は近い将来、非常に役に立つだろう。	= very useful
of late	最近 She has recovered from the disease of late. 彼女は最近、病気から回復した。	= recently

Track 343

熟語	語義／例文	同意表現／コメント
～ of one's own	～自身[自体]の～ I wish I could buy a house of my own. 自分の家を買えたらなぁ。	
of one's own ～ ing	～自身で～した He read to me a poem of his own writing. 彼は自分で書いた詩を私に読んで聞かせた。	
of one's own accord	自発的に I used to help my mother of my own accord. 私はかつて、自発的に母を手伝ったものだ。	= voluntarily
on [in] behalf of ～	～に代わって、～を代表して；～のために He was asked to attend the meeting on behalf of his boss. 彼は上司に代わって会議に出るように頼まれた。	= on [in] one's behalf
on ～ terms (with ～)	(～と)～な間柄で、～の関係で I was on close terms with him. 私は彼と親密な間柄だった。	
on a large [small] scale	大[小]規模に He is doing business on a large scale. 彼は大規模に事業を営んでいる。	
on account of ～	～のために He was compelled to resign on account of poor health. 彼は悪い健康状態のために辞任せざるを得なかった。	= because of ～
on and off	断続的に、時々 The girl was crying on and off while waiting for her mother to come. その女の子は母親が来るまで断続的に泣いていた。	= off and on
on board	(船・飛行機などに)搭乗して I was on board a plane for the first time when I was five. 私は5歳のときに初めて飛行機に乗った。	= aboard
on business	仕事で、商用で I have been to a number of different countries on business. 私は仕事で数多くの国に行ったことがある。	⇔ on vacation
on condition that ～	～という条件で、もし～ならば I will come on condition that she is invited too. 彼女が招待されているのであれば、私も行きます。	= if

熟語	語義／例文	同意表現／コメント
on duty	勤務中で，当直で You are not supposed to consume alcoholic beverages while on duty. あなたは勤務中にアルコール飲料を摂取するべきではない。	⇔ off duty while on duty は you are が省略されている。
on end	続けて，立て続けに I had to work until late at night for weeks on end. 私は何週間も続けて，夜遅くまで働かなければならなかった。	= continuously ⑤ 多忙であることの例を言うときに便利。
on foot	徒歩で You can go either by bus or on foot. あなたはバスか徒歩のどちらかで行くことができる。	= by foot
on no account	決して〜ない You should on no account come in late to the meeting. あなたは決してその会議に遅れてはならない。	= under no circumstances
on occasions	時々，時たま I see him on occasions. 私は時々彼に会う。	= now and then ／ from time to time
on one's [the] way (to 〜)	(〜への)途中で He was on his way to work. 彼は仕事に行く途中だった。	
on one's back	あおむけになって I like lying on my back on the bed. 私はあおむけになってベッドに寝るのが好きだ。	= face up ⇔ on one's stomach
on one's guard	用心して Be on your guard against thieves. 泥棒に用心しなさい。	= on alert
on one's own	1人で，独力で They should learn to do many tasks on their own. 彼らは1人で多くの仕事ができるようになるべきだ。	= by oneself
on one's part	〜の方[側]では There was nothing to do on my part. 私の方でできることは何もなかった。	= on the part of 〜
on one's stomach	腹ばいになって，うつぶせになって He lay on his stomach. 彼は腹ばいになった。	= on one's face

Track 345

熟語	語義／例文	同意表現／コメント
on purpose	故意に The excavated artefact was damaged on purpose. 発掘されたその遺物は故意に傷つけられた。	= intentionally R intentionally, deliberately との書き換えに注意。
on second thought(s)	考え直して On second thought, I gave it up. 考え直して，私はやめることにした。	= changing one's mind
on the [an] average	平均して On the average, I go to the movies twice a month. 平均して，私は月に2回映画を見に行きます。	on average と冠詞なしで使うこともできる。
on the contrary	それどころか He is not rich. On the contrary, he is deep in debt. 彼は金持ちではない。それどころか，借金だらけだ。	W1 使わない方がいい。on the other hand「もう一方で」と混同しないように！
on the go	（常に忙しく）活動中で She's always on the go. 彼女は働きづめだ。	
on the grounds that ～	～という理由で He quit his job on the grounds that the salary was not good enough. 彼は給料がよくないという理由で仕事を辞めた。	= because
on the increase	増加して The global population is on the increase. 世界の人口は増加している。	⇔ on the decrease
on the other hand	他方では On the one hand he is kind, but on the other hand he is lazy. 一方では彼は親切だが，他方では怠け者だ。	W1 つなぎ言葉として使える。
on the spot	即座に；その場で He agreed to pay the fine on the spot. 彼は即座に罰金を払うことに同意した。	= at once
on the tip of one's tongue	口先まで出かかって The name was on the tip of my tongue. その名前が私の口先まで出かかっていた。	
on the whole	概して，大体は On the whole, the experiment was successful. 概してその実験は成功だった。	= all in all

Track 346

熟語	語義／例文	同意表現／コメント
on time	時間通りに He worked so hard that the project was completed on time. 彼は一生懸命に仕事をしたので，プロジェクトは時間通りに終わった。	= punctually
on top of ～	～に加えて，～のほかに He is rude, and on top of that he is lazy. 彼は不作法なのに，加えて怠け者だ。	= in addition to ～ W2 口語表現なので使わない。furthermore, moreover を使う。
once and for all	きっぱりと，これを最後に They help people quit smoking once and for all. 彼らは人々がきっぱりと喫煙をやめるのを助ける。	= definitely
one after another	次から次へと，続々と They came up with new ideas one after another. 彼らは次から次へと新しいアイデアを思いついた。	= from one to the next
one of these days	近いうちに，そのうちに You'll get a good score one of these days. あなたは近いうちにいい点を取るだろう。	= sometime in the near future
or else	さもなければ，そうでないと You have to be careful, or else you will make the same mistake again. 気をつけなさい，さもないとあなたは同じ間違いを繰り返しますよ。	= otherwise
order A from B	A を B に注文する I ordered a drink from a bartender. 私はバーテンダーに酒を注文した。	S 「人に注文する」だが from を使う点に注意。
out of bounds	立ち入り禁止 The area is temporarily out of bounds. その地域は一時的に立ち入り禁止だ。	= off-limits
out of control	制御できなくて His temper sometimes gets out of control. 彼の気性は時々，制御できなくなる。	= uncontrollable ⇔ under control
out of date	時代遅れの Most of the software on my computer is out of date. 私のパソコンのソフトのほとんどが時代遅れだ。	= outdated ⇔ up to date

熟語	語義／例文	同意表現／コメント
out of fear	恐怖心から He ran away out of fear. 彼は怖くなって逃げ出した。	
out of order	故障して；順序が狂って The vending machine was temporarily out of order. その自動販売機は一時的に故障していた。	= not working ⇔ in order
out of reach of ~	~の手の届かないところに Dangerous items should be stored out of reach of children. 危険なものは子供の手の届かないところにしまうべきだ。	⇔ within reach of ~
out of sight	見えないところに He was waving his hand until the train went out of sight. 電車が見えなくなるまで彼は手を振っていた。	⇔ in sight
out of the question	問題外の；論外の；全く不可能な The advertising campaign was out of the question. その広告戦略は問題外だった。	= not in the options / impossible
out of work	仕事がない，失業中で The organisation helped provide food for his children while he was out of work. 彼が失業中，その団体が彼の子供たちに食べ物を提供するのを助けた。	= unemployed ⇔ in work
over and over (again)	何度も（繰り返して） Don't ask the same question over and over again. 同じ質問を何度も繰り返すな。	= again and again
owe A to B	AはBのおかげである；AをBに借りている I owe my success to you. 私の成功はあなたのおかげです。	= attribute A to B /ascribe A to B
owing to ~	~のために，~が原因で Owing to bad weather, we stayed home. 悪天候のため，私たちは家にいた。	= on account of ~ / due to ~ 不定詞ではないので to の後は名詞。
part from ~	~と別れる I parted from her at the airport. 私は空港で彼女と別れた。	= separate from ~
part with ~	~を手放す，~を売り払う I had to part with my property. 私は財産を手放さなければならなかった。	= relinquish

熟語	語義／例文	同意表現／コメント
participate in ～	～に参加する Many students participate in volunteer activities. 多くの学生がボランティア活動に参加する。	= take part in ～ participants in ～ 「～への参加者」でも前置詞は in。
pass away	亡くなる My grandfather passed away last year. 私の祖父は去年他界した。	= die
pass by	通り過ぎる；(時が)過ぎる Many years passed by. 何年もの時が過ぎた。	= go by
pass on A to B	A を B に伝える I'll pass on that information to them. 私はその情報を彼らに伝えます。	= inform B of A
pass out	意識を失う，気絶する The old man passed out from heat exhaustion. その老人は熱中症で意識を失った。	= faint away
pass through ～	～を経験する；～を経過する She passed through many hardships. 彼女は多くの困難を経験した。	= go through ～
pay A for B	B の代金として A を支払う I pay 500 dollars for the repair of my car. 私は車の修理代として500ドルを支払う。	
pay a visit to ～	～を訪問する The princess will pay a state visit to many nations. その王女は多くの国を公式訪問する。	= visit ～
pay attention to ～	～に注意を払う Pay more attention to the lecture. 講義にもっと注意を払いなさい。	= have an eye on
persist in ～	～に固執する，～をあくまでも主張する My father persisted in his belief. 私の父は自身の信念を貫いた。	= cling to ～
persuade [talk] 人 into ～ ing	人を～するように説得する Please persuade her into trying again. もう一度やってみるように彼女を説得してください。	⇔ persuade [talk] 人 out of ～ ing
persuade [talk] 人 out of ～ ing	人を～しないよう説得する I'll persuade him out of smoking. 私が彼をタバコを吸わないように説得する。	⇔ persuade [talk] 人 into ～ ing

Track 349

熟語	語義／例文	同意表現／コメント
pick up ~	~を取り上げる，~を拾う；~を(乗り物で)迎えに行く Let's pick up the trash. ごみを拾いましょう。	
place [lay / put] emphasis on ~	~を強調[重視]する Our company places huge emphasis on cost-efficiency. 我が社は費用対効果をとても重視する。	= emphasise ~
play a joke [trick] on ~	~をからかう Don't play a joke on your classmate. クラスメートをからかうな。	= make fun of ~
play a role (of ~)	(~の)役割を果たす[演じる] He played a role of a mentor. 彼は指導者の役割を果たした。	= play a part
play an important role [part] in ~	~に重要な役割を演じる[果たす] Sports play an important role in social life. スポーツは社会生活の中で重要な役割を果たす。	
plenty of ~	多くの~；十分な~ We have plenty of time to complete the project. 我々にはプロジェクトを終わらせるための十分な時間がある。	= a lot of ~
point of view	観点[視点]，見地，考え方 Let's discuss the issue from different points of view. 異なる視点からその問題を議論しよう。	= viewpoint
point out ~	~を指摘する My teacher often points out spelling errors. 私の先生はしばしばスペルミスを指摘する。	= point to ~
prefer A to B	B より A を好む The soldier will prefer death to dishonour. その兵士は不名誉よりも死を選ぶだろう。	= favour A over B prefer ~ ing to ~ ing や prefer to V rather than to V の形も覚える。
prepare for ~	~に備える，~の準備をする You should prepare for exams well in advance. あなたは前もって十分に試験に備えるべきだ。	= get ready for ~

369

Track 350

熟語	語義／例文	同意表現／コメント
prevent 人 from 〜ing	人が〜するのを妨げる[防ぐ] The noise prevented me from sleeping. その騒音が私の眠りを妨げた。	= keep [stop] 〜 from 〜 ing W2 フレーズで覚えれば使える場面は多い。
pride oneself on 〜	〜が自慢である，〜を誇りに思う He prides himself on the success. その成功が彼の自慢だ。	= be proud of 〜 / take pride in 〜
prohibit 人 from 〜ing	人が〜するのを禁じる Many nations prohibit teenagers from drinking alcohol. 多くの国が10代が飲酒することを禁じている。	= forbid 人 from 〜ing
prove to be 〜	〜であると判明する The theory eventually proved to be right. ついに，その理論は正しいことが判明した。	= turn out to be 〜
provide A with B [B for A]	AにBを与える The government should provide everybody with equal rights. 政府はすべての人に平等な権利を与えるべきだ。	= supply A with B [B to A] W2 provide 人 with モノ = provide モノ for 人 という形で覚える。
pull 〜 apart	〜を引き離す，〜をばらばらにする Don't pull a child apart from his family. 彼の家族から子供を引き離すな。	
pull one's leg	人をからかう They may be pulling our legs. 彼らは我々をからかっているのかもしれない。	= make fun of / tease
pull up (〜)	(車を)止める；(車が)止まる A patrol car pulled up in front of him. パトカーが彼の前で止まった。	= draw up (〜)
push forward 〜	〜を前面に押し出す，〜を注目させる The company plans to push forward the new product. その会社は新製品を前面に押し出す予定だ。	= put forward 〜
put [bring] pressure on 〜	〜に圧力をかける，〜を圧迫する They put pressure on him to resign. 彼らは彼に圧力をかけて辞任させた。	
put 〜 aside	〜を取っておく，〜をしまっておく Put some money aside for a rainy day. 万一のために少しお金を取っておきなさい。	

熟語	語義／例文	同意表現／コメント
put ~ in prison	~を投獄する The police put a thief in prison. 警察はどろぼうを投獄した。	= imprison ~ put ~ behind bars も同じ意味。
put ~ into effect	~を施行する，~を実施する The government put a new regulation into effect. 政府は新しい規則を施行した。	= enforce
put ~ to the test	~をテストする Let's put the new technology to the test. 新しい技術をテストしよう。	
put ~ to use	~を利用[使用]する You should put your time and money to good use. あなたは自身の時間とお金をうまく使うべきだ。	= make use of ~
put ~ together	~をまとめる，~を合わせる I put all the information together in a single file. 私はすべての情報を1つのファイルにまとめた。	= organise ~
put ~ into practice	~を実行する We will put a scheme into practice next month. 来月，我々はある計画を実行に移すだろう。	= practice ~
put A in touch with B	AがBと連絡をとれるようにする Can you put me in touch with him? 私が彼と連絡できるように取り計らってくれませんか。	
put A into B	AをBで表す It's difficult to put our feelings into words. 気持ちを言葉で表すのは難しい。	
put a question to 人	人に質問をする Let me put a question to you. あなたに質問があります。	= ask a question of 人
put an end to ~	~を終える[終わらせる] This evidence put an end to the argument. この証拠がその議論に決着をつけた。	= terminate
put away ~	~を片付ける Put away your toys before having a snack. おやつの前におもちゃを片付けなさい。	= clear
put down ~	~をけなす；書き留める His first novel was severely put down. 彼の処女小説はひどくけなされた。	= run down ~

Track 352

熟語	語義／例文	同意表現／コメント
put forth ~	~を発表する；~(芽・葉など)を出す Please put forth your ideas. あなたの考えを発表してください。	
put forward ~	(案など) ~を提出する They will put forward a new bill. 彼らは新しい議案を提出するでしょう。	= offer ~ / propose ~
put off ~	~を延期する We can no longer put off the deadline. 締め切りはこれ以上延ばせません。	= postpone ~ defer も同義語として覚える。
put on ~	~を身につける You had better put on your hat. 帽子をかぶった方がいいですよ。	⇔ take off ~
put oneself into someon's shoes	~の立場になって考える Put yourself into my shoes. 私の身にもなってくれ。	= consider oneself in someone's place
put out ~	(電灯・火など)~を消す Put out the lights before leaving the room. 部屋を出る前に明かりを消しなさい。	= extinguish ~ 火・照明の両方に使える
put up at ~	~に泊まる I always put up at this hotel. 私はいつもこのホテルに泊まる。	= stay at ~
put up with ~	~に耐える, ~を我慢する I can't put up with his rudeness any more. 私はこれ以上彼の無礼には我慢できない。	= endure ~ / bear ~
quite a few	かなり多く(の) There are quite a few children in the park. 公園にはかなり多くの子供たちがいます。	= not a few a few とは正反対の意味なので注意！
reach for ~	~に手を伸ばす She reached for a book on the shelf. 彼女は棚の本に手を伸ばした。	= put out one's hand
react to ~	~に反応する How did she react to the news? 彼女はそのニュースにどう反応しましたか。	= respond to ~
read between the lines	言外の意味を読み取る You should read between the lines of her letter. あなたは彼女の手紙の行間を良く読みとるべきだ。	= take a hint

Track 353

熟語	語義／例文	同意表現／コメント
recover from ～	～から回復する It's not easy to recover from an economic depression. 経済不況から回復するのは簡単ではない。	= get over ～
refer to ～	～を参照する；～に言及する Please refer to a dictionary. 辞書を参照してください。	= consult ～
reflect (up)on ～	じっくり思い返して；～についてよく考える We should reflect on the past and contemplate the future. 我々は過去を思い返して将来を見据えるべきだ。	= think over ～
refrain from ～	～を控える，～をやめる You should refrain from greasy food. あなたは脂っこい食べ物を控えるべきだ。	= abstain from ～ Please refrain from talking on the phone. は電車のアナウンスでおなじみ。
regardless of ～	～に構わず，～に関係なく The party will be held regardless of the weather. 天候に関係なく、そのパーティーは催されるでしょう。	= without reference to ～
relate A to [with] B	A を B と関連付ける[関連させる] You can't relate the result to a certain cause. その結果をある特定の原因に関連付けることは不可能だ。	= associate A with B
relieve A of B	A から[の] B を取り除く His boss relieved him of most responsibility. 彼の上司は彼のほとんどの責任を免除した。	= free A of B
rely on ～	～に頼る I can't rely on my parents any more. 私はこれ以上両親に頼ることはできない。	= depend on ～
remember A to B	B に（A のことを）よろしくと伝える Remember me to your family. 私のことをあなたのご家族によろしくお伝えください。	= give one's (best) regards to ～ ／ say hello to ～
remember to ～	忘れずに～する Remember to lock all the doors. 忘れずにすべてのドアに鍵をかけてください。	= don't forget to ～
remind A of B	A に B を思い出させる She reminds me of my mother. 彼女は私に母を思い出させる。	= bring one's mind back to ～
resort to ～	～に訴える；～に頼る Don't resort to arms. 武力に訴えるな。	= use ～ as a last resort

Track 354

熟語	語義／例文	同意表現／コメント
respond to ~	**~に答える，~に反応する** We should respond promptly to a request. 私たちは直ちに要請に応じるべきだ。	= reply to ~
rest on [upon] ~	**~にかかっている，~次第である** The success rests on us all. その成功は私たち全員にかかっている。	= depend on ~
result from ~	**~から生じる** Global warming results from greenhouse gases. 地球温暖化は温室効果ガスから生じている。	= arise from ~
result in ~	**~という結果になる** The attempt resulted in failure. その試みは失敗に終わった。	= lead to ~ / bring about ~ W2 分詞構文で, resulting in ~ が使えると応用表現として評価される。
right away [now]	**すぐに** I'll check it right away. 私がすぐに確認します。	= at once
ring [call] up ~	**~に電話をかける** I'll ring you up later. 私が後で電話します。	= make a call to ~ [英]では ring を使うことが多い。
rob A of B	**A から B を奪う** Someone robbed Mary of her wallet. 誰かがマリーから財布を奪った。	
rule out ~	**~を除外する** We can't rule out the possibility. 我々はその可能性を除外することはできない。	= exclude ~ R eliminate との書き換えに注意！
run [take] a risk	**危険を冒す** I don't want to run a risk. 私は危険を冒したくない。	= take chances
run across [into] ~	**偶然~に出会う** I ran across my old friend on the street. 私は旧友に道で偶然出会った。	= run into ~
run for ~	**~に立候補する** He decided to run for election. 彼は選挙に立候補することを決断した。	= become a candidate for ~
run out of ~	**~を切らす，~がなくなる** My mobile phone is running out of battery power. 私の携帯の充電がなくなってきた。	= run short of ~

熟語	語義／例文	同意表現／コメント
run over ~	~をひく He was run over by a car. 彼は車にひかれた。	= hit
say to oneself	（心の中で）思う He said to himself that he should do it. 彼はそうすべきだと心の中で考えた。	
scold A for B	BのことでAを叱る She scolded her child for telling a lie. 彼女は嘘をついたことで子供を叱った。	= admonish A for B
search for ~	~を探[捜]し求める Police are still searching for evidence. 警察はまだ証拠を捜している。	= quest for ~
second to none	右に出るものはいない He is second to none in mathematics. 数学で彼の右に出る者はいない。	= the best
see to it that ~	~するように気を配る；取り計らう I'll see to it that it never happens again. 私はそれが二度と起こらないように気を配ります。	= keep an eye on
see ~ off	~を見送る I went to the airport to see my best friend off. 私は親友を見送るために空港に行った。	⇔ meet ~
see much of ~	~によく会う I see much of him at the station. 私は駅で彼によく会う。	
see nothing of ~	~を全く見かけない I've seen nothing of him lately. 私は近頃はちっとも彼を見かけない。	
see the sights of ~	~（の名所）を見学する Let's see the sights of this town. この町の名所を見ようよ。	= sightsee in ~
see to ~	~を引き受ける；~に気をつける All right, I will see to it. よし，私がそれを引き受けますよ。	= take care of
seek for ~	~を求める；~を探す Many people are seeking for employment. 多くの人が職を求めている。	= quest for ~

熟語	語義／例文	同意表現／コメント
seize [grab, take] ~ by the collar	~のえり首をつかむ He seized the pickpocket by the collar. 彼はスリのえり首をつかんだ。	
sell out	売り切れる Tickets sold on the day sell out quickly. 当日券はすぐ売り切れる。	sell は自動詞で「(主語が)売れる」の意味もある。
send for ~	~を呼びにやる Send for the doctor right now! すぐに医者を呼びにやれ。	
separate A from B	AをBと分ける[切り離す] We need to separate politics from religion. 我々は政治を宗教と分ける必要がある。	
serve one's purpose [ends]	間に合う；目的にかなう It will serve our present purpose. 差し当たりこれで間に合う。	= be good enough
set ~ free	~を解放する, ~を放免する Set all the hostages free. 全ての人質を解放しなさい。	= liberate ~
set about ~	~に取り掛かる, ~を始める He has soon set about a new project. 彼は直ちに次の事業に取り掛かった。	= start ~
set forth [out]	(旅などに)出発する；門出する The expedition finally set forth to the South Pole. その探検隊はついに南極に旅立った。	= set off
set off ~	~を引き立たせる, ~を強調する The simple black dress set off her beauty. シンプルな黒のドレスが彼女の美を際立たせた。	= enhance
set up ~	~を設立する；身を立てる The entrepreneur has set up a new business. その企業家は新しい会社を設立した。	= establish
settle down	(身を)落ち着ける；静まる It takes a while to settle down in a new place. 新天地に身を落ち着けるのにはしばらくかかる。	= calm down
shake hands (with ~)	(~と)握手する The actor shook hands with many fans. その俳優は多くのファンと握手した。	= give ~ a handshake

熟語	語義／例文	同意表現／コメント
share A with B	A を B と共有する[分かち合う] I want to share this pleasure with you. 私はこの喜びをあなたと分かち合いたい。	⑤ 他の人とのエピソードで使えそう。
show A around B	A に B を案内する I'd love to show you around London. 私は喜んであなたにロンドンを案内しますよ。	= take 〜 around 〜
show off 〜	〜を見せびらかす He showed off his new car to others. 彼は人に新車を見せびらかした。	= make a display of 〜 人を主語にして使う。
show up	現れる She didn't show up at the party. 彼女はパーティーに現れなかった。	= show oneself
single out 〜	選び出す, 選抜する He was singled out from many applicants. 彼は多くの応募者の中から選び出された。	= choose
sit [stay] up (late)	夜更かしをする I had to sit up late to prepare for the presentation. 私はプレゼン準備のために夜更かしをしなければならなかった。	= keep late hours ⑤ 自分のことを話すときに使おう！
so far	今のところ So far, so good. 今のところ順調だ。	= up to now
some 〜 or other	何らかの〜 A man must have some occupation or other. 人は何かしら職業が必要だ。	
something is wrong with 〜	〜はどこか故障している Is something wrong with this PC? このPCはどこか故障しているの？	
something like 〜	およそ〜, ざっと〜 The cost will come to something like a million pounds. その費用はおよそ100万ポンドになるだろう。	= about 〜
something of 〜	ちょっとした〜 He is something of an artist. 彼はちょっとした芸術家だ。	
sooner or later	遅かれ早かれ Death comes to us all sooner or later. 遅かれ早かれ誰にでも死は訪れる。	= early or late

熟語	語義／例文	同意表現／コメント
speak ill of 〜	〜の悪口を言う Don't speak ill of your classmates. クラスメートの悪口を言うな。	= criticise 〜 ⇔ speak well of 〜
speak out [up]	思い切って意見を言う；大声で話す Now I'll speak out honestly. 私が思い切って本当のことを言いましょう。	
spend A (in [on, for]) 〜 ing 又は名詞	A を〜することに費やす We should spend more money exploring outer space. 我々は宇宙を探索することにもっとお金を使うべきだ。	[S] お金や時間に関して使う。
spoil oneself	破格に[我慢しないで]楽しむ We spoiled ourselves at a top hotel. 私たちは高級ホテルで破格に楽しんだ。	
stand by 〜	〜の味方をする My father has always stood by me. 父は常に私の味方をしてきてくれた。	= take someone's side
stand for 〜	〜を表す, 〜を象徴する；〜を支持する What does EU stand for? EUは何を表していますか。	= represent
stand on one's head [hands]	できる限りのことをする I'd stand on my head for you as I love you. 私は君のためなら何でもするよ, 愛してるから。	= do anything one can
stand on one's own feet	自立する You should stand on your own feet after graduation. 君たちは卒業後は自立するべきだ。	= become independent
stand out	目立つ, 際立つ His performance stood out on the stage. 舞台で彼のパフォーマンスが際立っていた。	= stick out
stand up for 〜	〜を擁護する, 〜を支持する You must stand up for your own rights. あなたは自身の権利を擁護しなければならない。	= support 〜
stare at 〜	〜をじっと見つめる, 〜をにらむ She stared at me in surprise. 彼女は驚いて私をじっと見た。	= gaze at 〜
starve to death	飢え死にする I'm starving to death. 私は腹が減って死にそうだ。	= die of hunger

熟語	語義／例文	同意表現／コメント
stay away from ～	～に近づかない；～を欠席する Stay away from any danger. いかなる危険にも近寄るな。	= keep away from ～
stem from ～	～に由来する The problem of obesity stems from the traditional diet. 肥満の問題は従来の食事に由来する。	= be derived from
step by step	一歩一歩, 少しずつ Progress is made in learning step by step. 学習は一歩一歩前進する。	= gradually
stick to ～	～に固執する, ～を守る；(仕事など) ～をやり通す Don't stick to the same technique. 同じやり方に固執するな。	= hold to ～ be wedded to ～ も同義語。
stop ～ ing	～するのをやめる She stopped talking to prick up her ears. 彼女は話すことをやめて聞き耳を立てた。	= quit ～ ing
stop to ～	立ち止まって～する, ～するために立ち止まる He stopped to have a smoke. 彼は立ち止まってタバコを一服した。	この不定詞は目的を表す副詞的用法。
struggle for ～	～のために奮闘する The parties struggled for political power. 各党は政権を求めて奮闘した。	
substitute A for B	Bの代わりにAを用いる We substitute margarine for butter. 私たちはバターの代わりにマーガリンを用いる。	= use A in place of B
succeed in ～ ing	～することに成功する He succeeded in obtaining the data. 彼はそのデータを手に入れることに成功した。	
succeed to ～	～の後を継ぐ The man shall succeed to the crown. その男に王位を継がせます。	= take over ～
such as ～	例えば～(のような) I've learned several languages such as English and Chinese. 私はいくつかの言語, 例えば英語や中国語を学んだ。	such as ～ は例を示し, like ～ は類似物を示す。
suffer from ～	～を患う, ～で苦しむ I'm suffering from depression. 私は鬱病で苦しんでいます。	= be afflicted with

熟語	語義／例文	同意表現／コメント
supply A with B [B to A]	AにBを支給する[供給する] We supply needy students with school uniforms. 我々は苦学生に制服を支給する。	= provide A with B
suspect A of B	AにBの疑いをかける The police suspected him of the murder. 警察は彼に殺人の疑いをかけた。	
sympathise with 〜	〜に同情する I sympathised with their plight. 私は彼らの窮状に同情した。	= commiserate with 〜
take [catch / get] hold of 〜	〜をつかむ Deep despair took hold of him. 深い絶望が彼をとらえた。	
take [go on] a trip (to 〜)	(〜へ)旅をする She took a trip to Hawaii on vacation. 彼女は休暇でハワイへ旅をした。	= go on a trip (to 〜) ⑤ 旅行の話題では絶対に使おう！
take [have] a look at 〜	〜を見る Take a look at this. これを見て。	= look at 〜
take 〜 aback	〜をびっくりさせる, 〜の不意をつく The news took everyone aback. そのニュースはみんなをびっくりさせた。	= bring 〜 to a stand 受身形の be taken aback「たじろぐ」も頻出。
take a spin	ドライブする We took a spin around the town. 私たちは町をドライブした。	
take 〜 by surprise	(不意をついて)〜を驚かせる His demise took the citizens by surprise. 彼の死は国民を驚かせた。	= catch 〜 by surprise
take 〜 by the hand	〜の手をつかむ They took each other by the hand. 彼らは互いに手を取り合った。	
take 〜 for example	〜を例にとる Let's take Japan for example. 日本を例にとってみよう。	= take 〜 for instance W2 例を書くときはこれを使わず, For example, で始めるように。
take 〜 for granted	〜を当然のことと思う We take health for granted. 我々は健康を当たり前のものだと思っている。	

Track 361

熟語	語義／例文	同意表現／コメント
take ～ into consideration [account]	～を考慮[配慮]する We should take everything into consideration. 我々はすべてのことを考慮するべきだ。	= take account of ～
take ～ off	(ある期間・日)を休みとして取る I'll take several days off next week. 私は来週数日間休みを取ります。	Ⓢ 仕事の話題で使えそう。
take a chance	思い切ってやる Let's take a chance. 思い切ってやってみよう。	= take the bet
take A for B	AをBだと思う；AをBと間違える At first, he took me for Chinese, not Japanese. 初め彼は私を日本人ではなく，中国人だと思った。	= regard A as B / mistake A for B
take advantage of ～	～を利用する He took advantage of his position as a leader. 彼はリーダーとしての地位を利用した。	= make use of ～
take after ～	(人が)～に似ている She takes after her mother. 彼女は母親にそっくりだ。	= resemble ～
take away ～	～を奪い[持ち・連れ]去る May I take away this dish? このお皿をお下げしてもよろしいですか。	
take care of ～	～の世話をする She took care of her young sisters and brothers. 彼女は幼い妹弟の世話をした。	= care for ～ / look after ～ / attend to ～
take charge of ～	～を管理[担当]する；～を預かる I will take charge of this class. 私がこのクラスを担当します。	= be assigned to ～
take courage	勇気を出す He took courage at her words. 彼は彼女の言葉で勇気づいた。	= try to be brave
take in ～	～を受け入れる；～を理解する Did you take in that request? あなたはその要求を受け入れたのですか。	
take it easy	気楽にやる；休養を取る I will take it easy today. 私は今日はゆっくりします。	= relax

381

熟語	語義／例文	同意表現／コメント
take it seriously	真に受ける, まじめにとる Don't take it seriously. 真に受けないでください。	= believe it
take leave of ～	～に別れを告げる He took leave of his beloved children. 彼は最愛の子供たちに別れを告げた。	= bid farewell to ～
take measures (to ～)	(～する)手段[措置]を講じる We should take measures to prevent a hostile takeover. 我々は敵対的買収を防止する措置を取るべきだ。	= take steps to ～
take note of ～	～に気づく；～に注意する Many scholars will take note of his discovery. 多くの学者が彼の発見に注目するだろう。	= take notice of ～
take notice (of ～)	(～に)気づく, (～を)気に留める Nobody took notice of his warning. 誰も彼の警告を気に留めなかった。	= take note of ～
take off (～)	離陸する；～を脱ぐ；～を取り去る Airplanes take off every five minutes. 飛行機は5分ごとに離陸する。	⇔ land / put on ～
take offense (at ～)	(～に)怒る He took offense at her attitude. 彼は彼女の態度に腹を立てた。	= get angry with
take on ～	～を引き受ける；～を帯びる He took on the difficult work. 彼は難しい仕事を引き受けた。	= assume W2 take on a role「役割を担う」を使おう！ 同義語の assume も盲点。
take one's time	ゆっくりする, ゆっくりやる Take your time. There's no hurry. ごゆっくりどうぞ。急ぎではありませんので。	
take someone's word for it	人の言葉を信用する Don't take her word for it. 彼女の言葉を信用するな。	
take over ～	～を引き継ぐ He took over his father's business. 彼はお父さんのビジネスを引き継いだ。	= assume ～
take pains	骨折る, 苦労する He took pains to educate his children. 彼は子供の教育に苦労した。	

Track 363

熟語	語義／例文	同意表現／コメント
take part in ～	～に参加する The athlete has taken part in the Olympics. その選手はオリンピックに参加したことがある。	= participate in ～ / join ～
take place	起こる；行われる The Olympic games take place every four years. オリンピックは4年に1度行われる。	= be held [W2]「(主語が)起こる」という使い方。他動詞の「～を引き起こす」ではない。
take pleasure in ～	～を楽しむ We took pleasure in driving in the country. 我々は田舎のドライブを楽しんだ。	= take delight in ～
take root	根付く How did the custom take root? その風習はどうやって根付いたのか。	
take shelter (from ～)	(～から)避難する The ship took shelter from the storm. その船は嵐から避難した。	= take refuge
take steps (to ～)	(～する)手段を講じる Police took steps to prevent such crimes. 警察が犯罪を防止するための手段を講じた。	= take measures to ～
take the [a] lead (in ～ing)	(～するのに)先頭に立つ He took the lead in carrying out the plan. 彼は先頭に立ってその計画を遂行した。	= head ～
take the initiative in ～ing	率先して～する She took the initiative in raising the fund. 彼女は率先して資金集めをした。	= initiate
take the place of ～	～に取って代わる Television can never take the place of books. テレビが本に取って代わることはあり得ない。	= take one's place / replace ～
take the trouble to ～	わざわざ～する He took the trouble to visit me in hospital. 彼はわざわざ見舞いに来てくれた。	= go out of one's way to ～
take to ～	～にふける；(習慣的に)～を始める；～が気に入る He has taken to evil courses lately. 彼は近頃悪い遊びにふけっている。	
take to one's heels	逃走する, 走り去る He took to his heels when he saw a policeman. 彼は警官を見て逃げ出した。	= run away

Track 364

熟語	語義／例文	同意表現／コメント
take turns in ～ing	交替で～する We took turns in driving all through the night. 私たちは夜通し交代で運転した。	= take it in turns to ～
take up ～	～（仕事など）を始める；～を占める He retired, and took up golf this spring. 彼は引退し，この春からゴルフを始めた。	
take 人 at one's word	人の言葉を真に受ける You must not take him at his word. 彼の言葉を真に受けてはいけない。	
talk over ～	～を討議する，～をよく話し合う It's important. We should talk it over. それは重要だ。きちんと話し合おう。	= discuss
talk 人 into ～ing	人を説得して～させる She talked her father into buying a new car. 彼女は父親を説得して新車を買わせた。	talk 人 against ～ing は「人に～しないよう説得する」。
tell A from B	AとBを区別する，AとBを見分ける Sometimes, it's difficult to tell right from wrong. 時に正と邪を区別するのは難しい。	= distinguish A from B
tell off ～	～を叱る The teacher told him off for being rude. 先生は無礼であると彼を叱った。	= reprimand ～
tell on ～	～にはこたえる，～に（悪く）影響する Age is telling on me. 年が私にはこたえてきた。	= affect ～
tend to ～	～する傾向がある His car tends to overheat even in winter. 彼の車は冬でもオーバーヒートする傾向がある。	= be inclined [likely] to 一般動詞なので be 動詞は不要。受動態にもしないように！
than ever before	以前よりも He is better off than ever before. 彼は以前よりも暮らしぶりがよい。	
thanks to ～	～のおかげで Thanks to your help, I succeeded. 私はあなたの助けのおかげで成功した。	= owing to ～
that is (to say)	つまり，言い換えれば I guess it's last Monday, that is to say the 4th of June. たぶん先週の月曜つまり6月4日だね。	= in other words

Track 365

熟語	語義／例文	同意表現／コメント
the other way round [around / about]	逆に，反対に Turn it the other way round. それを逆に回しなさい。	= conversely
there is no ~ ing	～することはできない There is no accounting for tastes. 人の好みは説明できない。	= it is impossible to ~
there is no need (for you) to ~	(あなたが)～する必要はない There is no need to worry. 心配する必要はない。	= (You) don't have to ~
There is something A about B	B にはどこか A なところがある There is something suspicious about that man. あの男には何か怪しいところがある。	
(the) same to you	あなたも(同じように) "Have a nice day!" "Same to you!" 「よい一日を！」「あなたもね！」	いいことにも悪いことにも使える。
think better of ~	～を考え直してやめる I was going to resign, but thought better of it. 私は辞職しようとしたが，考え直してそれをやめた。	
think highly [much] of ~	～を高く評価する，～を重視する Many people think highly of the university. 多くの人がその大学を高く評価している。	= make much of ~
think little of ~	～を軽んじる You should never think little of others. 絶対に他人を軽んじてはいけません。	⇔ think much [highly] of ~
think up ~	～を思いつく，～を考え出す He finally thought up a novel idea. ついに彼は斬新なアイデアを思いついた。	= hit on
think over ~	～についてよく考える Please think it over before you decide. それについては決断する前によく考えてください。	= reflect on ~
think twice	(行動する前に)よく考える Think twice before you buy it. それを買う前に，よく考えなさい。	= consider
this day week	来週の今日 We are supposed to take an exam this day week. 来週の今日，試験を受けることになっています。	= a week from today / today week

Track 366

熟語	語義／例文	同意表現／コメント
throw oneself into ～	～に没頭する The artist threw herself into that piece. 芸術家はその作品に没頭した。	= immerse oneself in ～
time after time	何度も The actor repeated the same line time after time. その俳優は同じセリフを何度も繰り返した。	= time and (time) again
to be frank with you	率直に言えば To be frank with you, I hate him. 率直に言えば，私は彼が嫌いです。	= frankly speaking
to do 人 justice	人を公平に見て，正しく評価すれば To do him justice, I agree with his opinion. 公平に見て，私は彼の意見に賛成だ。	= to do justice to 人
to make matters worse	更に悪いことには To make matters worse, the wrong diet impaired her health. 更に悪いことに，不適切な食事が彼女の健康を損ねた。	= what is worse W2 次の問題を導入するときのつなぎ言葉として使える。
to no avail	無益に，無駄で He made every effort, but it was to no avail. 彼はあらゆる努力をしたが無駄であった。	= in vain
to no purpose	無駄に，いたずらに He studied to no purpose. 彼は無駄に勉強しただけだった（報われなかった）。	
to one's heart's content	心ゆくまで Enjoy the dinner to your heart's content. 心ゆくまでディナーをお楽しみください。	= as much as one likes
to one's taste	～の好みに合って Jazz isn't to my taste. ジャズは私の好みに合わない。	
to say nothing of ～	～は言うまでもなく She can speak French, to say nothing of English. 英語は言うまでもなく，彼女はフランス語も話せる。	= not to mention ～
to some extent [degree]	ある程度は，ある程度まで Everyone is an amnesiac to some extent. すべての人がある程度は物忘れをします。	W2 to some extent I agree「ある程度は同意する」を自分の立場にすると書きやすいことも。
to the best of one's knowledge	～の知る限り To the best of my knowledge, she is from Manchester. 私の知る限り，彼女はマンチェスター出身だ。	= as far as one knows

熟語	語義／例文	同意表現／コメント
to the effect that S+V	〜という趣旨で He wrote her to the effect that he loved her. 彼は彼女を愛しているという趣旨の手紙を書いた。	
to the full	十分に，思う存分 We should exploit ocean energy to the full. 我々は海洋エネルギーを十分に活用すべきだ。	= fully
to the minute	きっかり She showed up on time to the minute. 彼女は時間きっかりに現れた。	= sharp
to the point	要領を得て His argument was to the point. 彼の議論は要領を得ていた。	⇔ beside the point [mark]
trouble A for B	A に B を求めて面倒[迷惑]をかける I have to trouble you for your help. 迷惑をかけるが私はあなたの助けが必要だ。	
trust A to B [B with A]	B に A を預ける I trust my money to that bank. 私はその銀行にお金を預ける。	
try on 〜	〜を試着する May I try on this dress? このドレスを試着してもいいですか。	代名詞では try this on の形になる。
try one's best	最善を尽くす Let's try our best for the victory. 勝利を求めて最善を尽くそう。	= do one's best
turn (A) into B	B に変わる；(A)を B に変える Caterpillars turn into butterflies. 毛虫は蝶に変わる。	
turn a deaf ear to 〜	〜に耳を貸さない My boss turned a deaf ear to my request. 上司は私の要求に耳を貸さなかった。	= refuse to listen to 〜
turn away (from 〜)	(〜から)顔をそむける；離れる He turned away from her. 彼は彼女から顔をそむけた。	
turn back (〜)	引き返す；〜を引き返させる；(元に)戻る He got tired and turned back halfway. 彼は疲れて途中で引き返した。	

Track 368

熟語	語義／例文	同意表現／コメント
turn down ～	～を拒否[拒絶]する，～を断る The professor turned down my request. その教授は私の依頼を拒否した。	= reject ～ / decline ～
turn off ～	～（電化製品など水道）を止める，消す I turned off the tap. 私は水道を止めた（蛇口を閉めた）。	
turn out (to) ～	～であること[すること]が分かる The rumour turned out false. その噂は事実無根であると分かった。	= prove
turn to 人 for ～	～を求めて人に頼る Many students turn to him for advice. 多くの生徒が忠告を求めて彼に頼る。	= depend on 人 for ～
turn up	現れる；出社する I had not waited long before she turned up. 私が待つまでもなく，彼女は現れた。	= show (up)
under [in] the control of ～	～に支配[管理]されて The department is under the control of the Ministry of Defence. その部門は国防省に管轄されている。	
under no circumstances	どんな事情があっても～ない，決して～ない Under no circumstances can we do such a thing. どんなことがあっても，我々はそんなことはできない。	= by no means R circumstances は通常は複数形で「状況」。
under way	進行中で The police investigation is still under way. 警察の捜査はまだ進行中である。	= in progress
up in the air	未決定で；(噂が)広まって Our plan of the new project is still up in the air. 我々の新事業の計画はまだ未定だ。	
up to ～	～次第で；～の責任で It's up to you. それはあなた次第だ。	= depend on ～
wait on ～	～に対応する，～に仕える The hotel needs more room clerks to wait on guests. そのホテルではゲストに対応する客室係がもっと必要だ。	= serve ～ / attend on ～ 「（レストランなどで）接客する」の意味が盲点。
warn A of B	B を A に警告する He warned me of the danger. 彼は私に危険を知らせてくれた。	

熟語	語義／例文	同意表現／コメント
way of ～ing	～する仕方, ～するやり方, ～する方法 This is the best way of dealing with the problem. これがその問題に対処する最善策だ。	
wear out ～	～を疲れさせる Stress wore me out. ストレスが私を疲労させた。	= tire out ～ / exhaust
well off	裕福な The family used to be very well off. その家族はかつてとても裕福だった。	⇔ bad (ly) off
what is more	さらに, その上 He is handsome, and what's more, he is well off. 彼は二枚目だし, その上裕福だ。	= in addition / moreover
what is the matter with ～?	～はどこが悪いのか[問題なのか] What's the matter with you? どこか悪いの（どうしたの）?	= What is wrong with ～
what we [they] call	いわゆる My son is what we call a bookworm. 私の息子はいわゆる本の虫だ。	= so-called
Why don't you ～?	～したらどうですか Why don't you take the day off? 今日は仕事を休んだらどうですか。	= had better
wipe out ～	～を絶滅させる；～を全滅させる They introduced new chemicals to wipe out insect pests. 彼らは害虫を絶滅させるための新しい化学薬品を導入した。	= kill off / exterminate
with [have] ～ in view	～を視野に入れて[心に抱いている] He works hard with money in view. 彼はお金のためにけんめいに働いている。	
with [in] regards [respect] to ～	～に関して What's your opinion with regards to the prices? 価格に関してどうお考えですか。	= about W1 as for ～ と同様に違う項目の話題に移るときに使える。
with ease	容易に, 簡単に She completed the assignment with ease. 彼女は容易にその課題を仕上げた。	= easily 〈with ＋ 名詞〉は副詞になる。
within easy reach of ～	～のすぐ近くに, ～の容易に手の届くところに The hotel was within easy reach of the station. そのホテルは駅のすぐ近くにあった。	

熟語	語義／例文	同意表現／コメント
within reach	すぐ近くに, 手の届くところに If you read in bed, keep a book within reach. ベッドで読書するなら, 本は手の届くところに置いておきなさい。	
without fail	きっと, 必ず I'll submit the report by the deadline without fail. 私は必ず期限までにレポートを提出します。	= surely
word for [by] word	一語一語, 逐語的に Don't translate English into Japanese word for word. 英語を日本語に逐語的に訳してはならない。	R L 1単語ずつではなく, 塊で意味を捉えるように！
work on ~	~に取り組む；~に影響を与える She started to work on the new project. 彼女は新しい企画に取り組み始めた。	= cope with ~ / tackle ~
work one's way (through ~)	苦労して進む；働いて~を出る He worked his way through college. 彼は苦学して大学を出た。	
work out (~)	~を解決する；うまくいく The two of us can work out the problem. 私たち2人ならその問題を解決することができる。	= solve ~
write down ~	~を書き留める, ~をメモする You may write down anything you need. 必要なら何をメモしても良いです。	= note ~ / take down ~
write to ~	~に手紙を書く I write to my parents once in a blue moon. 私は両親に手紙を書くことはまれである。	= write a letter to ~
yield to ~	~に屈服する, ~に敗れる He yielded to pressure. 彼は圧力に屈した。	= give in to ~

索引

INDEX

A

abandon	124	adequate	32	allocate	238
abate	200	adhesive	170	all of a sudden	299
abbey	144	adjacent	209	allot	294
abbreviate	259	adjunct	260	allowance	70
abdomen	102	adjust	33	allow for ~	300
abide	245	administer	179	all the same	299
abolish	158	admire	139	all the time	299
aboriginal	215	admittedly	114	all the way	300
above all	306	admonish	266	allure	265
abrupt	123	adobe	291	allusion	103
absent oneself from ~	298	adolescent	91	alongside	61
absorb	53	adopt	52	alter	24
abstract	120	adorn	262	alternate	87
absurdity	227	advance	16	alternative	160
abundant	33	advancement	53	altimeter	169
abuse	153	advantage	24	a man of ~	298
accelerate	169	advent	260	amass	220
acceptance	19	adverse	245	amateur	22
access	50	advertisement	41	a matter of course	298
accessible	62	advocate	191	ambience	281
accidental	27	aesthetic	245	ambiguous	157
acclaim	162	affectionately	226	ambivalence	266
accommodate	142	affiliation	223	ambulance	44
accompany	175	affirmative	265	amenable	287
accomplish	77	afflict	258	amid	98
accord	172	affluent	114	amorphous	197
accordance	118	afford	239	amount to ~	300
according to ~	298	after all	299	ample	65
account	129, 251	aftermath	89	anaesthetic	274
accountant	31	against one's will	299	analogous	272
account for ~	298	agenda	266	analogy	244
accredited	215	agent	93	analysis	60
accrue	279	aggravate	189	anarchy	203
accumulation	52	aggregate	290	ancestor	20
accurately	44	aggressive	59	anchor	247
accuse	101	agrarian	216	and yet	300
accuse 人 of ~	299	agree with ~	299	~ and so forth	300
accustom	113	aid	25	anecdotal	211
ache	41	aim	139	annihilate	234
acid	85	aim at ~	299	annotation	276
acknowledge	90	airborne	260	annual	117
acoustic	138	aisle	137	annum	277
acquire	69	akin	161	anomaly	282
acquisition	113	a large amount of ~	298	anonymous	218
acquisitive	276	a large number of ~	298	answer for ~	300
activate	57	alarmingly	29	anthropology	92
act on ~	299	alert	189	antibiotic	91
actual	74	algae	253	anticipate	183
acuity	263	alien	249	antidote	273
adaptation	62	alienate	273	antipathy	266
add A to B	299	align	290	antipode	91
addict	96	all along	299	antiquated	248
addictive	228	all but ~	299	antiquity	275
address	190	allergic	234	antiseptic	197
		alleviate	188	anxiety	73
		alley	184	anything but ~	300
		alliteration	202	a pair of ~	298

392

apart from ~	300	a sheet of ~	298	at leisure	304
apathy	266	ashore	111	at length	304
apologize to A for B	300	as is often the case with ~	301	atmosphere	19
apparatus	133	as it were	302	atomise	190
apparent	64	ask a favour of ~	302	at once	304
appeal to ~	300	ask for ~	302	at one's best	305
appease	266	aspiring	238	at one's convenience	305
appendix	265	as regards ~	302	at ones wits'	305
appetite	74	assassinate	294	at short notice	302
applicant	34	assault	104	at present	305
application	54	assay	275	at random	305
apply	248	assemble	144	atrophy	282
apply A to B	300	assent	267	attach	77
apply for ~	300	assert	123	attain	154
appointments	40	assess	235	attempt	43
apportion	272	asset	83	attest	264
appraise	253	assiduous	282	at the age of ~	305
appreciable	276	assign	62	at the back of ~	305
appreciate	49	assimilate	157	at the cost of ~	305
appreciation	236	associate	75	at the mercy of ~	305
apprehensive	247	assonance	103	at the minute	305
apprentice	182	as such	302	at the risk of ~	305
approve of ~	301	assumed	19	at the same time	305
approximately	81	assurance	155	at the sight of ~	306
aptitude	190	asteroid	243	at the top of one's voice	306
aquaculture	109	as the saying goes	302	at this rate	306
aquatic	262	asthma	96	attitude	44
A rather than B	298	as to ~	302	attract	17
arbitrary	240	astonishing	25	attribute	173, 274
arbitrate	267	astray	118	attribute A to B	306
archaeology	80	astronaut	129	at will	306
ardour	265	astronomer	143	at work	306
argue	171	as usual	302	audition	162
arise	135	~ as well	302	auditory	179
arithmetic	59	as yet	302	augment	265
army	156	asylum	232	auspicious	282
arouse	102	asymmetrical	259	authentic	246
arrange for ~	301	at a glance	303	authority	85
arrangement	135	at all times	303	autonomous	272
array	91	at a loss	303	autonomy	176
arrogance	102	at an end	303	autumn	21
artefact	102	at any cost	303	avail oneself of ~	306
arthritis	198	at any moment	303	avalanche	97
articulate	240	at any rate	303	a variety of ~	298
artifice	196	at any time	303	average	19
artificial	126	at a time	303	avert	260
artisan	162	at best	303	avid	248
as a matter of fact	301	at ease	303	await	99
as a result	301	at face value	303	awaken	79
as a rule	301	at first	304	award	41
as a token of ~	301	at first hand	304	awareness	174
as a whole	301	at first sight	304	a week from today	298
ascertain	102	at hand	304	awkward	247
ascribe	255	at heart	304	awry	275
ascribe A to B	302	athlete	60	axis	100
as far as ~	301	at issue	304		
as follows	301	at large	304	**B**	
as for ~	301	at last	304		
as good as ~	301	at least	304	bait	138

393

balance	49	be curious about ~	309	be liable to ~	314
balk	219	be cut out for ~	309	believe in ~	319
ban	186	be derived from ~	310	believe it or not	320
bandage	29	be determined to ~	310	be likely to ~	314
bankrupt	225	be different from ~	310	belly	73
bankruptcy	152	be disappointed at ~	310	belong to ~	320
barbed	184	be dressed in ~	310	be made from ~	314
barely	164	bedrock	99	be made of ~	314
barren	195	be due to ~	310	be made up of ~	314
barrister	232	be dying to ~	310	bend	76
barter	161	be eager for ~	310	beneath	81
basic	38	be endowed with ~	310	beneficial	80
basin	267	be engaged in ~	310	benign	205
basis	52	be entitled to ~	310	be nothing like ~	314
bask	165	be envious of ~	310	be obliged to ~	314
be above ~ ing	306	be equal to ~	311	be occupied with ~	314
be absorbed in ~	307	be equipped with ~	311	be of service to ~	315
be abundant in ~	307	be equivalent to ~	311	be of the opinion that ~	315
be accustomed to ~	307	be expected to ~	311	be on good terms with ~	315
be acquainted with ~	307	be faced with ~	311	be on the books	315
be adept at ~	307	be familiar to ~	311	be on the increase	315
be afraid of ~	307	be famous for	311	be on the point of ~ ing	315
be against ~	307	be fed up with ~	311	be on the rise	315
beak	185	be filled with ~	311	be on the verge of	315
be all ears	307	be fit to ~	311	be open to ~	315
be (all) Greek to ~	306	be fond of ~	311	be out of order	315
beam	248	be forced to ~	312	be particular about ~	315
be a match for ~	306	beforehand	38	be peculiar to ~	315
be anxious about ~	307	before long	319	be poor at ~	315
be anxious for ~	307	be free from ~	312	be popular with ~	316
be anxious to	307	be free to ~	312	be possessed of ~	316
be apt to ~	307	be gifted with ~	312	be proud of ~	316
bear	128	be grateful to A for B	312	bequeath	205
bear fruit	319	be hard on ~	312	be ready for ~	316
bear in mind	319	behave oneself	319	be reluctant to ~	316
be ashamed of ~	308	behind one's back	319	be representative of ~	316
beat around the bush	319	behind the times	319	be responsible for ~	316
be at home in ~	308	be ignorant of ~	312	be satisfied with ~	316
be attached to ~	308	be ill at ease	312	be second to none	316
be aware of ~	308	be impressed with ~	312	be sensible of ~	316
be based on ~	308	be incapable of ~ ing	313	be sensitive to ~	317
be bent on ~	308	be in charge of ~	312	be short of ~	317
be bound by ~	308	be inclined to ~	313	beside oneself (with ~)	320
be caught in ~	308	be in danger	312	Besides ~	320
because of ~	319	be in danger of ~ ing	312	besiege	266
be certain of ~	308	be in demand	313	be specific to ~	317
be characteristic of ~	308	be independent of ~	313	bestow	104
become of ~	319	be indifferent to ~	313	be strict with ~	317
be compelled to ~	308	be indispensable to ~	313	be subject to ~	317
be composed of ~	308	be in favour of ~	313	be suitable for ~	317
be concerned about ~	309	be inferior to ~	313	be superior to ~	317
be conditioned to ~	309	be in good health	313	be sure to ~	317
be confident of ~	309	be in the habit of ~ ing	313	be through with ~	317
be connected with ~	309	be involved in ~	313	be tired of ~	317
be conscious of ~	309	be jealous of ~	314	be to blame (for ~)	317
be considerate of ~	309	be (just) about to ~	306	be true of ~	318
be content to ~	309	be keen on ~	314	between ourselves	320
be content with ~	309	be keen to ~	314	between you and me	320
be crowded with ~	309	be lacking in ~	314	be under way	318

be up to ~	318	branch	21	by chance	322
be well off	318	breach	228	by comparison	323
be wide of the mark	318	breadbasket	248	by degrees	323
bewilder	253	break away (from ~)	321	by far	323
be willing to ~	318	break down (~)	321	by choice	322
be worn out	318	breakdown	122	by halves	323
be worried about ~	318	break into ~	321	by contrast	322
be worthy of ~	318	break out	321	by virtue of ~	322
be wrong with ~	318	break the ice	321	by means of ~	323
be yet to ~	318	breakthrough	154	by nature	323
beyond	20	breath	26	by no means ~	323
beyond words	320	breed	117, 191	by oneself	323
beyond description	320	brew	273	bypass	178
bias	162	bribe	42	by-product	132
bibliography	234	brief	17	by the time ~	323
bidding	112	brilliant	34	by the way	323
bill	115	bring about ~	321	by way of ~	323
billion	114	bring A home to B	321		
bind	182	bring oneself to ~	321	**C**	
binoculars	47	bring out ~	321		
biography	36	bring ~ to light	321	calamitous	270
bipedal	257	bring ~ to one's senses	321	calculate	78
bizarre	206	bring up ~	321	call for ~	323
blackout	227	brittle	244	call it a day	324
blame	62	broad	52	call off ~	324
blame A for B	320	broaden	226	call on ~	324
blanket	186	broadly	43	call up	324
blast	289	brochure	102	calm down (~)	324
bleach	39	bronchitis	274	camouflage	147
bleak	199	brush	293	campaign	234
bless	63	brush up ~	322	can afford to ~	324
blight	293	buckle	270	canal	47
blind	23	budding	204	canine	148
blossom	112	budget	26	cannot help ~ ing	324
blow up	320	buffer	207	capable	108
blueprint	261	buffet	129	capacity	55
blur	152	build-up	120	cape	145
board	145	bulky	133	capillary	264
boast	97	bulletin	153	capital	35, 232
boast of ~	320	buoyancy	249	capsize	222
bode	206	burden	159	captivity	266
bogus	237	bureaucracy	158	capture	187
bold	79	burgeon	286	cardiac	259
bombard	137	burglar	118	cardio-	277
bond	193	burn down	322	care for ~	324
book	131	burn off	30	cargo	98
boom	30	burrow	191	caring	139
boon	250	burst	25	carnivore	151
boost	151	burst into ~	322	carpentry	44
border	22	bury	148	carry out ~	324
botany	101	bush	80	carve	97
bother	34	bustle	227	case	211
boulder	156	buttress	270	cast	168
bounce	28	buzz	85	casualties	231
boundary	124	by accident	322	catalyse	286
bound for ~	320	by air	322	catastrophe	241
boundless	196	by all means	322	catastrophic	205
bout	273	by and large	322	catch	17
boxoffice	41	by birth	322	catch a glimpse of ~	324

395

catch on	324	civilization	33	come into view	326
catch ~ by the arm	324	claim	204	come near (to) ~ ing	326
catch sight of ~	325	clamour	203	come off ~	326
catch up with ~	325	clarify	228	come out	326
catch 人 ~ ing	325	clarity	83	comet	132
cater	138	clash	227	come to ~	327
caulk	251	class	25	come to an end	327
cave	40	classify A into B	325	come to light	327
cavity	244	clay	39	come to one's senses	326
cease	172	clear A of B	325	come to the conclusion that ~	327
cedar	214	clear one's throat	325	come true	327
ceiling	44	cleave	194	come up	327
celebrate	44	clientele	176	come up with ~	327
celebrity	139	cliff	145	comfort	33
celestial	247	clinch	267	command	111
cell	57	clinical	95	command a fine view	327
cement	48	clip	65	commence	107
cemetery	102	clone	213	commentary	88
censorship	228	close at hand	325	commission	162
census	149	close to ~	325	commit	76
centre	33	clout	282	commitment	124
cereal	237	clue	194	committee	39
certificate	131	clump	258	commodity	82
certify	215	coal	25	common	188
cetacean	262	coalesce	285	communal	216
chain	31	coarse	87	compact	150
challenge	144	coastline	48	companion	41
chamber	137	coating	174	comparable	170
change into ~	325	coercive	290	compare	24
channel	270	cognitive	273	compatible	169
chaos	42	coherent	228	compel	114
character	63	cohesion	107	compensate	92
characteristic	20	cohesive	228	competition	33
charge	68, 127	coin	199	competitive	139
charge 人 with ~	325	coincidence	93	compile	172
charter	158, 231	collaborative	107	complaint	188
cheat	63	collapse	168	complain to A about B	327
check into ~	325	collate	277	complement	181
chemical	98	collateral	292	complex	52
cheque	34	colleague	70	compliance	165
cherish	113	collection	37	comply	231
chew	53	collide	149	component	57
chick	35	collision	103	composite	255
chief	24	colloquial	202	composition	155
chilling	104	collude	281	composter	277
china	138	colonial	137	compound	100
choke	68	colour	113	comprehend	60
chronic	115	colourfast	215	comprehensive	245
chronological	251	combat	72	compressor	78
chunk	193	combine	77	comprise	103
cinema	39	combustible	236	compromise	129
cipher	256	come about	325	compulsion	226
circle	76	come across ~	326	compulsory	256
circuit	144	come before ~	326	concede	249
circulation	240	come by ~	326	conceit	265
circumference	230	come home (to ~)	326	conceivable	111
circumvent	290	come into being	326	concentrate (A) on B	327
cite	60	come into effect	326	concentration	28
civil engineering	214	come into existence	326	concern	78, 172

concert	288	construction	17	count for much with	328
concession	127	constructively	187	countless	130
concrete	147	consult	131	count on ~	328
concur	233	consume	239	courage	21
concussion	203	consumer	74	court	27
condemn	225	consumption	88	courteous	134
condensation	153	contact	49	courtesy	203
condense	190	contagious	263	coverage	161
condolence	263	contain	54	covert	263
conducive	260	contaminate	192	crack	66
conduct	73	contemporary	160	crackdown	186
conductor	79	contempt	166	craft	184
confectionery	271	content	16, 109	cram	160
confer	186	context	172	crammer	110
conference	69	contingency	295	cramped	259
confidence	61	contingent	279	crash	262
confidential	228	continuity	45	crater	252
configuration	178	continuum	288	creativity	17
confine	184	contour	226	creature	170
confirm	157	contract	143	credence	165
confiscate	287	contradict	181	credentials	239
conflict	88	contrary	175	credibility	90
conflicting	267	contrary to ~	328	credit	163
conform	84	contravene	281	creep	201
confront	192	contribute	53	crevice	153
confused	118	control	19	cripple	207
congenial	289	controversial	135	crippling	289
congestion	183	controversy	89	crisp	134
congratulate A on B	327	convection	260	criterion	123
conical	116	convene	294	critic	32
conifer	256	conventional	95	critical	61
conjunction	89	conversely	106	criticise	68
conquer	238	convert	77	crockery	200
consanguinity	282	convey	146	crop	78
conscious	83	convict	201	cross-section	178
consecutive	158	conviction	134	crouch	262
consensus	107	convince	108	crow	64
consent	188	convoy	200	crucial	253
consent to ~	327	cope	180	crude	200
consequence	89	cope with ~	328	crumble	195
conservation	213	coral	138	crumple	268
conserve	136	core	22	crusade	224
consider	20	corporal	281	crush	137
considerate	229	corporate	106	crust	97
consignment	210	corpse	260	crustacean	295
consist	17	correlation	23	cry for ~	328
consistency	275	correspond	137	crystal	77
consistent	175	correspond with ~	328	cub	177
consist in ~	328	corridor	116	cue	152
consist of ~	328	cosmic	144	culprit	204
consolidate	227	cosmopolitan	122	cultivate	69
consort	289	cost	177	culture	258
conspicuous	146	costly	32	cumbersome	250
conspiracy	257	cottage	38	cunning	64
constant	36	council	122	cupboard	120
constituent	220	count	241	curator	165
constitute	172	counter	89	cure	73
constitution	48	counterfeit	252	cure A of B	328
constraint	211	counterpart	185	curiosity	57

curious	224	degradation	195	destroy	87
current	74	degrade	136	destruction	22
cursory	291	degree	53	detachment	203
curtail	266	dehumanisation	103	detain	266
custodial	276	dehydrated	248	detect	58
custody	214	dehydration	272	detective	216
customary	114	delay	43	deter	108
customs	127	delegate	231	detergent	213
cut down ~	328	delete	159	deteriorate	203
cut in	328	deliberate	244	determinant	172
cutlery	200	deliberately	104	determination	69
cutting-edge	210	delicacy	292	determine	54
CV(curriculum vitae)	212	delight	24	deterrent	225
cylindrical	201	delineate	292	detour	199
		delinquency	280	devastate	205
		deliver	31	device	25
D		delta	133	devise	212
		delusion	196	devote	93
dairy	91	demand	41	devote A to B	329
damp	130	demanding	112	devote oneself to ~	329
dampen	255	demise	263	devour	109
dash	118	democratic	16	diagram	141
day after day	328	demographic	92	dialogue	68
daydream	251	demolish	226	diameter	170
dazzling	130	demonstrate	33	dictate	248
deadly	168	denial	88	dictation	71
deadstock	208	dense	30	die of ~	329
deal with ~	329	density	145	die out	329
debris	203	dent	212	diet	45
debt	23	depend on A for B	329	dietary	261
decade	73	depict	120	differ	18
decay	254	deplete	243	differ from ~	329
deception	90	depletion	273	differ in ~	329
decipher	259	deplore	237	diffusion	171
decisive	113	deploy	294	dig	81
declare	67	deport	281	digestion	74
decline	56	deposit	116	dignity	271
decode	263	deposition	293	dilapidate	283
decompose	191	depressed	84	dilute	209
decoy	209	depression	246	dim	104
decrepit	283	deprive	175	dimension	181
dedicate	149	deprive A of B	329	diminish	160
dedicate oneself to ~	329	deputy	264	dip	141
deduce	217	derive	112	diploma	130
deduction	274	dermal	293	dire	270
deductive	261	descend	80	direct A to B	329
default	103	desert	27	directory	128
defect	106	designate	189	disability	176
defendant	232	desire	18	disabled	137
defer	150	despair	88	disabuse	204
deference	289	despise	220	disapproval	142
defiance	237	despite	128	disaster	87
deficiency	86	despoiler	288	discard	155
deficient	94	despondency	195	discern	231
deficit	145	despondent	282	discharge	240
defined	193	destabilise	195	discipline	270
definite	125	destination	143	disclose	228
deflect	262	destine	235	discomfort	106
deforestation	164	destitute	291	discount	30
degenerative	198				

discourage	108	domain	42			**E**	
discourage 人	329	domesticate	34				
discourse	259	dominant	31	each other	331		
discrepancy	219	dominate	155	eagerly	70		
discrete	202	do more harm than good	330	earnest	176		
discursive	202	donate	36	eat up ～	331		
disdain	220	don't fail to ～	330	eclipse	246		
disguise	247	don't forget to ～	330	ecology	37		
disintegrate	169	doom	49	economy	161		
disintegration	89	doomsday	176	edible	148		
dislodge	292	dormant	245	edifice	258		
dismantle	294	dose	198	edit	149		
dismiss	155	double	22	editor	18		
disorder	129	doubt	182	eerie	254		
disorientated	205	doubt if ～	330	effectively	62		
disparity	197	dough	243	efficacy	280		
dispatch	250	do with ～	330	efficiency	62		
dispense	280	do without ～	330	effluent	200		
disperse	115	downside	114	egalitarian	186		
display	46	downturn	92	eject	155		
disposable	225	dozens of ～	331	elaborate	146		
disposal	249	do 人 a favour	330	elapse	221		
dispose of ～	330	draft	118	elastic	211		
disproportionate	163	drag	191	elderly	74		
disprove	106	drain	136	elicit	198		
dispute	94	drainage	186	eligible	127		
disrupt	180	dramatically	46	eliminate	168		
disseminate	224	drastic	58	elliptical	243		
dissent	146	draw	23	elucidate	278		
dissertation	212	drawback	118	elude	243		
dissipate	151	draw attention to ～	331	elusive	221		
dissolve	95	draw out ～	331	emancipation	244		
distant	27	dreadful	104	embark	239		
distinct	86	dream of ～	331	embed	226		
distinction	146	dress oneself	331	embellish	268		
distinctive	174	drip	224	emblazon	279		
distinguish	71	drive	92	embrace	147		
distinguish A from B	330	drive out (～)	331	embryo	287		
distort	101	drop ～ a line	331	emerge	184		
distract	180	drop in (on 人 /at 場所)	331	emergency	45		
distressing	189	droplet	77	emerging	110		
distribute	174	drop out (of ～)	331	emigrate	152		
distribution	164	drought	252	emission	183		
distributor	214	drowsiness	189	emit	157		
disturb	75	dubbed	214	emotion	19		
diverge	261	due	103	emotive	67		
divergence	285	due to ～	331	empathy	256		
diverse	146	dull	58	emphasis	63		
diversity	182	dump	229	empirical	221		
divert	262	dune	230	employment	41		
dividend	146	duplicate	181	empower	107		
division	110	durable	71	enclose	138		
divorce	43	duration	231	enclosure	217		
divulge	231	duty	19	encompass	252		
dizzy	156	dwelling	184	encounter	66		
do away with ～	330	dwindling	220	encourage	45		
dogma	150	dynamic	172	encroach	290		
do good to ～	330			encyclopaedia	40		
do harm to ～	330			endangered	61		

end in ~	332	essential	59	expedient	282
endorse	265	establish	180	expedition	99
endoscope	277	establishment	56	expel	138
endow	246	estate	121	expend	182
end up ~ ing	332	esteem	252	expenditure	94
end up with ~	332	estimate	54	experiment	17
endure	134	estuary	109	expertise	256
enduring	177	ethical	94	expire	146
enemy	18	ethnic	125	expiry	226
energetic	75	ethos	213	explode	89
engage	79	euthanasia	280	exploit	284
engraving	258	evacuate	231	exploitation	192
engrossed	272	evaluate	179	exploratory	184
engulf	260	evaporate	236	explore	164
enhance	171	evasive	103	explosive	181
enigma	197	eventuality	129	exponential	271
enigmatic	284	eventually	141	export-import	47
enjoy oneself	332	every inch	332	expose	59
enlightened	192	every other ~	332	expose A to B	333
enormously	141	every other day	332	exposure	174
enquire	209	every three days	332	extend	34
enquiry	115	evidence	17	extension	171
enrich	81	evident	56	extensive	91
enrollment	92	evil	67	extent	23
en-suite	216	evoke	189	extinct	114
ensure	55	evolution	66	extinction	173
entail	183	exacerbate	275	extinguish	231
enter into ~	332	exaggerate	187	extort	294
enthusiasm	172	examine	52	extract	173
enthusiastic	119	excavate	242	extraordinary	66
entice	223	exceed	18	extrapolation	272
entitle	116	excel	148	extraterrestrial	210
entity	286	except for ~	332	extravagance	223
entrepreneur	33	exceptionally	29	extremely	78
envious	170	excessive	62	extremities	275
envisage	270	excitable	139	extrinsic	271
envision	230	excite	289	exuberant	272
enzyme	265	exclude	102		
epicentre	293	exclusive	240	**F**	
epidemic	92	exclusively	182		
equate	147	excrete	270	fabric	38
equation	61	excruciate	280	façade	287
equator	28	excursion	125	face to face	333
equilibrium	241	excusable	209	facilitate	173
equip	172	excuse 人 for ~ ing	332	facility	80
equip A with B	332	exempt	242	faction	244
equipment	60	exercise	175	factor	19
equitable	134	exert	233	faculty	152
equity	178	exhaust	175	fade	44
equivalent	162, 170	exhibit	157	fade away	333
equivocal	260	exile	163	fair	94
eradicate	225	existence	27	fairground	221
erect	106	exorbitant	255	faith	90
erosion	192	exotic	161	fall short of ~	333
erudite	202	expand	58	fall in love with ~	333
erupt	97	expanse	261	fall into ~	333
eruption	257	expect	32	fall off (~)	333
escalate	33	expect A of B	333	fall on ~	333
escape	21	expectation	69	fall out with ~	333

fallow	275	fiscal	265	for one thing ~ and for	
famine	231	fixed	66	another ~	335
famished	242	flare	259	for or against	336
fan	134	flash	117	forsake	255
fanatical	112	flat	35	for sure	336
fare	134	flattering	156	forthcoming	191
far from ~	333	flat tyre	124	for the first time	336
farm	110	flawed	168	for the life of 人	336
fascinating	64	flee	196	for the most part	336
fashion	117	flexibility	76	for the purpose of ~ ing	336
fasten	70	flick	259	for the sake of ~	336
fatality	115	flinch	230	for the time being	336
fatigue	84	flooded	69	fortnight	218
fatty	117	flounder	274	fortunately	78
fault	291	flourish	49	fortune	39
favourably	134	flourishing	97	for all ~	334
fear	21	flow	45	fossil	80
feasible	248	fluctuate	229	foster	178
feat	222	fluctuation	152	found	95
feature	99	fluid	174	foundation	23
fee	35	fluorescent	273	foyer	214
feeble	217	flush	109	fraction	156
feed	109	flustered	278	fractured	105
feel at ease	333	flux	242	fragile	87
feel for ~	334	focal	193	fragment	102
feel free to ~	334	fold	89	fraud	101
feel ill at ease	334	foliage	230	free	86
feign	290	folk	43	free-range	232
fend	267	footnote	103	freight	241
ferment	262	for a change (of air)	334	frequency	180
fertile	87	forage	242	frequent	274
fertilise	208	for a rainy day	335	friction	161
fertility	277	for a while	335	frighten	111
fertilizer	49	force	79	frightening	196
fetch	239	force A on B	336	frigid	263
fete	206	for certain	335	from A to Z	337
fidelity	201	forecasting	111	from ~ ing	329
fierce	214	foreign	238	from now on	337
figural	259	foremost	164	from ~ point of view	337
figure	142	forensic	276	from time to time	337
figure out ~	334	foreseeable	61	frontal	83
fill in ~	334	foresight	66	frown	193
fill out ~	334	for ever	335	frustration	29
fill up (~)	334	for fear of ~ ing	335	fuel	111
filmy	256	forge	280	fugitive	242
filthy	212	forget ~ ing	336	fully	139
fin	139	forget to ~	337	fume	183
financial	159	forgive A for B	337	functional	66
find fault with ~	334	for good	335	fundamental	55
finding	93	for instance	335	fungus	210
find out ~	334	for lack of ~	335	furnish	145
fine	135	form	207	fusion	239
finite	175	former	81		
fir	213	formulate	156		
firefly	130	formulation	183		
firm	70	for nothing	335	gadget	117
firmly	71	for one's age	335	gain	70
firsthand	107	for oneself	336	gait	259
first of all	334	for one's part	335	gale	262

G

401

galvanise	289	
game	114	
gap	140	
gaping	133	
garbage	156	
garment	187	
gather	38	
gauge	169	
gear	190	
gender	74	
gene	158	
generalisation	63	
generate	79	
generation	61	
generosity	164	
genetic	52	
genetically	197	
genre	148	
genuine	188	
geometric	158	
geothermal	199	
germination	283	
get along with ~	337	
get A ready for B	337	
get at ~	338	
get ~ back on track	338	
get acquainted with ~	337	
get ~ under control	339	
get down to ~	338	
get in contact with ~	338	
get into ~	338	
get lost	338	
get married (to ~)	338	
get nowhere	338	
get on one's nerves	338	
get out of ~	338	
get over ~	338	
get A across to B	337	
get rid of ~	338	
get to one's feet	337	
get [stand] in the way of ~	337	
get the better of ~	339	
get through with ~	339	
get to ~	339	
get used to ~	339	
geyser	199	
gigantic	32	
gimmick	222	
girder	259	
give away ~	339	
give birth to ~	339	
give in to ~	339	
give off ~	339	
give rise to ~	339	
give the green light to	339	
give up (~)	339	
give way to ~	340	
give 人 a hand	340	
give 人 a ride	340	

give 人 up for dead	340	
glacier	168	
glamorous	137	
glance	57	
gland	170	
glaze	287	
glazing	209	
gleaming	227	
glide	78	
globalisation	30	
globe	88	
globule	270	
gloomy	179	
glossary	294	
glossy	223	
glow	129	
glue	116	
go bad	340	
go bankrupt	340	
go by	340	
go Dutch	340	
—goer	143	
go from bad to worse	340	
go on ~ ing	340	
go on to ~	340	
go out	340	
go over ~	341	
gorge	264	
go so far as to ~	341	
go through ~	341	
go through with ~	341	
govern	110	
go with ~	341	
go wrong	341	
gradation	236	
gradient	287	
gradually	46	
graduate from ~	341	
grain	28	
grand	98	
grant	122, 187	
granular	278	
grapple	280	
grasp	150	
grateful	38	
gravel	127	
grazing	236	
greet	26	
grid	230	
grind	230	
gross	90	
grossly	222	
ground	115, 169	
ground-floor	37	
gruesome	104	
guarantee	131	
guardian	38	
guilty	30	
gulf	90	

H

habitat	109	
habitual	64	
hail	224	
half the size of ~	341	
halt	196	
halve	92	
hamper	195	
hand down	341	
handful	81	
hand in hand	341	
handle	112	
handsome	139	
hand in ~	341	
handy	158	
hang	21	
hang up	341	
haphazard	262	
harass	240	
hard-wearing	215	
hard-wired	274	
hardy	129	
harmful	62	
harmless	38	
harness	253	
harsh	121	
harvest	170	
hassle	149	
hatch	216	
haul	222	
haunt	193	
have a good command of ~	342	
have a narrow escape	342	
have an effect on ~	342	
have an eye for ~	342	
have an influence on ~	342	
have a sweet tooth	342	
have a weakness for ~	342	
have difficulty (in) ~ ing	342	
have every reason to ~	343	
have words with ~	344	
have faith in ~	343	
have one's own way	342	
have had enough of ~	343	
have ~ in mind	342	
have little to do with ~	343	
have little in common	343	
have an impact on ~	342	
have no choice but to ~	343	
have no idea (~)	343	
have no say	343	
have nothing to do with ~	343	
have one's own way in	343	
have only to ~	343	
have one's say	343	
have second thoughts	344	
have some bearing on ~	344	
have something to do with ~	344	

have something to live for	344	horticulture	226	immunisation	216
have the right to ~	344	hospitality	131	immunity	164
have ~ to oneself	342	host	201	impact	161
havoc	275	hostile	101	impair	180
hazard	62	house	111	impart	233
head	126	household	93	impartial	219
head for ~	344	hover	99	impatient	115
headline	140	How come ~ ?	345	impede	247
hear from ~	344	huge	22	imperative	245
hear of ~	344	humanity	89	imperceptible	218
heartily	85	humankind	87	impetus	220
hectic	227	Human Resources	121	implement	230
hedge	86	humble	67	implication	98
height	36	humidity	152	implicit	217
heighten	93	humility	257	imply	26
help oneself to ~	344	hunger	105	impose	116
help 人 with ~	344	hurl	239	impose A on B	345
hemisphere	92	hut	105	imposing	139
hence	64	hybrid	194	impoverish	97
herd	42	hydrosphere	258	impressive	60
heredity	235	hydrothermal	99	improvement	75
heritage	97	hygiene	280	improvisation	252
hesitancy	94	hype	218	improvise	79
heterogeneous	204	hypnosis	222	impulsively	225
heyday	218	hypothesis	122	inability	112
hibernation	244	hypothesise	237	in accordance with ~	346
hiccup	106			in addition (to ~)	346
hide	117	**I**		inadequate	61
hierarchy	267			in advance	346
highland	22	iceberg	120	in a hurry	346
highlight	137	icecap	96	in a low voice	346
hilarity	202	identical	135	in a minute	346
hinder	148	identify	91	in a panic	345
hindrance	222	identity	60	in a sense	346
hinge	209	ideology	164	inaudible	229
hinterland	164	igneous	285	inaugurate	211
hire	75	ignite	221	in a word	346
hiss	290	ignorance	136	in-between	65
hitherto	204	ignore	72	incandescent	295
hit on ~	344	illegal	119	incapacitate	115
hive	155	illegible	225	in case of ~	346
hoard	292	illicit	285	incentive	149
hold	113	illiteracy	236	incidence	93
hold on	345	illiterate	211	incidentally	136
hold one's breath	345	illusion	176	incinerate	274
hold one's tongue	345	illustrate	141	inclined	76
hold onto ~	345	imaginary	236	inclusion	133
hold out	345	imaginative	63	income	26
hold the line	345	imbibe	257	in common (with ~)	347
hold true (for ~)	345	imitate	79	in comparison with ~	347
hold up (~)	345	immediately	99	inconclusive	123
holistic	233	immemorial	205	incongruity	278
hollow	220	immense	89	incongruous	223
homeopathy	276	immerse	271	in consequence	347
homogeneous	243	immigrant	40	inconsistency	93
hope for ~	345	immobile	115	in contrast (with ~)	347
horizontal	101	immobilise	239	incorporate	217
horrific	105	immortalise	188	incorrect	72
horrifying	195	immune	73	incredible	95

403

incubate	255	initiate	201	insufficient	116
incubation	284	initiative	58	insulate	248
indefinitely	90	injection	130	insulation	159
independence	19	injury	181	insulting	101
in-depth	138	injustice	151	insuperable	114
in detail	347	inlet	213	insurance	21
indicate	56	in line (with ~)	348	intact	190
indicator	45	inmate	243	intake	130
indict	293	innate	162	integral	81
indigenous	271	in need (of ~)	348	integrate	160
indispensable	175	inner	32	integrity	202
induce	182	in nine cases out of ten	348	intelligibility	229
inductive	273	innocence	48	intending	183
indulge	176	in no time	348	intense	76
indulge in ~	352	innovation	148	intensify	205
industrialisation	24	innovative	172	intensity	49
industry	185	innumerable	194	intensive	119
in earnest	347	in obedience to ~	348	intent	117
in effect	347	in one's company	348	interact	177
inequality	26	in oneself	349	interactive	49
inequity	179	in one's place	348	interest	23
inescapable	81	in one's teens	348	interfere	179
inevitable	52	in order	349	interior	28
in exchange for ~	347	in other words	349	interlink	188
inexorable	268	in part	349	intermodal	279
inexpensive	96	in particular	349	in terms of ~	350
inexperienced	76	in practice	349	internal	142
in fact	347	in proportion to ~	349	interpretation	63
infant	72	in prospect	349	interrupt	229
in fashion	347	in public	349	intervene	187
in favour of ~	347	inquiry	63	in the air	350
infection	183	in return for ~	349	in the course of time	350
infirmary	237	insatiable	187	in the dark	350
infirmity	223	inscribe	264	in the end	350
inflame	145	in search of ~	349	in the face of ~	350
inflammation	198	insect	64	in the first place	350
inflict	202	insecticide	198	in the future	350
influential	140	insecure	82	in the light of ~	351
influx	249	in short	349	in the long run	351
inform A of B	352	in short supply	350	in the main	351
informative	124	inside out	352	in the meantime	351
infrastructure	247	insight	212	in the name of ~	351
infringe	265	insist on ~	352	in the negative	351
in full	347	insolvency	233	in the presence of ~	351
in general	348	insomnia	188	in the process of ~	351
ingenious	185	inspection	56	in the way	351
ingestion	245	inspiration	73	in the world	351
ingrain	284	inspire	102	intimate	182
ingredient	25	in spite of ~	350	in time for ~	351
inhabit	168	in spite of oneself	350	intimidate	98
inhale	200	instalments	218	intoxicated	198
in harmony with ~	348	instance	83	intoxication	285
in haste	348	instantly	60	intricate	163
inherent	168	instead of ~	352	intrigue	237
inherit	159	instinct	72	intriguing	108
inhibit	154	institution	110	intrinsic	271
in honour of ~	348	instruction	65	introduce	25
initial	33	instrumental	91	introductory	41
initially	161	in succession	350	introvert	267

intrusive	264	keep company with ~	353	leaven	292
intuitive	250	keep early hours	353	leave nothing to be desired	355
in turn	351	keep in touch with ~	353	leave out ~	355
inundate	280	keep good time	353	leaver	186
in vain	352	keep one's word	353	ledge	258
invaluable	212	keep on ~ ing	353	legacy	42
invariably	151	keep to ~	353	legally	82
invention	18	keep ~ to oneself	353	legible	153
inventive	83	keep up with ~	354	legion	202
inventory	234	keep 人 company	354	legislation	165
inverted	221	kelp	271	legislative	250
in view of	352	kernel	293	legitimate	188
invigorating	218	kidney	31	lend ~ a hand	355
invisible	175	kill time	354	lengthy	96
invoke	273	kiln	256	lenticular	208
involve	84	kinetic	283	lessen	95
in regard to ~	346	knack	255	let alone ~	355
in youth	352	know a good deal about ~	354	let ~ down	355
ironically	17	know better than to ~	354	let go of ~	355
irrationally	112	know ~ by name	354	lethal	192
irrelevant	147	know one's way around ~	354	let out ~	355
irresistible	159			let up	355
irresponsible	136	**L**		leukaemia	286
irrevocable	288			level	78
irrigation	192	labyrinth	288	levy	293
irritable	59	laconic	199	lexical	218
irritation	193	laden	233	liability	250
isolated	96	laidback	122	liberal	55
isotope	200	lament	151	liberate	100
It goes without saying that ~	352	landfill	67	lie in ~	355
itinerant	285	landlord	37	life-size	217
itinerary	212	landmark	140	lifetime	18
		landscape	36	light	184
J		languish	233	lighthouse	44
		lapse	267	like a bolt from the blue	355
jam	70	larva	240	likelihood	82
jar	138	last	25	limb	182
jargon	213	last-minute	125	limit A to B	355
jeopardy	294	latently	254	liner	160
joint	61	lateral	66	liquor	142
jolt	255	lathe	291	literacy	197
jot	151	lather	213	literally	147
judge	38, 145	latitude	101	literati	206
jumble	256	latter	27	litter	185
jump at ~	352	launch	178	live from hand to mouth	356
jurisdiction	292	lava	96	live on ~	356
jury	210	lay aside ~	354	liver	31
just around the corner	352	layman	239	livestock	117
justify	32	lay off ~	354	live up to ~	356
just in case	352	laziness	75	lizard	132
juvenile	176	lead	29	load	127
		leak	161	lobbying	219
K		leap	141	localise	155
		learn ~ by heart	354	locomotion	252
kaleidoscope	178	lease	29	logging	79
keen	80	leathery	87	logical	32
keep abreast of ~	353	leave A for B	354	logistics	124
keep an eye on ~	353	leave A to B	355	longevity	90
keep away from ~	353	leave ~ behind	354	longitude	201

long for ~	356
look after ~	356
look back on (upon) ~	356
look down on (upon) ~	356
look for ~	356
look forward to ~	356
look ~ in the face	356
look into ~	357
look over ~	357
look to ~	357
look up ~	357
look on (upon) A as B	356
look up to ~	357
look out for ~	356
loophole	232
loot	151
lose no time (in) ~ ing	357
lose (one's) face	357
lose one's temper	357
lose one's way	357
lose sight of ~	357
loss	31
low-lying	88
low-profile	206
loyalty	186
lucrative	206
ludicrous	278
lunar	157
lunatic	219
lung	30
lure	227
lurk	264
lush	195
luxury	26
lyric	241

M

magical	40
magnificent	121
magnify	108
mains	208
maintenance	22
maize	207
majesty	211
major	127
major in ~	357
majority	31
make	124
make a choice	358
make a contribution to ~	358
make a difference	358
make a fool of oneself	358
make A from B	358
make A into B	358
make allowance(s) for ~	358
make an appointment (with ~)	358
make an effort (to ~)	359
make a noise	358

make a point of ~ ing	358
make believe ~	359
make (both) ends meet	357
make do with ~	359
make one's living	358
make for ~	359
make friends with ~	359
make fun of ~	359
make good	359
make it a rule to ~	359
make money	359
make much of ~	359
make no difference	359
make oneself at home	360
make oneself heard	360
make oneself understood	360
make one's way (to ~)	359
make out ~	360
make progress (in ~)	360
make a face	358
make room for ~	360
make sense (of ~)	360
make sure that ~	360
make the most of ~	360
make up ~	360
makeup	164
make up for ~	360
make up one's mind to ~	360
make use of ~	361
make way for ~	361
malfunction	146
malicious	226
malleable	288
malnutrition	95
mammal	56
mandatory	160
manifest	294
manifestation	168
manipulative	223
manmade	20
manner	72
manoeuvre	253, 272
manual	110
manufacture	17
manufacturing	157
map	47
margin	117
marginal	229
mark	126
marked	58
markedly	254
marsh	127
marshal	216
marsupial	283
marvel	262
marvellous	135
masonry	284
masterpiece	44
mate	176

materialistic	140
maternal	158
matinee	277
mature	76
maverick	199
maze	105
meadow	82
meaningful	43
means	174
meanwhile	71
measure	93
mechanical	154
medical	25
medication	96
mediocre	238
medium	183
meek	105
meet the demands	361
memorable	45
memorise	22
menace	208
menial	166
mentally	29
mention	43
mentor	186
mercenary	282
merchant	47
merely	53
merge	133
merger	247
meritocracy	282
metabolise	249
metabolism	106
metamorphosis	289
meteor	250
meteorite	217
meteorologist	206
methodology	63
meticulous	247
microorganism	100
midst	105
migraine	274
migration	40
migratory	126
milestone	227
mill	154
millennium	162
mimetic	257
mimic	170
mine	148
minimal	119
mining	192
minority	60
mint	283
miraculous	85
miraculously	203
misfortune	119
missionary	151
mistake A for B	361

mite		196
mitigate		244
mixture		173
mobility		141
mock		255
mode		69
moderate		82
modest		163
modification		204
modify		64
module		107
moist		54
molar		293
molecule		94
molten		159
monitor		173
monochrome		157
monolingual		122
monologue		45
monotonous		190
mood		59
moody		180
moon		200
moraine		276
morale		279
morbid		204
more often than not		361
more or less		361
more than 人 can help		361
morphology		289
mortal		134
mortality		196
moss		54
motivation		20
mould		177
mounting		180
move to ～		361
mucus		197
muddle		215
muggy		179
multiple		85
multiply		81
mummy		101
mundane		218
municipal		133
mural		243
murky		273
murmur		97
mutate		220
mute		154
mutually		80
myriad		287
myth		63
mythology		206

N

naive		64
name ～ A after B		361
namely		136
nanny		144
nap		75
narcotic		266
narration		140
narrow		122
nasty		122
native		101
nature		125
navigate		153
nearly		74
neat		71
negative		16
negligence		159
negotiate		214
nerve		57
net		70
neurologist		188
neutral		150
nevertheless		54
next to impossible		361
next to nothing		362
nil		216
nip		185
noble		132
nocturnal		285
nod		77
no less than ～		362
no longer ～		362
nomad		154
nomadic		212
nominal		246
no more than ～		362
none of one's business		362
nonetheless		112
none the less for ～		362
nook		263
norm		114
notably		138
note		130
noteworthy		123
nothing but ～		362
noticeable		140
notification		131
notion		90
notoriety		234
nourish		35
nourishment		111
novel		160
novelty		166
now and then		362
nuance		251
nuclear		27
nucleus		137
nuisance		193
numeration		222
numerical		149
numerous		123
nursery		116
nursing		41
nurture		219
nutrient		86
nutritional		173

O

oath		244
obedient		133
obesity		203
objective		43
object to ～		362
obligation		55
oblige		225
oblique		199
obscene		240
obscure		86
observation		63
obsess		284
obsolescence		280
obsolete		234
obstacle		115
obtain		53
occasional		68
occupancy		141
occupy		162
occur		173
odd		72
odour		98
offence		189
off-limits		112
offset		244
offshoot		213
offside		136
offspring		191
of great interest		362
of great use		362
of late		362
～ of one's own		363
of one's own accord		363
of one's own ～ ing		363
omit		52
on account of ～		363
on a large scale		363
on and off		363
on board		363
on business		363
once		49
once and for all		366
on condition that ～		363
on duty		364
one after another		366
on end		364
one of these days		366
one-sided		140
on foot		364
ongoing		94
on behalf of ～		363
online		39

on no account	364	outflow	128	paramount	252
on occasions	364	outgrowth	238	paraphernalia	276
on one's back	364	outing	263	parasite	160
on one's guard	364	outlay	209	parole	284
on one's own	364	outline	58	part from ~	367
on one's part	364	outlook	159	participate in ~	368
on one's stomach	364	outnumber	121	particle	77
on one's way (to ~)	364	out of bounds	366	particular	56
on purpose	365	out of control	366	partly	24
on second thought(s)	365	out of date	366	part with ~	367
on ~ terms (with ~)	363	out of fear	367	party	113
on the average	365	out of order	367	passage	37
on the contrary	365	out of reach of ~	367	pass away	368
on the go	365	out of sight	367	pass by	368
on the grounds that ~	365	out of the question	367	passionate	36
on the increase	365	out of work	367	pass on A to B	368
on the other hand	365	output	192	pass out	368
on-the-spot	68, 365	outrageous	241	pass through ~	368
on the tip of one's tongue	365	outset	238	pasture	80
on the whole	365	outskirts	210	patent	71
on time	366	outstanding	181	path	142
on top of ~	366	outstrip	230	patriot	154
onwards	174	outward	82	patronage	27
opaque	257	outweigh	251	pay A for B	368
operate	207	over and over (again)	367	pay attention to ~	368
operation	79	overcome	58	pay a visit to ~	368
opt	236	over-confidence	32	peak	56
optical	153	overestimate	113	peck	240
optimal	258	overflowing	132	peculiarity	153
optimisation	285	overhang	243	pedestrian	140
optimistic	59	overlap	81	pedigree	278
optimum	87	overlook	224	peer	107, 234
optometrist	293	overpopulation	22	penalise	135
orbit	136	overrun	211	penetrate	157
order	55	overstocking	82	peninsula	145
order A from B	366	overstretch	125	pensioner	127
orderly	241	overtake	142	pepper	180
ordinance	252	overtax	154	per	23
ordinary	59	overthrow	251	per capita	261
ore	241	overweight	46	perception	180
or else	366	overwhelm	146	perch	238
organ	174	overwhelming	205	perennial	279
organic	49	overwork	45	peril	242
organism	100	owe A to B	367	perimeter	209
orientate	121	owing to ~	367	period	41
-orientated	177	oxidise	155	periodic	178
-oriented	204			periodically	149
origin	21	**P**		periphery	163
original	39			perish	252
originally	150	packed	163	perk	189
originate	193	paddle	152	permanency	274
ornament	137	paediatric	196	permanent	20
orphanage	190	palatable	207	permeate	205
ostrich	117	pale	117	permission	76
otherwise	63	pane	133	permit	21
ought	114	pant	220	permutation	275
outbreak	154	paradigm	283	perpetuate	179
outcome	171	parallel	132	perplex	246
outermost	237	paralyse	215	persevere	189

408

persistence	106	plenty of ~	369	predatory	272
persist in ~	368	pliable	185	predecessor	219
personnel	120	plot	100	predicate	273
perspective	151	plough	192	predictable	84
persuade	107	pluck	244	prediction	170
persuade 人 into ~ ing	368	plummet	281	predispose	204
persuade 人 out of ~ ing	368	plunge	229	predominantly	91
pertinent	258	poet	27	predominate	16
pervasive	217	pointed	229	preeminent	254
perverse	278	pointer	185	preferably	110
pessimistic	87	point of view	369	prefer A to B	369
pest	94	point out ~	369	preference	75
pesticide	161	polar	36	pregnant	34
petal	194	polarise	189	prehistoric	31
petition	224	poll	113	preliminary	250
petrol	126	pollination	286	premiere	236
pharmaceutical	207	pollutant	100	premise	73
pharmacy	85	pollute	240	premium	194
phase	215	pollution	16	preoccupation	209
phenomenal	179	polygon	254	prepare	38
phenomenon	84	ponder	155	prepare for ~	369
philanthropic	237	ponderous	202	preponderance	281
photosynthesize	109	pop	163	prerequisite	228
physical	80	popularity	77	prescribe	198
physician	26	portend	288	prescription	130
physics	85	portfolio	125	preservative	254
physiology	73	portrait	36	preserve	62
pick up ~	369	portray	121	preside	283
pie chart	142	pose	253	prestige	110
pier	247	positive	29	prestigious	241
piety	240	possession	113	presume	150
pigment	256	possibly	59	pretentious	217
pile	121	postcode	37	prevailing	72
pill	27	posterity	286	prevalence	93
pillar	263	postgraduate	125	prevention	24
PIN	137	postulate	253	preventive	23
pinnacle	292	posture	116	prevent 人 from ~ ing	370
pioneer	61	potential	16	preview	43
pity	35	potentially	91	pride oneself on ~	370
pivotal	295	poultry	208	primarily	75
placebo	276	pounce	264	primary	16
place emphasis on ~	369	pound	165	primate	256
placement	126	practice	19	principal	34
plagiarise	217	practitioner	115	principle	175
plague	238	pragmatic	162	print	39
plain	124	prairie	48	priority	55
plaintiff	247	praise	26	proactive	233
plane	156	preamble	237	probation	242
plaster	152	precarious	284	probe	246
plastic	18	precede	104	procedure	107
plateau	205	precedent	156	proceeding	109
platform	147	precious	44	proceeds	190
plausible	219	precipitate	245	process	53
play a joke on ~	369	precipitation	123	procrastination	210
play an important role in ~	369	precise	54	prodigious	243
play a role (of ~)	369	preconception	91	prodigy	263
pleasant	74	precondition	24	productive	31
pledge	228	precursor	255	professional	37
plenty	67	predator	184	proficiency	122

profit	20	pull up (~)	370	raft	130
profound	88	pulmonary	285	rage	103
profuse	205	pulse	34	raid	152
profusion	287	punchline	278	raise	120
progression	65	punctual	130	rally	265
progressive	19	punish	19	ramification	196
prohibit 人 from ~ ing	370	pup	177	range	31
project	125	pupa	259	rank	47
proliferation	258	pupil	37	rapidly	46
prolong	134	purify	93	rate	53
prominence	101	pursuit	151	ratify	234
promote	37	push forward ~	370	ratio	99
promotion	171	put A into B	371	ration	233
prompt	68	put A in touch with B	371	rationale	189
promptly	144	put an end to ~	371	rationalise	71
prone	233	put a question to 人	371	ravage	198
pronounce	22	put ~ aside	370	raw	52
pronounced	283	put away ~	371	reach for ~	372
-proof	171	put pressure on ~	370	reactive	59
proof	65	put down ~	371	react to ~	372
proofreading	35	put forth ~	372	read between the lines	372
prop	261	put forward ~	372	ready-made	17
propagation	271	put ~ in prison	371	reagent	194
propel	108	put ~ into effect	371	realisation	56
proper	55	put ~ into practice	371	real-life	229
property	66	put off ~	372	realm	138
prophecy	113	put on ~	372	rear	30, 208
proponent	94	put oneself into someon's shoes	372	reasonable	140
proportion	55	put out ~	372	reasoning	154
proportionally	207	put ~ together	371	reassurance	201
propose	74	put ~ to the test	371	rebel	159
proprietary	286	put ~ to use	371	rebellion	264
propulsion	264	put up at ~	372	rebound	60
prosaic	287	put up with ~	372	recalcitrant	280
prosecute	232			receptor	249
prospect	68	**Q**		recession	232
prospective	204			recipient	165
prospector	292	qualification	68	reciprocal	178
prosper	131	qualitative	123	reckless	136
prosperity	238	quantity	82	reckon	197
prototype	221	quantum	290	recognise	53
protrude	291	quay	226	recoil	199
prove	17	query	116	record	21
prove to be ~	370	questionnaire	116	recount	203
provide A with B	370	queue	118	recover	21
provided	206	quibble	281	recover from ~	373
provision	175	quite a few	372	recreational	26
provoke	156	quota	279	recruitment	18
prowess	177	quotation	42	rectangular	127
proximity	197	quote	213	recur	292
prune	195			redemption	206
pseudo	289	**R**		reduce	62
publicise	223			redundant	223
publicity	122	rabies	286	reef	44
pudding	34	race	16	refer	119
pueblo	286	radiant	256	referee	42
puerile	277	radiation	54	referendum	279
pull ~ apart	370	radically	29	refer to ~	373
pull one's leg	370	radius	216	refine	121

410

reflection	149	renowned	72	retrenchment	279
reflective	172	rent	40	retrieve	67
reflect (up)on ~	373	reorient	156	return	78
reflex	278	repatriate	278	reunion	48
refrain	224	repeal	251	reuse	68
refrain from ~	373	repel	243	reveal	65
refresher	209	repellent	293	revelation	272
refreshment	120	repercussion	208	revenue	232
refugee	89	repertoire	163	revere	190
refundable	40	repetitive	83	reverse	90
refurbishment	281	replace	37	revert	195
refuse	60, 261	replenish	215	revision	69
regardless	58	replicate	169	revitalise	144
regardless of ~	373	represent	95	revival	96
regenerate	242	representation	254	revive	182
regime	225	reproduce	53	revolution	32
regimen	279	reptile	132	revolve	88
region	142	requirement	39	revulsion	277
regional	235	requisite	202	reward	83
register	40	resemble	56	rhetoric	265
regulate	159	reservoir	77	rib	67
regulation	37	reside	230	rickety	277
reign	234	residence	119	ridge	232
reimburse	212	resident	28	right	55
reinforce	150	residue	192	right away	374
reiterate	271	resign	69	rigorous	184
rekindle	181	resin	152	ring	33
relate A to B	373	resistant	170	ring up ~	374
relative	80, 173	resolute	218	riot	180
relentless	267	resolve	107	ripple	235
relevant	183	resort	103, 216	ritual	83
reliable	70	resort to ~	373	roam	191
reliant	253	resource	53	roaring	111
relic	264	resourceful	65	rob	35
relief	125	respectable	73	rob A of B	374
relieve	72	respectively	143	rodent	246
relieve A of B	373	respiratory	176	rogue	291
religion	16	respondent	113	rotate	193
relish	206	respond to ~	374	rote	171
relocate	130	rest	140	roughly	140
reluctance	110	restless	157	roundabout	120
rely on ~	373	restoration	198	routine	141
remain	61	restore	135	row	64
remains	168	restraint	85	rub	126
remark	56	restrict	136	rubbish	67
remarkable	64	restriction	48	rubble	236
remedy	95	rest on ~	374	rugged	290
remember A to B	373	result from ~	374	ruin	254
remember to ~	373	result in ~	374	rule out ~	374
remind A of B	373	resurface	111	run	152
remnant	219	resurgence	198	run across ~	374
remote	36	resurrect	186	run for ~	374
removal	82	retail	38	runoff	160
remuneration	279	retain	66	run out of ~	374
render	240	retard	223	run over ~	375
rendering	227	retirement	18	run a risk	374
renew	39	retract	246	rural	25
renounce	242	retractable	214	rust	86
renovate	146	retreat	150	rusty	157

411

S

sabbatical	287
sabotage	98
sac	85
sacred	96
sail	30
saline	267
sanction	234
sanitation	211
satellite	52
satire	235
satisfy	16
saturate	237
save	257
savings	143
saw	146
say to oneself	375
scale	246
scallop	165
scan	235
scant	100
scapegoating	294
scarce	55
scarcity	261
scavenger	295
scenario	22
scenery	120
scented	194
sceptical	180
scheme	121
scholar	143
scholarship	40
school	114
scold A for B	375
scope	124
scorching	284
scour	221
scrub	191
scruffy	281
scruple	295
scrutinise	250
sculpture	48
seal	57
seam	291
search for ~	375
seasick	39
secede	286
seclusion	294
second to none	375
secrete	171
secular	235
sediment	99
sedimentary	245
seed	28
seedling	251
seek	30
seek for ~	375
see much of ~	375

see nothing of ~	375
see ~ off	375
seep	201
see the sights of ~	375
see to ~	375
see to it that ~	375
segment	74
segregation	154
seismic	100
seize ~ by the collar	376
seldom	81
selective	26
self-catering	129
self-contained	210
self-esteem	209
self-evident	132
self-fulfilling	112
self-reliance	133
self-sufficient	158
self-sustaining	81
sell out	376
semester	35
send for ~	376
senior	165
seniority	186
sensational	119
sense	111
sensitive	57
sensory	178
sentence	106
separate A from B	376
sequel	226
sequence	85
sequential	185
serial	184
servant	34
serve one's purpose	376
service	35
set about ~	376
set forth	376
set ~ free	376
set off ~	376
settle	123
settle down	376
settlement	20
set up ~	376
severely	84
sewage	127
sewer	186
sewerage	288
shade	219
shady	86
shake hands (with ~)	376
shallow	21
share A with B	377
sharply	46
shatter	133
shed	252
sheer	223

shelf	169
shellfish	109
shelter	93
shift	60
shipping	120
shipwreck	124
shoot	159, 190
shoplift	231
shore	54
shortage	88
shortcoming	185
shorthand	144
short-sighted	98
shot	147
shove	224
show A around B	377
show off ~	377
show up	377
shrink	52
shroud	286
shrub	86
shudder	221
shy	258
sibling	91
siege	291
signal	30
signature	260
significance	24
significantly	57
signpost	123
silt	286
similarly	86
simmer	213
simulate	237
simulated	107
simultaneously	225
single out ~	377
sink	46
sip	228
sit up (late)	377
skew	197
skyrocketing	224
slab	285
slash	68
sledge	120
sleeveless	42
sliding	23
slot	49
sluggish	241
slumber	215
slump	46
smother	283
smuggle	294
sneeze	143
sniff	139
snowfall	36
soak	163
soar	142
sober	251

412

sobriquet	289	squeamish	289	straightforward	116
so-called	43	squeeze	118	strain	207
sociable	141	squirt	288	strand	109
so far	377	stabilise	153	strategy	141
solace	203	stag	280	stray	153
solicit	189	staggering	277	streak	109
solicitor	232	stagnate	238	stream	77
solid	85	staircase	37	strengthen	72
solitary	214	stalemate	295	stricken	176
soluble	220	stall	122	stride	179
solvent	270	stand	95	strife	234
some ~ or other	377	standard	23	strike	71
something is wrong with ~	377	standardise	84	striking	110
something like ~	377	stand by ~	378	stringent	288
something of ~	377	standby	131	strip	98, 208
sooner or later	377	stand for ~	378	strive	151
soothe	235	standing	214	stroke	71
soothing	126	stand on one's head	378	struggle for ~	379
sophisticated	65	stand on one's own feet	378	stubborn	97
sort	150	stand out	378	stumble	148
soul	158	standstill	135	stump	149
souvenir	45	stand up for ~	378	stun	222
span	108	staple	246	stunning	121
spark	255	star	73	sturdy	210
sparse	153	stare at ~	378	subconscious	193
sparsely	191	stark	227	subcontractor	187
spasm	208	startle	238	subduction	284
spawn	160	startling	104	subdue	267
speak ill of ~	378	starvation	136	subject	45
speak out	378	starve to death	378	sublime	102
specialisation	66	state	55	submerge	261
species	64	static	92	submerged	132
specific	57	station	132	submit	119
specimen	174	stationary	253	subordinate	82
spectacular	87	stationery	161	subsequent	97
speculate	148	statistics	76	subsidence	270
speculation	168	status	58	subsidise	239
spell	241	statute	203	subsidy	277
spend A (in) ~ ing	378	stay away from ~	379	subsist	239
spew	201	steeply	142	substance	54
sphere	100	stem	175	substantial	276
spill	98	stem from ~	379	substantially	248
spinal	249	step by step	379	substitute	170
spine	115	sterilise	284	substitute A for B	379
spiral	105	stethoscope	285	subterranean	291
spit	139	stick	83, 211	subtitled	39
split	77	stick to ~	379	subtle	106
spoil oneself	378	sticky	84	subtract	75
spontaneous	141	stiff	132	suburban	75
spore	272	stiffen	236	subway	48
sport	147	still	145	succeed	70
spot	108	stimulate	96	succeed in ~ ing	379
sprawl	182	stimulus	177	succeed to ~	379
spring	28, 71	stock	42	succinct	254
sprinkle	126	stocky	229	succulent	195
sprout	147	stop ~ ing	379	such as ~	379
spur	254	stop to ~	379	suckle	178
spurious	283	store	83	sufferance	282
squander	200	storey	212	suffer from ~	379

413

suffice	222	tactics	181	tapered	274
sufficiently	20	tag	164	tardy	161
suffrage	247	take ~ aback	380	tariff	90
suicide	59	take a chance	381	taunt	224
suitable	69	take advantage of ~	381	tax	47
sum	70	take A for B	381	tear	65
sundries	211	take after ~	381	tease	57
superannuation	281	take a spin	380	tedious	171
superficial	193	take away ~	381	teem	252
superiority	97	take ~ by surprise	380	tell A from B	384
supernatural	40	take ~ by the hand	380	teller	118
supervise	128	take care of ~	381	tell off ~	384
supplant	251	take hold of ~	380	tell on ~	384
supply A with B	380	take charge of ~	381	temper	179
supportive	45	take courage	381	temperate	138
suppress	178	take ~ for example	380	temporary	40
surge	157, 206	take ~ for granted	380	tenacious	274
surgery	74	take a trip (to ~)	380	tendency	75
surmise	201	take a look at ~	380	tender	208
surpass	62	take in ~	381	tendon	283
surplus	162	take ~ into consideration	381	tend to ~	384
surrender	219	take it easy	381	tenement	288
surrogate	270	take it seriously	382	tense	208
surround	46	take leave of ~	382	tension	59
surveillance	263	take measures (to ~)	382	tentacle	244
survey	42	take note of ~	382	tentative	155
survival	20	take notice (of ~)	382	term	216
susceptible	194	take ~ off	381	terminal	225
suspect	76	take off (~)	382	terminology	241
suspect A of B	380	take offense (at ~)	382	terrain	290
suspend	105	take on ~	382	terrestrial	253
sustain	48	take one's time	382	territory	28
sustainable	123	take over ~	382	tertiary	275
sustenance	173	take pains	382	testimony	236
swallow	108	take part in ~	383	texture	229
swamp	128	take place	383	than ever before	384
swat	245	take pleasure in ~	383	thanks to ~	384
sway	225	take root	383	thatch	291
sweep	89	take shelter (from ~)	383	that is (to say)	384
swell	271	take someone's word for it	382	thaw	253
swift	187	take steps (to ~)	383	theft	119
swipe card	128	take the lead (in ~ ing)	383	theme	46
switch	31	take the initiative in ~ ing	383	theology	143
swivel	222	take the place of ~	383	theorem	291
swollen	88	take the trouble to ~	383	the other way round	385
symmetrical	185	take to ~	383	therapeutic	187
symmetry	145	take to one's heels	383	thereby	219
sympathetic	118	take turns in ~ ing	384	there is no ~ ing	385
sympathise with ~	380	take up ~	384	there is no need (for you) to ~	385
symptom	95	take 人 at one's word	384	There is something A about B	385
synchronisation	233	tale	29	thermal	86
synthesise	194	talk over ~	384	thermometer	28
synthetic	169	talk 人 into ~ ing	384	(the) same to you	385
system	26	tame	79	thesis	235
		tan	42	think better of ~	385
		tangible	239	think highly of ~	385
T		tangle	187	think little of ~	385
		tantalise	256	think over ~	385
table	142	tap	84, 169	think twice	385
tackle	173				

think up ~	385
this day week	385
thorn	184
thoroughly	144
threaten	82
threshold	204
thrive	160
throughout	78
throw oneself into ~	386
thus	47
thwart	292
tick	125
tidal	148
tide	168
tiered	281
tight	126
tightrope	103
till	226
tilt	169
time after time	386
timepiece	163
tingling	205
tint	195
tiny	20
tip	153
tissue	108
to be frank with you	386
toddler	187
to do 人 justice	386
toil	251
token	228
tolerance	194
tolerate	148
toll	196
to make matters worse	386
tomb	44
tone	125
to no avail	386
to no purpose	386
to one's heart's content	386
to one's taste	386
top-notch	235
topographical	199
topography	290
torso	285
to say nothing of ~	386
to some extent	386
to the best of one's knowledge	386
to the effect that S+V	387
to the full	387
to the minute	387
to the point	387
touchstone	218
tough	54
tout	223
tow	124
toxic	249
toxin	290

trace	99, 102
track	80
tract	293
traditional	16
traffic	292
trail	78
trait	191
tram	133
trample	249
trance	230
tranquillity	257
transaction	118
transcend	227
transform	169
transgenic	198
transient	278
transit	49
transition	260
transitional	135
transmission	185
transoceanic	202
trap	100
traverse	200
treason	149
treatment	27
trek	123
tremendous	100
trend	47
tribe	48
tributary	287
trickle	245
tricky	94
trigger	158
tripod	165
trouble A for B	387
troublesome	128
trunk	79
trust A to B	387
try on ~	387
try one's best	387
tuck	221
tuition	23
tumble	105
tun	199
tune	150
turbulence	105
turbulent	257
turmoil	287
turn a deaf ear to ~	387
turn (A) into B	387
turn away (from ~)	387
turn back (~)	387
turn down ~	388
turn off ~	388
turnout	214
turn out (to) ~	388
turnround	143
turn to 人 for ~	388
turn up	388

tutorial	131
twig	67
twist	111
typify	210

U

ulcer	188
ultimate	119
ultimately	18
ultrasonic	220
ultraviolet	58
unadorned	250
unbeatable	128
unbiased	183
uncanny	261
uncertainty	112
uncharted	99
uncomfortable	28
unconscious	95
underestimate	176
undergo	78
underground	47
under the control of ~	388
underlie	242
underlying	96
undermine	215
underneath	99
under no circumstances	388
underscore	248
undertake	147
under way	388
undoubtedly	24
undue	147
unemployment	47
unfold	165
unforeseen	131
unit	84
unite	84
universal	171
unmanned	210
unmatched	162
unorthodox	181
unparalleled	220
unpleasant	35
unprecedented	249
unpredictable	177
unprejudiced	183
unpromising	86
unquestionably	57
unravelled	224
unsatisfactory	42
unsound	211
unstable	46
unsung	257
unwarranted	249
unwise	46
upcoming	127
uphill	104

415

up in the air	388	vice versa	213	welfare	34
upright	87	vicinity	235	well	65
uptake	221	vicious	110	well-balanced	43
up to ~	388	victim	67	well-being	129
up-to-date	29	vigilant	196	well off	389
upward	32	vigorous	164	well-rounded	145
urban	24	vigour	134	wharf	150
urbanisation	165	vine	105	what is more	389
urgent	131	vineyard	144	what is the matter with ~ ?	389
urine	158	violation	76	what we call	389
usage	68	viral	215	wheat	48
usher	171	virtually	200	wheel	25
utensil	135	virtue	83	wheelchair	41
utilise	173	viscosity	288	whereabouts	254
utopia	207	viscous	278	whereas	101
utterly	121	visible	18	whereby	163
		visual	126	whilst	276
		vital	58	whim	222
		vocational	129	whip	108
V		voice	217	whirl	255
vacancy	135	volatile	28	whisper	143
vaccinate	250	volcano	27	whole	56
vacuum	35	voluntary	61	wholesale	231
valid	128	voracious	257	wholesome	174
valuable	29	vote	43	Why don't you ~ ?	389
vanguard	282	voucher	128	widespread	72
vanish	182	vow	245	width	36
vapour	190	vulgar	218	wield	92
variable	177, 181	vulnerable	207	wilderness	210
variation	30			window	272
varsity	284			windscreen	124
vary	69	**W**		wipe out ~	389
vascular	264			wisdom	181
vast	67	wag	177	withdraw	90, 149
vault	258	wage	69	with ease	389
veer	199	waggle	262	with ~ in view	389
vegetation	131	wait	144	withhold	246
vegetative	279	wait on ~	388	within easy reach of ~	389
vehicle	143	wander	191	within reach	390
velocity	243	warn A of B	388	with regards to ~	389
venom	276	warning	41	without fail	390
venomous	260	wart	230	withstand	174
vent	201	wary	94	witness	104
ventilation	98	waterborne	92	[wit's] end	305
venture	194	watercolour	36	wobble	261
venue	119	waterfowl	128	wonder	70
verbal	179	watertight	197	woodland	47
verbally	104	waterway	126	word for word	390
verdict	232	way of ~ ing	389	workforce	132
verge	233	weaken	73	workmanship	65
verify	156	weak-willed	106	work on ~	390
versatility	242	wealthy	33	work one's way (through ~)	390
verse	248	wean	216	work out (~)	390
vertebrate	217	wear off	134	worn-out	129
vertical	155	wear out ~	389	worthy	32
vessel	188	weathering	250	wreak	275
vested	275	weave	212	wreck	88
veterinarian	266	wed	207	wring	221
vex	273	wedge	66	write down ~	390
viable	271	weigh	71		

416

write to ~	390
wryly	197

Y

yield	192
yield to ~	390
youngster	38

あとがき

　本書籍の作成には，林，小玉以外にも，留学試験対策専門校LINGO L.L.C.の常勤教職員全員が深く関わりました。候補単語・熟語の選別からエクセルによる分類，校正，録音音声の確認，各種の連絡，メール便・宅急便の手配など，本書作成のあらゆる局面でLINGO L.L.C.教職員の真摯な汗が飛び散りました。よってここに各位のお名前を列挙し，そのご尽力に心から感謝致します。

　　秋本　陽二／庄司　恵里子／山本　卓／桝井　雅之／松倉　英栄

　　　　　　　　　　　　　　　　　　　　　　　　　　　　林　功

著者略歴

林　功（はやし いさお）

- 早大一文中退。サザン・イリノイ大英文科卒。
ワシントン大大学院比較文学科修士課程修了（学位：MA in Comparative Literature）。
留学試験専門校 LINGO L.L.C. 代表。筑波大大学院共通科目客員講師。
長年にわたって、高校生からビジネスマンまで、TOEFL テスト受験対策を中心に英語を教え続け、「ヒゲの林」の愛称で親しまれている。今では 10000 人以上の教え子が国内外で活躍中。2004 年に他校に先駆けて IELTS 対策カリキュラムを企画し、レベル別対策講座を開講、現在に至る。
- 著書『CD BOOK 改訂新版 TOEFL TEST 必須英単語 5600』『CD BOOK TOEFL iBT 頻出英単語 1700』『CD BOOK アメリカの中学教科書で英語を学ぶ』（以上ベレ出版）、
『全問正解する TOEFL ITP TEST 文法問題対策』（語研）、
『ETS 公認ガイド TOEFL iBT CD-ROM 版』（監訳、ETS/McGraw-Hill）。

小玉　英央（こだま ひでお）

ニューヨーク州立大学プラッツバーグ校卒（学位：BA in Communication）。
民間企業に勤めた後、教員免許を取得して中学・高校で英語講師として勤務。
その後、LINGO L.L.C. に入社し、現在は IELTS 主任講師として IELTS や TOEFL の講座を担当。その実践的で分かりやすい授業は、確実に得点力を伸ばしてくれると、5.5、6.5、7.5 クラスのいずれにおいても定評がある。

音声の内容

タ　イ　ム：10 時間 34 分
ナレーション：Emma Howard ／ Guy Perryman ／久末絹代

IELTS 必須英単語 4400

2016 年 5 月 25 日	初版発行
2025 年 7 月 12 日	第 11 刷発行
著者	林　功・小玉　英央
カバー・本文デザイン	竹内　雄二
DTP	WAVE 清水　康広

©Isao Hayashi / Hideo Kodama 2016. Printed in Japan

発行者	内田　真介
発行・発売	ベレ出版

〒162-0832　東京都新宿区岩戸町12 レベッカビル
TEL.03-5225-4790　FAX.03-5225-4795
ホームページ　https://www.beret.co.jp/

印刷	株式会社モリモト印刷
製本	根本製本株式会社

落丁本・乱丁本は小社編集部あてにお送りください。送料小社負担にてお取り替えします。

ISBN 978-4-86064-472-7 C2082　　　　　　編集担当　脇山　和美

留学試験対策専門校
LINGO L.L.C.（リンゴ・エル・エル・シー）
We respect what makes man man.

受講生の目標得点到達を確実にし、真の英語運用力獲得と夢実現を可能にする少人数クラス
- TOEFL(R) 対策講座
  Course 100・80・65・Speaking 各クラス
- IELTS(TM) 対策講座
  Course7.5・6.5・5.5・Speaking(Academic・General) 各クラス
  LINGO L.L.C./ リンゴ・エル・エル・シー

〒160-0023
　東京都新宿区西新宿 3-2-7　KDX 新宿ビル 1F
　JR・小田急線・地下鉄各線新宿駅南口徒歩約 8 分
　Tel 03-6279-4340　Fax03-6279-4350
　ホームページ：http://www.lingollc.com
　　　　　　　e-mail:ryugaku@lingollc.com

● 音声のダウンロード方法

- 音声は MP3 ファイル形式です。
- 音声内容：収録音声の英語部分はすべて，英国人のネイティブスピーカーによって読まれています。

● 「見出し語」→「見出し語の例文和訳」→「見出し語の英語例文」の順に録音
● Speaking / Writing 用に和訳から英語フレーズを作る練習が可能

ダウンロード方法

1. パソコンのウェブブラウザを立ち上げて「ベレ出版」ホームページにアクセス（www.beret.co.jp）
2. ホームページ内の検索欄から『IELTS 必須英単語 4400』の詳細ページへ
3. 「音声ダウンロード」ボタンをクリック
4. 8 ケタのダウンロードコードを入力してダウンロード，音声ファイルを解凍
   ダウンロードコード　`vakf3Xxa`　（＊半角英数字で入力してください）
   （＊ダウンロードには時間がかかる場合があります）
   （＊音声ファイルは zip 形式でダウンロードされます）
5. パソコン，もしくは MP3 音声対応のプレーヤーに転送して再生

❖ お願いと注意点について

音声のダウンロードは，スマートフォン，タブレットには対応しておりません。パソコンからのダウンロードをお願いします。
デジタルオーディオ(iPhone, iPod, WALKMAN 等)への転送方法，ご使用されているパソコンやアプリケーションの操作方法についてのお問い合わせは，小社では対応できません。取扱い説明書，もしくは製造元にお問い合わせください。
音声は本書籍をお買い上げくださった方へのサービスとして，無料でご提供させていただいております。さまざまな理由により，やむを得なく終了することがありますことをご了承ください。

アメリカの中学教科書で英語を学ぶ

林功 著

A5 並製／本体価格 2200 円（税別）　■ 344 頁
ISBN978-4-86064-042-2 C2082

本書は歴史・数学・英語（Writing）・科学・課外授業の 5 つの Chapter に分かれています。少しアカデミックで身近なものを扱うジュニア・ハイの英語は日本人の学習者にも最適。各科目の学習事項を英語を使って考える、内容を確認しながら聞き、イディオムや語彙などの知識も同時に覚える構成。中学で学ぶ知識を英語で読み直す大人の復習帳。

英文徹底解読 スティーブ・ジョブズのスタンフォード大学卒業式講演

畠山雄二 著

A5 並製／本体価格 1400 円（税別）　■ 224 頁
ISBN978-4-86064-443-7 C2082

プレゼンのとき以上にことばを選び、ことばの力だけで自分自身を全力でプレゼンしたことがジョブズには一度だけあります。それが伝説とまで言われるスタンフォード大学の卒業式でのスピーチです。あまりにも有名なスピーチですが、ほとんどの人がわかったつもりになっているだけで、ジョブズの背景と英文法の知識を駆使してちゃんと読むと、誤解していたこと、メッセージをちゃんと受け取れていなかったことに気づかされます。理論言語学の専門家であり、ジョブズ信者でもある著者が完全解釈し、徹底解剖して、深く深く掘りさげていきます。

英語はつおんワークブック

マクラフリン愛菜 著

A5 並製／本体価格 1900 円（税別）　■ 232 頁
ISBN978-4-86064-455-0 C2082

すべての発音記号を平均的に練習するのではなく、著者が指導経験の中から培ってきたノウハウを用いて、ピンポイントで日本人が苦手とする音を矯正していきます。発音のコツを簡潔に示しつつ、音の比較練習を繰り返すことで、「通じる英語発音」を効率的に身につけられます。カラフルでイラスト満載、一見児童書のようにも見える本書ですが、子どもから大人まで、楽しくトレーニングをするうちに通じる英語発音をいつの間にか身につけられ、さらに一歩進んで、スペルから正しい発音を予測する力も養えます！　発音を学ぶ最初の一冊に最適です!!

とにかく600点突破！TOEIC TEST 大特訓

濵崎潤之輔 著

A5 並製／本体価格 2300 円（税別） ■ 496 頁
ISBN978-4-86064-379-9 C2082

有名企業や大学で TOEIC の講義をし、連続受験と 990 点満点記録を更新中の著者が書く目標点数別 TOEIC シリーズ第1弾。本番レベルの質のよい模擬問題と、厳選の必須単語、パート別に実力養成トレーニングを行ない、目標点数を突破できる力を徹底的に鍛えてつけていきます。特にリスニング対策はこれまでなかった、視覚イメージを連動させた劇的点数アップが狙える対策を紹介。自身の体験はもちろん、TOEIC 本を作り、教えてきた経験のすべてが込められた一冊！

ぜったい900点突破！TOEIC TEST 大特訓

濵崎潤之輔 著

A5 並製／本体価格 2300 円（税別） ■ 424 頁
ISBN978-4-86064-380-5 C2082

"TOEIC 界の有名人、また、高得点のテクニック解説や学習指導に定評のある著者が書く 900 点突破のための一冊。今や TOEIC を教え自身は満点記録を更新中だが、もとはふつうに仕事をしながら少ない時間を勉強にあて、900 点の壁を超えられずあがいた経験を持つ。限られた時間を最大限に活かす効率的な対策と、必須の知識のすべてがまとめられている本書は、それらの経験が活かされている。900 点を超えるという目標に特化した総合対策＆トレーニング本、本番さながらの良質の模試付きです。

TOEIC Test 900点突破 必須英単語

石井辰哉 著

四六並製／本体価格 1900 円（税別） ■ 464 頁
ISBN978-4-939076-30-5 C2082

難しい単語を必死に覚えても、実際のテストで役立つ確率はそう高くはありません。本書は、英文を読んで文脈からキーとなる単語の意味を推測する練習をすることで、スコアアップにつながる単語力をつけられるようになっています。高得点を目指すレベルでは、この方法が一番効率の良い有効な勉強法です。収録単語の出題率の高さは実証済みです。

TOEFL iBT 頻出英単語 1700

林功 著

A5 並製／本体価格 2100 円（税別）　■ 320 頁
ISBN978-4-86064-132-0 C2082

本書は iBT テストを徹底的に分析してできた単語集です。テストに最もよく出る単語 1700 を同意語・例文と一緒に基本語から段階的に ABC に分類して載せています。新しく導入されたスピーキングを分析し、またライティングで使える語彙が充実した、総合能力を試す新試験に完全対応した一冊です。CD2 枚に見出し単語、日本語訳、同意語を収録。

改訂新版 TOEFL TEST 必須英単語 5600

林功 著

四六並製／本体価格 2500 円（税別）　■ 552 頁
ISBN978-4-86064-282-2 C2082

10 年間ロングセラーとして多くの TOEFL 受験者に愛読された『TOEFL Test 必須英単語 5000』が新しくなりました。「聞くことと読むことを通して文脈から単語を定着させる」というコンセプトは同じですが、5 年前に実施された iBT という難解なテストをさらに分析しさらに進化したのが本書です。iBT 本試験に毎回のように出題される単語群、頻出ジャンルの英文の追加、キャンパス用語リストを追加した本格的な TOEFL 対策本です。